ALAN RO

Good Cam

France 1996

Contents

Published by: **DENEWAY GUIDES & TRAVEL LTD**
Chesil Lodge, West Bexington, Dorchester, Dorset DT2 9DG
Tel: (01308) 897809 Fax: (01308) 898017

Printed by: BPC Wheatons, Exeter
Covers: Jayne Homer - Maps: Charles Broughton
Cover photograph is of Camping Soleil Plage,
by courtesy of Eurocamp Independent

Sales: **Derek Searle Associates**
The Coach House, Cippenham Lodge
Cippenham Lane, Slough SL1 5AN
Tel: (01753) 539295 Fax: (01753) 551863

Distribution: **Bookpoint Ltd**
39 Milton Park
Abingdon, Oxon OX14 4TD
Tel: (01235) 835001 Fax: (01235) 861038

Foreword

To say that 1995 was a bad year for French campsite operators so far as British visitors were concerned is something of an understatement! The strong franc, and/or the weak £ sterling, antipathy towards nuclear testing in the Pacific and a summer when the weather was as good (i.e. hot) in the UK as it was in France, all contributed to a significant downturn in British visitors to what is normally the number one camping and caravanning destination.

Hopefully the 100 or so `value for money' municipal sites which we introduced into our Guide for the first time in 1995 went at least some way to address the problem of cost for our readers visiting Europe's most popular camping and caravanning country last year and let's hope that by 1996 the exchange rate is somewhat more favourable. The probability of Britain enjoying another summer like 1995 next year is statistically remote, so we are reasonably confident that things should look up so far as camping and caravanning in France in 1996 is concerned.

For 1996 we have made some significant changes and improvements, which are worth describing in some detail. By far the most important development is the introduction, with co-operation from **Brittany Ferries**, two insurance companies and some of our featured campsites, of a **Readers' Discount Voucher Scheme,** whereby readers of our 1996 edition will be able to enjoy a range of discounts, on ferry fares, travel and breakdown insurance, caravan or motorcaravan insurance and on site fees at a good few of the sites featured in this Guide. Full details are shown on the Discount Voucher included in the Guide.

Another important change is the decision to amalgamate the 100 or so better municipal sites, which we introduced as a separate section last year, into the main body of the Guide for 1996. The introduction of a municipal section last year was prompted by the fact that more and more readers were asking us for `value for money' sites without `frills' - i.e. sites which provide good facilities in terms of pitches and sanitary facilities, at a reasonable price and preferably with a genuinely `French flavour', but not necessarily with lots of other amenities such as swimming pools, restaurants, shops or entertainment.

The introduction of these sites into the Guide has been well received, but some readers have asked "why are these municipals in a separate section rather than arranged with the rest of the sites, which would make using the guide easier?" Well, we do really pay attention to your concerns, so for 1996 you'll find our reports on the municipals amongst all the rest of the sites in any given area, but still distinguishable from commercial sites by virtue of having been given a Site Number suffixed with an `M'.

Regular readers will also notice that we have changed the layout of the Guide somewhat (again in response to readers suggestions) by listing sites by Département rather than by Region. This is quite handy in France where each Département can be listed alphabetically, and by its official number. We have still mentioned in which Region each Département, and the individual sites within it, are located.

We hope you will find our new edition not only better and more interesting than ever, but a real help too in terms of financial savings.

Lois Edwards MA, FTS
Clive Edwards BEd, FTS
Sue Smart   Directors

The Guide's Aims and Principles

Our selective site guides are designed to provide the sort of information and guidance which we, as campers and caravanners ourselves, would wish to know before committing ourselves to staying on a site which we did not know personally. In assessing our sites (all of which are of course inspected by us before selection, and regularly monitored by further visits, questionnaires, etc.) we pay particular attention to:

- the site itself, and its individual pitches
- the sanitary facilities
- the `hospitality'

Only after satisfying ourselves that these basic necessities are of a good standard do we consider a site for selection, irrespective of whether or not it has an extensive range of other facilities. If a site does have additional facilities then of course these too must all be of an at least acceptable standard. The same principles apply in respect of the municipal sites featured in the Guide, but readers should understand that, in general, facilities in municipal sites tend to be somewhat more `utilitarian' than in the better commercial sites and less `luxurious' - this needs to be balanced against the generally lower charges - you do tend to get what you pay for!

Of course most site guides provide at least some information on these subjects, often by reference to symbols and a key, a system which many people don't seem to like, and which is often difficult to operate in a moving vehicle, but the most important difference with our approach is that it allows us far more freedom to comment on QUALITY than does a system of stars or other symbols, which are really designed only to inform the reader (de-coder!) whether or not a particular facility is provided, without any reference to the quality.

Every site in our Guides is known to us personally; they are not selected from official lists, or written about at second-hand. Even when we get readers suggestions couched in glowing terms we only include a site after we ourselves have visited it - this ensures a degree of uniformity in our reports, as what appeals to one person may prompt an opposite reaction in another.

All our sites are chosen on merit alone, the only criterion being that they meet our standards; no payment is required of a site for inclusion in the Guide, so no camp can buy its way into the Guide.

Reference has already been made to our rigorous inspection process, but of course we are not infallible, and occasionally we get caught out by an unexpected mid-season change in ownership or management of a site, so we do appreciate the invaluable feedback we receive from readers each year. Unlike some other guides we do not have an army of inspectors operating what seems to be an essentially bureaucratic approach to assessment, but rather we have a small dedicated team of Site Assessors, all of whom are experienced campers and caravanners themselves, with a breadth of relevant individual expertise.

The many positive readers letters which we receive suggest that our choice of sites meets with general approval; we always try to visit sites in the season, and if staying overnight, to stay under exactly the same conditions as our readers, but obviously we cannot visit every site between mid-July and mid-August when there is the greatest pressure on both staff and facilities; so far as seaside sites in particular are concerned, our advice would be to avoid this period if you possibly can - the French themselves tend to holiday in that period, and for those restricted to school holidays the last two weeks of August and first week of September are usually quieter than the previous four weeks.

How to use the Guide

The Regions and Départements of France

France is divided administratively into 95 'départements' (including Corsica) which are approximately the equivalent of our counties but with rather more autonomy. The départements are numbered in alphabetical order and these numbers form the first two digits of all post codes within each département. For example, the Dordogne is département 24, so every large town in the Dordogne has a post code commencing 24. We have adopted a similar system for numbering our French campsites; thus all our sites in the département of Dordogne start with the numbers 24.

Our Guide is now organised in départements for ease of use. The layout is therefore numerical and alphabetical: 01 Ain, 02 Aisne, etc. For the benefit of the majority of readers who are not experts on French geography, we include the map below indicating the location of each département, together with its official number. The map also shows in which Region each département is situated. We have also included a (necessarily very brief) description of each Region on pages 209-213.

The Regions of France

France is also divided into larger areas known as Regions, each of which consists of several départements. For example, the Region known as Normandy comprises five départements (76 Seine-Maritime, 27 Eure, 61 Orne, 14 Calvados and 50 Manche). Although this may seem a little confusing, it is actually quite straightforward and more definite than the English equivalent (for example, East Anglia comprises Norfolk, Suffolk and Essex, but also arguably Cambridgeshire). The Regions, listed alphabetically with the Départements (each with its official number) within each, are:

ALSACE: 67 Bas-Rhin, 68 Haut-Rhin

AQUITAINE: 24 Dordogne, 33 Gironde, 47 Lot-et-Garonne, 40 Landes, 64 Pyrénées-Atlantiques

AUVERGNE: 03 Allier, 63 Puy-de-Dôme, 15 Cantal, 43 Haute-Loire

BRITTANY: 35 Ille-et-Vilaine, 22 Côtes d'Armor, 29 Finistère, 56 Morbihan

BURGUNDY: 21 Côte d'Or, 71 Sâone-et-Loire, 58 Nièvre, 89 Yonne

CHAMPAGNE-ARDENNE: 08 Ardennes, 51 Marne, 10 Aube, 52 Haute-Marne

CÔTE D'AZUR: 06 Alpes-Maritimes

FRANCHE-COMTÉ: 90 Tre. de Belfort, 70 Haute-Sâone, 25 Doubs, 39 Jura

LANGUEDOC-ROUSSILLON: 48 Lozère, 30 Gard, 34 Hérault, 11 Aude, 66 Pyrénées-Orientales

LIMOUSIN: 23 Creuse, 19 Corrèze, 87 Haute-Vienne

LOIRE VALLEY: 28 Eure-et-Loir, 45 Loiret, 18 Cher, 36 Indre, 37 Indre-et-Loire, 41 Loir-et-Cher

LORRAINE VOSGES: 57 Moselle, 54 Meurthe-et-Moselle, 88 Vosges, 55 Meuse

MIDI-PYRÉNÉES: 46 Lot, 12 Aveyron, 81 Tarn, 31 Haute-Garonne, 32 Gers, 90 Ariège, 65 Hautes-Pyrénées, 82 Tarn-et-Garonne

NORD/PAS-DE-CALAIS: 62 Pas-de-Calais, 59 Nord

NORMANDY: 76 Seine-Maritime, 27 Eure, 61 Orne, 14 Calvados, 50 Manche

PARIS/ILE DE FRANCE: 75 Paris, 77 Seine-et-Marne, 78 Yvelines, 91 Essonne, 95 Val d'Oise, 92 Hauts-de-Seine, 93 Seine-St-Denis, 94 Val de Marne

PICARDY: 80 Somme, 02 Aisne, 60 Oise

POITOU-CHARENTES: 79 Deux Sèvres, 86 Vienne, 16 Charente, 17 Charente-Maritime

PROVENCE: 05 Hautes-Alpes, 04 Alpes-de-Haute-Provence, 83 Var, 84 Vaucluse, 13 Bouches-du-Rhône

RHÔNE VALLEY: 01 Ain, 69 Rhône, 26 Drôme, 07 Ardèche, 42 Loire

SAVOY/DAUPHINY ALPES: 38 Isère, 74 Haute-Savoie, 73 Savoie

WESTERN LOIRE: 53 Mayenne, 72 Sarthe, 49 Maine-et-Loire, 85 Vendée, 44 Loire-Atlantique

CORSICA: 20 Corse-Sud, Haute-Corse

Page Headings in the Guide, are in numerical order by **Département** and these indicate the Département(s) in which sites featured on that page are situated.

The campsite **title line** at the start of each report gives the **site number** (also indicated on the Site Map, see pages 216-217) and a combination of nearby village/adjacent town. These are listed alphabetically in the Town Index (starting on page 218).

This system should enable the reader to quickly identify the approximate location of any site.

How to use the 1996 Discount Voucher !

The Discount Card/Vouchers are in three parts:

Part 1   should be retained and must not be removed from the Guide. You should complete it by adding your name, address and signature. This part includes the printed Card Number, and should be shown to those parks indicating special offers for our readers as identified by an Alan Rogers' logo in the Guide.

Part 2   should be completed by adding your name, address and your signature. This part may then be used to claim your discount(s) for travel, breakdown, caravan or motorcaravan insurance.

Part 3   should be completed by adding your name, address and your signature. This part may then be used to claim your FERRY DISCOUNT as directed.

Note that the Discount Cards are valid from **1 January - 31 December 1996 only**

Notes on Information Provided in Camp Site Reports

`Site' and `Pitch'
Throughout the reports we have used the word site in the sense of a camping site: that is to say the camp itself, not your own individual place in the camp. The latter we have called a pitch.

Distances
All distances are given in kilometres and metres to correspond with those on Continental maps and signposts.

Opening dates
We give the **advertised** opening dates of sites. If we know that the shops, meals service, swimming pool, etc. (if they exist) are open for a shorter period than the site itself, we have so indicated. However on occasion site owners will close or open earlier or later than stated and it is wise to check with the site if you intend to visit in the period immediately following the stated opening date, or immediately prior to the stated closing date.

Sanitary facilities
Here we have tried to give the most important and variable information on sanitary facilities without expanding it into a detailed survey. All the sites featured in the main section of the guide have a majority of `British style' WCs (i.e. pedestal type with lifting seat), plus a variety of `continental' toilets (seatless or reverse bowl pedestal), or the `Turkish' type. The word `Turkish' is normally used to mean the squatting type with hole at ground level and two raised foot stands; if you do use this type of 'loo, beware of the flush, which often resembles a small tidal wave! It is also worth noting that some sites still do not provide toilet paper, so take your own. In regard to personal washing facilities, on the plus side we mention particularly if private cabins are provided and on the minus side, for example, if the facilities are not under cover. All the sites included in this guide have at least some hot showers, and also special sinks for washing-up dishes and for washing clothes, and normally also points for electric razors and hair dryers, or even provide coin operated hair dryers. One peculiarity you may encounter at French campsites is the provision in washbasins of only warm/hot water which leaves you searching for a cold tap for teeth cleaning. If we say that the showers are `fully controllable', this means that they have either two taps or a multipurpose tap which enables the temperature and flow to be controlled (as distinct from premixed hot water with push-button or chain control).

Electrical connections
The vast majority of sites featured in this guide have at least some electric hook-ups, although the amperage may vary from 2A to 10A - with the introduction of more and more electrical gadgets, we have started to give details of the current rating (i.e. amperage) where possible, but we would warn readers to be careful to avoid using domestic electrical appliances, such as household electric kettles, that are not specifically designed for use in caravans, etc. as in many cases these will seriously overload the supply and blow the fuse in the connection box or worse!

Whilst there is now a European Standard for connectors (CEE 17) this is not retrospective, so you will undoubtedly find sites where your UK 3-pin (CEE 17) connector will not fit. Adapters are required in many such cases, by far the most common being the `2-pin plus earth' type (available from many accessory shops in the UK) which is particularly useful (probably essential) for France. Holland, Norway, Sweden and some sites in Germany still require a `German' (2-pin plus 2 earth connections) adapter, and Denmark sites often require a special small 3 pin adapter.

Serviced Pitches
Various terms are used to describe pitches which provide services in addition to an electrical supply. In the context of this guide these services include water and drainage - in France, pitches providing these three services are graded `Grand Confort'.

Idiosyncrasies!
Of course, most campsites in France, as elsewhere, have their own rules and regulations which are too complex and varied to include in this Guide. However, it is worth noting one or two rules in particular which are becoming rather more commonplace. For example, many French campsites now ban the wearing of `boxer' shorts in swimming pools on hygiene grounds. Our advice would be to ensure that everyone takes a proper swimming costume. Similarly it is worth noting that many campsite swimming pools (where the general public are not admitted) are designated as `private' and are not required under French law to be supervised.

Charges
Few French campsites fix their prices for the following year before our press date and most charges refer to 1995. Where 1995 or 1996 prices were not available we try to give an indication of their usual level by providing a `charges guide'. The prices are given in French Francs. We would emphasise that the prices which we quote are merely a guide as many campsites have complicated charging systems and the limited space available to us means that we cannot do more than provide a summary or outline of charges - if you need to get an exact quotation you should write to the site specifying your precise requirements, and ask for a quotation (we provide a sample letter at the back of the guide). In this edition we include whether payment can be made by credit card. Lack of space precludes us giving full details about exactly which of the many different credit cards, debit cards or charge cards are accepted.

Reservations
This is a somewhat vexed subject and difficult to deal with comprehensively in terms of the variety of different systems operated by individual campsites in our reports. Our reports therefore indicate whether or not the camp will make reservations and, if so, to give any important special features of their system, such as whether they keep a particular place, whether there is any minimum period of stay, and whether any deposit or fee is payable. A fee of course is lost if the booking is cancelled whereas a deposit is deducted from your bill, though there could be cases where a camp objects to returning your deposit - for example, if you book for a precise period and then want to leave early because it starts to rain. Because of the many different systems and conditions, it is best not to send any money until the camp has confirmed your reservation. Write first to the site asking for a reservation, and if they can offer you what you want they will normally write back confirming it and telling you how much they want by way of deposit and fee. Then arrange either for your bank to make the necessary payment or simply send the site a Eurocheque for the required amount, in French Francs.

Reservation for campsites in most areas of France is only really necessary in the main season (mid-July to mid-August), so if you are travelling at any other time, our advice is to consider the continentals' practice of taking a look round a site before making a decision to stay, or parting with any payment. If you feel that it's really necessary to book up in advance, you ought to take out travel insurance to include cancellation cover - travel insurance is a wise precaution anyway and if you wish to take out cover you can arrange this through your travel agent, motoring organisation or through the publishers of this Guide who are agents for one of the best and most competitive of the several specialist travel and breakdown insurance companies. Details are given in the colour section between pages 16 and 17; we even provide you with a 10% discount on this insurance with the voucher provided in this Guide!

UK Reservations services
Several organisations offer a service in the UK for booking pitches at French sites. We have worked very satisfactorily with Select Site Reservations and Eurocamp Independent for some years and their addresses and telephone numbers can be found in their advertisements in this Guide. Several organisations also offer a reservations service for booking the range of `static' accommodation which has become a feature of many French sites; again you will find advertisements for several of these organisations in the guide, all of whom we have found to provide a satisfactory service.

Naturist Sites

During the past three years we have had very favourable feedback from readers concerning our choice of Naturist Sites, which we first introduced in our 1992 edition, and over the last three years we have gradually added a few more, including two in Corsica.

Apart from the need to have a `Naturist Licence' (see below), there is no need to be a practising naturist before visiting these sites. In fact, at least as far as British visitors are concerned, many are what might be described as `holiday naturists' as distinct from the practice of naturism at other times. The emphasis in all the sites featured in this guide at least, is on naturism as `life in harmony with nature', and respect for oneself and others and for the environment, rather than simply on nudity. In fact nudity is really only obligatory in the area of the swimming pools.

There are a number of `rules', which amount to sensible and considerate guidelines designed to ensure that no-one invades someone else's privacy, creates any nuisance, or damages the environment. Whether as a result of these `rules', the naturist philosophy generally, or the attitude of site owners and campers alike, we have been very impressed by all the naturist sites we have selected. Without exception they had a friendly and welcoming ambience, were all extremely clean and tidy and, in most cases, provided much larger than average pitches, with a wide range of activities both sporting and cultural.

The purpose of our including a number of naturist sites in our guide is essentially to provide an `introduction to naturist camping in France' for British holidaymakers; we were actually surprised by the number of British campers we met on naturist sites, many of whom had `stumbled across naturism almost by accident' but had found, like us, that these sites were amongst the nicest they had encountered. We mentioned the Naturist Licence - French Law requires all campers over 16 years of age on naturist sites to have a `licence'. These can be obtained in advance from either the British or French national naturist associations, but are also available on arrival at any recognised naturist site (a passport type photograph is required).

Travel Information

The following is a resume of some of the more important considerations in connection with travel to France, and those seeking more detailed advice and guidance on specific subjects should contact:

French Government Tourist Office, 178 Piccadilly, London W1V 0AL Tel: 0891 244123

Passports

Visitors to France must hold a valid full (10 year) passport. The 1 year British Visitors Passport is being abolished from 1 January 1996, and will only be valid for journeys **completed** by 31 December 1995.

Health

There are no obligatory inoculations and, as Britain enjoys reciprocal agreement with France for health care, it is possible to obtain treatment in France by producing Form E111, obtainable in advance in the UK through post offices. As only about 80% of the cost of treatment is covered in this way, personal travel insurance, including medical expenses cover, is a wise precaution.

Insurance

Third party motor insurance is obligatory and a Green Card is strongly recommended; you should contact your motor insurance company or broker for details. Comprehensive personal travel and break-down insurance, including cancellation cover is a sensible precaution - several organisations can arrange cover to suit virtually every need. Details and a proposal form for one of the best of the travel and breakdown insurance services are included in this Guide (see colour section between pages 16 and 17). You can claim your special reader's discount by using the Discount Voucher included with this Guide!

Finance

There is no limit to the amount of Sterling which you may take into France and you can change Sterling notes at banks or bureaux de change once there. Most holidaymakers prefer to take French currency or Travellers Cheques with them, and most banks in the UK provide a foreign currency service, although smaller branches may need a few days notice of your requirements. Eurocheques, backed up by a Eurocheque Card, are accepted at many establishments and can be used to obtain cash at most banks in France. French banking hours differ from the UK - they normally open Mon - Fri, 9.00-12.00 and 14.00-6.00, but close either on Saturday **or** on Monday.

They also normally close at midday the day prior to a public holiday. Bank Holidays in France are different from the UK and full details can be obtained from the French Government Tourist Office in London - the most important are:

New Year's Day	Easter	Labour Day (1 May)
Liberation Day (8 May)	Ascension Day	Whit Monday
Bastille Day (14 July)	Assumption Day (15 Aug)	All Saints Day (1 Nov)
Remembrance Day (11 Nov)	Christmas Day.	

The major (i.e. Access, Visa, American Express and Diners Club) credit and charge cards are acceptable at many establishments (including a good few campsites - see individual Site Reports) throughout France. However we have heard of instances where credit cards issued in Britain have been refused by French retailers; this is because French credit cards have a microprocessor built in, whereas British cards have a magnetic stripe. If you do encounter any difficulty (and in many visits every year we have never personally encountered such a problem) Visa International says there is no reason for the French to refuse British cards, and recommends the following statement:

"Les cartes brittaniques ne sont pas des cartes a puce, mais a piste magnetique.
Ma carte est valable et je vous serais reconnaissant d'en demander la confirmation
aupres de votre banque ou de votre centre de traitement"

Shopping

French shopping hours vary considerably, although shops are often open later than in the UK, and many close for lunch, often for up to two hours. Supermarkets and hypermarkets are normally open until 8-10 pm (20.00 - 22.00 hrs).

Customs

With the introduction of the open market in 1993, formalities for EC residents travelling between the UK and France are now minimal - it is however important to distinguish between `duty free' goods (where the limits are more or less unchanged) and `duty paid in the EC' goods which are no longer subject to strict limits.

Motoring Information

Both the AA and the RAC can provide full details of continental motoring regulations, including those applying in France, but the following points should be borne in mind in particular:

Documentation: It is advisable to carry your vehicle registration document and/or, if the vehicle is not registered in your name, a letter of authority signed by the registered owner to the effect that you have permission to take the vehicle abroad. A valid full (not provisional) UK driving licence is required and car drivers must be over 18 years of age. An International Driving Licence (obtainable from the AA or RAC) is not required for France, but may well be necessary if you intend to make excursions into neighbouring countries, such as Spain. You must have valid third-party insurance cover as a minimum requirement. An International Green Card (obtainable from your insurers) is strongly recommended and comprehensive breakdown insurance is also a wise precaution. An International Camping Carnet is not essential but can usually be deposited at Camp Reception as security, if you dislike handing over your passport for this purpose. Camping Carnets are obtainable from the motoring organisations, and from the G.B. Car Club, PO Box 11, Romsey, Hants (see advertisement on page 18).

Vehicle: You should display a GB plate or sticker on the rear of your vehicle and you should carry a spare set of light bulbs and a red warning triangle for use in the event of an accident or breakdown. Similarly you should ensure that your headlights dip to the RIGHT (conversion kits are available from motor accessory shops). Riders and passengers of motorcycles exceeding 50 cc. must wear crash helmets and special speed limits apply to machines up to 80 cc.

Drinking and Driving: Until recently the French were pretty relaxed about this, irrespective of the fact that they had laws not unlike ours. However, since August 1994, French drink and drive laws, and their implementation, have been considerably tightened up (the alcohol limit is now LOWER than in Britain) and they are now implementing their new law with some enthusiasm! The upshot is that if you have a couple of glasses of wine at lunchtime you are probably no longer (legally) fit to drive for the rest of the afternoon at least. Similarly speed limits are also being enforced more rigorously with hefty (we mean huge) on-the-spot fines for offenders.

Taking your caravan: Touring caravans may visit France for up to six consecutive months without formalities, but the following regulations apply:

* any vehicle towing a caravan must be fitted with adequate mirrors
* maximum dimensions are 2.5 m. wide, 11 m. long (for vehicle and trailer, max. length is 18 m).
* no passenger may be carried in a moving caravan.
* outside built-up areas the driver of the towing vehicle is required by law to keep a distance of 50 m. between him/herself and the vehicle ahead.
* vehicles towing caravans are not allowed into central Paris, or in the outer lane of 3 lane motorways.
* on narrow roads you are required to give way to vehicles wishing to overtake by slowing down or pulling into the side.
* in case of breakdown you MUST display a warning triangle at least 30 m. behind you (irrespective of hazard lights).
* if the caravan is hired or borrowed, you must have written authorisation from the registered owner.
* if the maximum gross weight of the caravan does not exceed the kerb weight of the towing vehicle, speed limits are the same as for cars. If the weight of your caravan is greater than this, graduated speed limits, from 65 kph. apply according to the caravan/car weight ratio.

Overnight parking: Strictly speaking, overnight parking is not allowed in lay-bys, but in the case of fatigue you should pull off the road and stop to rest. On Autoroutes you should not look upon the rest areas (Aires de Repos) as alternative camp sites, and your toll (péage) ticket is only valid for 24 or 48 hours, depending on the particular Autoroute concerned - check your ticket for details.
The Federation de Camping et Caravaning (FFCC) publish a 'Camping Car' guide to Aires de Service where there are facilities for overnight stops - see advertisement between pages 16 and 17.

Roads: France has a comprehensive road system, ranging from motorways (Autoroutes), Routes National (N roads), Routes Departmental (D roads) down to purely local C class roads; the Autoroute system is extensive but expensive! The use of Autoroutes nearly always involves the payment of substantial tolls and it is a matter of personal choice as to whether you prefer to use the normally much faster Autoroute, and pay the tolls, use the equivalent N road, or even avoid main roads altogether. Autoroutes are expensive, but they are fast and some savings in terms of the cost of overnight stops can sometimes offset the cost of tolls on a long journey. Up-to-date information on the prevailing toll charges is available from the French Government Tourist Office.

Maps and Guides: We have relied on Michelin maps for France ever since I first drove over there 30 something years ago, but in recent years the need for lots of maps has been obviated by the introduction of the Michelin Motoring Atlas covering all of France on 1:200,000 scale pages. Excellent value, easy to use and almost indispensable unless you intend to stick to main roads only! Arguably the spiral-bound version is the best. For users of personal computers, we also recommend Microsoft's Autoroute Express programme which we have found very useful for assistance in navigating around France.
Your interest and enjoyment of travelling in or through France can be much enhanced by use of a 'travel guide', of which of course there are lots to choose from; our own favourites are the books by fellow rally enthusiast Richard Binns (e.g. French Leave, and French Leave Encore) and his latest book 'Allez France' is actually directly related to the individual pages of the Michelin Atlas, as well as including an excellent 'Rapport Qualité-Prix' section on good value restaurants.

Post
Post Offices and many Tabacs (tobacconists) sell stamps; charges are roughly similar to those in the UK.

Telephone
To telephone the UK from France during 1996 you still need to dial 19 44 followed by the UK exchange code MINUS the first 0, followed by the subscriber's number. e.g. to telephone our office (01308 897809) from France you would dial: 19 44 1308 897809. Most French 'phone boxes now take 'phone cards not coins; 'phone cards (Telecartes) can be bought at post offices, tabacs and at most campsites. To call France from the UK, the code is now 00 33 followed by the local number in full. All Paris numbers are prefixed by '1'.

Car Ferry Services

The number of different services from the UK to France provides a wide choice of sailings to meet most needs. The actual choice is a matter of personal preference, influenced by factors such as where you live, your actual destination in France, cost and whether you see the channel crossing as a potentially enjoyable part of your holiday or, (if you are prone to sea-sickness) as something to be endured!

In terms of providing helpful information concerning ferries in this Guide, we have provided a summary of services likely to be operating in 1996 on information available at the time of going to press (Oct 95), together with a number of reports on those services which we have used ourselves during the last two years. Detailed up-to-date information will be available from Ferry Operators themselves, the Motoring Organisations and Travel Agents early in the New Year when the 1996 schedules are finalised; the information produced here is intended only as a provisional guide.

ROUTE	OPERATOR	SEASON	FREQUENCY	TIME
Dover-Calais	P&O Ferries	all year	up to 25 daily	75 mins
Dover-Calais	Stena Line Stena Lynx II	all year all year	up to 25 daily up to 7 daily	90 mins 45 mins
Dover-Calais	Hoverspeed	not January	up to 27 daily	35 mins
Folkestone-Boulogne	Hoverspeed	not January	up to 6 daily	55 mins
Ramsgate-Dunkirk	Sally Line	all year	up to 5 daily	150 mins
Ramsgate-Ostend	Ostend Line	all year	up to 6 daily	4 hours
Newhaven-Dieppe	Stena Line Stena Lynx II	all year from Jun 96	up to 4 daily up to 4 daily	4 hours 120 mins
Portsmouth-St. Malo	Brittany Ferries	all year	up to 2 daily	9/11 hours*
Portsmouth-Caen	Brittany Ferries	all year	up to 4 daily	6/7 hours*
Portsmouth-Le Havre	P&O Ferries	all year	up to 4 daily	5¾ hours
Portsmouth-Cherbourg	P&O Ferries	all year	up to 4 daily	5/9 hours*
Southampton-Cherbourg	Stena Line	all year	up to 3 daily	6/8 hours*
Poole-Cherbourg	Truckline	all year	up to 4 daily	4/7 hours*
Poole-St. Malo	Brittany Ferries	mid May-Sept.	up to 4 weekly	8/9 hours*
Plymouth-Roscoff	Brittany Ferries	all year	up to 3 daily	6/8 hours*
Cork-Roscoff or St. Malo	Brittany Ferries	May-Sept.	weekly	13 hours
Rosslare-Cherbourg	Irish Ferries	all year	varies	18 hours
Cork-Le Havre	Irish Ferries	from 25 March	varies	18+ hours

the longer time is for night sailings

Brittany Ferries
Millbay Docks, Plymouth PL1 3EW
(01752) 221321

P & O European Ferries
Channel House, Channel View Road,
Dover CT17 9TJ (01304) 203388

Stena Sealink Line
Charter House, Park Street, Ashford TN24 8EX
(01233) 647047

Sally Ferries
Argyle Centre, York Street, Ramsgate CT11 9DS
(01843) 595522

Hoverspeed
Maybrook House, Queens Gardens,
Dover CT17 9UQ (01304) 240241

Irish Ferries
2/4 Merrion Road, Dublin 2
(016) 610511

Ferry Reports

Even though we travel to France frequently in respect of our extensive Site Inspections Programme, we do not use all the various services summarised every year, and our reports therefore cover those services which we have used over the past two years.

 ## Hoverspeed Sea-Cat Service - Folkestone / Boulogne

The speed and comfort of the Sea Cat may well make it a realistic competitor to the Tunnel. There is easy access at Folkestone and the professionalism and courtesy of the staff is impressive. Embarkation is quick and efficient, obviously facilitated by the comparatively small number of vehicles accommodated. Once aboard the certain resemblance to air travel in terms of the seating arrangements is noticeable, but there is plenty of space and we had no trouble getting a seat, buying our `duty frees' or getting a snack and a drink from the bar. Admittedly the range of products is limited, but in view of the speed of the crossing and the extensive facilities (including a good duty free shop) at Boulogne, this is no great problem. The staff were all pleasant and helpful and the journey sped by in well under the hour (the Sea-Cat holds the cross-channel record for the quickest passenger vessel crossing, other than by hovercraft). The safety procedures were well demonstrated by an audio-visual presentation. There are two excellent observation areas on board - at the stern and immediately behind the bridge, where you can see the captain and crew at work navigating across the busiest sea lane in the world. A word of caution - don't stand on the stern observation deck when the engines are being started, especially if you're wearing light-coloured clothing! Disembarkation at Boulogne is quick and efficient, and this crossing makes a most relaxing stress-free start to a holiday.

 ## Truckline Service - Poole / Cherbourg

To be honest this is our favourite service, partly because we live less than an hour's drive from Poole, which is a small and easily accessible port, with facilities that are adequate and friendly. Since it started some years ago this service has offered good value for money, comfortable onboard facilities and good restaurants, and the introduction of the brand new `Barfleur' onto the route a couple of years ago has introduced a degree of luxury to rival any cross channel service. The main restaurant, for example, provides a variety of set menus in very pleasant surroundings and a standard of food and service which, on quite a few occasions, we have found to be consistently excellent and which represents very good value - not cheap, but value for money. The self-service cafeteria is also good, with reasonable prices, but tends to become more crowded. The ships, the good facilities and service, the interesting voyage along the Dorset coast for some miles and the very competitive fare structure combine to make this service well worth serious consideration. Cherbourg itself is worth a visit (the old town in particular) and there is a huge new hypermarket on the outskirts for stocking up with wine, etc. but be prepared for long (I mean around half an hour!) queues at the checkouts at busy times. The port facilities at Cherbourg were moved to a completely new terminal last year which includes the offices of the various operators, waiting room, toilets, restaurant, boutiques, bureau de change, phones, cashpoint machines, tourist information office, etc.

 ## Sally Line - Ramsgate / Dunkirk

As Ramsgate is a long way from Dorset, we seldom use this route, but on the occasions during the last two years when we have done so we have been well satisfied and, were it not for the long journey to Ramsgate, would probably use it more often.

The roads through Kent to Ramsgate have been greatly improved and access to the port is easy, although the final approach road is somewhat twisty and the check-in is rather exposed to the elements. Loading was quick and simple and, once on board (at the height of the season this year) the facilities and service were both good. We have eaten both in the large self service restaurant, and in the excellent but more expensive fixed price Smorgasbord. The food in the self-service restaurant was of a good standard, with a range of choices to suit most tastes and the self-service arrangements were if anything better than average. In common with most others in the peak season, the self-service restaurant was both busy and quite noisy, which doesn't encourage one to linger. The Smorgasbord offers substantial meals at a choice of two fixed prices, in more luxurious surroundings.

One criticism we have is the system whereby professional drivers (who share the same dining facilities) have vouchers for their meals and are thus able to `jump the queue' - there may be arguments in favour of this in terms of their having a job to do, whereas most passengers are on holiday and are thus deemed to be in less of a hurry (and not so hungry?!) but this isn't necessarily true. If commercial travellers and holidaymakers are to share the same facilities, then I think they should be afforded exactly the same treatment. The crossing (about 2 hours) is shorter than we're accustomed to on the western Channel routes, and disembarkation at Dunkirk presents no problem and fairly easy access to the Autoroutes.

 ## P & O European Ferries - Dover / Calais

With 20 sailings each way from October to March and 25 each way from April to September, Fares at a reasonable level, the use of 'super ferries' which make the crossing in 75 minutes and check-in time of 20 minutes, P & O are taking on the Channel Tunnel head on to ensure a competitive alternative to the latest method of reaching mainland Europe. Although prior booking is advisable, the space on each vessel means that, except perhaps at peak times, one can just turn up and cross on the next sailing.

The A20 extension to the M20 Folkestone to the Eastern Dock entrance at Dover and the direct access to the French Autoroute system at Calais with the pleasant 'cruise' across the channel in between, now make for a hassle free beginning to the holiday and a smooth start on the continental journey. This also helps the transition to driving on the right as, by the time one needs to use 'ordinary' roads, one has become used to overtaking on the left. Apart from these advantages, the ferries have been modernised to the highest standards with waiter and self-service restaurants, shops selling a wide range of duty-free and other goods, comfortable bars and lounges and 'Club Class' at a small supplement for those who want peace and quiet away from the bustle on the decks below. Boarding and leaving the ships has been made simple by the use of double width ramps on two levels.

 ## P & O European Ferries - Portsmouth / Le Havre

The `Pride of Portsmouth', one of the new super ferries which operates this service, is most impressive and provided us with very comfortable crossings in late September and early October, despite gale warnings, when we attended the Castels et Camping convention at Disneyland Paris. We were fortunate perhaps to have been travelling on night services with excellent cabins, and thus able to enjoy a good night's rest in spite of the weather. This is probably one of the few services whereby one can travel overnight to France returning the next night and still have plenty of time to visit Paris for a day without a too exhausting drive. We were able to enjoy an excellent meal in the main restaurant, and a plus point on this night service is the fact that the duty free shop, restaurant etc. are all open as soon as you board, which means you can get a meal, do some shopping, and still get to bed at a reasonable hour.

 ## Brittany Ferries - Poole / St. Malo

Although a long crossing (some 8 hours), facilities on this new service were very good, especially with the added attraction of a cinema on board showing new releases, an ideal means to while away a couple of hours; another two hours or so in the restaurant, and the trip is half completed.

The staff were exceptionally helpful and friendly, and generally the ship was both spacious and very comfortable - this is certainly a convenient and relaxing route which will be of particular interest to those visiting Brittany or the Vendée, especially if you prefer smaller and quite attractive ports, of which both Poole and St. Malo are good examples. The excellent service throughout was what we have come to expect from Brittany Ferries, and for those of us living west of Southampton, services from Poole are a real convenience, and whilst on the face of it they are not the cheapest crossings, the savings in time, fuel and stress associated with travelling to ports further east more than compensate for the somewhat higher fares.

The Channel Tunnel
"Le Shuttle"

Eurotunnel has certainly had its problems both with constructing the under channel link, getting the trains up and rolling and in getting its finances right. However, the first two difficulties have now been overcome and that is all that will worry those who wish to journey quickly and smoothly beneath the waves rather than on them. Hailed as one of the wonders of the modern world this joint British/French initiative proved to be more difficult than experienced engineers could foresee and although it took longer to achieve than had been anticipated, is a tribute to imagination and skill.

Access to the terminals on both sides of the channel is from motorways. On the British side it is served from junction 11a of the M20 London/Folkestone motorway and junction 13 of the A16 Calais/Boulogne autoroute in France. It is a slick operation and now caravans and motorcaravans, as well as cars and lorries may use this service. *Le Shuttle* is essentially a "turn up and go" operation but it is still worth booking in advance as, from time to time special promotion offers are available only for those who pre-book. Price structure depends on season, duration of stay abroad and time you will pass through tollbooths, not actual time of departure. An inclusive price is charged for the vehicle and for up to the number of passengers legally allowed to travel in the vehicle.

Unlike lorries which travel in open-sided wagons, cars, caravans and motorcaravans make the journey in closed trucks. Double-deck carriages are used for cars and single-deck for other vehicles. As it is not possible to offer the shopping and other services available on a conventional ferry during the crossing, there are Service Areas at both terminals. These are situated between the tollbooths and the reporting area for vehicles, necessitating a short, well sign-posted, detour on the route to the boarding points to purchase duty-free products, have a snack or meal, change currency and use toilets. At Folkestone, in addition to a well stocked duty-free shop, W.H. Smith, Boots, the AA and RAC, Hamleys, Tie Rack have retail outlets along with souvenirs, a coffee bar, Burger bar and Tavern which also offers meals. On the French side the mix is slightly different but, at the terminal complex, there is a large hypermarket [also available to those not using the shuttle] with about 100 shops, bars, restaurants etc. and a large cinema with a range of programmes.

The route to the Folkestone terminal is straightforward from exit 11a of the M20 travelling from the London direction and well signed if approaching from Dover. On approaching the line of tollbooths, signs direct drivers to head for an available booth shown with a green arrow on the gantry. Checking-in is easy and efficient and, once through here, one either heads direct for the boarding point or drives via the services area. Once through passport/customs check, vehicles queue in a boarding line. Signs show the next loading and departure time. Loading commences about 20 minutes before the shuttle departs. Following the number shown overhead, drivers proceed to the train, enter at a reasonable angle and continue driving along the train until an attendant signals a halt. About 5 cars are accommodated in each section between shutters which are then lowered. The carriages are well-lit, have a walk way on each side of the vehicle with toilets available. Printed instructions request drivers to secure car in gear with hand-brake on and windows and vents open. Smoking is not allowed either in the service area or on the train. Messages are relayed on an overhead strip screen during the journey. A special VHF radio service is available during the crossing although this had broken down during my return crossing. Attendants pass up and down the train during the journey.

Driving off is a matter of following the car in front and, because customs and immigration procedures have been completed at the start of the crossing, exit into the terminal area is quick and simple. Roads linking with the motorway/autoroute are well signed. Caravanners and motor caravanners are catered for with toilet emptying points at both terminals. Before the start of each crossing, gas bottles and caravan doors are sealed to prevent their use during the journey.

The 35 minute crossing quoted refers to the time the train starts moving until it stops on the other side and one can expect to be away from the arrival terminal very quickly. However, the time taken from tollbooth to final exit depends on how long is taken driving to the boarding point, the wait to board and the frequency of the service. The day I travelled two consecutive trains were cancelled and there was an hours delay between the time I was ready to leave Folkestone and the next train.

Once one gets going, the crossing is quick and efficient although I found it rather boring without the on-board diversions of a conventional ferry. The young staff on duty were all very helpful, pleasant and efficient. *Le Shuttle* provides an excellent alternative means of crossing to France particularly for those averse to sea crossings and those who dislike the bustle of crowds milling around on boats.

Gerry Ovenden
who travelled as a guest of Eurotunnel.

Eurostar
The Channel Tunnel Rail Link - London / Paris

The opening of the Channel Tunnel was long awaited. However, now it has been completed it offers travellers an alternative to crossing the channel by ferry over the unpredictably choppy seas, which is good news for all those who suffer from sea-sickness. Others may comment on Le Shuttle, the car train, but I would like to share with you my experiences of Eurostar, the rail passenger service.

Eurostar may not be of immediate interest to those towing caravans or trailer tents, but we found that our family could still get fully together for its annual camping holiday by using its speed and convenience. I'm afraid I was the problem... after my GCSE exams I had the customary long wait for results and college to start and, in order to get a summer job, my holiday window was restricted to just the one week. I certainly didn't want to spend half of it travelling! We live in Weymouth, and luckily trains from here come in just a few platforms away from the Eurostar terminal at Waterloo.

The train leaves from Waterloo station and travellers are asked to check-in at least twenty minutes before the departure of the train. Once you have worked out exactly how to enter your ticket into one of the many hi-tech machines at the entrance to the platforms, and once you have found out that the machine wont accept your ticket, and once you have had it checked in manually by one of the staff on hand, you enter, through posh automatic doors into a room which is so bright and clean you are lead to believe you are making the journey from earth to heaven rather than London to Paris. It is this room in which your luggage and yourself are scanned for any concealed weapons you are trying to smuggle to France. It is at this point that you should, to avoid any embarrassment, remove all large metal objects from your person. I myself was called back because of a harmonica in my back pocket, although some would describe such an object as a lethal weapon. The Eurostar staff had obviously never heard me play or they would have never let me have it back!

The next cryptic puzzle that confronts you involves choosing one of four elevators from the information given on as many monitors. At this point in time, struggling to match up the data on your ticket with that of the monitors whilst juggling with your luggage, you are likely to be descended upon by the most helpful and careful of people that are the Eurostar stewards and stewardesses. These smiling faces will tell you where to go and what to do which leaves you wondering what the point was in having the monitors in the first place.

Once on the train you can dump your luggage, help yourself to a newspaper, sit back, relax and perhaps find out that you have a seat next to an American student who has set himself the objective of chatting up the pretty French stewardess who walks up and down the surprisingly wide isle with a drinks and snacks trolley. The items on the trolley can be paid for with French or English money. One of the first things you notice about the train is how comfortable the seats are. While the train glides out of the station, if you are lucky enough to have a window seat, you can gloat at all the passengers in the British Rail trains who won't be in Paris in a few hours. After which you can enjoy the scenery en route to Dover.

On the hour you arrive at the entrance to the tunnel and for just twenty minutes are robbed of the outside world. However, almost before you can say 'Isn't it dark in here', you are blinded by a rush of light, and if you think that was quick - you ain't seen nothin' yet.

It is not long before you are informed that the train has reached it's top speed of 186 mph and as you gently tilt into the bends you realise why this train makes a good old British Rail train seem like a bathtub on wheels. An hour and forty minutes later, only three hours into the journey and shortly after you have got over the awesome realisation of how fast you are going, you arrive in Paris. You jump off the train with a feeling you haven't had since you were eight years old just after your first fairground ride. The only thought in your head being 'Again, Again'!

The difference between first and second class is that with first class you have slightly wider seats, designer upholstery and electric blinds. You also get a free meal of limited choice but of a high quality. The facilities are excellent and include desks, lights, air conditioning and arm rests to all seats. Although the boarding system is confusing and the technology a bit bewildering there is always a member of staff who will be only too glad to help. For business trips the train is perfect, but the barrier that is having to get to London (or indeed Paris) first means that you have to plan the rest of your travels around the trip.

Having arrived at the Gare du Nord, my journey was to continue on to Brive-la-Gaillard, just north of the Dordogne area. A brave choice was to walk across Paris, the only problem being how to navigate the streets of the busy Capital. The map and a few helpful Parisians helped me find the Gare d'Austerlitz... about an hour's walk. A less scenic but also less tiring alternative would be to take the metro. The SNCF train took just under four hours to travel the considerable distance, rather quicker than Intercity, but an equivalent comfort level.

Let's review the situation. I was able to travel up to London the night before and stay with my aunt, catch the 8.30 am. from Waterloo to Paris, walk between stations, catch the train to Brive, and meet my parent at 6 pm. French time. Only the hour time difference made the overnight in London preferable. On the way back, the hour worked in my favour.... I left Brive at 10 am, was in Paris at 1.50, had three hours sightseeing, zoomed back to Waterloo, changed platforms, and arrived back home in Weymouth in time for Match of the Day!

Many families find that older children can't go on holiday for the full duration due to other commitments. Most of these older children appreciate a bit of time `home alone', but those of us who have camped in Europe before don't want to miss out completely. Eurostar represents a valuable link which saves considerable time, and makes it feasible to join the rest of the family for a week or so. A one way trip, going out with the family and coming back by train is maybe the best option pricewise and timewise, but I enjoyed it so much I hope to travel both ways again next year!

Chris Aylott
who travelled as a guest of Eurostar.

eurostar

Useful telephone numbers:

British Rail International 0171 834 2345 (for times and fares in Europe)
Eurostar Information and bookings 0345 300 003.

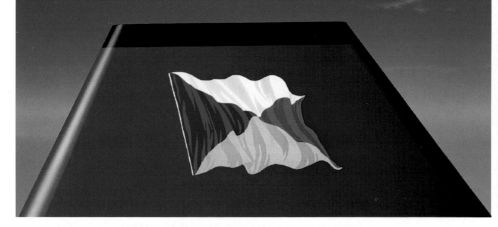

CHANNEL CROSSING IN
THE CONTEMPORARY STYLE

Sally Ferries has Channel crossing down to a fine art. So why not take advantage of our excellent prices and service and cruise across to France or Belgium?

For more information or to make a booking, call us now on 01843 595522, or contact your local travel agent.

For frequent travellers abroad...

ANNUAL POLICY

If you or your family are frequent travellers abroad you will probably save money by taking out our Gold Cover ANNUAL Policy. You will be covered for all your trips abroad up to an overall limit of 178 days with no one trip exceeding 91 days. The cover for each trip is as outlined under Gold Cover in the previous pages.

PREMIUM TABLE All rates include Government Insurance Premium Tax of 2.5%

HOLIDAY INSURANCE	Insured only	Family *	MOTORING SERVICE – Europe only	
EUROPE only	£ 88	£145	Vehicle	£99
WORLDWIDE (Excluding USA/Canada/Caribbean)	£135	£215	Caravan/Trailer	£40
WORLDWIDE	£165	£285		

Children under 4 are included free. *Family defined as two adults plus dependant children under the age of 18 and in full time education.

APPLICATION FORM
BLOCK CAPITALS PLEASE

Please complete and return to Deneway Guides, Chesil Lodge, West Bexington, Dorchester DT2 9DG

Cover Required (tick appropriate box)

Holiday Insurance – Europe only ☐

Holiday Insurance – Worldwide ☐
(excluding USA/Canada/Caribbean)

Holiday Insurance – Worldwide ☐

Motoring Service – Europe only ☐

Caravan//Trailer ☐

Date cover to commence [   ]

(Remember you are not covered for cancellation costs until cover commences)

Name of Proposer in full (Mr, Mrs or Miss)	Age	Premiums
		£
Less 10% Special Discount Due		£
TOTAL Premium Due		£

ADDRESS IN FULL

Postcode

Daytime Tel No.

Details of other people to be insured (continue on second sheet of paper if not enough room)

Name	Age	Name	Age
1.		3.	
2.		4.	

PAYMENT. Choose your method of payment and tick appropriate box.

☐ I enclose cheque for £[   ]   Cheques made payable to Deneway Ltd

☐ Debit my Access/Visa
Credit Card No. [   ]   Expiry Date [   ]

Name of
Cardholder [   ]   Signature [   ]   Date [   ]

● Holiday travel insurance   ● Covers all your holidays and trips abroad
● Personal emergency service   ● Optional Motoring breakdown and accident service

FOR IMMEDIATE COVER PHONE 01308 897809

GOLD COVER INSURANCE

for all Motoring Holidays

SPECIAL READER 10% OFF OFFER

DON'T LET AN EMERGENCY RUIN YOUR HOLIDAY

- Holiday insurance
- Optional motoring (and caravan) breakdown and accident service
- Personal emergency assistance

How Gold Cover gives you the best protection

HOLIDAY INSURANCE and Personal Emergency Assistance per person

- Cancellation costs, plus additional expenses from delay (including missed Motorail connections) due to illness, blockade, strike or breakdown etc.

- Medical expenses, repatriation etc – up to £2 million.

- 24 hour help service for all emergencies.

- Personal accident – up to £20,000. There is an age limit of 75 for this part only and for motor cyclists the cover is halved.

- Baggage and personal money up to.£1,250.

- Legal liability – up to £2 million.

- Legal expenses – up to £25,000.

MOTORING SERVICE

- Cover starts 7 days BEFORE you travel. Allows you to hire a car if your own vehicle becomes unusable.

- Roadside assistance for motoring breakdown or accident with emergency repairs and towing – up to £250.

- Obtaining replacement parts (but not the cost of them – no limit).

- Vehicle hire up to £750 (or £1500 if Supplement purchased).

- Cost of repatriating vehicle if repairs cannot be done abroad – up to market value of vehicle.

- Alternative accommodation up to £100 per person (or £200 if Supplement purchased).

- Vehicle hire in UK, if delay in repatriation – up to £150.

- Provision for alternative driver – no limit.

- Bail bond, legal advice and legal expenses – up to £2,000.

The policy document will be sent to you, details the cover in full and contains a 14 day Money Back Guarantee if for any reason you are not happy with the policy.

See over for application form:▶

for all Motoring Holidays

Use the application form below to claim 10% discount on your Gold Cover insurance protection for your holiday in 1996.

SPECIAL READER 10% OFF OFFER

EASY COST CALCULATOR TABLE including Government Insurance Premium Tax of 2.5%							
HOLIDAY INSURANCE EUROPE	Period up to 3 days	Period up to 6 days	Period up to 9 days	Period up to 17 days	Period up to 24 days	Period up to 31 days	Each Extra Week or Part
ADULTS CHILDREN	£	£	£	£	£	£	£
1 0	7.50	10.50	13.50	21.00	24.00	28.00	5.50
1	13.13	18.38	23.63	36.75	42.00	49.00	9.63
2	18.75	26.25	33.75	52.50	60.00	70.00	13.75
3	24.38	34.13	43.88	68.25	78.00	91.00	17.88
4	30.00	42.00	54.00	84.00	96.00	112.00	22.00
2 0	15.00	21.00	27.00	42.00	48.00	56.00	11.00
1	20.63	28.88	37.13	57.75	66.00	77.00	15.13
2	26.25	36.75	47.25	73.50	84.00	98.00	19.25
3	31.88	44.63	57.38	89.25	102.00	119.00	23.38
4	37.50	52.50	67.50	105.00	120.00	140.00	27.50
3 0	22.50	31.50	40.50	63.00	72.00	84.00	16.50
1	28.13	39.38	50.63	78.75	90.00	105.00	20.63
2	33.75	47.25	60.75	94.50	108.00	126.00	24.75
3	39.38	55.13	70.88	110.25	126.00	147.00	28.88
4	45.00	63.00	81.00	126.00	144.00	168.00	33.00
4 0	30.00	42.00	54.00	84.00	96.00	112.00	22.00
1	35.63	49.88	64.13	99.75	114.00	133.00	26.13
2	41.25	57.75	74.25	115.50	132.00	154.00	30.25
3	46.88	65.63	84.38	131.25	150.00	175.00	34.38
4	52.50	73.50	94.50	147.00	168.00	196.00	38.50

Double these rates for Winter Sports. Multiply rates by 2½ for Worldwide Cover.
For UK & N.Ireland 40% reduction and S. Ireland 25% reduction on these rates.

MOTORING SERVICE (only for vehicles up to 15 years 11 months old (back to 'W' registration)	22.00	27.00	35.00	44.00	48.00	50.00	10.00
SUPPLEMENT	9.00	10.50	11.50	15.00	17.50	19.00	4.50
CARAVAN/TRAILER	14.00	14.00	14.00	14.00	14.00	14.00	NO CHARGE

INSTRUCTIONS

1. Work out the period of insurance you will need – be careful, departure sailing on the 2nd June, with return sailing on the 11th June is 10 days NOT 9 days.

2. Using the line in the table opposite which corresponds with the number in your party, will tell you the cost of the Holiday Insurance for the 'Period' you will need. Don't include children under 4 – they go free!

3. Add the Motoring Breakdown Service cost (if needed) and, if you wish to take the Supplement (increases hire limit to £1,500 and accommodation limit to £200 per person) or include your caravan or trailer, add the cost for these.

FOR IMMEDIATE COVER PHONE
01308 897809

APPLICATION FORM
BLOCK CAPITALS PLEASE

If you would like the protection Gold Cover Insurance can offer please complete the application below and return to Deneway Guides, Chesil Lodge, West Bexington, Dorchester DT2 9DG

HOLIDAY DETAILS
Outward Voyage — Day | Month | Year

Inward Voyage — Day | Month | Year

No of Adults in party

No of Children in party (4 & under 14)

Tick if cover required for Winter Sport Activities

Name

Address

Postcode

Daytime Tel No.

COVER REQUIRED
Please insert premium in box(s) for cover required   PREMIUM

Holiday Insurance £

Motoring Service £

Motoring Supplement (Only available in conjunction with Motoring Service) £

Caravan/Trailer (Only available in conjunction with Motoring Service) £

TOTAL PREMIUM £

LESS 10% SPECIAL DISCOUNT DUE £

NET DUE £

PAYMENT
Choose your method of payment and tick appropriate box:

I enclose cheque for £
Cheques payable to Deneway Ltd.

Access/Visa Credit Card

Expiry Date

Name of Cardholder

Signed

Date

19

FRENCH FLAVOUR HOLIDAYS

DISCOVER THE REAL TASTE OF RURAL FRANCE

ALL INCLUSIVE LOW SEASON CARAVANNING
MOTOR CARAVANNING AND CAMPING HOLIDAYS
TO BURGUNDY AND THE ALPS

- TOP QUALITY 4 STAR CAMPSITES
- FREE CROISSANTS & BREAD delivered daily to your pitch
- FREE LOAN OF BICYCLES THROUGHOUT YOUR STAY
- FREE REGIONAL GUIDES AND MAPS
- DISCOUNTS OF UP TO 50 % on entry fees to local attractions
- ESCORTED VINEYARD AND CHATEAU VISITS
- GASTRONOMIC DINNERS featuring regional specialties
- WINE AND LOCAL PRODUCE TASTINGS
- PETANQUE MATCHES, evening entertainment ...

and much more to enjoy

FOR AN UNFORGETTABLE HOLIDAY
IN THE GROUNDS OF A MEDIEVAL CHATEAU OR
AMIDST THE BREATHTAKING SCENERY OF THE FRENCH ALPS

CALL FOR A FREE COLOUR BROCHURE

TELEPHONE : (UK) 0171 229 1464

or write to French Flavour Holidays Gigny sur Saône 71420 FRANCE

0101M Camping Municipal Montrevel, Montrevel en Bresse

This is a large site with over 500 marked and numbered pitches (all with 6 or 10A electricity). The majority are of a good size, hedged and on flat grass, with reasonable shade in most parts. Although large, the site is spacious and certainly did not feel too pressurised when we visited in late June. It is on the edge of a large, 250-acre lake with its own beach and adjacent public beach, and a variety of watersports, including sailing, windsurfing, and, on another part of the lake, water-skiing. Campers may bring boats, but **not** motor boats. Minigolf and tennis courts, etc. are on or adjacent to the site. Adventure play area on beach. A restaurant and shop adjacent to the site open in the main season, but Montrevel is an attractive, small town, only 300 m. walk. Sanitary facilities are in nine rather elderly blocks, with some newer ones in the course of completion. The facilities are functional and include hot showers with dividers, some washbasins in cabins, British type WCs, washing machines and dryer. All have a slightly institutionalised feel but seem adequate. The site is used by tour operators.

Directions: Site is approx. 20 km. east of Macon. From the A40 autoroute, take exit 40 (Bourg Nord) but travel north on the D975 for 10 km. to Montrevel. Site is signed on the D28 in the direction of Etrez.

Charges guide:
-- Per unit incl. electricity Ffr. 37.40 - 52.80; person 17.60 - 19.80; child (2-7 yrs) 8.80 - 9.90.
Open: 15 April - 30 Sept.
Address: Base de Plein Air, 01340 Montrevel en Bresse.
Tel: 74.30.80.52. FAX: 74.30.80.77.
Reservations: Required for mid July - mid Aug - write to site with 25% deposit.

0200 Camping Caravaning du Vivier aux Carpes, Seraucourt-le-Grand

Small, quiet site, close to A26, two hours from Calais, ideal for overnight stop or longer stay.

This relatively new site is imaginatively set out taking full benefit of large ponds which are well stocked for fishing. There is also abundant wild life. The 60 spacious pitches, all at least 100 sq.m. are on flat grass and dividing hedges are growing. All have electricity (6A), some with water points and there are special pitches for motorcaravans. The site has a spacious feel although it is close to the village centre. The sanitary block is spacious and spotlessly clean, with separate, heated facilities for handicapped visitors, also available to other campers in the winter months. Laundry facilities. Upstairs there is a large TV/games room with table tennis and snooker. Small children's play area and a petanque court. There is, however, plenty to see in the area, with the cathedral cities of St Quentin, Reims, Amiens and Laon close, Disneyland is just over an hour, Compiegne and the World War 1 battlefields are near and Paris easily reached by train (1¼ hrs from St. Quentin). Day trips arranged to Paris (Ffr 160 p.p) or to Disneyland with English speaking guide. The enthusiastic owners speak excellent English and are keen to welcome British visitors. Although there is no restaurant on site, good and reasonable hotels are close. We were impressed by the ambience created and would recommend this site to those seeking tranquillity in an attractive setting. Gates close 10.30 pm, office open 10.00-11.30 am, 5-7 pm. Motorcaravan service point. Caravan storage available. Rallies welcome.

Directions: Leave A26 (Calais-Reims) road at exit 11 and take D1 left towards Soissons. On entering Essigny-la-Grand (4 km.) turn sharp right on D72 signed Seraucourt-le-Grand (5 km). Site clearly signed - it is in the centre of the village.

Charges 1996:
-- Per unit incl. 2 persons and electricity Ffr 80.00; extra person 15.00; child (under 10 yrs) 10.00; pets 5.00.
-- Discounts for students with tents.
Open: All year.
Address: 10 Rue Charles Voyeux, 02790 Seraucourt-le-Grand.
Tel: 23.60.50.10 (French) or 23.60.51.02 (English). FAX: 23.60.51.69.
Reservations: Recommended for peak season.

0201M Camping de Parc de l'Ailette, Chamouille, nr Laon

The Parc de l'Ailette and the purpose built campsite are approached through an area of France which has many war cemeteries, within the triangle formed by the towns of Laon, Soissons and Reims. The development offers many leisure opportunities but also forms a most attractive nature reserve with abundant wildlife. The 500 acre lake forms the centre for many of the activities, including watersports (over some of its area only and no motor boats) and swimming from a sandy beach. Here also are minigolf, tennis and a playground. Elsewhere are boat hire, horse riding, a jogging track, 18 hole golf course, fishing and miles of signed walks. Adjacent to the beach is the well designed campsite with 180 large, numbered pitches, all with electricity and marked by growing hedges of ornamental shrubs. Arranged in groups with excellent access roads and well kept grass, most have lovely views over the lake. Site buildings are modern and include three sanitary blocks, each divided into small rooms containing either toilets or showers and washbasins (some in cabins). Hot water is free. Dishwashing outside each block, laundry and facilities for the handicapped by reception. Snack bar with takeaway and shop (limited hours out of main season). Restaurants at the nearby hotel and in the local villages. A few seasonal units. The Parc and site are said to be crowded in high season. Good security.

Charges 1996:
-- Per pitch Ffr. 25.00; extra tent 11.00; car 16.00; m/cycle 10.00; adult 20.00; child (4-7 yrs) 10.00; electricity 17.00; local tax 1.00.
-- Credit cards accepted.
Open:
6 April - 15 September.
Address:
Camping de l'Ailette, 02860 Chamouille.
Tel:
23.24.83.06.
FAX: 23.24.75.80.
Reservations:
Essential in high season and made with Ffr. 20 fee - details from site.

Directions: Follow signs to Parc Nautique des Vallées l'Ailette from N2, N44 and N31 roads connecting Soissons, Laon and Reims. Chamouille is on D967.

0205M Camping Municipal La Cascade, Hirson

Approached by an 800 m. private road, and close by the river l'Oise, but near to a railway line, this is a pretty little site. On two levels, it provides 100 marked pitches, all with 6A electricity, on gently sloping ground. It has the advantage of a small swimming pool, but the young trees provide little shade - not too critical in this northern area probably! The single, rather elderly, sanitary block is just about adequate, but the men's WCs are all of the Turkish variety (the women's are British type) and the few hot showers are on payment (Ffr. 3.25 token from reception) Similarly hot water for washing up requires payment (1.75). Given the low tariff, these charges are more of an irritant than a serious consideration. Apart from the pool, there is a children's play area and half-court tennis, and some nice walks by the river to the waterfalls that give the site its name. There are few other facilities, and the town of Hirson is about 2-3 km. distant by road.

Charges guide:
-- Per person Ffr. 7.30; child (4-7 yrs) 3.65; pitch 5.50; car or m/cycle 4.90; pet 1.80; electricity (6A) 12.00.
Open:
23 April - 25 September
Address:
02500 Hirson
Tel:
23.58.18.97 (low season: 23.58.26.01).
Reservations:
Not normally made or needed, if in doubt ring.

Directions: Site is just off the N43, 1 km. northwest of Hirson, clearly marked with a banner. Follow signs for 800 m. down private road, through ford.

0303 Camping Les Acacias au Bord du Lac, Bellerive, Vichy

Well tended site quite close to town with swimming pool adjacent.

Quietly situated on the edge of the town and with few on-site activities, this small site has a well kept and peaceful look and very helpful owners. There are 90 individual pitches with electricity, of good size and separated from each other by neat full hedges. Of these 60% have TV (satellite) and water connections also. The site, which extends to the edge of the river, is in two parts separated by an access road. With a sanitary block (recently renovated) in each part, there should be an ample coverage. They have continental style toilets, washbasins in private cabins with free hot water, and a good supply of free hot showers with immediate hot water. No shop but supermarket and restaurants close. TV room with BBC by satellite. Table tennis. Laundry facilities. Vichy is a well kept town with select parts, comprehensive sporting facilities and a wide range of entertainment in season. Large open-air and heated covered municipal pools are a short walk and a small pool with tiled floor and surrounds (15/6-15/9) has been installed on site. Mobile homes for hire. Site is full for most of July/Aug.

Charges 1996:
-- Per person Ffr. 26.00; child (under 7 yrs) 13.00; pitch 32.00; electricity (6A) 14.00.
-- Less in low seasons.
-- Credit cards accepted.
Open:
1 April - 8 October.
Address:
03700 Bellerive sur Allier.
Tel:
70.32.36.22 (winter: 70.32.58.48).
Reservations:
Made without deposit.

Directions: Site is on south side of town in suburb of Bellerive just south of the river; cross river by Pont Bellerive bridge, turn left, and follow camp signs.

Alan Rogers' discount
Low season discounts

0301 Camping de la Filature, Ebreuil

Small peaceful riverside site with a difference.

Situated near the spa town of Vichy and bordering the Massif Central area, this site provides the opportunity to explore this lesser known and unspoilt area of France known as the Auvergne. Originally developed around a spinning mill (even today the hot water is provided by log burning - note the chimney), the site has an individuality not normally evident in French sites. This is being perpetuated by its new English owners with their artistic flair.

The site lies beside the River Sioule and there are 50 spacious, grassy pitches with some shade from mature fruit trees. All can be supplied with electricity (3 or 6A). At the time of our visit a rare orchid had been discovered by the river bank and indeed the whole area is a naturalist's paradise. The sanitary facilities, converted from the original buildings, are all individual, opening into an alley way with gaily painted arches and now completely refurbished. Well cleaned they provide free hot water, continental and British style toilets, 8 showers and a bathroom, washcabins and hairdrying facilities. River bathing is said to be possible but it may be a little shallow at the height of the summer and there are fishing facilities on site (drying room, permits, tackle, etc). Bicycle hire - many tracks for mountain biking nearby. Riding, canoeing and tennis nearby. Washing machine and ironing facilities. Bread can be ordered. Takeaway food - traditional French cooking or straight forward English (10/5-20/9) and a bar. A site speciality is selling local wine. Minigolf. Table football. Children's play area. Table tennis. Barbecue facilities. Rooms and 3 mobile homes for hire.

Charges 1995:
-- Per unit incl. 2 persons Ffr. 70.00; extra person (over 10 yrs) 20.00, (under 10 yrs) 10.00; electricity 3A 9.00, 6A 16.00.
-- Less in low season.
-- Credit cards accepted.
Open:
1 April - 30 September.
Address:
03450 Ebreuil.
Tel:
70.90.72.01.
FAX: 70.90.79.48.
Reservations:
Made with deposit (Ffr 200 per week of stay or full amount if stay costs less).

Directions: Site is signed at exit 12 of new A71 autoroute to Clermont Ferrand in the direction of Ebreuil. Site is west of Ebreuil beside the river.

DON'T WAIT TO DIE TO GO TO HEAVEN,
COME TO THE CAMPING DE LA FILATURE!

- HOT hot water, *even in low season.*
- VERY clean facilities.
- New bar and terrace.
- Take-away food and home made pizza.
- Spacious plots beside one of the cleanest rivers in Europe, one of France's finest trout rivers.

For information in the U.K., ring Stamford (01780) 55857

REDUCED RATES IN LOW SEASON

Camping de la Filature
★ ★ ★ ★
Tel: (00 33) 70 90 72 01
FAX: (00 33) 70 90 79 48

0302 Castel Camping-Caravaning Château de Chazeuil, Varennes s. Allier

Useful night-stop in central France, adjacent to main road.

Although adjacent to the main N7, this site is attractively situated in a large park and traffic noise should be no problem. The site is established around the château with a range of good quality amenities including a new sanitary block with modern fittings and facilities, with provision for the handicapped and a swimming pool (open 15/6-15/9). Pitches are marked and 60 have electricity (4-10A), with many mature trees providing shade. Reading room. Children's play area. Fitness track (2 km.) in wood. Table tennis. This site should provide a pleasantly relaxing night-stop or a base to explore the Bourbonnais region.

Charges 1995:
-- Per person Ffr 26.00; child (under 7) 16.00; pitch 21.00; car 18.00; m/cycle 10.00; animal 6.00; electricity 18.00.
Open:
15 April - 15 October.
Address:
03150 Varennes/Allier.
Tel:
70.45.00.10.
Reservations:
Made for min. 3 days with Ffr. 300 deposit.

Directions: Site is on the eastern side of the main N7, 25 km south of Moulins, almost opposite the D46 turning for St Pourcain.

0304 Camping Champ de la Chapelle, Braize, nr St Bonnet Troncais

Very quiet, rural site with large pitches in the 10,500 hectare Forest of Troncais.

This small site is the perfect answer for those who want to get away from it all. With only 80 pitches set in 5.6 hectares, they are large (up to 250 sq.m.) with plenty of shade and open space. It is the policy of the owner to keep the site small, quiet and unsophisticated. The reward is the wealth of wild life that abounds here - you may see red squirrels, deer, bee-eaters or hoopoes. Of the 80 pitches, 62 have electricity (16A) and water. There are only 7 static pitches and no tour operators. The sanitary block is new and well appointed with British toilets. Washbasins are in private cabins and have razor points, mirrors, shelves and hot water. Showers are pre-set, pushbutton type with dressing area, hooks and shelves. There are low toilets for children. Dishwashing facilities are good and there is a washing machine and dryer. Small snack kiosk selling croque monsieur, pizza, quiche, soft drinks, ices, etc. Bread is sometimes available but there is no shop - the nearest supermarket is 5 km. away at St Bonnet. Swimming pool, children's play area and courts for volleyball, flipball and petanque. Mountain bikes may be hired by the day or half day. There are many lakes in the area - one at 5 km. offers fishing, bathing, pedaloes, canoes, sail-boarding, minigolf, volleyball, tennis and, in high season, organised rambles every day. At 6 km. there is horse riding and archery and the whole area is a paradise for nature lovers, cyclists and walkers.

Directions: From the N144 Bourges-Montlucon road take the D978A eastward and then the D28 to Braize from where the site is signed.

Charges 1996: -- Per unit incl. 1 person Ffr. 44.00; extra person over 5 yrs 12.00, under 5 yrs 6.00; electricity 14.00.
Open: 1 May - 15 September.
Address: Braize, 03360 St Bonnet Troncais.
Tel: 70.06.15.45.
Reservations: Made for any period with deposit (Ffr. 300) and fee (60).

0320M Camping Municipal du Lac, Neris Les Bains

This is a modern site on the edge of a very attractive, small spa town. Offering a total of 150 mainly flat, grassy pitches, all with 10A electrical connections, this site is actually a combination of two smaller sites. Situated within walking distance of the centre of the town, it is on two levels alongside a small lake and is pleasantly laid out with pitches mainly in small bays. The three sanitary blocks, of modern purpose-built construction are of a generally good standard which varies slightly from block to block. They provide some British type WCs, hot showers with dividers, hooks, etc., washbasins in private cabins, washing machine and dryer. Although close to the town's many and varied facilities, the site has its own attractive bar with snacks and restaurant, beside a stream which runs through the lower part of the site.

Directions: Site is 500 m. from the RN144, signed in the town centre.

Charges guide: -- Per unit incl. 1 person and electricity Ffr. 49.00; extra person 18.40; child (4-10 yrs) 9.20; plus local tax.
Open: 1 April - 30 October.
Address: Avenue Marx-Dormoy, 03310 Neris les Bains.
Tel: 70.03.17.69 or 24.70.
Reservations: Contact site.

0403 Camping Lac du Moulin de Ventre, Niozelles, Forcalquier

Small, peaceful lakeside site, close to the Luberon.

Near Forcalquier, a busy French town, this is an attractive site situated beside a small lake offering opportunities for swimming (supervised in season), canoeing or for hiring a pedalo and 28 acres of wooded, hilly land available for walking. Trees and shrubs are labelled and the herbs of Provence can be found growing wild. A nature lover's delight - birds and butterflies abound. Some 75 of the total of 100 level, grassy pitches have electricity (6-10A) and there is some shade from the variety of trees. This is a family run site, providing an ambience which will appeal particularly to families with younger children. There is a bar/restaurant with waiter service and takeaway meals. Pizzeria. Entertainment for children (July/Aug) and playground. Sanitary facilities are good, with hot showers, washbasins in cabins and some en-suite cubicles with showers and washbasins. Facilities for the disabled, baby bath, washing machines and fridges for hire. Shop for essentials; supermarket 5 km. Library. Fishing. Apartments, bungalows and caravans to let. Swimming pool with large shallow area. Barbecues permitted in special area only. Used by a tour operator (10%).

Directions: From A51 autoroute take exit for village of Brillanne and follow N100 east for 3 km. Site is signed near Forcalquier, 3 km. ESE of Niozelles.

Charges 1996: -- Per unit, incl. 2 persons Ffr. 105.00; extra person 30.00; child (under 4 yrs) 18.00; dog 20.00; electricity (6A) 20.00.
Open: 1 April - 25 September.
Address: Niozelles, 04300 Forcalquier.
Tel: 92.78.63.31.
FAX: 92.79.86.92.
Reservations: Made with deposit (30% of charge) and fee (Ffr. 10+0).

0401 Hotel de Plein Air L'Hippocampe, Volonne, nr Sisteron - see editorial report on page 49

0402 Castel Camping du Verdon, Castellane - see editorial report on page48

N0404 Domaine Naturist Castillon de Provence, Castellane

Very large naturist site with spectacular views.

One hundred pitches in 45 hectares of fairly wild Provencal countryside near the Gorges du Verdon (the French answer to the Grand Canyon and nearly as spectacular) make this a site for naturists who are also nature lovers. Quite apart from the size of the terrain, this is an unusual site and is perhaps of more interest to experienced naturist campers - the access road is narrow, steep and twisting - no problem for smaller caravans, trailer tents or small motorhomes, but probably rather daunting for larger units. The setting and the views are spectacular, and whilst the site has only a tiny pool for children (from July), there is a large lake within hard walking distance (2 km. and hilly, but we did it!) where swimming and canoeing, etc. are possible from the naturist 'beach' (motor boats forbidden). The pitches are unmarked and scattered around the hilly terrain - they are really as large as you want - and 2 or 3A electrical connections are available on over 30%; long cables may be required (the site operators offered to lend us one when we visited, but our 50 m. cable was sufficient). You should be able to find a flat pitch even though a lot are not, although nobody seemed too bothered by this. The facilities are surprisingly extensive and include a bar/restaurant (with limited menu and take your own crockery and cutlery!), takeaway, shop (all from June. bread available all season) and a quite varied range of activities including entertainment and a children's club in the main season. The sanitary facilities were very clean and typically rural naturist site in style - mainly open shower and washbasins - hot showers in one block (on payment in high season) - but elsewhere only cold water. WCs of the Turkish variety, apart from the one British type in the handicapped toilet and spotlessly clean when we visited on Bastille Day. There is nothing 'manicured' about this site, but if you like unspoiled and fairly wild (but not inhospitable) countryside and appreciate a warm welcome from the French owner and Dutch assistant, this could be a very attractive proposition.

Charges 1996:
-- Per adult Ffr. 36.00 + local tax; child (4-14 yrs) 15.50; electricity 12.50.
Open:
Easter - end September.
Address:
La Grande Terre,
La Baume,
04120 Castellane.
Tel:
92.83.64.24.
Reservations:
Made with deposit (Ffr. 500 paid by Eurocheque).

Directions: From Castellane take the D955 before turning left onto the CD402 to the site. This is a very narrow road with few passing places and caravanners are asked to arrive **after** 14.00 hrs or to phone the site to check that no-one is about to travel in the opposite direction!

0405M Camp Municipal Les Relarguiers, Beauvezer, nr St Andre Les Alpes

This pleasant, clean site has around 100 pitches, some seasonal. The central ones are on gravel covered stone, in bays separated by low shrubs, while pitches around the outside are unmarked on sparse grass with a stony underlay. Rock pegs and a heavy hammer are essential for the erection of awnings and tents and there can be a strong wind blowing down off the mountains. Pitches furthest away from the main road are shaded by tall trees. Electricity (5, 10 or 16A) is available in the central area. A single sanitary block has free hot showers but no washbasins in cubicles. Washing machine, iron and board. A small shop on site sells basics and occasionally stocks locally produced dishes. Ice pack service. Small shop in village, supermarket, etc. in St Andre, hypermarket in Digne-les-Bains. Small children's playground. Swimming pool 150 m. Direct access to River Verdon with trout fishing. Jazz entertainment is often staged in the village, which is also home to one of France's finest chefs (M. Thiorne). A good area for summer walking or winter skiing. The site manager, who speaks no English, is wonderfully welcoming but rather eccentric!

Charges guide:
-- Per adult Ffr. 18.00; child 10.00; caravan 20.00; electricity 12.00.
Open:
All year.
Address:
04370 Beauvezer.
Tel:
92.83.47.73.
Reservations:
Policy not known, contact site.

Directions: Follow the D955 north from St Andre Les Alpes towards Colmar, Col d'Allos and Barcelonnette. Beauvezer is approx. 22 km. north of St Andre and 7 km. south of Colmar. Site is on right on entering village from the south on D955, well signed and with wide entrance.

0500 Camping des Princes d'Orange, Orpierre

Attractive, terraced site within walking distance of interesting medieval village.

Orpierre, an attractive village of old, narrow streets and small houses, is situated in the Buĕch valley, 700 m. above sea level. The site is on the hillside above the village and the 100 pitches are all shaded and of an adequate to good size on five terraces. All have electrical connections (4A). The very friendly owners make visitors extremely welcome and are keen to maintain a balance of different nationalities on their site. Sanitary facilities, which are very clean and adequate, but not luxurious, are accessible to all the terraces. Laundry facilities. There is a good range of on site activities - tennis, table tennis, boules, soccer, a games room and a twice weekly disco. The site also arranges walks, tournaments and other activities. Swimming pool (20 x 10 m.), separate paddling pool and small water slide (1/6-30/9). Children's play area. No shop but bread is available each morning. Limited shopping in Orpierre; nearest supermarket and wider range of shops in Laragne (12 km). Takeaway and welcoming bar (both 1/6-30/9). Only gas barbecues permitted. Within easy walking and/or driving distance is some lovely countryside. The nearby gorges have good swimming and the lavender fields make excellent picnic spots. Orpierre is a renowned rock climbing centre and the area is famous for hang gliding. Opportunities for walking are endless, with marked footpaths crossing the area. The site is attractive and well run but may not suit everybody because of the steepness of the terrain and its rather out of the way, rural location. Used by a tour operator (20%).

Directions: Turn off the N75 road at Eyguians onto the D30 - site is signed at turning in centre of village of Orpierre.

Charges 1996:
-- Per unit incl. 3 persons Ffr. 105.00, 2 persons 102.00; extra person 22.00; child (under 7 yrs) 14.00; electricity 14.00; local tax (over 16 yrs) 1.00.
-- Less 25% in low season.
Open:
1 April - 31 October.
Address:
05700 Orpierre.
Tel:
92.66.22.53.
Reservations:
Made with deposit (Ffr. 500) and fee (50).

 Alan Rogers' discount Special price outside July/Aug

0601 Domaine Sainte Madeleine, Sospel

Attractive, peaceful site, with swimming pool, in spectacular mountain scenery.

A few miles inland from Menton, and very near the Italian border, the approach to this site is not for the faint-hearted although, to be fair, the road is actually not as bad as it looks and the site itself makes the effort worthwhile. Although terraced, manoeuvring within the site presents no problem and the pitches, whilst not marked, offer sufficient space on fairly level well drained grass, with electricity to 70 of the 90 pitches, varying shade and marvellous views. There is a 140 sq.m. swimming pool (heated spring and autumn). The single sanitary block is of excellent quality, with seatless toilets, washbasins in private cabins, and good hot showers, although, unusually for France, these are on payment (Ffr 3.00) and there is no shelf or seat. Laundry facilities with two washing machines. Although there are no catering facilities on the site, the attractive small town of Sospel is only a short, fairly easy drive and here can be found a quite wide variety of restaurants, bars, cafés and shops. Caravans and chalets for hire (April-Oct, depending on the weather) and rooms in the house. Car wash area, motorcaravan service point and chemical toilet disposal. Some English spoken.

Directions: Site is on D2566, some 4 km. north of Sospel. The D2566 can be reached from either A8 autoroute via the Menton exit, or from the N7 at Menton.

Charges 1995:
-- Per unit, incl. 2 persons Ffr. 75.00; extra adult 15.00; child 9.00; electricity 12.00.
Open:
All year.
Address:
06380 Sospel.
Tel:
93.04.10.48.
Reservations:
Necessary for July/Aug. and made with Ffr. 300 deposit.

0602 Caravan Inn, Opio, nr Grasse

Good quality site for caravans only, with large plots and swimming pools.

Near the hills around Grasse and 18 km. inland from the sea at Cannes, Caravan Inn has 120 plots which are appreciably larger than one usually finds on touring sites. They are mostly about 150-180 sq.m. and partly terraced on a naturally wooded, gently sloping hill. All have electricity and with water laid on, with much shade available and landscaped with hand -hewn stone. Half are kept for permanent caravans, the other half for tourists - caravans and motor caravans are taken, but not tents. The site has an attractive bar/restaurant (open July/Aug.) with a terrace, providing good value waiter service and takeaway meals and there are two swimming pools (unheated) one for adults and one for children, (pools open 15/6-15/9).

Charges guide:
-- Per unit incl. 4 persons, electricity (2A) Ffr 155.20, 174.30 or 193.80, acc. to pitch type; extra person 17.00, or child (under 6 yrs) 8.50; extra small tent 9.20 - 15.50; electricity 4A 12.40, 10A 15.50.
-- Less in low seasons.

continued overleaf

0602 Caravan Inn continued

A small mobile shop calls. Amenities include tennis, volleyball and table tennis with golf and riding nearby. Children's playground. TV on request in bar for big events. The four toilet blocks, though not large, are of good quality and are being progressively renovated. Between them they give a good coverage to the site. One building can be heated. British toilets, individual basins in cubicles with mirror, shelves, and free hot water in basins, sinks, showers and ladies' baths. English spoken. Gas barbecues only. Nearby are an 18 hole golf course and horse riding.

Directions: Turn off the A85 road 9 km. east of Grasse onto D7 and D3 and continue to site. Site is on D3 road (Châteauneuf de Grasse - Valbonne), signed from Châteauneuf.

Open: Easter - 15 September.
Address: B.P. 31, 18 Rte de Cannes, 06650 Opio.
Tel: 93.77.32.00.
FAX: 93.77.71.89.
Reservations: Made with 25% deposit and fee (Ffr 100); Sat. to Sat. only in July/Aug.

0605 Camping La Vieille Ferme, Villeneuve Loubet Plage, nr Antibes

Family owned site with good facilities, open all year, in popular resort area.

La Vieille Ferme has been developed and improved over the years and now provides over 100 level, grass pitches with some shade. These range from a special 'camping car' pitch, tarmaced and with water, drainage and electricity laid on, other special pitches with all facilities neatly hedged (some for winter camping), to simple terraced pitches for small tents. The toilet facilities in five units (one new) provide British toilets, washbasins with pre-mixed hot water in a general wash room or in private cabins, and well equipped showers. Two units are heated for winter use. Facilities for the handicapped and children's toilets. There is a shop in high season but a drinks, sweets and ices machine is situated in the TV room for all year use and essentials are kept in the office. The swimming pool (20 x 10 m.) is also heated and covered for winter use (closed mid Nov-mid Dec), with a children's pool and jacuzzi in summer. Table tennis. Boules. Refrigerator hire. Laundry facilities. Safety deposit and exchange facilities. The site is making every effort to provide facilities all year round within commercial viability and special rates are available for long stay winter visitors. A long pebbly beach is a 1 km. walk away or drive via a railway underpass (motorhomes take care). Parking is usually possible even in high season. English spoken at reception. Chalets to let, for winter use as well.

Directions: From west take Antibes exit from Esterel autoroute and turn left towards Nice when joining the N7 outside Antibes. After 3½ km. on N7 turn left for site. From east take N7 towards Antibes and turn right after Villeneuve Loubet Plage. The turning off the N7, though signed, is not easy to see particularly at busy times but, coming from Antibes, it is on the left, between the Bonne Auberge and the Parc de Vaugrenier. Site is 150 m. on right. (Note: avoid N98 Route du Bord de Mer.) Site has its own small, yellow site signs.

Charges 1996: -- Low season prices in brackets. Per pitch incl. up to 3 persons (2 persons in low season): tent Ffr 120.00 (78.00); with electricity 120.00 (80.00), all services 149.00 (90.00); extra person 24.00 (19.00); child (under 5) 18.00 (13.00); extra car 22.00 (15.00); electricity 15.00 (2A) - 23.00 (10A); local tax 1.00. -- Less 10-20% for long stays in low season. -- Credit cards accepted.
Open: All year
Address: Bvd. des Groules, 06270 Villeneuve Loubet Plage.
Tel: 93.33.41.44.
FAX: 93.33.37.28.
Reservations: Advisable over a long season and made with 25% deposit and Ffr. 120 fee (high season).

0603 Camping-Caravaning Domaine de la Bergerie, Vence, nr Nice

Large but quiet family type site attractively situated in hills behind Riviera.

La Bergerie is a family owned and run site, situated in the hills about 3 km. from Vence and 10 km. from the sea at the nearest point, at Cagnes sur Mer. It is a very extensive site, left very natural in a part grassy and part lightly wooded, quiet and rather secluded situation about 300 m. above sea level. Most parts have shade. However, even if it is less crowded than the coastal sites, it is difficult enough to find a pitch here in high season. There are 67 special pitches with water, drainage and electricity. The original sanitary facilities have been supplemented by a large new, tiled block of a good standard with hot water throughout, washbasins in cabins and the largest number of facilities (toilets, basins and showers) for the handicapped we have seen in France. Good provision also for children. Improvements generally to the site continue to be made. There are two chalets to rent on the site, but no tour operators or organised activities. However, there is an attractive small bar/restaurant, takeaway and shop (1/5-30/9). Children's playground and paddling pool. Tennis courts. Table tennis. 10 shaded boules pitches, lit at night with competitions in season. Winter caravan storage. Telephones (6). Bus service from site to Vence every hour except Sundays.

Directions: From the autoroute take the Cagnes exit in the direction of Vence. Site is west of Vence and it is necessary to follow `toutes directions' signs around the town to join the D2210 Grasse road. Follow this to roundabout (2 km.), turn left and follow site signs for 1 km. Site is on left in light woodland.

Charges 1995:
-- Per unit with up to 3 persons, simple pitch Ffr. 58.00 - 77.00; with electricity (2A) 74.00 - 93.00; with 3 services 90.50 - 110.00; extra person 19.00; child (under 5) 12.50; extra car 12.00; electricity (5A) 10.00; local tax (over 18) 1.00.
-- Rates available from site for seasonal pitches.
-- Credit cards accepted.
Open:
15 March - 31 October.
Address:
Rte de la Sine, 06140 Vence.
Tel:
93.58.09.36.
Reservations:
Necessary only in July/Aug. for special pitches; made with 25% deposit and Ffr. 85 fee.

0604 Le Grand Saule, Cannes-La Bocca

Agreeable, small site with swimming pool, within Cannes limits.

This little site is in a pleasant setting and, although only 200 m. from a busy through road, the intervening wooded area seems to give it sufficient screening to make the camp itself quite peaceful. It is only 1½ km. from the beach at La Bocca and 4 km. from Cannes town centre, so its position is unusually handy for one of the show-places of the Riviera. A bus stop is close to the entrance gate. There is a small swimming pool of irregular shape on site, beside an attractive terrace bar (pizzeria/grill within close walking distance). With its situation, the site obviously deals with much transit trade and many backpackers. It therefore has `young people' areas, formally designed for tents, and a `family area' with individual pitches separated by hedges and with electricity, water points and drainage, all with good shade, with a total of 55 units taken. There are also 25 small apartments to let for self-catering. The small toilet block, though kept busy, is usually well kept and clean, with British WCs, free fully controllable hot showers, washbasins with cold water (some in private cabins) and with hot water in clothes/dishes sinks and a washing machine. No shop - many very close. Tennis club adjoining, open to clients. Table tennis. Children's frames. Sauna. Only gas barbecues are permitted. Being very close to Cannes, the site is naturally not cheap, but it is easily accessible.

Directions: From A8 autoroute take Cannes-Ouest exit, turn towards Cannes, passing airport, left into Ave. de Coubertin, then into Ave. Jourdan; cross under autoroute, then 300 m. to camp on right. Le Grand Saule is signed from most main junctions in La Bocca.

Charges 1996:
-- Per unit incl. 2 persons Ffr. 89.00 - 127.00, incl. 3 persons 127.00 - 167.00; car 19.00; electricity 19.00.
-- Credit cards accepted.
Open:
1 April - 30 September.
Address:
24-26 Bd. Jean Moulin, 06110 Le Cannet-Cannes.
Tel:
93.90.55.10.
FAX: 93.47.24.55.
Reservations:
Recommended and made from any day with refundable deposit equivalent to 1 weeks stay.

Alan Rogers' discount
Ask at site for details

Remember - to claim your discount you will need to show your 1996 discount voucher

0606 Camping-Caravaning Le Moulin Noù, Gilette, nr Nice

Family riverside site beside mountains, about 15 minutes inland from Nice.

Extensively used by British and Dutch tour operators, this is a well maintained, attractive site, conveniently situated for Nice and the coast, but in more peaceful inland surroundings beside the rocky River l'Esteron valley. Facilities include a tennis court, medium sized swimming pool and children's' pool, boules, volley-ball, table tennis, children's play area and games room. A small bar/pizzeria-grill and shop are on site and facilities for fishing, horse riding and canoeing are near. There are 172 marked, divided and level pitches of reasonable, variable size, all with electricity (3, 4 or 6A) and some fully serviced. Access is via tarmac roads and there is some shade from a variety of trees, hedges and flowering shrubs. The sanitary facilities, in two blocks, are of a good standard, although some are more modern then others, with large showers (ample hooks and dividers), washbasins in private cabins and British style WCs. Dishwashing and laundry needs (including machines, ironing boards, etc.) are well provided for. Generally this is an attractive site that will appeal particularly to those who enjoy the company of other British holiday makers.

Directions: Take the Grenoble/Digne exit from the A8 autoroute and follow the N202 past St Martin du Var. Turn left over the bridge onto the N209 signed Gilette and follow camp signs for 1½ km.

Charges guide:
-- Per pitch incl. 2 persons Ffr. 65.80 - 130.50; extra person 18.60 - 19.30; child (under 5) 12.90 - 13.50; car 12.20 - 12.70; electricity 14.00 - 16.50; local tax (over 15) 1.00.
Open:
1 April - 30 September.
Address:
Rte. de Carros, 06830 Gilette.
Tel:
93.08.92.40.
FAX: 93.08.44.77.
Reservations:
Only necessary for July and August.

N0607 Domaine Naturiste Club Origan, Puget-Theniers, nr Nice

Spectacularly situated naturist site in the mountains behind Nice.

Despite its rather spectacular location, Origan is easily accessible from the coast and you only discover that you are at a height of 500 m. when you arrive! The terrain within the extensive confines of the site is fairly wild and the roads distinctly stony - watch your exhaust system especially if, like us, you visit with a classic sports car. The scenery is impressive and footpaths in and around the site offer good, if fairly strenuous walks up to a height of 1,000 m. The nearby small town of Puget-Theniers is very pleasant and offers a choice of bars, cafés, etc. although Origan itself provides both a bar/restaurant (open all season) and takeaway facilities. The site shop opens 15/6-31/8. There are two swimming pools, one for children, a jacuzzi and even a disco in the cellars. The pitches, some with the possibility of electric hook up (by long cables) are in three different areas with many wild flowers. They are of irregular size and shape and all have good views. Sanitary facilities were exceptionally clean when we visited and of a standard and type associated with most good naturist sites - mainly British type WCs, mostly open plan hot showers and ample washbasins with hot and cold water.

Directions: Site is just off the N202, 47 km. from Nice, to the right.

Charges 1995:
-- Per unit incl. 2 persons Ffr. 91.00 - 126.00, 3 persons 120.00 - 165.00; child (3-8 yrs) 15.00 - 20.00; electricity 19.50; dog 9.00 - 11.00; entertainment free - 5.00 per adult/per night.
-- Credit cards accepted.
Open:
15 April - 30 Sept.
Address:
06260 Puget-Theniers.
Tel:
93.05.06.00.
Reservations:
Contact Nat' Azur, 23 ave J. Médecin, 06000 Nice. (Tel: 93.88.28.61. Fax: 93.87.47.49).

0702 Camping-Caravaning L'Ardechois, St. Sauveur-de-Montagut

Well equipped site in spectacular setting.

This site is quite a way off the beaten track with a steep and windy approach road (now improved). It is worth the effort, however, to find such an attractive hillside site offering good amenities and a variety of different types of pitch. All 95 pitches have electricity (3, 6, 10 or 15A) and are said to be 100 sq.m. Some are situated alongside the small fast-flowing river, while the rest (60%) are on higher, sloping ground nearer the restaurant/bar with steep, gravelled access roads which are not so good for large units. Many are separated by trees and plants. The main sanitary block, bar/restaurant, shop and `salle de jeux' (more or less sound-proof!) have been created by the careful conversion of old buildings and provide modern amenities in an attractive style. (Shop from 15/6, restaurant from 1/5). TV. Table tennis. Heated swimming pool (from 1/5) with bar, snack bar and terrace. The sanitary facilities, all recently renovated, are good and provide British toilets, hot showers, washbasins in private cabins etc, and include dishwashing and laundry facilities. A sanitary block of equal quality is near to the riverside pitches. It includes facilities for the handicapped and a laundry. Chalets and mobile homes for hire. The site owners have developed an extensive and unusual excursion programme for exploring this attractive area on foot or by car. Used by tour operators and popular with the Dutch.

Directions: Approaching from the north, follow the N86 south from Valence for about 12 km. Turn right onto the D120 to St. Sauveur de Montagut, thence onto the D102 (alongside which the site is situated) in the direction of Mezilhac. This was a very narrow twisting road alongside the river, needing care but it has now been much improved.

Charges 1996:
-- Per unit incl. 2 persons Ffr 98.00; extra person (incl. children) 20.00; pet 10.00; electricity (5A) 18.00.
-- Less 20-30% on pitch fee outside July/Aug.
-- Special rates for senior citizens.

Open:
6 April - 25 September.

Address:
07190 St. Sauveur-de-Montagut.

Tel:
75.66.61.87.
FAX: 75.66.63.67.

Reservations:
Write with deposit (Ffr. 500) and fee (100).

Alan Rogers' discount
Less 5-10% reserved stays (7-10 days)

0704 Camping La Rouveyrolle, Casteljau, nr Les Vans

Attractive, family run site in peaceful surroundings beside the Chassezac river gorge.

Family run and aimed at families, this is a very tranquil site by the river in attractive countryside with vineyards and orchards. There are 100 good sized pitches here, all with electricity (4 or 5A), on flat grass, some with ample shade and others with less for those preferring the sun. The site has a relaxed atmosphere and provides good facilities for families, including an attractively shaped swimming pool, positioned to catch the sun all day. It was built by the site in 1990 after the water level in the river dropped following the building of a dam upstream. The site offers a pleasant bar/restaurant (13/6-15/9) serving a `dish of the day' and including takeaway, and animation (July/Aug). The sanitary facilities are situated in two modern blocks providing free hot showers in cubicles with separator, and some continental, seatless WCs although the majority are Turkish type. There are part covered washing up and laundry areas, including a washing machine. Shop in July/Aug. (8-12.30 and 4.30-7.30) - the village is 500 m. Tennis courts and a children's playground. River beach (100 m.) with swimming and canoeing in July/Aug. The Cévennes and the Gorges of the Ardèche (20 km) are near. Riding, pot-holing and rock climbing (with guides) are available nearby. Excursions can be arranged. Mobile homes (6 persons) for hire.

Charges 1996:
-- Per unit incl. 2 persons Ffr. 115.00; extra person 28.00; child under 7 yrs free, 7-16 yrs 23.00; electricity 18.00; local tax 1.00.
-- Less 20-30% in low seasons.
Open:
1 April - 30 September.
Address:
Casteljau, 07460 Berrias et Casteljau.
Tel:
75.39.00.67.
FAX: 75.39.07.28.
Reservations:
Write to site.

Directions: From the A7 at Montélimar, take the D102 west to Aubenas, then the D104, south through Joyeuse and the hamlet of Chandolas. Turn right just after the bridge over the Chassezac and right again to site.

Alan Rogers' discount
Less 10% at certain times

0703 Camping Soleil Vivarais, Sampzon, nr Ruoms

Attractively situated site beside the Ardèche river, with good swimming pools.

Although in a rural setting, this site offers a range of activities and facilities which will appeal to families with teenage and younger children. These include a large modern swimming pool (22½ x 10½ m.), with ample sunbathing areas, a smaller children's pool (100 sq.m.) and a pebbled beach area bordering the Ardèche. A feature of the site is its very modern and attractive bar/restaurant with several terraces, offering a wide range of meals including takeaway, pizzas, etc. There is also a quite large disco (soundproofed we understand) adjacent to the bar/restaurant. The site provides some 200 pitches, all with electricity (6-10A) and 33 fully serviced. Four modern sanitary blocks with facilities for the disabled, excellent babies room, dishwashing (H&C), 2 washing machines and free hot water. One block (including the babies' room) is heated for Easter. In addition to the disco, in high season the site provides an `animation' programme, mountain biking, climbing, pot holing and canoeing and rafting on the river, a mini-club and evening entertainment. Large shop. Sports include tennis, archery, handball, water polo, minigolf, table tennis, volleyball, basketball, badminton and petanque. Children's playground and child minding. Games room. TV. Bicycle hire. Riding, fishing and golf near. Chalets, mobile homes and tents to hire. Motorcaravan service point. Used by tour operators (35%).

Charges 1996:
-- Per unit incl. 2 persons and electricity Ffr. 107.00 - 163.00; extra person 25.00 - 34.00; child (under 10 yrs) free - 34.00; water and drainage free - 22.00; animal free - 14.00; local tax 1.00.
-- Cedit cards accepted.
Open:
29 March - 30 September.
Address:
Sampzon, 07120 Ruoms.
Tel:
75.39.67.56.
FAX: 75.93.97.10.
Reservations:
Write with deposit (Ffr 500) and fee (80).

Directions: At St. Just on the RN86 (on west side of the Rhône, south of Montélimar) take the D290 westward to Vallon Pont d'Arc, then via the D579 towards Ruoms, turning left to site across the river (controlled by traffic lights). Alternatively via Villeneuve-de-Berg take N102 and D579 to Ruoms.

See advertisement on opposite page

0706 *Mondial Camping, Riviére Ardèche, Vallon Pont d'Arc - see editorial report on page 48*

0705 Camping-Caravaning Le Ranc Davaine, St Alban Auriolles, Ruoms

'Lively but tasteful' - family oriented site in southern Ardèche.

This is a quite large site with an extensive programme of entertainments, especially for families with small children. Although lively, there is nothing 'tacky' about it - even the background music in the attractive partly open air restaurant beside the pool was Baroque, and listening to Bach, Handel and Vivaldi makes a change from Johnny Halliday. The 300 pitches, all of at least reasonable size, are all supplied with electricity (3, 6 or 10A.) and are on fairly flat, rather stony, ground under a variety of trees giving plenty of shade. There is an attractive, large, irregularly shaped swimming pool overlooked by terraces and the bar/restaurant which serves a good range of meals in very pleasant surroundings, made more attractive in the evenings by the lighting and floodlighting. The entertainment programme (July/Aug) is extensive and varied with a particular emphasis on the participation by younger children in a quite imaginative way. The five sanitary blocks are all of a good standard, with British seatless WCs, hot showers with dividers and many washbasins in private cabins. Washing machines, dryer and irons. The amenities include a restaurant, pizzeria and takeaway, large shop, children's play area, tennis, table tennis, archery, minigolf and an extensive programme of watersports and excursions on and to the river Ardèche. Popular with tour operators (30-40%).

Charges 1996: -- Per unit incl. 2 persons Ffr. 135.00, with electricity 157.00; extra adult or child 31.00. -- Less outside high season. **Open:** 1 April - 20 September. **Address:** St Alban Auriolles, 07120 Ruoms. **Tel:** 75.39.60.55. FAX: 75.39.38.50. **Reservations:** Made with deposit (Ffr 600) and fee (170). Write or fax site.

Directions: Continue south on D111 after Ruoms. Turn left on D246 just before Grospierres, across bridge and then left in the direction of Chandolas to site.

CAMPING-CARAVANING
LE RANC DAVAINE ★★★★
Open from 1 April to 20 Sept

Shop ~ Bar ~ Restaurant ~ Heated swimming pool low season
Chalets ~ Mobile Homes ~ Tents to rent

07120 St-Alban-Auriolles
Tel 75 39 60 55   Fax 75 39 38 50

How to use the 1996 Discount Voucher !

The Discount Card/Vouchers are in three parts:

Part 1 should be retained and must not be removed from the Guide. You should complete it by adding your name, address and signature. This part includes the printed Card Number, and should be shown to those parks indicating special offers for our readers as identified by an Alan Rogers' logo in the Guide.

Part 2 should be completed by adding your name, address, the card number as shown in part 1, and your signature. This part may then be used to claim your discount(s) for travel, breakdown, caravan or motorcaravan insurance.

Part 3 should be completed by adding your name, address, the card number as shown in Part 1, and your signature. This part may then be used to claim your FERRY DISCOUNT, as directed.

Note that the Discount Cards are valid from **1 January - 31 December 1996 only**

0707 Camping Les Ranchisses, Chassiers, Largentière

Family orientated site on the Route de Valgorge.

The Chevalier family (no relation to Maurice, as far as we know!) combine farming and wine-making with running a family orientated campsite and an Auberge. In a somewhat lesser known area of the Ardèche at Chassiers, on the route de Valgorge, the site started life as a `camping a la ferme' but has now developed into a 130 pitch family campsite with an extensive range of facilities. These include a medium sized pool with sunbathing areas and, somewhat apart from the pitches, an Auberge developed from the original 1824 building used to house silk-worms. Open to the public, traditional dishes are served at lunch-time and in the evenings in very attractive surroundings, both indoors and outside. The good sized, level, grassy pitches are in two main areas, one older (the original camping a la ferme) and well shaded, the other newer and with recently planted small trees. The great majority have 6A electrical connections, with a few being fully serviced. There is frontage onto a small lake which is connected to the river, providing opportunities for simple canoeing and, judged by appearances, at least one part is pretty safe for youngsters. There are two sanitary blocks, one excellent new one with the latest fittings, the other older, smaller one renovated and refurbished to acceptable present day standards. Washing machine - `buanderie'. Both were immaculate when seen in high season.

Directions: From Largentière take the Route de Valgorge (D24) and Les Ranchisses is the first site on the left hand side.

Charges 1995:
-- Per unit incl. 2 persons Ffr. 90.00; extra person over 7 yrs 22.00, under 7 yrs 18.00; animal 5.00; electricity 15.00.
-- Low season less 20%.
Open:
Easter - end September.
Address:
Route de Valgorge, Chassiers, 07110 Largentière.
Tel:
75.88.31.97.
FAX: 75.88.32.73.
Reservations:
Contact site for form; made with Ffr. 500 deposit.

0801M Camping Municipal du Mont Olympe, Charleville-Mézières

Superbly situated alongside the Meuse River, within easy walking distance across a footbridge to the centre of this surprisingly attractive town, this site provides some 100 numbered pitches, most with the possibility of electrical connection, on level grass and among a variety of trees providing ample shade. The pitches are of irregular size and shape. There is a mobile bar/snack-bar on site, although the town's shops are within a 5 minute walk. The municipal indoor pool is adjacent and boat trips operate on the river virtually from the site. By comparison, the sanitary facilities are rather disappointing, the two purpose blocks being of a somewhat strange '60s design - mainly turkish style WCs, with washbasins grouped in rather cramped rooms, but the hot showers, although somewhat elderly, are excellent with a good supply of hot water. Generally this is a very attractive site, unusually quiet and secure for a town centre location and conveniently situated for exploring the town and surrounding area.

Directions: Site is north of Charleville on the island of Montcy St Pierre and is signed from the city centre `Mont Olympe'. From the north D988/D1 follow the river, over the bridge, then immediately left. From the southeast (A203/N51/ N43) head from `Gare' then follow Avenue Forest north and over the bridge.

Charges guide:
-- Per person Ffr. 10.00; child (2-7 yrs) 5.00; pitch 5.60; vehicle 5.60; supplement for mobile home or caravan over 5 m. 3.80; electricity (10A) 12.00.
Open:
Easter - 15 October.
Address:
Rue des Paquis, 08000 Charleville-Mézières.
Tel:
24.33.23.60 or 24.32.44.80.
Reservations:
Contact site.

0802M Camping des Lac des Vielles-Forges, Les Mazures, Revin

An attractive lakeside site with top quality amenities, du Lac provides 300 large pitches, all with electricity (3-10A). They are mainly on individual, gravel hardstandings, arranged on several terraces, but easily accessible via tarmac approach roads, with good shade. The attractively arranged pitches offer ample shade from a variety of trees and shrubs. It is situated only a 100 m. or so back from the large lake which offers a variety of watersports, and its somewhat remote location is approached by a road which forms part of the Route des Fortifications. The several purpose built sanitary blocks are of excellent quality providing modern facilities in terms of showers, WCs, washbasins in private cabins, washing machines, dryers, etc. Tennis, table tennis and mountain biking.

Directions: From the N43, 11 km. northwest of Charleville-Mézières, take D40 north in the direction of Revin for approx. 8 km. The lake is signed on the left - follow the lakeside road to the site; a one way system operates in high season.

Charges guide:
-- Per person Ffr. 15.60; child (under 7 yrs) 7.80; pitch 8.60; large vehicle plus 7.80; electricity 3A 10.50, 5/6A 13.50, 10A 22.50; pet 4.80.
Open:
All year.
Address:
85000 Les Mazures.
Tel:
24.40.17.31.
Reservations:
Not normally made or necessary, but if in doubt 'phone.

N0901 Domaine Naturiste de Pauliac, Saverdun

Superbly situated, Dutch owned naturist site with glorious views.

Situated in attractive countryside, the views from the terrace and swimming pools at this site are exceptional including the distant Pyrénées across the Ariège landscape. The 286 pitches, on generally hilly terrain, (many of which have electricity) are informally arranged on small terraces at various levels throughout the large and varied grounds which include semi-wooded and more open areas giving a choice of amount of shade. The site and swimming pools have been attractively landscaped around the old manor house (Domaine) and outbuildings which now form the reception, bar, restaurant and the oldest of the several sanitary blocks. The conversions have been sympathetically carried out with the result that the appearance of the old and attractive buildings is largely unimpaired.

The bar provides quite a focal point for informal gatherings and is pleasantly cool, while the smart French restaurant specialises in a number of well prepared dishes at reasonable prices. There is a well stocked shop including fresh bread, essential because the nearest village is some kilometres away. The sanitary facilities, in two blocks, provide the usual naturist site style open-plan hot showers, British and Turkish WCs, washbasins (open and in private cabins), dishwashing and laundry facilities (including washing machine) under cover and facilities for the handicapped. Both have winterised sections. In the height of the season an extra mobile block is provided in the wooded area. At most naturist sites, particularly the larger ones, the range of leisure activities (sporting and cultural) on offer is extensive and Domaine de Pauliac is no exception. Apart from two large swimming pools, plus a child's pool and sauna, there are facilities for boules, table tennis, volleyball and archery. Drawing, painting and pottery classes in the main season. Further afield, the site owners organise mountain walking, climbing, caving, canoeing and cycling. The site is also quite conveniently situated for day excursions to places such as Carcassonne, the Route of the Cathars, the Pyrénées or even Andorra. Bungalows, cabins, mobile homes and tents to let. **Note**: Some pitches are not so easily accessed but the views are worth it and the site tractor can be booked for siting.

Directions: Approaching from Auterive, turn right at restaurant/tabac in centre of Saverdun then left before bank (Credit Agricole). Continue up hill for 1 km. until road levels out and watch for sign 'de Pauliac' to left. Follow this unmarked road for 7 km. (road surface OK). The site operates a one way system so units leave in the opposite direction.

Charges 1995:
-- Per pitch Ffr. 45.00; person 30.00; child (2-12 yrs) 18.00; animal 10.00; electricity 18.00.
-- Discounts (except electricity) 20-30% outside high season.
Open:
All year.
Address:
09700 Saverdun.
Tel:
61.60.43.95.
Reservations:
Made with deposit (50% of charges) plus Ffr. 85 fee.

0905M Camping Municipal, Sorgeat, nr Ax-les-Thermes

Superbly situated high up on the mountainside overlooking the valley, this small site provides just 40 pitches on terraces. Very well supervised, with the warden present all evening, it is kept very clean. It has a rather small sanitary block with only two showers and two WCs in each half. However, standards are very high - there are even clean foot towels in the showers. Hot water is provided for dishwashing. Facilities for the disabled are also very good with special hand-basin and a very large shower suite. Electrical connections (5 or 10A) available.

Directions: From the N20 road through Ax-les-Thermes, take the D613 northeast to Sorgeat (hairpin bends) for 5 km. Site is signed.

Charges guide:
-- Per pitch Ffr. 13.50; adult 12.50; child 7.00.
Open:
All year.
Address:
09110 Sorgeat.
Tel:
61.64.36.34.
Reservations:
Adviseable for high season (15/7-15/8) - contact site.

1001 Camping du Tertre, Dienville
Pleasant, privately run site, ideal for watersports enthusiasts.

This is a modern (1989) campsite which is situated opposite a major watersports centre on Lac du Temple, and also within easy distance of Lac d'Orient, the former for motorboats and waterskiing, the latter for sailing, windsurfing, etc. The site provides 143 large pitches of which 102 have electrical connections (4A). They are on mainly level grass, separated by hedges and with some young trees which, as yet, do not provide much shade. The modern sanitary blocks, all to a good standard, provide hot showers, with dividers and hooks, some washbasins in private cabins, British type WCs, washing-up facilities and a washing machine. There is a bar/snack bar, open from 1/6 at weekends only, but daily in the peak season, when there is also some entertainment. A baker calls daily; there is a variety of restaurants, shops, etc. at the watersports centre opposite and the village is about 5 minutes walk away.

Directions: Dienville is 5-6 km. south of Brienne le Château (with its Napoleon connections) and the site is opposite the port. From the A5 autoroute take the exit for Vendeuvre sur Barse and follow D443 north for approx. 23 km.

Charges 1995:
-- Per pitch Ffr. 22.00; person 15.00; child (4-10 yrs) 10.00; animal 2.00; electricity 10.00.
-- Less for longer stays.
-- Credit cards accepted.
Open:
15 March - 15 October.
Address:
10500 Dienville.
Tel/Fax:
25.92.26.50.
Reservations:
Required for Jul/Aug. and made for min. 7 nights with deposit (FFr. 400) and fee (70).

1005M Camping Municipal de Troyes, Troyes
A typical town site, this is close to the River Seine, but separated by allotments!. The 100 or so grassy pitches, all with electricity, are of reasonable size, on fairly level ground and are situated around the large central facilities buildings. These include the sanitary block, table tennis area, meeting room, etc. The pitches are numbered and separated by young, small hedging plants and there is some shade from mature trees. Sanitary facilities are ultra-modern and include hot showers with dividers, hooks, etc., washbasins in private cabins, British type WCs, undercover dishwashing sinks and laundry sinks - all of a very high standard and with free hot water. There are few other facilities, apart from a games room and small children's play area, but bread is delivered to order and there is a restaurant and a supermarket nearby. The town, famous for its knitwear, is about 20 minutes walk away (3 km). Barrier operated by card (deposit Ffr. 100).

Directions: From town centre take Chalons sur Marne direction (2 km). Site is on northeast outskirts of town in Pont-Sainte-Marie area. The easy way is from new A26 (exit Troyes) and follow signs for Pont-Sainte-Marie and site.

Charges guide:
-- Per person Ffr. 22.50; child (under 7) 10.00; caravan 25.00; tent 10.00; motorcaravan 26.00; electricity 15.50.
Open:
1 April - 15 October.
Address:
7 Rue Roger-Salengro, 10150 Pont-Saint-Marie.
Tel:
25.81.02.64 (Tourist office: 25.73.00.36).
Reservations:
Probably unnecessary, but if in doubt 'phone.

1102 Camping Le Moulin du Pont d'Alies, Axat, nr Quillan
Site for visiting the Pyrénées or night halt on the way to Spain.

For those travelling from Toulouse to the Spanish frontier at Le Perthus, the route via Limoux and Quillan is more pleasant than the main road, though not so quick. This site is on this route and makes a good night stop, or a base for exploring the Pyrénées. It is on a flat piece of ground between the N117 road and the river Aude, and 1½ km. north of Axat. Shade is available and many electrical connections. A small swimming pool (open 20/6-31/8). There are two sanitary blocks which have been refurbished, part tiled, with vanity style washbasins, some in private cabins, seatless toilets and free hot showers. Cleaning may be variable. Improved washing up and laundry sinks. Facilities for the disabled. Washing machine. Small shop and snack bar. Large general room with bar. TV room. Table tennis. Mountain walks. Trout fishing. Children's playground. Watersports including canoeing, rafting, hydrospeed. Caving and climbing nearby and the site is popular with young people for canoeing. Chalets and mobile homes for hire.

Directions: Site is off the N117, 11 km. east of Quillan, by junction with N118.

Charges 1995:
-- Per pitch Ffr. 35.00, with electricity 49.00; person 15.00; child (under 10) 10.00; car 10.00; dog 6.00.
-- Credit cards accepted.
Open:
All year.
Address:
St Martin Lys, 11140 Axat.
Tel:
68.20.53.27.
FAX: as phone.
Reservations:
Made if some deposit sent.

11 Aude

1101 Camping Eden II, Villefort, nr Chalabre

Most attractive site in spectacular scenery, near the Pyrénées.

Set in beautiful surroundings, this well equipped modern site is situated in the foothills of the Pyrénées and provides an ideal location to explore this area; there is a ski station 30 km. away. Growing trees planted around the site provide a number of shady pitches. When visited there were 75 large marked pitches on mainly level ground, all with electricity and the majority having drainage, of which 8 are 'super-pitches' with their own sanitary facilities, including hot showers. These and the main, large sanitary block have been built to very high standards; the amenities include a small unit for the disabled, laundry and ironing facilities and even hairdryers. There is an attractive, partly shaded, swimming pool and sun bathing terrace adjacent to the small bar/restaurant and takeaway. Mini-shop at present. Refrigerator for ice packs. Archery. Table tennis. Volleyball. Tennis. Golf practice. Children's playground. Bicycle hire. Riding, fishing, watersports near. Comprehensive literature and ideas about activities in the area are provided. Mobile homes and chalets for hire.

Directions: Site is between Quillan and Lavelanet, off the D117. Take the D16 north at Puivert towards Chalabre; site is on left before village of Villefort.

Charges 1995:
-- Per pitch, incl. 2 adults: basic Ffr 54.00 - 65.00; with electricity (6-10A) 75.00 - 91.00; 3 services 96.00 - 118.00; plus individual sanitary facility 119.00 - 145.00; extra person 14.00 - 15.00; local tax 1.00.
Open:
15 April - 1 October.
Address:
Villefort,
11230 Chalabre.
Tel:
68.69.26.33.
FAX: 68.69.29.95.
Reservations:
Made for Sat. - Sat. with min. Ffr. 200 deposit.

1104 Camping Le Martinet Rouge, Brousses-et-Villaret, nr Carcassonne

Very pretty, rather quaint retreat in Aude countryside north of Carcassonne.

This is a very pretty little site and the new owners have been working hard to improve the facilities. The three sanitary blocks have British WCs, large hot showers, washbasins (hot water) in private cabins, facilities for the disabled, baby bathroom and dishwashing and laundry facilities, including a washing machine. The most striking features of the site are the massive granite boulders (outcrops of smooth rock) throughout the area used for sunbathing and for children's games. The site offers only 35 pitches, all with electricity, in two contrasting areas - one is well secluded with irregularly shaped, fairly level, large pitches created amongst a variety of trees and shrubs, while the other is on open meadow with mature oaks more typical of English rather than French sites. This has an unusual inflated swimming pool (15/6-15/9), semi sunk in, which the owners say is very good for young children and provides a pleasant area for parents to relax and watch them. Table tennis. Small 'pub' bar with terrace serving snacks (chicken and chips to order), barbecue area and shop. Restaurants 50 m. Useful also as a possible overnight stop. Tennis, swimming, riding, fishing quite close. Caravans (4) and bungalows (2) to let.

Directions: Using N113 going west from Carcassonne, turn right onto the D48 just after the village of Pezens (6 km). Follow D48 for approx. 10 km. (surface not so good) and site is signed just before the village of Brousses-et-Villaret.

Charges 1995:
-- Per standard pitch incl. 2 persons and car Ffr. 58.00, with electricity 73.00; extra person 18.00; child (under 7 yrs) 11.00; animal 5.00.
Open:
1 April - 31 October.
Address:
Brousses-et-Villaret,
11390 Cuxac-Cabardes.
Tel:
68.26.51.98.
Reservations:
Made with deposit of 20%.

1106 Camping Au Pin d'Arnauteille, Montclar, nr Carcassonne

Peaceful, spacious, developing site with superb views to the Corbières and beyond.

Enjoying some of the best and most varied views of any site we have visited, this rather unusual site is ideally situated for exploring, by foot or car, the little known Aude Dèpartement, the area of the Cathars and for visiting the walled city of Carcassonne (a 10 minute drive). However, access could be difficult for large, twin axle vans. The site itself is set in 115 hectares of farmland and is on hilly ground with the original pitches on gently sloping, lightly wooded land and the new `grand-confort' ones semi-terraced, on level, hedged places with 3 or 6A electricity, lacking shade at present. A swimming pool (25 x 10 m.) with paved sunbathing area is in a hollow basin surrounded by green fields and some of the newly developed pitches. Sanitary facilities are modern and unisex, the main block part open, part enclosed, with another under the pool, one behind reception and a new small block in the developing area. Well located for all areas, with modern facilities including British WCs, hot showers , washbasins in cabins, dishwashing under cover (with hot water) and laundry facilities. Facilities for the handicapped and a baby bath are other features in what is a good overall provision. A restaurant constructed in a converted stable block has snacks and plat de jour, grills and takeaway (15/6-15/9). The reception building is vast; originally a farm building, subsequently a new top floor being added by former owners (to create a nursing home) but later converted to apartments. Although architecturally rather strange, from some angles it is quite attractive and mature trees soften the outlines. Shop. Table tennis. Volleyball. Horse riding. Fishing 2 km. Rafting and canoeing near. Chalets, mobile homes and bungalow tents to let. Used by tour operators (20%). A developing site with enthusiastic owners for whom riding is the principle theme with stables on site.

Directions: Using D118 from Carcassonne, after bypassing the small village of Rouffiac d'Aude, there is a small section of dual carriageway. Before the end of this, turn right to Montclar up a rather narrow road for 3 km. Site is signed sharp left and up hill before the village.

Charges 1995:
-- Per pitch incl. 2 persons Ffr. 65.00 - 77.00, pitch with electricity 81.00 - 93.00, pitch with water and drainage 103.00 - 113.00; extra person 17.00 - 20.00; child (under 7 yrs) 11.00 - 13.00; extra car 10.00 - 12.00; dog 5.00 - 6.00.

Open:
1 April - 30 September.

Address:
11250 Montclar.

Tel:
68.26.84.53.
FAX: 68.26.91.10.

Reservations:
Made with deposit of 35% of charges.

◢u Pin d'◢rnauteille

11250 MONTCLAR

(15 mins from the city of Carcassonne)

At the heart of a 115ha. estate with 5ha. for camping in an exceptional setting with magnificent views of the surrounding hills. 25m swimming pool, walking, rambling & riding. Comfortable sanitary facilities. Snackbar & Shop. Caravans, mobile homes, chalets and Andrè Trigano canvas bungalows, all fully equipped to hire.

☎ 68 26 84 53   Fax: 68 26 91 10

1103M Camping Municipal La Pinède, Lézignan-Corbières

Within walking distance of the little town and only 35 km. from Narbonne Plage, La Pinède is laid out in terraces on a hillside, with good internal access on made-up roads. The 94 individual pitches vary in size and are divided up mainly by various shrubs and bushes with electricity available. Outside the gates are a municipal swimming pool (1/7-31/8) and tennis courts. Three sanitary blocks are a plentiful provision of quite reasonable quality with free hot water. Small shop with bar and hot food (1/7-31/8). Washing machine. Mobile homes for rent.

Directions: Access directly off main N113 on west side of Lézignan-Corbières

Charges 1995:
-- Per adult Ffr. 16.50; child 10.00; pitch 16.50; electricity 15.00.

Open:
1 April - 15 October.

Address:
11200 Lézignan.

Tel:
68.27.05.08.

Reservations:
Advisable in season.

1105M Camping Municipal La Bernede, Rennes les Bains

In a sheltered position alongside the river, within 10 minutes walking distance (along either river bank) of the town, this is a small site ideal for a visit to this interesting little spa town and little known area steeped in Cathar history. The 50 pitches are of reasonable size, all with electricity (10A) and on fairly level grass with easy access, although access to the site itself is over a rather narrow, unfenced, low bridge/ford. There is a modern sanitary block with British and Turkish style WCs, hot showers, washbasins (3 with hot water) and washing up facilities. Although there is no restaurant or shop on site, bread is delivered daily and the site is within easy reach of the several bars, restaurants and shops in Rennes Les Bains, including the local bar/restaurant in the town square which we found to offer good value. Readers tell us there is a good English owned restaurant further up the valley at Bugarach. It is also possible to use the thermal pool and other facilities (cheaper rates over longer periods) which are open 10/4-6/11. Campers have free use of the tennis courts.

Charges 1995:
-- Per pitch Ffr. 18.00; person 14.00; child (under 12) 9.00; animal 7.00; electricity 10.00.
Open:
All year except Dec. and Jan.
Address:
c/o Les Thermes de la Haute Vallée, Grand rue des Thermes, 11190 Rennes les Bains.
Tel:
68.69.87.01.
FAX: 68.69.80.38.
Reservations:
Write to site

Directions: Using D118 from Carcassonne, 12 km. before Quillan going south, turn right on D613 at Couiza. Turn right again after 5½ km. to Rennes-les-Bains (3 km.). Follow through village and site is signed on left past the houses.

1107 Camping Les Mimosas, Narbonne

Lively site on the Mediterranean littoral, close to beaches at Narbonne Plage and Gruissac.

Being some 6 km. inland from the beaches of Narbonne and Gruissac, this site benefits from a somewhat less hectic situation than others in the popular seaside environs of Narbonne. The site itself is, however, quite lively with plenty to amuse and entertain the younger generation while, at the same time, offering facilities for the whole family. Some 75% of the 250 mainly good sized pitches (including a few `grand confort' ones) have 6A electrical connections and benefit from a reasonable amount of shade. Facilities at the site include a large swimming pool and a smaller one with sunbathing areas, overlooked by a mezzanine level which includes a small lounge, amusements, etc. There are three tennis courts, a sauna, gym and mini-golf, with a riding stable nearby. A lagoon for boating and fishing is accessible via a footpath (about 200 m). The site also includes a rather attractive Auberge offering a comfortable environment and interesting menu for meals. There are four sanitary buildings, the newest of which offers `state of the art' facilities, and whilst the other three are beginning to show their age, the facilities are adequate. These include showers with dividers, some British WCs, washbasins in cabins, etc, all clean when seen in high season. This could be a very useful site offering many possibilities to meet a variety of needs - on-site entertainment, easy access to popular beaches and to interesting towns such as Narbonne itself, Beziers or even Carcassonne.

Charges 1995:
-- Per basic pitch incl. 1 or 2 persons Ffr. 58.00 - 78.00, pitch with electricity 72.00 - 92.00, pitch with electricity, water and drainage 87.00 - 107.00; extra person 13.00 - 21.00; child (2-7 yrs) 5.00 - 10.00; animal 7.00; extra tent 16.00; extra vehicle or trailer 5.00.
Open:
1 April - 31 October.
Address:
Chaussée de Mandirac, 11100 Narbonne.
Tel:
68.49.03.72.
FAX: 68.49.39.45.
Reservations:
Made with deposit (Ffr. 500) and fee (80).

Directions: From the A9 take Narbonne Sud exit and follow signs to La Nautique from where site is well signed (6 km. from autoroute).

1200 Camping Peyrelade, nr Millau

Attractive site by a pebble beach in the Gorges du Tarn.

Peyrelade is at the foot of the Tarn Gorges, dominated by the ruins of Château de Peyrelade, with the site situated on a bend in the river which has thrown up a natural pebble beach. Bathing is safe and the water is clean. Canoes can be hired and the site can arrange for rafting trips and 'canyonning' excursions. There are 180 level, grassy tourist pitches, all with electricity, marked by trees and shrubs. Shade is very good in most parts. Two conveniently placed toilet blocks, one refurbished to a high standard with special miniature facilities for little people! Washing machine. Small, attractively designed pool and children's pool (from 15/5). Children's play area. The site nicely abuts a leisure centre with minigolf and tennis which can be booked at the camp reception. Friendly, comfortable bar and restaurant/pizzeria with full takeaway (all from 6/6). Barbecue area. Games room and mini club. Guided walks and fossil hunting are organised. The site is ideal for visiting the Tarn Gorges and other attractions in the area include Roquefort of cheese fame, La Couvertriade (Knights Templar village) and the eastern Cevennes. The Mediterranean coast is just within range for a day trip. A few tour operator pitches (15%).

Charges 1996:
-- Per unit incl. 2 persons Ffr. 84.00 - 105.00; extra adult 16.00 - 19.50; child (under 5) 12.00 - 15.00; dog 7.00; electricity (5A) 18.00; tax 1.00.
-- Credit cards accepted.
Open:
15 May - 15 September.
Address:
12640 Rivière-sur-Tarn.
Tel:
65.62.62.54 (low season: 65.60.08.48).
FAX: 65.61.33.59.
Reservations:
Made with deposit (Ffr. 450) and fee (100).

Directions: From N9 Sevérac-Millau road, turn east from Aguessac (Gorges du Tarn signs). Site is 2 km. past Rivière sur Tarn, on right - access is quite steep.

Alan Rogers' discount
Free bottle of local wine

1201 Castel Camping Val de Cantobre, Nant d'Aveyron

Attractive, terraced site in the valley of the Dourbie.

This site which has been imaginatively and tastefully developed by the Dupont family over a 23 year period, offers a bar, restaurant, pizzeria and takeaway facility. In particular, the magnificent carved features in the bar create a delightful ambience, complemented by a recently added terrace. True, the ground is hard in summer but reception staff supply robust nails if your awning pegs prove a problem. Most of the pitches (which all have electricity and water), are peaceful, generous in size and blessed with views of the valley. The three adjoining swimming pools now have a new surround, bedecked by flowers and crowned by a large urn which dispenses water into the paddling pool. The shop, although small, offers a wide variety of provisions including many regional specialities. Although there are tour operators on many pitches (45%), the terrace design assures peace and privacy. The new sanitary block is impressive and is beautifully appointed, with a huge indoor dishwashing area on one hand, or grubby children on the other. Adventurous visitors relish sports like river rafting, white water canoeing, rock climbing or jumps from Millau's hill tops on twin seater steerable parachutes. Around 15 such activities, all supervised by qualified instructors, are arranged. Passive recreationists would appreciate the scenery, especially Cantobre, a medieval village that clings to a cliff in view of the site. Nature lovers will be delighted to see the vultures wheeling in the Tarn gorge alongside more humble rural residents. Butterflies in profusion, huge edible snails, glow worms, beavers and the natterjack toad all live here. It is easy to see why - the place is magnificent. Mobile homes and chalets for hire.

Charges 1995:
-- Per unit incl. 2 persons and 4A electricity 120.00 - 140.00; extra person (4 yrs and over) 20.00 - 30.00; extra car or pitch 10.00; electricity 10A 10.00.
-- Credit cards accepted.
Open:
15 May - 15 September, with all facilities.
Address:
12230 Nant d'Aveyron.
Tel:
65.62.25.48.
FAX: 65.62.10.36.
Reservations:
Made for any length with deposit (Ffr. 82) and fee (18).

Directions: Site is 4 km. north of Nant, on D991 road to Millau.

1203 Camping Val Fleuri, Belmont-sur-Rance

Satisfactory small, grassy site close to town centre.

Belmont is somewhat remote, either from through routes or the well known tourist attractions, yet it is nonetheless a pretty little town and this part of Avreyon is well worth a short stay. The site is on the banks of the river (though bathing at this point is not recommended) and is well grassed with small hedges between the 69 flat, fairly standard sized pitches, mostly arranged in pairs. 44 pitches have electricity (2, 4 or 6A) and shade is minimal. With the town so close there are few on-site amenities, but the restaurant/bar (Relais Routiers) opens at lunch times and evenings all the year. **continued overleaf**

Charges guide :
-- Per pitch incl. 1 or 2 persons Ffr. 52.00; extra person 20.00; electricity 2A 8.00, 4A 10.00, 6A 12.00; pet 7.00.
Open:
15 March - 31 October.

1203 Camping Val Fleuri continued

The single sanitary block in two parts is not luxurious but is well cleaned and just about adequate for the numbers. Toilets are the seatless type, washbasins are in private cabins. Dishwashing and laundry sinks (with H&C). Ironing room. Facilities for the handicapped. Fishing from site. Good large grassy play area. Children's pool. Swimming pool, tennis, canoe school, karting, riding and town facilities close by. Boules. Table tennis. 3 bungalows and 3 tents for hire.

Directions: Site is on the south bank of the Rance on the road to Lacaune.

Address:
12370
Belmont-sur-Rance.
Tel:
65.99.95.13.
Reservations:
Made for min. week
with 20% deposit.

1202 Les Rivages, Millau

Large site on town outskirts close to Tarn Gorges with good range of sporting facilities.

This site is well organised and is very popular, being close to the high limestone 'Causses' and the various river Gorges, particularly the Tarn, and their associated attractions, such as caves, remote villages, wildlife refuges, etc. Some 314 pitches occupy flat ground adjacent to the Dourbie river, close to its confluence with the Tarn. There is safe river bathing from the river beach. Pitches in the older part of the site are arranged in fours and tend to be a little crowded, with a bare 100 sq.m. space. In a newer, though less shaded part of the site (Camp 2), campers have more room. All pitches have electricity (6A) whilst 98 also include water and drainaway points. Pitch quality varies and shade is available according to taste. Sanitary facilities are good, the four modern blocks providing washbasins in private cabins, showers and toilets (British and continental), dishwashing and laundry sinks, rooms for the handicapped, and a super new block especially for children with baby baths, small showers, children's toilets and ironing facilities - very nice for mother and from next year it will have a play area beside it. The current management is committed to providing a wide range of sporting and cultural options (said to be 26 different activities, even demonstrations of artificial fly making). On site are indoor and outdoor tennis courts, 2 badminton courts, 2 squash courts, volleyball and two swimming pools. Table tennis. Football. Petanque. Activities on the river, mountain biking, walking, bird watching, fishing and many more. Cyclo-cross track. All are exclusively for campers in high season. Children's play area and entertainments - child minding (3-6yrs) is available. Off-site organised activities are extremely varied and efficiently publicised. Shop. Snack bar. Restaurant. Gates shut 10 pm. - 8 am, with nightwatchman. A few pitches (15%) occupied by tour operators.

Directions: Site is on the Nant (D991) road out of Millau.

Charges 1995:
-- Per pitch incl. 2 persons: normal Ffr 67.00 - 99.00, with electricity 79.00 - 115.00, with all services 88.00 - 125.00; extra person (over 3 yrs) 18.00 - 20.00; pet 12.00 - 14.00; local tax (15/6-15/9) 1.00.
-- Credit cards accepted.
Open:
1 May - 30 September.
Address:
Ave. de l'Aigoual, Rte. de Nant, 12100 Millau.
Tel:
65.61.01.07.
FAX: 65.60.91.40.
Reservations:
Advisable for Jul/Aug. with deposit (Ffr. 400) and fee (100).

1205 Camping Les Terraces du Lac, Pont de Salars, nr Rodez

Family run site overlooking lake between Millau and Rodez.

At an altitude of some 2,000 ft. on the plateau of Le Lévézou, this site enjoys attractive views over Lac de Pont de Salars. The site is terraced, providing 180 good sized, level pitches with or without shade, all with electricity. The site seems largely undiscovered by the British. There is an attractive, quite large (200 sq.m.) pool and children's pool (open 15/6-15/9), with paved and grass sunbathing terraces and good views over the lake which has direct access from the site at two places - one for pedestrians and swimmers, the other for cars and trailers for launching small boats. A large bar/restaurant with a lively French ambience serves full meals in high season and snacks at other times, with takeaway. Shop (July/Aug). Four sanitary blocks, all quite modern include a new 'state of the art' one. All have free hot showers, seatless WCs and some washbasins (H&C) in private cabins, plus washing up areas under cover and laundry facilities. Solarium. Children's playground. Volleyball. Pétanque. Table tennis. Billiards. Games and TV rooms. Tennis 3 km. Entertainment and activities in high season. This site is well placed for excursions into the Gorges du Tarn, Caves du Roquefort and nearby historic towns and villages.

Directions: Using D911 Millau - Rodez road, turn north at Pont de Salars in the direction of the lake on the D523. Follow camp signs. Ignore first site and continue following lake until Les Terraces (approx. 5-6 km).

Charges 1996:
-- Per pitch incl. 2 persons Ffr. 65.00 - 95.00; extra person 16.00 - 20.00; child (under 7 yrs) 11.00 - 14.00; electricity (6A) 18.00; water, drainage and electricity 25.00; local tax 1.00.
-- Credit cards accepted.
Open:
15 June - 15 September.
Address:
Rte. du Vibal,
12290 Pont de Salars.
Tel:
65.46.88.18.
FAX: 65.46.85.38.
Reservations:
Made with deposit (Ffr. 400) and fee (70).

1204 Castel Camping Les Tours, St Amans des Cots

Attractive, friendly and efficiently run site on shores of Lac de la Selves.

This is an impressive campsite, set in beautiful countryside very close to the Truyère Gorges, Upper Lot valley and the Aubrac Plateau. There are 250 pitches, all of approx. 100 sq.m. and with 5A electrical connections, some bordering the lake, the rest terraced and hedged with views of the lake. About 100 pitches also have individual water points. About 20% of the pitches are for static caravans - reserved for tour operators or owned by the site, but these are well spaced. The site has a spacious feel about it, enhanced by the thoughtfully planned terraced layout. The sanitary facilities are good, with four blocks including an excellent new one of unusual round design. All have free hot showers, individual washing cubicles, British style toilets, and seem more than adequate for the number of campers. They were spotlessly clean when seen in main season. The central complex, with office, restaurant, bar, swimming pools (650 and 40 sq.m.), shop and modern children's play area is most attractive. Volleyball, tennis courts, putting green, football area and table tennis. The site arranges a varied programme of daytime and evening activities, some of which are held in a very attractive, converted barn, a little away from the other facilities, so no noise. Lake activities available include canoeing, pedaloes, windsurfing, water ski-ing and there is provision for launching small boats. Riding and golf near. Takeaway. Shop and greengrocer. Exchange facilities. The owner and his staff are helpful. Used by tour operators (30%).

Directions: Take D34 road from Entraygues-sur-Truyere to St. Amans-des-Cots (14 km.). In St. Amans turn right onto D599 (site is signed), then left on a narrower road around lake and site. Alternatively, if using autoroute A75, take St. Flour exit and follow D921 south for 41 km. 1½ km. past Lecalm turn right on D34 signed St. Amans-des-Cots. Follow signs for 23 km.

Charges 1996:
-- Per unit, incl. 2 persons Ffr. 124.00, 3 persons 148.00; extra person 24.00; child 17.00; electricity 15.00; services 8.00.
-- Less 20% outside July/Aug.
-- Credit cards accepted.
Open:
20 May - 15 September, full services 21/5-10/9.
Address:
12460 St Amans-des-Cots.
Tel:
65.44.88.10.
FAX: 65.44.83.07.
Reservations:
Made and are advisable for July/Aug. - write for details.

1210M Camping Municipal du Lauradiol, Campouriez, nr Entraygues

A strikingly neat and pretty little site, tucked into a wooded gorge in the Aveyron hills, Lauradiol is alongside the La Selves river, 500 m. from the Cambeyra barrage. The 37 pitches (21 with electricity) are arranged on flat grass, neatly separated by trim hedges. Many are quite large, although those actually along the river bank are somewhat smaller. There is quite good shade from a variety of trees. Surprisingly for such a small site, there is even a swimming pool, plus paddling pool, and a well kept tennis court - both free to campers. There is not much else by way of facilities, but there are several villages within 5-6 km. for restaurants, shopping, etc. Sanitary facilities include hot showers, some washbasins in private cabins, and at least one, somewhat cramped, British WC (others are Turkish style) - all very clean when inspected.

Directions: Site is 5 km. northeast of Entraygues sur Truyère. Follow the D34 in the direction of St Amans-des-Cots.

Charges guide:
Per caravan incl. 2 persons and electricity Ffr. 75.00; tent incl. up to 2 persons 55.00.
Open:
20 June - 10 September.
Address:
12460 Campouriez.
Tel:
65.44.53.95. (winter La Mairie): 65.44.85.31.
Reservations:
Write or phone La Mairie de Campouriez.

1301M Camping Municipal Les Romarins, Maussane-les-Alpilles, nr Arles

This is one of those neat, well kept and orderly municipal sites that has been in the guide for several years and readers who have reported have always been satisfied. The 130 pitches, on flat ground adjoining made-up access roads, are of good size and enclosed by hedges, with 6A electrical connections available everywhere. The three modern toilet blocks are good ones and should be large enough with continental seatless toilets; washbasins in cubicles with shelf, mirror, free hot water; free pre-set hot showers with chain operation, and are well maintained. On-site amenities are limited (pleasant reading room with fireplace for cool days, telephone, 2 tennis courts and a children's playground), but there are others only a short walk away; the municipal swimming pool very close, and shops and restaurants in town. Les Baux and St. Remy-de-Provence are just a short drive away. Les Romarins becomes full from 1 July - late August.

Directions: Site is within the little town of Maussane on the eastern edge.

Charges guide:
-- Per pitch, incl. 2 adults, 1 child Ffr 65.00; extra person 15.00; child (under 12) 8.50; electricity 13.00 - 15.00.
Open:
15 March - 15 October.
Address:
13520 Maussane.
Tel:
90.54.33.60.
Reservations:
Any length with fee (Ffr. 52 in low season, Ffr. 115 high season).

1302 Camping Arc-en-Ciel, Aix-en-Provence

Well shaded site, with pool, within walking distance of the centre of Aix-en-Provence.

Family run, this site is a good base for discovering Aix, the centre of which is about a 20 minute walk away, or there is a bus service. Close to a main road, there may be traffic noise in some areas. The 65 pitches (all with electricity and water) are arranged amongst a variety of trees and shrubs and a small river with ducks, and crossed by a bridge, divides the site, making an attractive feature, especially for a town site. Whilst many city sites are noisy, not only from traffic, but from groups of youngsters, this site caters particularly for families and does not accept groups. No bicycles are to be ridden after 7 pm. There is a heated swimming pool (electronically controlled), table tennis and table football, with tennis, golf, river walks and fishing nearby. The sanitary facilities, in two blocks with en-suite cabins (British WC, shower and washbasin), are kept clean but are beginning to show their age. Laundry area with sinks and washing machine. There is no shop or restaurant on the site, but a supermarket and numerous restaurants catering for all tastes and pockets are within easy reach. Bread is available on site each morning. Gates closed 8 pm. (electronic key provided).

Charges 1995: -- Per person Ffr. 28.00; local tax 1.00; pitch 27.00; electricity (6A) 15.00.
Open: 15 March - 31 October.
Address: Pont-des-Trois-Sautets, 13100 Aix-en-Provence.
Tel: 42.26.14.28.
Reservations: Necessary for July/Aug. and made with no deposit.

Directions: From the Paris - Nice autoroute, take the Trois-Sautets exit onto the RN7 to Nice/Toulon (take RN7 also from Aix town centre), keep right and site is signed to the right after the Gendarmerie.

1303 Camping Rio Camargue, Port St. Louis du Rhône

Recently developed site on southeastern edge of the Camargue.

Situated close to the Rhône estuary, this is a somewhat unusual site with a number of excellent features including a large swimming pool and a crèche. The buildings, recently constructed in Camargaise style, include a large bar/restaurant providing welcome relief from the hot sun, particularly as there is little shade and the 100 sq.m. pitches are mainly on gravelled hardstanding, which emphasises the heat. The site is divided into two main areas (one having the official 4 star grading, the other being 3 star). The 4 star pitches all have electricity and drainage points as do some of the 3 star ones. The two sanitary blocks, one in each area, are modern and functional rather than luxurious. They were clean when visited and provide hot showers, some washbasins in private cabins, British WCs and also WCs for children. There is also a well equipped nursery with qualified staff (on payment). Other facilities include a café, shops, takeaway, laundry facilities, a fitness club, minigolf, tennis, table tennis, volleyball and basketball. Activities, excursions and entertainment programmes. Mobile homes and apartments for rent. This area of the Camargue is close to several industrial complexes, although it does make a very convenient base for exploring this interesting part of France. There is a large flat beach of hard sand (the Plage Napoleon) some 5 km. distant and the site provides cards giving free access to the beach car parking. A typically 'estuary type' beach, it does enjoy some good views and bathing is said to be clean and safe.

Charges guide: -- Per unit Ffr. 25.00 - 50.00, acc. to season; small tent 18.00 - 35.00; person 15.00 - 30.00; child (under 7 yrs) 10.00 - 20.00.
Open: All year.
Address: Route Napoleon, 13230 Port St. Louis du Rhône.
Tel: 42.86.06.06. FAX: 42.86.33.13.
Reservations: Write for booking form (deposit Ffr. 500).

Directions: From village of Port St. Louis du Rhône, drive through the village one way system. Turn right after lifting bridge and site is on left beside the river.

The sites featured in this Guide are regularly inspected by our team of experienced site assessors, but we welcome your opinions too.

Please see Readers' Reports on page 205

1305M Camping Municipal Mas de Nicolas, St Rémy de Provence

On the edge of the deservedly popular village of St. Rémy de Provence, this pretty and spacious site is one of those 'magnificent municipals' at which the French excel, although it must be said that it is let down somewhat by rather utilitarian sanitary facilities which, whilst giving adequate provision in terms of hot showers, with dividers and shelves, some washbasins in cabins, also include some of the most cramped WCs we have encountered. However, you should not let this put you off because in all other respects the site is excellent, with wide access roads, marked and mainly hedged pitches (some irregular shapes and slightly sloping ground in parts) all with very pretty surroundings and with some good views. All the 140 pitches have 6A electrical connections. Nearby, in the village itself, there are several historic attractions. Tennis, a Wednesday market, fishing, riding several festivals during the year and a variety of restaurants, shops, etc. Unusually for a municipal, the site has its own swimming pool (open 1/06 - 30/09), a TV lounge and children's play area.

Directions: St Rémy de Provence is situated where the D571 from Avignon connects with the D99 Tarascon - Cavaillon road. Site is signed from the village centre on the north side. Leave autoroute A7 at Cavaillon or Avignon-Sud.

Charges guide:
-- Per unit incl. 2 persons Ffr. 72.00; extra adult 21.00; child (under 10 yrs) 11.00; animal 9.00; electricity 16.00.
Open:
15 March - 31 October.
Address:
Av. Théodore Aubanel, 13210 St. Rémy de Provence.
Tel:
90.92.27.05.
Reservations:
Necessary for main season and made with Ffr. 110 fee.

1401 Camping de la Côte de Nacre, St Aubin sur Mer, nr Caen

Large new site just back from the sea, with swimming pool.

This stretch of the Normandy coast comprises a long series of towns which tend to run together. Nonetheless, the beaches and bathing are good, and they are within walking distance of the site. There are some standard sized, disc marked pitches here, laid out adjacent to semi-circular gravelled access roads; 200 of them have electricity (4, 6 or 10A). Some 100 holiday statics are placed around the perimeter of the flat, open site. Because it is fairly new, the trees and shrubs planted have not yet had much time to grow so there is little to separate pitches or to give shade and shelter, with a somewhat bare appearance at present. The two sanitary blocks are of modern construction and style. Washbasins are in cabins and all hot water is free. On site activities are not extensive although there is a small pool (no shorts) with child's pool, a children's playground and some animation and excursions are organised in season. The reception complex houses a restaurant/bar (open all season), TV and games room and a small shop. Boules. Table tennis. Bicycle hire. Used by tour operators.

Directions: Site is on southern side of town centre relief road, well signed from the approach roads to St Aubin, but make sure you leave the adjacent towns first.

Charges 1995:
-- Per pitch Ffr 28.00 - 35.00; adult 22.00 - 25.00; child (under 7) 12.00 - 15.00; electricity 18.00 - 32.00, acc. to amps; local tax 1.60.
Open:
1 April - 31 October.
Address:
Rue du Camping, BP 18, 14750 St. Aubin sur Mer.
Tel:
31.97.14.45.
FAX: 31.97.22.11.
Reservations:
Advisable for July/Aug. and made with deposit (Ffr. 400) and fee (100).

1402M Camping Municipal, Bayeux

Whether or not you want to see the tapestry, this site makes a very useful night stop on the way to or from Cherbourg, and in addition it is only a few kilometres from the coast and the landing beaches. Pleasantly laid out with grassy lawns and bushes, its neat, cared for appearance make a good impression. The 225 pitches are in two areas. In the main area 27 new hardstanding pitches have been created, with the remaining pitches well marked and generally of good size, 170 with electricity. The three toilet blocks have British and continental WCs, washbasins in cabins in the main block, free, roomy hot showers, units for the handicapped, and are of good quality. A large public indoor swimming pool adjoins the site with children's pool and jacuzzi. Takeaway food, snacks and small shop for basics 15/6-15/9, but large supermarket very close (closes 8 pm). Two children's playground. Reading room with TV. Games room. Laundry room. The site is busy over a long season - reservation, particularly for electricity, is advised. Used by tour operators (5%). There is a full time site warden from 15/6-15/9, otherwise reception is only open for one hour in the morning and two in the evening.

Directions: Site is on the south side of northern ring road to town.

Charges 1996:
-- Per person Ffr 15.00; child (under 7) 8.10; pitch and car 18.40; electricity 15.30.
-- Less 10% for stay over 5 days.
Open:
15 March - 15 Nov.
Address:
14400 Bayeux.
Tel:
31.92.08.43.
Reservations:
Made for min. 3 nights without deposit. (See editorial).

Camping de la Vallée

★★★★

SHOP □ BAR □ GAMES ROOM
HEATED SWIMMING POOL □ TENNIS
CHILDREN'S POOL □ ENTERTAINMENT

88, Rue de la Vallée – 14519 Houlgate
Tel: 31.24.40.69

1403 Castel Camping de Martragny, Martragny, nr Bayeux

Site adjoining château in parkland setting, close to Bayeux and D-Day landing beaches.

Martragny is particularly convenient for those using the port of Cherbourg and has facilities to encourage longer stays as well as stopovers. Taking 160 units on the pleasant lawns approaching and surrounding the château, it does not have marked out pitches and can be very busy in peak season. There are 140 electrical connections. The sanitary installations are constructed to top standards and a further block is provided in the extension. Kept very clean, the facilities include British toilets, individual basins mainly in private cabins with mirror and light and free hot water in basins, showers and sinks. Provision is made for the handicapped. There is a free swimming pool (16½ x 6 m.), open from mid-May with a children's paddling pool. Shop and hot takeaway all season. Play areas. Minigolf. Bar, games and TV room, table tennis and billiards. Bed and breakfast (bathroom en-suite) in the Châteaux available all year - reservation essential. Laundry facilities. Quietly situated, the site is 12 km. from the sea, and one can visit the Bayeux tapestry, Caen, and the wartime landing beaches and Arromanches museum. The site is popular with tour operators (25%).

Directions: Site is off N13, 8 km. southeast of Bayeux. Take Martragny exit from dual carriageway.

Charges 1996:
-- Per person Ffr. 25.00; child (under 7) 16.00; simple pitch 55.00 - 60.00; extra car 10.00; electricity (6A) 18.00.
-- Credit cards accepted.
Open:
15 May - 15 September.
Address:
14740 Martragny.
Tel:
31.80.21.40.
FAX: 31.08.14.91.
Reservations:
See text - made for min. 3 nights; deposit and small fee required.

1405 Castel Camping-Caravaning Le Colombier, Moyaux, nr Lisieux

Normandy site with swimming pool and other installations of high quality.

Le Colombier is a quality site with the aspect of a spacious country estate. Pitches are large and it has a free heated swimming pool (25 x 12m.) in a very attractive landscaped setting between the manor house and the `colombier' - a circular building which houses the bar, library and TV room. The 170 pitches, all with electricity, some with water connections also, are marked by trees at the corners but otherwise have nothing between them. The central toilet block is of the very best quality, with everything in cabins and free hot water throughout. A new smaller block of similar quality is on the opposite side of the site, mainly for the benefit of the new extension, with British toilets and a good unit for the disabled. Shop. Crêperie. Takeaway in main season. Special dinners (limited numbers) served some days in château. Bar open latter part of evening. TV room. Large general room for reading, cards, etc, with TV. Tennis court. Minigolf. Volleyball. Free fishing on nearby lake. Washing machine and dryer. Baby sitting available.You do pay for the quality, but there are no off-peak reductions, but all the main amenities open for the whole season and the château and its surroundings do have a certain elegance. Used by a tour operator (8%). American motorhomes not accepted. Lisieux is 16 km., and places on the coast such as Deauville and Honfleur 30 to 40. Excursions to Paris available.

Directions: Site is 3 km. northeast of Moyaux on the D143, well signed from the Cormeilles-Lisieux road.

Charges 1996:
-- Per person Ffr 30.00; child (under 7) 15.00; pitch 66.00; electricity (12A) 15.00.
-- Credit cards accepted.
Open:
1 May-15 September, with all services.
Address:
Le Val Séry.
14590 Moyaux.
Tel:
31.63.63.08.
FAX: 31.63.15.97.
Reservations:
Made for min. 5 days with Ffr. 150 fee.

1407 Camping de la Vallée, Houlgate

Fresh, well kept site, close to lively little resort of Houlgate.

Camping de la Vallée's owners provide a warm welcome to all visitors and the attractive site has good, well maintained facilities. Situated on a grassy hillside overlooking Houlgate, the 270 pitches are large and open, with hedging planted and all have electricity. Part of the site is sloping, the rest level, with gravel or tarmac roads. An old farmhouse has been converted to house a rustic bar and comfortable TV lounge and billiards room. A heated swimming pool (from 15/5) and a tennis court have been added. Shop. Small snackbar with takeaway in season (from 15/5). A large grassy area has a children's playground, volleyball and a football field. Tennis. Bicycle hire. Petanque. Organised entertainment in Jul/Aug. There are three toilet blocks of a good standard with free hot water in the controllable, well fitted showers; washbasins in cabins; mainly British toilets. Facilities for the handicapped are provided. Washing up and laundry provision with machines, dryers and ironing boards (no washing lines allowed). Motorcaravan services. The beach is 1 km, the town 900 m. and a championship golf course is nearby. English spoken in season. Popular with tour operators (30%).

Directions: Site is 1 km. from Houlgate, along D24A (route de Lisieux). Turn right onto D24, rue de la Vallée and look for site sign.

Charges 1996:
-- Per person Ffr. 28.00; child (under 7) 20.00; pitch 40.00, with services 45.00; dog 10.00; extra car or boat 10.00; electricity 2A 12.00, 4A 16.00, 6A 25.00, 10A 30.00; local tax 2.00.
-- Low season less 10%.
-- Credit cards accepted.
Open:
1 April - 30 September.
Address:
88 rue de la Vallée, 14519 Houlgate.
Tel:
31.24.40.69.
FAX: 31.28.08.29.
Reservations:
Write to site.

1410M Camping Municipal du Château, Falaise

The location of this site is really quite spectacular, lying in the shadow of the Château Falaise, in the old part of the town - the `coeur de Normandie'. The site itself is small, with only 66 pitches (all with 5A electricity). It has a rather intimate `up-market' feel about it, rather different from the average municipal site. With good shade, tarmac roads and easy access, it was well recommended by the British campers we met there. However, we were concerned that the sanitary facilities could be insufficient in terms of quantity when the site is full - perhaps it never is - campers we met felt they were adequate. The quality was reasonable, with free hot showers and British style WCs, and they were well cleaned. That misgiving aside, whatever this site lacks in size and facilities it makes up for in its situation. Close to the town centre, the swimming pool and tennis club and near to the river for fishing, the charges are reasonable and the reception friendly - who minds waiting a while for a shower?

Directions: Site is on the western side of town (signed) via the N138 road.

Charges guide:
-- Per pitch Ffr. 14.00; adult 16.00; child (under 10 yrs) 11.00; electricity 13.00.
Open:
Easter - 30 September.
Address:
14700 Falaise.
Tel:
31.90.16.55.
Reservations:
Contact site.

1411M Camping Municipal Le Traspy, Thury-Harcourt

Somewhat akin to a tiny nature park, close to a lake (reputedly excellent for fishing) and with a small stream running through it, this secluded site is resplendent with mature tall trees. The 92 pitches are on two levels, both flat, with a choice of 6 or 10A electrical connections. There is some traffic noise but it is not obtrusive. Sanitary facilities include both British and Turkish type WCs, free hot showers and some washbasins in private cabins. External dishwashing facilities and a laundry room. There is no on-site restaurant or shop, but the village facilities are only about 500 m. away. A useful site for night stops, or for longer stays for keen anglers!

Directions: Site is signed in the town of Thury-Harcourt on the D562 Caen - Vire road, 26 km. from Caen.

Charges guide:
-- Per pitch Ffr. 19.50; adult 19.50; child (under 7 yrs) 13.00; electricity 17.00 - 19.50.
Open:
Probably April - Sept. (not finalised at time of going to press).
Address:
14220 Thury-Harcourt
Tel:
31.79.70.45 (Mairie).
Reservations:
Contact site.

1501 Le Belvédère (Camping-Hôtel), Pont de Lanau, Lanau, nr St Flour

Peaceful, terraced site with fine views in picturesque Auvergne south of St. Flour.

Situated in a pleasant mix of high country, lakes and deep valleys, La Belvédère used to be difficult to reach but recent road improvements make this peaceful site much more accessible. The region has plenty to offer the discerning visitor interested in nature, ie. birdwatching, walking, etc. Wild flowers are profuse (and the wild strawberries are excellent!). The 150 or so pitches are all on flat terraces on a quite steep hillside with good views. They vary in size and most are well shaded. The highest ones are only for tents, leaving about 80 (some higher ones with difficult access) for caravans; these all have electrical connections, 36 with water also. Four new pitches of 150 sq.m. have been added by extending the terraces. These have little shade but do have their own private sanitation. The two original toilet blocks, which have been renovated, and a third new one have a mixture of WC types; washbasins in cubicles or cabins with very hot water, mirror and shelf, and a good quota of fully controllable hot showers. These facilities now include provision for the handicapped, for hairdressing, baby baths and a covered laundry. There is a swimming pool (14 x 6 m.) plus a children's pool (8 x 4). In addition to the up-and-down walking on the site itself, many good walks are available from the site and numerous excursion possibilities. A nearby lake can be used for sailing, windsurfing and fishing. Self-service shop. Restaurant/bar/pizzeria, with limited food available each day and takeaway. Laundry facilities. Large new children's playground. Animation in high season. Table tennis. Sauna. Hotel rooms, mobile homes and studios to let. Friendly reception. Tour operators take about 20% of the pitches.

Charges 1996:
-- Per unit incl. 2 persons: simple Ffr. 105.00, with electricity 120.00, with 3 services 125.00, pitch with barbecue 145.00; extra person (over 2 yrs) 25.00.
-- Less 20% in June and Sept.
-- Credit cards accepted.
Open:
15 May - 15 September.
Address:
15260 Lanau.
Tel:
71.23.50.50.
FAX: 71.23.58.93.
Reservations:
Made for min. 1 week with deposit (Ffr. 900), fee (100) and cancellation insurance.

Directions: Site is on D921 road south of St. Flour, about halfway between Neuvéglise and Chaudes-Aigues.

N1502 Domaine Naturiste de la Taillade, Neuvéglise

Delightful naturist site in superb Cantal surroundings.

In the words of the jovial and enthusiastic owner, Noel Brun, "this is a site where comfort comes second to activities" - this may be partly true, as the activities are very important, but we spent a very comfortable 36 hours here doing very little! Approached along a **very** minor road, through beautiful countryside, this is a superbly situated site, with wonderful views across the Auvergne landscape and part of the Gorges de la Truyère. For such a rural site it is surprisingly large, with 120 reasonably flat pitches, of variable size, on several terraces, many of which enjoy those superb views. A fair number have electrical connections. Facilities include an attractive swimming pool with sunbathing area, small epicerie for basics and a snack bar - the epicerie and snack bar are open only in the main season.

Sanitary facilities are in three small blocks, one of which is of the `portaloo' variety. These are fairly basic, but provide all the essentials, with typically naturist open showers as well as traditional, private (hot) indoor ones, some British style WCs, washbasins, washing up sinks (both with H&C), etc. For those looking for a hide-away in glorious countryside, with the possibility of a range of activities, from the energetic (eg. canoeing or sailing in the lake, hill walking, horse riding, rock climbing) to studying the flora and fauna, this site has a lot to offer. In particular it may appeal to the first time naturist as, although the campsite itself is naturist, the activities take place mainly in the non-naturist surrounding countryside. Chalets to let.

Charges guide:
-- Per pitch incl. 2 persons Ffr. 100.00; extra person (over 3 yrs) 10.00.
-- Less 10% for stays over 10 days.
Open:
15 June - 31 August.
Address:
15260 Neuvéglise.
Tel:
71.23.80.13.
FAX: 71.23.86.94.
Reservations:
Advised from mid-July. and made with Ffr. 500 deposit.

Directions: Site is signed from the D921 at Pont de Lanau (alongside entrance to Camping Hotel Belvedere, no. 1501) via a small, unclassified road through the hamlet of Gros. Follow site signs carefully - about 5 km. from the main road.

1510M Camping Municipal de l'Ombrade, Aurillac

This is a fairly typical, good quality municipal site of some 200 pitches, about half of which have electricity. The site is divided into two parts either side of a river, one half being on flat grass with well marked, and partially separated, level pitches, with good shade, the other half being on terraces with less obvious marking and not a lot of shade. There are no less than nine sanitary blocks of slightly elderly construction, but with adequate facilities in terms of hot showers, British type WCs, some washbasins in cabins, etc. - not luxurious, but quite acceptable. There is not a lot by way of other facilities, as the town's amenities are mostly within walking distance, but there is the ubiquitous `salle de reunion' (we're never entirely sure what these rooms are actually used for, but wardens on French municipals are always at pains to point them out!) This could be a useful and quite comfortable site for exploring this area, and/or for overnight stops.

Directions: Site is well signed from town centre, on the northwest outskirts, and from various other junctions too.

Charges guide:
-- Per adult Ffr. 9.50; child (4-7 yrs) 4.25; pitch 6.00; car 6.00; m/cycle 3.40; motor-caravan 15.00; local tax 1.00; electricity 8.00.
Open:
1 May - 30 September.
Address:
12 Rue du Gué, Bouliaga, 15000 Aurillac.
Tel:
71.48.28.87.
Reservations:
Advised for July/Aug. Contact site.

1602 Castel Camping Gorges du Chambon, Eymouthiers, nr Montbron

Attractive family site in Charente countryside.

The British owners have further developed this site around a restored Charente farmhouse and outbuildings and it provides high quality facilities in an attractive setting. There are some 120 large marked pitches with electrical connections, on gently sloping grass (shade in parts) and enjoying extensive views over the countryside. The two sanitary blocks are of a good standard with British style WCs, hot showers and washbasins in private cabins. It is a good provision for the number of pitches. There are facilities for the disabled, a baby bath and laundry facilities, including a tumble dryer. The swimming pool (18 x 7 m.) has an adjacent bar selling drinks, snacks and ices. There is a bar and restaurant (in main season only) converted from the barn with an interesting gallery arrangement. Games room with soft drinks, ice creams, TV and table tennis, etc. Games for children are organised daily. Takeaway including pizzas (1/6-1/9). Small shop for basics in reception. Tennis. Minigolf. Children's play area. Used by tour operators (33%). Caravans and gite to let. No animals accepted.

Directions: From Montbron village, follow D6 in direction of Piegut-Pluviers. Site is signed.

Alan Rogers' discount
7th night free in May & June

Charges 1996:
-- Per pitch Ffr 38.00; person 28.00; child (under 7 yrs) 14.00; car 12.00; electricity (6A) 20.00; local tax 1.00.
-- Less 15% in low season (not electricity).
-- Credit cards accepted.
Open:
15 May - 10 September.
Address:
Eymouthiers, 16220 Montbron.
Tel:
45.70.71.70.
FAX: 45.70.80.02.
Reservations:
Necessary for July/Aug. Write with min. Ffr. 200 deposit and fee (80).

0402 Castel Camping du Verdon, Castellane

Good site with swimming pool close to `Route des Alpes' and Gorges du Verdon. Although it is an inland site, Camp du Verdon is in a popular holiday area and now has two heated swimming pools (both 19 x 7 m., one deeper than the other), open from mid-June to at least late Aug. In fact most visitors are here for a period, although it also has transit trade. It is very big and is sheltered, on flat ground which is part meadow and part wooded. The 500 pitches are numbered and vary in size and type, most with 6A electricity. The sanitary blocks, three fair-sized and two smaller, have been improved and are of very good quality. They have mostly continental toilets, individual basins with mirrors and shelves (cold water); free pre-set hot showers, free hot water for sinks and facilities for the disabled, kept spotless by resident cleaners. Traditional restaurant (very popular) and separate fast food service in July/Aug. Pizzeria/crêperie with terrace. Bar and special room with fireplace for early season. Takeaway. Children's playgrounds. Volleyball. Archery. Minigolf. Football field. Games room. Lake for trout fishing; another for small boats; access to River Verdon at end of site with stone beach and river pools. Rafting nearby. Horse riding. In July/Aug. organised sports in daytime; dancing/disco twice weekly. Washing machines, dryers and ironing facilities. Bureau de change. Ice boxes for hire. Mobile homes for hire. There is usually space except right at the peak, though not perhaps on the pitch that you would choose. Torches required at night. Used by main tour operators (20%). A busy but well run site.

Directions: From Castellane take D952 towards Gorges du Verdon/Moustiers.

This site has asked to appear out of order - it should be on page 24

Charges 1996:
-- Per unit with up to 3 persons Ffr. 93.00 - 180.00, acc. to season, size and facilities; extra person over 2 yrs 33.00 - 35.00; extra car, tent or caravan 15.00; dog 13.00; local tax 2.00.
Open:
15 May - 15 September.
Address:
Domaine de la Salaou, 04120 Castellane.
Tel:
92.83.61.29.
FAX: 92.83.69.37.
Reservations:
Any length with fee (Ffr. 130) and deposit - details from site.

 Alan Rogers' discount
Discounts in May & Sept

1601M Camping Municipal de Bourgines, Angoulême

This little site on flat grassy terrain provides a convenient and satisfactory night halt close to the town and to the main routes to the southwest. With the municipal swimming pool complex next door (full prices payable), you might even stay an extra day or so. There are 197 pitches of which 40 have electricity (5 or 15A). They include many of the individual type with hedge separators for tourists as well as an open meadow. A second toilet block has been built, giving a satisfactory total supply from the two blocks. Nearly all continental WCs; washbasins in cubicles with free hot water; hot showers on payment, with taps in the old block, chain operated in the new. No shop. Children's playground and entertainment in high season. Table tennis. Good security.

Directions: Site is near the Angoulême western by-pass (and the main N10 route to Bordeaux) on the west bank of the Charente river. There is now no sign from the by-pass, only from the town centre.

Charges guide:
-- Per pitch Ffr. 25.00; adult 13.00; child (under 7 yrs) 6.00; electricity 5A 16.00, 15A 26.00; water connection 5.00.
Open:
14 March - 2 November.
Address:
Ile de Bourgines, 16000 Angoulême.
Tel:
45.92.83.22.
Reservations:
Write to site.

1605M Camping Municipal de Cognac, Cognac

If you're a lover of brandy, this area is a must, with abundant vineyards and little roadside chalets offering tastings of Pineau (a Cognac based aperitif) and a vast range of Cognacs. This municipal site, with 165 large pitches separated by small shrubs and with 5A electricity, is convenient as a night stop or longer stay to visit the area, and for sleeping off the effects of the `tastings' - you probably won't even notice the noise from the nearby road! Three modern toilet blocks have mixed British and Turkish style WCs, pushbutton showers with hot water, some washbasins in cabins, dishwashing and laundry sinks and a washing machine. The municipal swimming pool is nearby. Restaurants, bars and shops may be found in the town centre, but the site has a snack bar and entertainment in July/Aug. Bicycle hire, volleyball, table tennis, children's play area on grass and a sand pit. Motorcycles are restricted. The famous Cognac Houses (Pineau, Hennessy, Martell, Remy Martin, etc.) and the Cognac Museum may be visited (no public transport to the town centre 2.3 km).

Directions: Site is signed from Cognac town centre on N141 Angoulême road.

Charges:
Not available.
Open:
May - 15 October.
Address:
Bvd. de Chatenay, Rte. de Ste-Sévère, 16100 Cognac.
Tel:
45.32.13.32.
Reservations:
Recommended in high season. Write for more information to:
Office de Tourisme de Cognac, 16 Rue du 14 Juillet, 16100 Cognac.

l'Orée du bois

★ ★ ★ ★ *Hotel de plein air*

Camping Caravaning
17570 Les Mathes - France

Bonne Anse Plage
★★★★
40% Discount Low Season

Camping, Caravanning
17570 Les Mathes
FRANCE

GORGES DU TARN
MILLAU GORGES DE LA DOURBIE

Gorges du Tarn, Lozére

1200 Camping Peyrelade****
1201 Castel et Camping Val de
Cantobre****
1202 Camping Les Rivages****

The Region of the Gorges du Tarn
and these three Campings offer you
a tourist environment: rivers,
gorges, causses, historic sites,
heritage…

Outdoor activities: canoeing,
rafting, caving, paragliding,
climbing, mountain biking,
rambling, walking, fishing…

Sports and Leisure: tennis,
swimming, volley-ball

CAMPING CLUB ✩✩✩✩ NN LE NAPOLEON

FAMILY CAMPING - VERY SHADY - HEDGED PITCHES
TO LET - COMFORTABLE APARTMENTS T2 (6 PERSONS) -
T3 (8 PERSONS) BATHROOM, KITCHENETTE
WOODEN CHALETS - MOBILE HOMES - CARAVANS -
TRIGANO TENTS
LOW SEASON - 50%

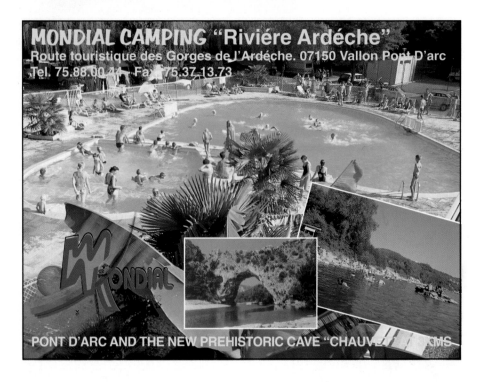

0401 Hotel de Plein Air L'Hippocampe, Volonne, Sisteron

Attractive, friendly site with good pool complex and sports opportunities.

Haute-Provence is one of the most beautiful and unspoilt regions of France and the proprietor here has arranged access to some of the most intriguing ways of exploring the many canyons and mountains in easy reach from the site - guided rafting expeditions, the new sport of 'canyonning' and treks with pack mules. The famous Gorges du Verdon are not far away and there are more than 100 other canyons in the area. The site is well run and has a family atmosphere. There are tour operator tents but the vast majority of the 447 pitches are for touring units, 370 with electricity (6A). Pitches are numbered and well marked by bushes, olives and cherry trees which not only make an attractive setting but also provide some shade.

The site retains a Provencal ambience whilst having a wide range of good facilities for visitors. Five toilet blocks, two larger and rather more modern, have free hot water in showers and washbasin cabins; WCs are mostly British style (possibly under pressure in main season). Friendly bar (1/5-30/9), reasonably priced self-service restaurant, pizzeria and takeaway (1/6-15/9). Small shop (July/Aug). Good sports facilities and some instruction (English spoken). The attractively designed pool complex (heated from 1/5) is excellent, comprising a fairly deep swimming and diving pool, another large pool not quite so deep and a paddling pool for young children. Tennis (free outside 3/7-21/8). Table tennis. Archery. Soundproof disco. Animation in season, aerobics sessions, some in water and mini-club for 7-12 year olds. Tourist information office with reservations service. Washing machines. The village is 600 m. Mobile homes (with phone and satellite TV) for rent. The site abuts a lake, really a wide stretch of the Durance, and pedaloes can be hired from the beach. A busy site, increasing in size, with lots going on for teenagers.

Directions: From the north turn off N85 across river bridge to Volonne, then right to site. From the south right on D4 1 km. before Château Arnoux.

This site has asked to appear out of order - it should be on page 24

Charges 1995:
-- Per unit with 2 persons basic pitch: Ffr. 58.00 - 115.00, with electricity 72.00 - 140.00, with water and drainage 72.00 - 153.00, large (140 sq.m.) with all services 72.00 - 173.00; extra person (over 2 yrs) 11.00 - 18.00; extra car or m/cycle 10.00 - 12.00; extra caravan or tent and car 20.00 - 50.00; dog 8.00 - 10.00; local tax 0.50 - 1.00.
-- Low season offers.
-- Credit cards accepted.

Open:
1 April - 30 September.

Address:
04290 Volonne.

Tel:
92.33.50.00.
FAX: 92.33.50.49.

Reservations:
Made with deposit and booking fee (Ffr. 120).

Alan Rogers' discount
4th day free outside July/Aug

0706 Mondial Camping, Riviére Ardèche, Vallon Pont d'Arc

Attractive family run site beside the river, close to popular resort.

Essentially this is a good quality family run site catering for families! It is close to the popular Ardèche resort of Vallon Pont d'Arc but is much less frenetic than some of the other sites in this area, with only 10% of its 240 pitches taken by tour operators. The majority of the pitches have good shade from mature trees. Neatly arranged in short rows, all are of a good size, level and with 6 or 10A electricity. The site itself is quite long and narrow with direct access at the far end to the river for bathing or canoeing (canoes for hire from the site), or just watching the river activity. There is a modern bar/restaurant, takeaway and pizzeria and an attractive heated swimming pool with sunbathing areas (all from 1/4), plus tennis, volleyball and a children's play area. The three modern sanitary blocks are of a good standard, very clean when inspected in high season and with unusually good facilities for the disabled. They have comfortable hot showers, a mixture of British and Turkish WCs, washbasins in private cabins, washing machine and dishwashing facilities. Motorcaravan service point. The pretty village, with shops, restaurants and bars, is just a short walk from the site, the famous Pont d'Arc is 3 km.

Directions: From Vallon Pont d'Arc take the D290 in the direction of Pont St. Esprit - site is on the right hand side of this road.

This site has asked to appear out of order - it should be on page 32

Charges 1995:
-- Per unit incl. 2 persons Ffr. 70.00 - 155.00; extra person 26.00 - 30.00; child (under 5) 18.00 - 23.00; electricity 19.00; water/ drainage 30.00; local tax 2.00 (over 10).

Open:
15 March - 10 October.

Address:
Rte Touristiques Gorges l'Ardèche, 07150 Vallon Pont d'Arc

Tel:
75.88.00.44.
FAX: 75.37.13.73.

Reservations:
Made with deposit (Ffr. 500) and fee (100).

1603M Camping Municipal Le Champion, Mansle

Le Champion is a convenient stop-over on the N10 or a good base to explore the northern Charente area. Beside the Charente river, the site has a cool, relaxing and peaceful atmosphere created by its attractive location, with a natural combination of trees, weirs and running water - ideal for fishermen, and canoes are also allowed. The site itself is mostly open with little shade and has 100 standard sized pitches, all with electricity (10A) and water points. The main sanitary block is kept in immaculate condition and is modern, tiled, with free hot water throughout. There is an additional smaller, older block in the tenting area at the rear of the site. These provide pushbutton showers, washbasins in cabins, British WCs and facilities for the disabled. Dishwashing and laundry facilities also. Two privately owned restaurants are situated at the site entrance. One is attractively tented and both have al fresco facilities and snack bar priced food. The town and shops are 200 m. over the bridge (but bread van calls in mornings) with a market on Tuesday and Friday mornings and farm produce on Saturday mornings. Swimming pool in town, recreational area and sports ground next to the site, with plenty of space for children (where most of the town's social activities are held). The local Syndicate d'Initiative calls at the site to advise on trips and activities, eg. cycle tracking (one or two days), coach trips, open air cinema, climbing tuition, canoeing courses, etc. Trout fishing in nearby lake and river fishing (permits necessary). Canoe and bicycle hire.

Directions: Site is well signed off the N10 (in town of Mansle), 30 km. north of Angoulême.

Charges 1995:
-- Per pitch Ffr. 15.00; adult 10.00; child 5.00; motorhome, caravan or tent 10.00; vehicle 10.00; electricity 15.00.

Open:
15 May - 15 September.

Address:
16230 Mansle.

Tel:
45.20.31.41.
FAX: 45.20.30.40.

Reservations:
Bookings accepted without deposit on Alan Roger's booking form, although not usually necessary.

Mansle Town   Charente River   Le Champion Camp Site

17 Charente-Maritime

1701 Camping Bois Soleil, St. Georges-de-Didonne, nr Royan

Large site with various amenities by sea south of Royan.

Bois Soleil is a large site long patronised by the British (English is spoken), although other nationalities also find it attractive. The site is in three separate parts. The two nearest to the beach, La Mer and Les Pins, consist entirely of 350 special pitches for caravans and some tents, for which one pays an all-in charge including electricity and water. The third and largest part (La Forêt), mainly for statics, is on the far side of the main road, some way from the beach and shops, although prices are lower. This can also be used for both tents and caravans. Some pitches here are very sandy although they are now stabilised. The site has an hotel-type reservation system for each caravan pitch and can be full mid-June - late August. The areas are well tended with pitches, all with names not numbers, cleared and raked between clients and there is good shade. The sandy beach here is a wide public one with direct access from one of the caravan areas, and a very short distance from the other. It is sheltered from the Atlantic breakers but the sea goes out some way at low tide. The sanitary installations consist of 10 blocks of varying size, type and quality. They have been considerably improved recently and there are some hot showers, and hot water in some if not all washbasins, in all the blocks except one. Continental and British toilets. Individual basins in private cabins or cubicles and facilities for the disabled. `Parc des jeux' with tennis, table tennis, children's playground (main season). Amusements and video games in a separate area. Launderette. Safe deposit. A busy little shopping area beside reception, an upstairs restaurant and bar with terrace and an excellent takeaway facility (all from 1/4) complete the provision. Doctor visits daily. No charcoal barbecues but gas ones can be hired by the evening. No dogs. A swimming pool is planned. This site offers a terrain for everyone, whether they like beach, forest or socialising in the main area - it is best to book for the area you prefer.

Charges guide:
-- Per unit with 3 persons: tent Ffr. 90.00 - 97.00 (acc. to location of pitch), caravan with 2A electricity, water and drainage 105.00 - 116.00, with 4A electricity, water and drainage 128.00; extra adult 21.00; child (2-7 yrs) 12.00, under 2 yrs 5.00; local tax 1.30.
-- Less in low seasons.
Open:
Easter/1 April - 30 Sept.
Address:
2 Ave.de Suzac, 17110 St. Georges-de-Didonne.
Tel:
46.05.05.94.
FAX: 46.06.27.43.
Reservations:
Made with no min. stay with deposit (Ffr. 400) and fee (130).

Directions: From Royan keep along coast road to south until camp signs.

1702 Airotel Le Puits de l'Auture, St Palais sur Mer, nr Royan

Good seaside site on La Grand Côte, to west of Royan and St Palais.

This popular region has a good, sunny climate and this camp is well situated in 10 acres of parkland with the sea right outside its gates just across the road, with a long sandy beach starting 400 m. away. Attractively laid out, flower beds and shrubs giving it a well cared for look. The 400 pitches, which are of varied but sufficient size, are on flat ground largely covered by tall trees and most have some shade. Numbered but not separated, with electrical connections in most areas, 200 have water and drainage also. There are now six sanitary blocks, which should be a good provision, although they might be pressured in the busiest times. Some are more modern than others and they vary in type. Half British WCs, half continental; most basins are in private cabins and all have free hot water, as do showers and sinks. Most showers are pre-set. Facilities for babies and washing machines. There is a good self-service shop with delicatessen and butcher, takeaway food, bar (all from 1/6), table tennis, volleyball, games room and children's play area. Excellent swimming pool complex of three pools. Doctor visits. A launderette and phone boxes are on site. Tennis, horse riding and 18 hole golf course nearby. Several good restaurants specialising in seafood are a few minutes walk away. No dogs taken. Barbecues not permitted except in a special area. The site is popular with British visitors and reservation is essential for main season. A few tour operator pitches (5%); mobile homes and large caravans for hire.

Charges 1996:
-- Per unit incl. up to 3 persons Ffr.105.00 - 150.00; with electricity (5A) 130.00 - 170.00, with water and drainage 160.00 - 190.00; extra person (over 3 yrs) 26.00 - 32.00; extra vehicle 16.00 - 22.00; electricity (10A) 30.00; plus local tax.
-- Credit cards accepted.
Open:
1 May - 30 September.
Address:
La Grande Côte, 17420 St Palais sur Mer.
Tel:
46.23.20.31.
FAX: 46.23.26.38.
Reservations:
Made for min. 5 days with exact dates; deposit and fee required.

Directions: Site is 2 km. from St Palais and 8 km. from Royan. From north Royan take back road to St Palais, going past it following La Palmyre signs, then turn back left towards Grande Côte and St Palais at junction with D25.

1703 Camping L'Estanquet, Les Mathes, La Palmyre, nr Royan

Pleasant modern site a short drive from seaside town of La Palmyre.

This attractive site lies in beautifully wooded grounds approximately 5 km. from the sandy beaches of the `Côte Sauvage', although the safest swimming is at La Palmyre (3½ km). There are 420 good sized individual pitches separated by small hedges, all of which have electricity and some 150 can be linked up to water and drainage. Set amongst tall pine trees the ground is flat and sandy, and almost all pitches have some shade. The sanitary installations are of good quality providing plenty of hot water in basins, showers and sinks, which are thoroughly cleaned daily.

The reception staff are friendly and helpful and, in the main season, speak English. There is now a large swimming pool, small pool with water slide and a small children's pool, with paved surrounds for sunbathing. A card system involving a deposit is required for pool users. The bar/restaurant overlooks the pool. Shop. Takeaway. Tennis. Volleyball. Table tennis. Bicycle hire. Laundry facilities. Children's playground. Three discos per week during July/Aug (finish at 11.45 pm). Mobile homes to let. The use of barbecues is limited. We notice that the site has become very popular with British tour operators (30-40%) but it still maintains its high class image.

Directions: From the north and east follow D14 (Saujon-la Tremblade) road, turn south onto D141 at Arvert; turn east in Les Mathes, from where camp is signposted. From south take D25 from Royan, turn north at La Palmyre for Les Mathes and proceed as above. Note: there is now a new roundabout with a boat on it - if sign for La Tremblade, then follow. Site is signed from this road, and this way is said to be quicker.

Charges 1995:
-- Per pitch, incl. 2 persons Ffr. 120.00; extra person 22.00; child (under 4) 12.00; electricity (6A) 22.00.
-- Less in low seasons.
Open:
15 May - 15 September.
Address:
La Fouasse, 17570 Les Mathes-La Palmyre.
Tel:
46.22.47.32.
FAX: 46.22.51.46.
Reservations:
Made with deposit (20%) and fee (Ffr. 120) for min. 1 week.

1705 Camping L'Orée du Bois, La Fouasse, Les Mathes

Large, attractive site amidst beautiful pines and oaks of the Forêt de la Coubre.

L'Orée du Bois has 400 pitches of about 100 sq.m. in a spacious, pinewood setting, including 40 with individual sanitary facilities (shower, toilet, washbasin and washing up sink). Pitches are on flat, sandy ground, separated by trees and shrubbery and all have electrical connections (6A). The forest pines offer shade. There are 45 mobile homes (for hire) set apart and several tour operators use the site. The four large, sanitary blocks of modern construction, have free hot water to the controllable showers and the washbasins (in private cabins). Three of the blocks have a laundry room and washing up is under cover. All have fully equipped units for the disabled.

The excellent bar, restaurant and crêperie have terraces overlooking the large swimming pools, including a new water toboggan, and children's paddling pool (proper swimming trunks, not shorts). Takeaway service available and very well stocked self service shop. Other amenities include a tennis court, boules, games room, TV lounge (with satellite), bicycle hire, 2 sand based children's play areas, volleyball and table tennis. Twice weekly discos and free, all day children's entertainment are organised in July/Aug. Exchange facilities. Nearby are sandy beaches (lifeguard in season); walking, riding and cycling in the 10,000 hectare forest; fishing; sailing and windsurfing; golf and the zoo at La Palmyre. Site rules are quite specific about total silence between 22.00 and 07.00 (except when entertainment is organised). Because of the forest setting only gas barbecues are allowed, with four communal barbecue areas provided.

Directions: From the north follow D14 (La Tremblade) and at Arvert turn onto D141 then east at Les Mathes. From the south, at Royan take D25 to La Palmyre, then in the direction of Les Mathes from where site is signed. Note: there is now a new roundabout with a boat on it - if sign for La Tremblade, then follow. Site is signed from this road, and this way is said to be quicker.

Charges 1996:
-- Per unit incl. 2 persons Ffr 80.00 - 150.00, with private sanitary facilities 120.00 - 200.00; extra person (over 3 yrs) 22.00; local tax 2.00 (child 4-10 yrs 1.00); extra vehicle 22.00; animal 10.00.
Open:
13 May - 15 September.
Address:
La Fouasse, 17570 Les Mathes.
Tel:
46.22.42.43.
FAX: 46.22.54.76.
(Low season:
45.83.15.81,
Fax: 45.83.15.87).
Reservations:
Made with 30% deposit plus fee (Ffr 130).

see advert in previous colour section

1704 Camping International Bonne Anse Plage, La Palmyre

Spacious, well organised, family run site amongst shady pine trees with large pool.

Bonne Anse is a gently undulating site in a pine wood, 500 m. from the beach, with its own heated swimming pool complex with a pool (35 x 25m), two water toboggans and a splash pool with water slide. The 850 pitches, of which 600 have electricity (6-8A), are clearly marked and are level and grassy, if a little sandy. On site facilities are neat and well kept. The seven sanitary blocks, including two new ones, provide free hot water, washbasins all in cabins with mirror, shelf and electric point, British style toilets with a few continental, hot (controllable in the new blocks) and cold showers and facilities for the handicapped and babies. Covered washing up sinks and laundry facilities, including washing machines.

There is a pleasant bar/restaurant with a terrace overlooking the boules area, a shop complex, crêperie and takeaway (all open all season). With organised activities, entertainment and dancing arranged in the season, the site generates a holiday park image but the family owners are keen to promote the peace and tranquility they can offer their clientele, many of whom return. Children's playground. Amusement arcade. TV (satellite). Mini car racing circuit. Volleyball. Table tennis. Pétanque. Bicycle hire. The site has direct access to the beach and to cycle tracks, avoiding the main road. Boating, tennis, golf, fitness track and horse riding available nearby. Motorcaravan service point. Exchange facilities. No dogs are accepted. Many (140) mobile homes for rent. Favoured by tour operators (over 20%), this is a busy site in an area popular with the British. English spoken. Rallies welcome with visit programmes organised.

Directions: Leave A10 autoroute at Saintes and head for Royan (N150). In Royan take signs for La Palmyre (D25). At La Palmyre roundabout, site is 1 km. on left, following signs for Ronce-les-Bains.

Charges 1995:
-- Per unit incl. 3 persons Ffr. 143.00; per unit incl. 1 or 2 persons 120.00; local tax 2.00 or child (4-10 yrs) 1.00; extra person (over 1 yr) 34.00; extra car 10.00; electricity (6A) 22.00.
-- Low season discounts of up to 40%.
-- Credit cards accepted.
Open:
25 May - 8 September.
Address:
La Palmyre,
17570 Les Mathes.
Tel:
46.22.40.90.
FAX: 46.22.42.30.
Reservations:
Min. 3 days - phone, fax or write for details.

see advert in previous colour section

1706 Airotel Domaine de Montravail, Château (sur Ile) d'Oléron

Attractive site on the Ile d'Oléron with riding stables and swimming pool.

The Ile d'Oléron is an `island' onto which you drive across a long viaduct with a toll. The west side of the island has wide sandy beaches and Atlantic seas; the east side more like a tidal estuary with gentle safe sandy bathing at high tide and an expanse of mud flats at low tide. Fishing and boat trips are available. It is a friendly, traditional site with all you could want except perhaps that it is a bit back from the sea, but it does have a swimming pool (open 15/5-30/9) alongside the bar, restaurant (both open 15/6-1/9) and TV room. Quietly situated, it is 1 km. to the east side of the Château d'Oléron beach (5 km. to the west side). The site has 200 large pitches of about 100 sq.m., all marked out, with some mature trees and newer bushes and shrubs and many electrical connections. It can be full in high season but there may be odd vacancies; reservations are made for longer stays. American motorhomes accepted for minimum 5 days. There are two toilet blocks with British and continental toilets, individual basins with shelf and mirror, some in private cabins for ladies and free hot water in basins, sinks, and in the showers which have preset hot water. They should be sufficient in high season, although a reader reports that cleaning can be variable. Children's playground. 2 tennis courts. Montravail particularly features equitation, having a good-class riding establishment attached to the site (site entrance adjoins the stable yard), and it has something of an `olde world' farm atmosphere, with a friendly welcome. A further attraction is the abundant wildlife, particularly peacocks which wander freely (can be noisy at 6.30 am!) Bungalows and rooms to let. Used by tour operators (18%).

Directions: Turn right to Château d'Oléron immediately after the viaduct and follow camp signs at junctions.

Charges 1995:
-- Per unit incl. up to 3 persons Ffr. 108.00; extra person 30.00; local tax in July/Aug. 1.00 for over 14s, 0.50 for child; extra car 15.00; dog 13.00; visitor 20.00; electricity (6A) 25.00; water 5.00; drainaway 20.00.
-- Less 30% outside 15/6-15/9.
-- Credit cards accepted.
Open:
1 March - 15 October.
Address:
17480 Château d'Oléron.
Tel:
46.47.61.82.
FAX: 46.47.79.67.
Reservations:
Made for exact dates (min. about one week in Aug.) with deposit (Ffr. 470) and booking fee (130).

17 Charente-Maritime

1707 Camping de L'Océan, La Couarde-sur-Mer, Ile de Ré
Interesting site on the attractive Ile de Ré.

Now joined to the mainland at La Rochelle by a toll bridge (expensive - at least Ffr. 110 for a car, 220 for car and caravan), the Ile de Ré is an attractive and understandably popular holiday area for the French although, as yet, largely unknown to the British. L'Océan is a somewhat unusual site offering a variety of pitches. Some are in long-established areas affording plenty of shade, others in newer areas without much shade. In total there are 330, all with electricity (3-10A). The site is some 100 m. from a sandy beach, quite near to the attractive old town and harbour of St. Martin-en-Ré. There are currently three sanitary blocks, of satisfactory rather than good quality (cleaning reported to be variable), with hot showers, basins in private cabins, and both British and continental WCs. Bar and restaurant complex (all season) with games and entertainment rooms and two attractively landscaped swimming pools, partly heated (1/5-30/9). Entertainment for children (free). Fishing lake planned (to be free in low season). TV room. Small supermarket (15/6-15/9). Tennis. Bicycle hire. Large children's play area. Mobile homes, chalets and bungalows to rent.

Directions: Site is 3 km. beyond town of La Couarde, towards Ars-en-Ré, just past the turning to Loix.

Charges 1996:
-- Per unit incl. 3 persons high season Ffr 145.00 - 162.00, low season incl. 2 persons 81.00; extra person 22.00 - 35.00; animal 10.00- 15.00; electricity (3A) 18.50.
-- Credit cards accepted.
Open:
1 April - 30 September.
Address:
17670 La Couarde.
Tel:
46.29.87.70.
FAX: 46.29.92.13.
Reservations:
Necessary for July/Aug only - with deposit (Ffr. 100) and fee (50).

 Alan Rogers' discount
Less 10% in low season

★ ★ ★ ile de ré
CAMPING DE L'OCEAN
17670 LA COUARDE SUR MER
Tél: 46 29 87 70
Facing the sea and only 50m from one of the most beautiful blue flag beaches, this rurally situated campsite is well equipped to a very high standard. Very comfortable toilet facilities with baby changing room, washing machines, quality furnishings, mini-market, take-away, bar and restaurant.
As for the leisure facilities, they are numerous: tennis, table tennis, volley ball, boules, evening entertainment and games area. Landscaped swimming pool.
Mobile homes and bungalows to rent.

1708 Camping Les Chirats, Angoulins-sur-Mer, nr La Rochelle
Quiet site with first class amenities and swimming pool, near La Rochelle.

Good quality sites near large towns or cities are hard to find and so we were pleased to locate such a site near La Rochelle. Situated only 50 m. from the beach at Angoulins sur Mer (bathing only possible at high tide but with no sand then) and about 15 minutes drive from the centre of La Rochelle, this site has 246 marked pitches, 100 in a new extension. Electricity (6A) is available. The site is new but there is some shade now as the trees and hedges that have been planted grow. The owners are continuing to improve the site and its facilities. Two good sanitary blocks have British WCs, hot showers, washbasins in cabins and a washing machine in each block. There is a good medium sized heated swimming pool with water slide and a shallow children's pool (open 15/5). Snack restaurant, bar and takeaway in high season. Barbecues permitted. Children's play area on grass. Boules, games room and table tennis. Small shop. Entertainment programme in season. 8 wooden bungalows and 6 caravans for hire. Watersports close by. Gates are locked at night in July/Aug.

Directions: From N137 La Rochelle-Rochefort road, follow signs for Angoulins-sur-Mer into village centre, then signs for 'Plage' to site.

Charges 1996:
-- Per pitch, incl. 1 or 2 persons Ffr 61.00 - 82.00, with electricity 79.00 - 100.00, water and drainage 83.00 - 109.00; extra adult 20.00 - 22.00; child (0-10) 14.00 - 17.00.
-- Credit cards accepted.
Open:
Easter - 30 September.
Address:
Rte de la Platère, 17690 Angoulins-sur-Mer.
Tel:
46.56.94.16 or 46.56.95.17.
Reservations:
Write with deposit (Ffr. 500) and fee (50).

1709M Camping Le Soleil, La Rochelle

Le Soleil has been neatly and attractively landscaped and has 155 grassy and level pitches, 25 with electricity (8A). Some have hardstandings. The four toilet blocks provide seatless toilets, pre-set hot water, some washbasins in cabins and 12 hot and 2 cold showers. There are facilities for the disabled and all is regularly cleaned and maintained. Hot water for clothes and dishwashing sinks. There is likely to be some noise from the road and an industrial area nearby, but accessibility to the amenities of the town balance this to a degree (5 mins. to grassy picnic areas by the harbour and 20 mins to the town centre shops, restaurants and bars or to the beach). Delivery vans call with bread, milk, etc. Launderette near. Table tennis. Half hourly bus service to town from outside site and ferry service across harbour to town. For information or reservation contact: Service de Campings, B.P. 1541, 17086 La Rochelle Cedex 02.

Charges 1995:
-- Per unit incl. 1 person Ffr. 23.50 - 32.00; child (under 10 yrs) 5.80 - 10.00; electricity 15.00 - 17.00; local tax 1.00.
Open:
10 May - 20 September.
Address:
Ave. des Minimes, 17000 La Rochelle.
Tel:
46.44.42.53.
Reservations:
See above.

Directions: From the ring road (peripherique), take the first exit signed 'Gare' or 'Centre-Ville' and follow signs to 'Vieux Port', 'Port les Minimes' and site.

1801M Camping Municipal de Bellon, Vierzon

This is an acceptable site to be found in the town of Vierzon on the Cher river, a tributary of the Loire. It has 98 pitches separated by low hedges, some with shade and all with water and electricity connections (although a few require a long lead). Two clean, sanitary blocks have washbasins in cubicles, showers, British and continental style WCs, plus a shower and toilet for the disabled. Stainless steel dishwashing and laundry sinks with hot water, also a chemical disposal unit and a motorcaravan service point. Whilst the nearest shop is 500 m, on site catering offers snacks, chips, etc. and a bar. Boules area, table tennis. Sand based play house and slide for children. Access is possible to the River Cher for canoeing or enjoying the park area with its picnic tables. Close by are opportunities for walking or cycling in the forest areas or on quiet roadways.

Charges 1995:
-- Per person Ffr. 14.50; child (under 10) 7.00; caravan 20.00; tent 15.00; electricity 12.50.
Open:
30 April - 30 Sept.
Address:
Rte. de Bellon, 18100 Vierzon.
Tel:
48.75.49.10 (low season: 48.52.65.24).
FAX: 48.71.62.21.
Reservations:
Contact site.

Directions: Site is signed from Vierzon on old N20 towards Châteauroux. From Vierzon centre take D918 towards Issoudun. Turn left onto D27 and second left off D27 at Intermarche supermarket sign.

1901 Camping Intercommunal de l'Abeille, Merlines, nr Ussel

Pleasant site for a short halt between Clermont-Ferrand and Brive.

This camp is part of a 'village de vacances' complex which has many solidly built bungalows. The site itself is fairly small, having around 75 individual pitches, all with hardstandings (a little weedy) and a grassy area for tents, with about 34 electrical connections in one section. There was some space in early August. The two modern small toilet blocks have continental toilets for men, British for women, washbasins with shelf, mirror and cold water, some in private cabins, and pre-mixed free hot showers. To use the facilities of the village de vacances, which include restaurant, bar and organised activities for both the young and adults, you have to join the Association that runs it, at a fee which would probably only be justified for stay of a few days or more. It is possible that the small swimming pool in the village section may be free to campers. Laundry room with dryer. Canoes for hire on nearby lake. Mountain bike hire. Tennis. Riding nearby. 10 chalets for hire.

Charges guide:
-- Per pitch incl. 4 persons Ffr. 45.00 - 58.00; extra adult 12.00; child 6.00; electricity 12.00; pet 10.00.
Open:
mid-June - mid-Sept.
Tel:
55.94.31.39.
Reservations:
Write to Village VAL 'L'Abeille', 19340 Eygurande or phone 73.43.00.43 (head office in Clermont-Ferrand) or site in season. Probably easiest just to turn up.

Directions: Site is signed on the eastern edge of village of Merlines which is 20 km. northeast of Ussel on the N89 road.

1905M Camping Municipal de la Riviere, Donzenac

The Corrèze is not nearly as well known as the Dordogne to the immediate south, but it is, in fact, a beautiful area, deserving of more attention. Donzenac is an attractive small town with a variety of shops, restaurants, etc. The municipal site is on the outskirts, less than a mile from the centre (an uphill walk). The site is quite small with 77 fairly large pitches on level grass, the majority with electricity and many with shade from tall trees.

Charges guide:
-- Per person Ffr. 11.00; child (under 9 yrs) 5.00; pitch 16.00; electricity 11.00; dog 3.00.
Open:
20 June - 30 September.

continued overleaf

1905M Camping Municipal de la Riviere continued

Next door to the tennis courts and swimming pool, it also has a children's play area, table tennis and a small takeaway. Other facilities are all close by in the town and a baker calls daily at the site. The sanitary facilities have all been recently modernised and are good. Laundry room.

Directions: Site is 9 km. north of Brive on the D920 before Donzenac (high on a hill). Alternatively it is signed from the dual-carriageway N20.

Address:
19270 Donzenac.
Tel:
55.85.63.95.
Reservations:
Probably unnecessary, but if in doubt 'phone.

CORSICA

Corsica is deservedly known as the Isle of Beauty - about half of its 220,000 inhabitants live in the towns of Ajaccio and Bastia, leaving much of the 8.68 sq.km. island (the fourth largest in the Mediterranean) very thinly populated. Although much of the island is covered with vegetation, pine trees, oaks, chestnut and the famous 'maquis', the variety of scenery is spectacular with mountains rising to 2,706 m and a coastline of 965 km. both dramatic and serenely beautiful. The highest mountains lie to the west, the gentler ranges, weathered in strange and often bizarre shapes, lie to the south and a continuous barrier forms the island's backbone. Beaches curve around scenic bays of white sand and the clear blue waters of the Mediterranean contrast with the stone pines that line the beaches and the multi coloured flowers that flourish on the sandy terrain. The entire island is ablaze with exotic flowers, aided by Corsica's excellent sunshine record. The summer months are hot and dry, July and August being the most popular, making the idea of an early or late holiday appealing.

Roads in Corsica vary from being broad and well surfaced to being narrow and treacherous, particularly in the mountains, so care should be exercised. Travel to and from Corsica by ferry is not difficult and SNCM operate a choice of routes from mainland France. On our recent visit we travelled from Nice to Bastia on a comfortable overnight sailing. The fare structure is quite complicated but a study of the ferry guide is worthwhile and can mean picking up a special offer if prepared to travel on given dates and specified sailings. There are also several services to Corsica from mainland Italy and Sardinia. Part of any stay on Corsica should include the 11 km. ferry trip from Bonifacio to Santa Teresa in Sardinia. Many make this short crossing to appreciate the incredible sight of Bonifacio from the sea, one of the most surprising and spectacular ports in Europe to sail into. For ferry information between France and Corsica contact:

SNCM Southern Ferries, 179 Piccadilly, London WIV 9DB. Tel. 0171 4914968.

2000 Camping Caravaning U Farniente, Pertamina Village, Bonifacio

Well designed, attractive site only 4 km. from Bonifacio.

Irrespective of whether or not you are using the ferry to Sardinia, Bonifacio deserves a visit and it would be difficult to find a more attractive or convenient site than this one at which to pitch for a night stop or longer stay. The 130 pitches, many with electricity, are partially terraced and are hedged with trees and bushes, providing reasonable shade. Fairly flat, they vary in size, many being well over 100 sq.m. A central feature is the large attractive swimming pool, surrounded by terraces and a bar, with a good restaurant serving set meals and an a la carte selection at reasonable prices (shorter opening hours in May, June and Oct). Pizzeria and takeaway and self-service shop. Sanitary facilities are in two blocks with free hot showers (cabins without dividers), washbasins in semi-private cubicles, British and Turkish style WCs, dishwashing, washing machines and ironing facilities. Children's play area. Tennis. Table tennis. TV room. Mobile homes and chalets for hire. Used by a tour operator.

Directions: Site is on the RN198, 4 km. north of Bonifacio on the right. Watch for the sign - you come on it quite suddenly.

Charges 1995:
-- Per caravan or tent incl. 2 persons Ffr. 70.00; motorcaravan 80.00; extra person 23.00; child (under 7) 13.00; electricity 16.00.
Open:
All year.
Address:
Pertamina Village, 20169 Bonifacio (Corse).
Tel:
95.73.05.47.
FAX: 80.59.12.58.
Reservations:
Contact site.

N2005 Camping Naturiste Club La Chiappa, Porto-Vecchio

Extensive site set in a naturist reserve with 3 km. of private beach.

This holiday paradise stands in a magnificent setting on the Chiappa Peninsular, which juts out into the bluest of seas. There are 220 pitches for caravans and tents, plus 250 bungalows to hire. Even when full, there should be lots of space and something to suit all tastes - in fact, here you can be as private and relaxed or as convivial as you wish. There are three beaches of golden sand where you are sure to find a quiet spot and where it is safe to swim, or alternatively enjoy the swimming pool. There are extensive grounds and gardens and, for the sports enthusiasts, riding, mountain biking, tennis, diving, water skiing, keep fit and much more (some at extra cost). For children: a mini-club, play area and indoor/ outdoor theatre with a daily programme of events. The pitches are large, part shaded and level, and some have 6A electrical connections. There are more than enough sanitary blocks and open plan facilities, which include showers, British style WCs, washbasins, etc. which are clean and modern. Plenty of dishwashing sinks, washing machines and chemical disposal points. If you don't want to cook, there are restaurant meals, snacks and three bars and a baby sitting service is available. Well stocked shop. No dogs accepted.

Directions: South from Bastia on N198, continue through Porto-Vecchio for 2 km. Left on unclassified road signed `Pnte de la Chiappa' and follow camp signs.

Charges 1995:
Per pitch, car/caravan or motorcaravan Ffr. 40.00 - 70.00; pitch, car and tent 35.00 - 60.00; adult 10.00 - 50.00; child (4-16 yrs) 18.00 - 25.00.
Open:
29 April - 20 October.
Address:
20137 Porto-Vecchio.
Tel:
95.70.00.31.
FAX: 95.70.07.70.
Reservations:
Contact site.

2006 Camping-Caravaning La Vetta, Trinité de Porto-Vecchio

Family run site in country park setting, yet only minutes from the sea.

In a pleasing position to the north of La Trinité village and only 3 km. from Porto-hio and a sandy beach, this 6 ha. campsite enjoys a tranquil setting. A part sloping, part terraced site, which seems to stretch endlessly, it is well maintained and has an abundance of tree varieties including cork oaks. It gives the impression of being off the beaten track, yet many of the delights of Corsica are only a short drive away. If you want to do no more than relax there is much on offer: a swimming pool for hot days, plenty of trees for shade and a patio area for cool drinks. For the young there is table tennis, snooker table, a play area and children's entertainment in high season. The site has 100 pitches, most with 16A electrical connections. The clean, modern sanitary facilities are more than adequate and include hot showers, open plan washbasins plus cabins with mirrors and shaver points, British WCs, chemical disposal, dishwashing and laundry sinks and also a washing machine. The entrance to the site is directly off the main road with security gates closed 11 pm-7 am.

Directions: Site is on left off the RN198, north of La Trinité village.

Charges 1995:
-- Per adult Ffr. 30.00 - 32.00; child (under 7 yrs) 15.00 - 16.00; pitch 10.00, with electricity 24.00; car 10.00; motorcaravan 20.00; local tax 1.00.
Open:
1 June - 30 September.
Address:
Trinité,
20137 Porto-Vecchio.
Tel:
95.70.09.86.
FAX: 95.70.43.21.
Reservations:
Made with 30% deposit.

2007 Camping Santa Lucia, Sainte-Lucie-de-Porto-Vecchio

Friendly, family run site in a delightful southern Corsican setting.

This well appointed campsite is set in a cork oak forest just off the main road. The entrance is enhanced by a huge palm tree which characterises the approach to reception. At this point you also find the restaurant and bar which overlook the swimming pool - particularly pleasant in the evening when ornamental lamps light up the patio area. There are 160 pitches, 46 with 6A electricity. Pitches are numbered and some are in little enclosed bays which offer privacy. Two sanitary blocks, one to the right of the site, the other on the far left towards the rear, house British WCs, washbasins (some cubicles), dishwashing and laundry sinks (no washing machines) also a chemical disposal point. Apart from the restaurant, bar and takeaway, there is a small shop selling bread, milk, etc. A supermarket is opposite the site entrance. Other on site activities include table tennis, volleyball, minigolf and a children's play area. Six timber bungalows to rent blend unobtrusively with the setting. You are only minutes by car from Porto Vecchio which is surrounded by lovely beaches.

Directions: Site is at the south end of Sainte-Lucie-de-Porto-Vecchio village, off the N198, well signed.

Charges 1995:
-- Per adult Ffr. 24.00 - 32.00; child 12.00 - 16.00; pitch 12.00 - 17.00; car 8.00 - 12.00; motorcaravan 20.00 - 29.00; electricity 16.00.
Open:
15 April - 15 October.
Address:
RN 198 Mulindinu,
20144 Ste-Lucie-de-Porto-Vecchio.
Tel:
95.71.45.28.
FAX: as phone.
Reservations:
Contact site.

2008 Camping-Caravaning Bon'Anno, Favone

Friendly site opposite a magnificent stretch of coastline.

This site makes an excellent base for touring the southeastern side of the island with Porto-Vecchio within 35 km. and Bonifacio 62 km. Emphasis here has to be on the reception where you are sure of a warm greeting, albeit we called just as the season was getting under way and the staff were not being stretched. It is a typical 'in the trees' site which offers plenty of shade, often welcome when temperatures soar. There are 150 pitches, 64 with 4A electricity, and two sanitary blocks. These have British WCs, washbasins with mirrors, electric points, showers with hooks, etc. Dishwashing and laundry sinks are outside but under cover, plus a washing machine. Around the reception is a small shop, bar and takeaway service. An attractive patio area is garlanded with climbing flowers and shrubs around a trellis. Children can enjoy a play area in the cool of the trees or the delightful sweep of Favone sandy beach (200 m).

Directions: Site is 200 m. off the N198 road, clearly signed at the south end of Favone village.

Charges 1995:
-- Per person Ffr. 29.00; child (under 7 yrs) 14.50; car 9.00; caravan 15.00; electricity (4A) 16.00; local tax 1.00.
Open:
1 June - 30 September.
Address:
20144 Favone.
Tel:
95.73.21.35.
Reservations:
Necessary for July/Aug.

2001 Camping Arinella Blanca, Ghisonaccia

Very well designed, family run, beach side site on Corsica's east coast.

This site is a tribute to its owners design and development skills as it appears to be in entirely natural 'glades' where, in fact, these have been created from former marshland with a fresh water lake. The 300 marked pitches, all with 6A electricity, are on flat grass among a variety of trees and shrubs, providing ample shade. They are irregularly arranged, but are all of a good size. The site is right beside a beach of soft sand which extends a long way either side of the attractive central complex of restaurant, shop, bar, amphitheatre, snack bar, etc. (all from 10/5) which, together with the addition of a swimming pool in 1995, form the hub of this site. There are four open plan sanitary blocks with free pre-set hot showers in larger than average cubicles (some with dressing area), washbasins in private cabins and mainly British seatless WCs. Open air washing up areas and a laundry with washing machines and ironing boards. There is a large range of sports and leisure facilities at or adjacent to the site, including windsurfing, canoeing, volleyball, bicycle hire, tennis, riding, children's mini-club and play area and a disco, plus an entertainment programme in the main season. Used by tour operators (20%).

Directions: From N198 after entering Ghisonaccia look out for 'Route de la Mer' (D144) and site is on left approaching south end of village.

Charges 1996:
-- Per person Ffr. 42.00; child (up to 7 yrs) 21.00; pitch 18.00; car 9.00; electricity (6A) 17.00; local tax 2.00 (child 1.00).
-- Credit cards accepted.
Open:
Easter - 30 September.
Address:
20240 Ghisonaccia.
Tel:
95.56.04.78 or 95.56.12.54.
Reservations:
Write to site.

N2004   Camping Naturiste de Riva Bella, Aleria

Relaxed, informal naturist site beside glorious beach.

Arguably this is camping and caravanning at its very best. Although offering a large number and variety of pitches, they are situated in such a huge area of varied and beautiful countryside and seaside that it is difficult to believe it could ever become overcrowded. The site is divided into several distinct areas - pitches and bungalows, alongside the sandy beach, in a wooded glade with ample shade, behind the beach, or beside the lake/lagoon which is a feature of this site. The ground is undulating, so getting an absolutely level pitch could be a problem in the main season. Although electric hook-ups are available in most parts, a long cable is probably a necessity. The sanitary facilities, which are being extended, are in several blocks and are fairly typical of naturist sites, with British WCs, hot water to open plan washbasins and free hot showers in open plan cubicles. The temperature of the showers is said to be controllable (once you have learned the knack). Besides the beautiful beach, (with sailing school, fishing, sub-aqua and other watersports) there is a wide variety of activities available including volleyball, aerobics, table tennis, archery, half-court tennis, etc. You can even spend your time observing the llamas. An excellent restaurant with reasonable prices overlooks the lagoon, as well as a snack bar beside the beach during the main season. Large well stocked shop. There is an interesting evening entertainment programme. Noël Pasqual is fully proud of his site and the fairly unobtrusive rules are designed to ensure that everyone is able to relax, whilst preserving the natural beauty of the environment. There is, for example, a restriction on the movement of cars in certain areas, although there is ample free parking. The police/fire service ban barbecues during the summer as a safety precaution, but generally the ambience is relaxed and informal with nudity only obligatory on the beach itself.

Directions: Site is approx. 8 km. north of Aleria on the N198 (Bastia) road. Watch for signs and unmade road to it and follow for 4 km.

Charges 1995:
-- Per unit Ffr. 59.00 - 96.00, acc. to season; extra person 23.00 - 33.00; child (0-7 yrs) 13.00 - 19.00; extra tent 23.00 - 30.00; electricity 18.00; local tax 1.00

Open:
10 May - 15 October.

Address:
20270 Aleria.

Tel:
95.38.81.10 or 95.38.85.97.
FAX: 95.38.91.29.

Reservations:
Made with deposit (Ffr. 500) and fee/cancellation insurance (160).

2003   Camping Merendella,   Moriani, nr San Nicolao

Attractive smaller site with direct access to beach.

This is a smaller, family run site with the advantage of direct access to a pleasant beach. It is peacefully situated on level grass with many trees and shrubs providing shade and colour. There are 140 pitches of a min. 100 sq.m. with electricity available on practically all, albeit with the necessity for longish cables. The sanitary facilities are in one main block, apart from a couple of individual cabin units near the beach with 2 showers, 2 washbasins and toilet. Facilities are modern and include free hot showers and washbasins in private cubicles. Some British WCs plus further Turkish style ones. There are also washing up and laundry areas including 2 washing machines. The site is about 800 m. from the village but also has its own well stocked shop. Chalets to hire. Amenities nearby include tennis, riding and various watersports. Snack bar. TV and games room. No dogs or cats are accepted.

Directions: Site is to seaward side of the RN198, immediately (800 m.) south of Moriani Plage.

Charges 1995:
-- Per person Ffr. 29.50 - 35.00; child (2-12 yrs) 19.00 - 21.00; pitch 10.00 - 10.50; vehicle 12.00 - 13.50; m/cycle 9.50 - 11.00; motor-caravan 22.00 - 26.00; caravan 12.50 - 14.00; tent 9.00 - 10.50; electricity 15.00 (2A), 17.00 (5A); local tax (1/7-15/9) 1.00.

Open:
1 May - 15 October.

Address:
20230 Moriani-Plage.

Tel:
95.38.53.47.
FAX: 95.38.44.01.

Reservations:
Advisable; write to site.

20 Corsica

2009 Aire Naturelle de Camping, Venaco
Idyllic small campsite in the mountains.

Just as spectacular as the coastline is Corsica's mountainous interior and by getting off the N200 this exceptional little campsite can be discovered. In a clearing among the trees are 25 pitches, many with a 20A electrical connection. Whilst the view, peace and tranquillity are cause enough to be here, the enthusiastic young couple, Mathieu and Angele who run the site have already made it noteworthy. They offer visitors a restaurant service with cuisine of Corsica, prepared from their own farm produce - Mathieu works on the farm, as well as being the chef. The small restaurant is a delight with neatly laid tables, an old stone fireplace, wall hangings and bric a brac all creating a special atmosphere. The local cheeses and wines are superb, but don't expect chips. Farm produce and bread each day are available in the shop. The single sanitary block is clean and provides washbasins with mirrors, hot showers and British style WCs. Around the site are picnic tables, water points, night lighting and a central rubbish point. You are not totally isolated at this site - Venaco (with doctor, chemist, boulangerie, etc) is only 4 km. away.

Directions: From Corte centre take N200 in the direction of Aleria. After 15 km. turn east on the D143 and site is on left after 4 km.

Charges 1995:
-- Per adult Ffr. 22.00; child (3-7 yrs) 11.00; tent 15.00; car 10.00; caravan 17.00; motorcaravan 25.00.
Open: April - 30 October.
Address: La Ferme de Peridundellu, 20231 Venaco.
Tel: 95.47.09.89.
Reservations: Write to site but probably not necessary.

2010 Camping-Caravaning Santa Barbara, Corte
Developing campsite in Corsica's mountainous interior.

Corte, the historical capital of the island, stands at 396 m. altitude in the central mountains where you get a feel of the real Corsica. Camping Santa Barbara is 3 km. east of the town. Already established as a restaurant/bar, the campsite is being developed, with 25 level pitches at present but plans for 50 when the work is completed. They are separated by young shrubs and there are 12 electrical connections (12A) (will be 18). The sanitary facilities are also being extended, adding to the already modern and spotlessly clean units with showers, British WCs, facilities for the disabled, dishwashing and laundry sinks, with a washing machine to be installed at a later date. An excellent swimming pool is an established focal point and very welcome in this hot, mountainous region. The patio area, which overlooks the pool, is popular. The restaurant offers a varied menu and a pizza style hut is outside near the pool. A reception and mini-market are being added alongside the attractive, well kept restaurant building. Children's play area, table tennis and pool table. The owners are friendly and helpful.

Directions: Site is 3 km. southeast of Corte by the N200 Aléria road.

Charges 1995:
-- Per adult Ffr. 29.00; child (under 7) 17.00; tent 16.00; caravan 24.00; car 16.00; motorcaravan 36.00; local tax 1.00; electricity 24.00.
Open: April - 31 October.
Address: RN200 Rte. d'Aléria, Aérodrome de Corte, 20250 Corte.
Tel: 95.46.20.22. FAX: 95.61.09.44.
Reservations: Write to site.

2011 Camping-Caravaning Village de l'Ostriconi, Palasca, nr Belgodère
Scenically located campsite with access to the beach.

Where the scenic stretch of the N1197 winds around the magnificent bay of Perajolo on Corsica's northwest coast, this site is clearly signed and visible from the road. The 134 pitches are on rough, dry ground among the trees which offer shade. We were told that 30 have 2A electricity connections, but many pitches would require long cables. There are two sanitary blocks, one of an unusual rectangular design with WCs and showers to the outside and an open area for washbasins, etc. and, in the middle forecourt, flower beds and shrubs. Wooden shelving and doors have a weathered look giving a run down appearance, but apparently the facilities are cleaned three times daily in season. The smaller block is heated by solar panels, the other by electricity. The restaurant/bar area to the right of reception is more modern and attractive and is also where the swimming pool is located. Takeaway, shop selling basic foodstuffs, bread, etc. The restaurant menu is varied and entertainment is organised two evenings a week in July/Aug. Access to the beach from the site makes this an attractive base, plus the fact that Ile Rousse is only minutes away by car, its harbour on an island and its old streets leading to a square surrounded by plane trees.

Directions: From L'Ille Rousse take N197 road east for 8 km. to join the N1197. Proceed for 4 km. and site is on the seaward side.

Charges 1995:
-- Per person Ffr. 28.00; child (2-7 yrs) 14.00; pitch with tent or caravan 11.00; car 11.00; m/bike 9.00; motorcaravan 22.00; electricity (2A) 18.00.
Open: 1 May - 31 October.
Address: Palasca, 20226 Belgodère.
Tel: 95.60.10.05. FAX: 95.60.01.47.
Reservations: Write to site.

2012 Camping-Caravaning Le Panoramic, Lumio

Simple, family run site in a quiet, elevated position.

On the scenic route that winds inland and upwards from the coast between Calvi and Ile Rousse, Le Panoramic, as its name suggests, enjoys magnificent views across the Golfe d'Ambroggio. The 150 pitches are laid out in named avenues (e.g. Rue Josephine) and the marked places are shaded by many trees and vegetation, with quite a number having 15A electricity connections. Whilst the ground is level, the site is terraced and hard going if climbing from the bottom towards reception. There are four sanitary blocks and, although the site was not officially open when we visited, the facilities were of a good quality and very clean. They include British WCs, hot showers, washbasins, plus sinks for dishwashing (no washing machines, launderette 4 km). Chemical disposal can be arranged through reception. Good sized shop, takeaway and a bar. Caravans to hire. Amenities include a swimming pool, table football, pool table and a children's play area. A recommended scenic drive is the 5 km. climb to St Antonino, a mountain village piled upon a rock face.

Directions: From Calvi take the N197 towards Ile Rousse. Proceed for 10 km. to village of Lumio, then east on D71 and site is 2 km. on the left.

Charges 1995:
-- Per adult Ffr. 27.00; child (under 7 yrs) 13.50; caravan 17.00; tent 12.00; car 8.00; electricity 19.00; local tax 1.10.
Open:
15 June - 15 September.
Address:
Rte de Belgodère, Lumio, 20260 Calvi.
Tel:
95.60.73.13 (or when closed: (1) 40.95.16.01. FAX: (1) 40.95.16.01.
Reservations:
Pnone or write.

2101M Camping Municipal Louis Rigoly, Châtillon-sur-Seine

This well kept little municipal site has 60 pitches, mainly individual ones with separators between them on fairly flat grass, 48 with electricity. Mature trees provide shelter. The main toilet block, at one end of site, is satisfactory with plentiful washbasins in cubicles with free hot water and pre-set free showers; also a small central unit. New facilities for the disabled. Adjoining the site is the municipal swimming pool complex with both indoor and outdoor pools (on payment), and minigolf. No shop, but town is close. Snack bar in July/Aug. The site, which has much transit trade, can become full by evening in season.

Directions: On northeast outskirts of town; site is signed from centre.

Charges 1996:
-- Per person Ffr. 13.00; child (under 7) 8.00; car 7.00; m/cycle 5.00; pitch 10.00; electricity 2A 11.00, 4A 20.00.
Open:
1 April - 15 October.
Address:
Esplanade Saint-Vorles, 21400 Châtillon.
Tel:
80.91.03.05.
Reservations:
Not officially made, but if you write shortly before your visit, they will reserve until 7 p.m.

2102M Camping Municipal Les Cent Vignes, Beaune

A well kept, 2 hectares site, this has 116 individual pitches of good size, separated from each other by neat beech hedges high enough to keep a fair amount of privacy. Rather over half of the pitches are on grass, ostensibly for tents, the remainder on hardstandings with electricity for caravans. The two sanitary blocks, one of which can be heated, are well constructed modern ones which should be large enough. Mainly continental toilets; washbasins now nearly all in private cabins with shelf and light. Free hot water for these, and for the pre-set showers and the sinks. Shop, restaurant with takeaway (all 1/4-30/9). Children's playground, sports area with tennis, boules and table tennis. Washing machines. A popular site, within walking distance of the town centre, Les Cent Vignes becomes full mid-June to early Sept. but with many short-stay campers there are departures each day and reservations can be made. Beaune is of course in the Burgundy wine producing area, and several 'caves' in the town can be visited.

Directions: From the autoroute exit follow signs for Beaune centre then pick up Dijon road and camp signs.

Charges 1995:
-- Per person Ffr. 15.00; child (2-7 yrs) 7.50; local tax 2.00; pitch 22.00; electricity (6A) 19.00.
Open:
15 March - 30 October
Address:
10 Rue Auguste Dubois, 21200 Beaune.
Tel:
80.22.03.91.
Reservations:
Made before 30 May without deposit.

2103M Camping Municipal, Savigny-les-Beaune, nr Beaune

This popular site is ideally located for visiting the Burgundy vineyards, for use as a transit site or spending time in the town of Beaune. It offers an alternative to our already popular site (no. 2102). During the high season it is full every evening, so it is best to arrive by 4 pm. The 91 level pitches are now marked and numbered, with electric hook-ups and room for an awning. If reception is closed when you arrive, you find a pitch and report later, otherwise `Madame' will allocate a place. Sanitary facilities, which are kept very clean and have been renovated and extended, are housed in a modern building behind reception. Hot water is free. Additional WCs are placed towards the middle of the site. The bureau staff are pleasant and, if required, a bottle of local wine, soft drinks and ice can be purchased. Whilst the famed wine region alone attracts many visitors, Beaune, its capital, is unrivalled in its richness of art from times gone by. Narrow streets and squares are garlanded with flowers, pavement cafés are crammed with tourists and overlooking the scene is the glistening Hotel Dieu.

Directions: From Beaune follow directions for Dijon (N74). Take the first left at traffic lights approaching a church, then first right signed Savigny-les-Beaune. Site is on the left through the village.

Charges 1995:
-- Per person Ffr. 8.75; child (under 7 yrs) 4.30; car 4.30; pitch 5.65; electricity 12.90.
Open:
1 May - 30 September.
Address:
21420
Savigny-les-Beaune.
Tel:
80.21.52.35 or
80.21.51.21.
Reservations:
Not accepted.

2104M Camping Municipal de Fouché, Arnay le Duc

Useful as an overnight stop en-route to or from the Med. or indeed for longer stays, this quite large but peaceful, lakeside site has good facilities and the added advantage of being open all year. Of the 190 good sized pitches, on fairly level grass and mostly with electricity, about a dozen are taken by a British tour operator, which gives some indication of the range of facilities and the growing popularity of this part of Burgundy. Arnay le Duc itself is an attractive little town with an interesting history and is renowned for its gastronomy, with many hotels and restaurants. The site itself is within walking distance of the town centre, where there also an indoor swimming pool, tennis courts, etc. The pitches, many of which are hedged, offer a choice of shade or more open aspect. The five sanitary blocks, although fairly elderly, have modern fittings and include free hot showers, some British WCs, washbasins in cabins, a washing machine and under cover dishwashing facilities.

Directions: Site is on the east side of town - well signed.

Charges 1995:
-- Per person Ffr. 9.40; vehicle 4.80; pitch 6.60; electricity 10.10.
Open:
All year.
Address:
21230 Arnay-le-Duc.
Tel:
80.90.02.23.
Reservations:
Contact site.

2200 Camping des Vallées, Saint Brieuc

Neat attractive site, set in a wooded valley.

Previously run by the municipality, this site is now privately managed. It has 108 good size pitches, 70 with electrical connections. set mainly on flat terraced grass and separated by shrubs and bushes. There are 14 pitches with hardstanding and electricity, water and sewage connections. Mature trees are plentiful, providing shade if required, and a small stream winds through the middle of the site. Two main sanitary blocks provide pre-set showers, some washbasins in private cabins and British WCs. Facilities are provided for the disabled and there is also a baby room and laundry with machines and dryer. A further smaller block is situated at the bottom of the site. A lane leads from the site to a large, outdoor public swimming pool (50 x 20 m.) with a children's pool and water slide, minigolf, football pitch, tennis courts, all free of charge to campers except tennis. These facilities are open 25/6-1/9. A compact bar is on site and a shop with basic provisions, with a small restaurant planned. Animation is organised in peak season, also weekly pony days arranged for the children. Children's play area and arcade games. Caravans (3), mobile homes (2) and chalets (2) for hire. A key system operates for the access gate (closed 2230-0700 hrs). The site is only 800 m. from Saint Brieuc, but still manages to create a quiet, peaceful atmosphere. No tour operators.

Directions: From the east, on entering St Brieuc, look for the sign to the railway station and from there, signs for site.

Charges 1995:
-- Per pitch incl. car and 1 adult Ffr. 43.00; extra adult 16.00; child (under 7 yrs) 10.00; extra car 10.00; animal 7.00; water and drainage 33.00; electricity (10A) 16.00.
-- Credit cards accepted in July/Aug.
Open:
Easter - 15 October.
Address:
Chemin des Vallées, 22000 Saint Brieuc.
Tel:
96.94.05.05.
Reservations:
Made with deposit (Ffr. 200) and fee (70).

2201 Camping Les Capucines, St. Michel-en-Grève, nr Lannion

Family run site, 1 km. from the beach and in good central location for touring Brittany.

Quietly situated 1 km. from the village of St. Michel with its good, sandy beach, this attractive site has 100 pitches on flat or slightly sloping ground. All are well marked out by hedges and many mature trees and 70 have electricity, water and drainaway. The two modern toilet blocks give a good supply, with British WCs, washbasins with free hot water mainly in private cabins set in flat surfaces, controllable free hot showers and facilities for babies and the disabled. There is a swimming pool (14 x 6 m.) with a small children's pool, solar heated and open from June. Small shop for essentials, fresh bread to order. Takeaway. Bar. Washing machine. Tennis. Minigolf. Bicycle hire. Children's playground. General room with table tennis amd table football.

Directions: Turn off main D786 road northeast of St. Michel where signed and 1 km. to site.

**Alan Rogers'
discount**
Less further
10% in low season

Charges 1996:
-- Per person Ffr. 25.00; child (under 7) 15.00; tent 40.00, caravan 55.00; electricity 10.00 - 18.00 acc. to amps.
-- Less in low season.
-- Credit cards accepted.
Open:
15 May - 8 September.
Address:
St. Michel-en-Grève, 22300 Lannion.
Tel:
96.35.72.28.
Reservations:
Any length with deposit (Ffr. 200) and fee (30).

2203 Camping Nautic International, Caurel, Mur-de-Bretagne, nr Pontivy

Small, friendly, lakeside site in central Brittany with facilities for watersports.

Nautic is attractively situated on the north shore of the long, sinuous Lac de Guerledan, which is used for all sorts of watersports. There are pleasant walks around the shores and through Breton countryside and forests. The site is terraced down to the shore of the lake and provides 120 quite large pitches - all with electricity, 5 with hardstanding - in beautiful peaceful surroundings. A range of boating activities is possible on the lake (small boats may be launched) and there is a floating pontoon available (charged for daily). In addition, an imaginatively designed swimming pool (25 x 6 m.) and smaller pool (6 x 6 m), heated by a wood burning stove (from June). The toilet facilities in two blocks have been modernised and provide mostly British toilets, hot showers, some individual wash cabins, one toilet for the disabled and facilities for babies with a playpen. Shop and takeaway (July/Aug), TV and video room. Sauna, solarium and fitness room. Children's play area. Games room. Fishing. Tennis. Table tennis. Volleyball. Watersports and riding near. Motorcaravan service point.

Directions: Turn off the N164 between Mur-de-Bretagne and Gouarec to village of Caurel. Follow camp signs from there.

Charges 1995:
-- Per person Ffr. 24.00; child (under 7) 16.00; local tax (July/Aug, over 10 yrs) 1.00; pitch 34.00; car 10.00; electricity (6A) 16.00.
Open:
1 April - 25 September.
Address:
Route de Beau-Rivage, 22530 Caurel.
Tel:
96.28.57.94.
FAX: 96.28.02.00.
Reservations:
Write to site.

2204 Camping Le Chatelet, St. Cast-le-Guildo, nr St. Malo

Pleasant site with views over the bay and steep path down to beach.

Le Chatelet is pleasantly and quietly situated with views over the estuary from many pitches. It is well laid out, mainly in terraces with 190 individual pitches of good size marked out by hedge separators; all have electric points and 30 water and drainage also. The two toilet blocks, one above the other but with access at different levels, have British WCs, plentiful washbasins in private cabins and preset free hot showers. There are also small units for night use at extremities of the site. A little lake with some pitches around it can be used for fishing. Heated swimming pool, with children's pool (12/5-15/9). Small children's play area (above the lake and unsupervised). Shop. Bar lounge and general room with satellite TV, pool table; dancing weekly in June, July and Aug. Hot food service to take away or eat on spot (12/5-5/9). Games room with table tennis, amusement machines. Organized games and activities for all the family in season. A path leads down direct to a beach from camp, about 150 m. but including steps. St. Cast, 1 km. away to the centre, has a very long beach with many opportunities for sailboarding and other watersports. A high percentage of British tour operator pitches (45%). Mobile homes for hire.

Directions: Turn off D786 road at Matignon towards St. Cast; just inside St. Cast limits turn left at sign for `campings' and follow camp signs on C90.

Charges 1996:
-- Per person Ffr 21.00 - 27.00; child (under 7) 13.00 - 17.00; pitch 63.00 - 82.00; electricity 6A 18.00, 10A 20.00; local tax 2.00.
Open:
6 April - 15 September.
Address:
Rue des Nouettes 22380 St. Cast le Guildo.
Tel:
96.41.96.33.
FAX: 96.41.97.99.
Reservations:
For July/Aug - made (min. 1 week) with deposit (Ffr. 200) and booking fee (120).

2205 Camping Le Vieux Moulin, Erquy, nr St Brieuc

Family run site with individual pitches and reasonable prices, 1 km. from sea.

About 1 km. from a beach of sand and shingle, this site is probably the best along this stretch of coast. It has recently been extended to provide a total of 250 pitches, about 150 of which have electricity. They are of good size, in square boxes, with trees giving shade in many places and the newer pitches arranged around a pond. There are two sanitary blocks of good quality with mostly British toilets and plenty of individual basins (with preset warm water and some in private cabins) and free hot pre-set showers. Facilities are provided for the disabled and for babies. A further small block provides toilets and dishwashing only. A smart crêperie with takeaway food completes the new developments. Solar heated swimming pool and childs' pool. Tennis. Shop. Bar lounge (discos in high season) overlooking the pool. Small gym. 2 children's playgrounds. TV room. Games room with table tennis. Washing machines and dryer. The site becomes full, busy and possibly noisy late at night in July and August. Used by tour operators (20%).

Directions: Site is 2 km. east of Erquy. Take minor road towards Les Hôpitaux and site is signed from the junction of D786 and D34.

Charges 1996:
-- Per person Ffr. 26.00; child (under 7) 18.00; car 17.00; motorcaravan 17.00; pitch 45.00; electricity 18.00.
Open:
1 April - 15 September.
Address:
22430 Erquy.
Tel:
96.72.34.23 (winter: 96.72.12.50).
Reservations:
Made for min. 1 week.

2206M Camping Municipal La Hallerais, Taden, nr Dinan

As well as being an attractive old town itself, Dinan is quite a short run from the resorts of the Côte d'Emeraude. A well regulated, municipal site in attractive part of northern Brittany, the Hallerais site is just outside Dinan, beyond the little harbour on the Rance estuary. There is a pleasant riverside walk where the site slopes down towards the Rance. The 200 pitches, all but 20 with electricity, water and drainaway, are mainly on shallow terraces, with trees and hedges giving a park-like atmosphere. The three toilet blocks are of very good quality, and are well heated in cool seasons. British toilets. Individual basins in washrooms and in private cabins with shower, shelf, mirror and light. Free hot water everywhere. Self-service shop (July/Aug). Café/bar with takeaway service. Small swimming pool with separate children's pool (16/6-15/9). Tennis courts. Minigolf. Fishing. Games/TV rooms. Children's playground. Laundry room. Mobile homes (8) to let.

Directions: Taden is northeast of Dinan; on leaving Dinan on D766, turn right to Taden and camp before reaching big bridge and N176 junction. From N176 take Taden/Dinan exit.

Charges guide:
-- Per unit incl. 1 person and all services Ffr. 70.00 - 90.00; extra adult 20.00; child (under 7) 10.00.
-- Less in low seasons or for longer stays.
Open:
15 March - 31 October.
Address:
Taden, 22100 Dinan.
Tel:
96.39.15.93.
FAX: 96.39.86.77.
Reservations:
Made for min. 1 week with deposit of Ffr 100.

2207 Castel Camping Manoir de Cleuziou, Louargat, nr Guingamp

Quiet site, rurally situated in grounds of Breton manor house.

Located 20 km. from the north Brittany coast, this site is in the grounds of the attractive, rather imposing, 16th/18th century Manoir de Cleuziou which is now used as an hotel and restaurant. The site offers a solar heated pool and children's pool (open 15/5-30/9) with a terrace beside the house and a small bar, but will probably suit those who like a quieter site. There are 200 large, secluded and well tended pitches, all with electricity and water, separated by tall hedges, shrubs and roses, on two flat, grassy fields. Sanitary facilities consist of two blocks (one in each field) with good, free hot showers and washbasins in cabins (unisex), plus several small, neat toilet blocks within easy reach of all pitches and one unit for the disabled. There are further facilities at the pool, together with washing machines and dryers. Small shop in high season only (bread and milk to order at other times) and takeaway food to order. Campers may use the hotel restaurant (prices start at Ffr. 90). Tennis. Children's play area and club in July/Aug. Mobile home, caravans and tents to rent. One British tour operator.

Directions: From N12-E50 take exit for Louargat. Site is signposted in town centre on Route de Tegrom. After 1 km. turn right, then 2 km. to site following brown signs to 'Cleuziou'.

Charges 1995:
-- Per unit incl. 2 persons Ffr 80.00 - 90.00; extra person 28.00; child 14.00; pitch with electricity, water and drainage 25.00; extra car 12.00; dog 6.00.
Open:
15 March - end Nov.
Address:
22540 Louargat.
Tel:
96.43.14.90.
FAX: 96.43.52.59.
Reservations:
Made with deposit (30%).

22 Côtes d'Armor

2209 Camping Château de Galinée, St Cast le Guildo

Well kept family run site 8 km. from St Cast.

This site is in a parkland setting on level grass with numerous and varied mature trees. It has 272 pitches, all with electricity (6A), water and drainage and separated by many newly planted shrubs and bushes. The top section is mostly for mobile homes which are for hire. The main tiled, modern sanitary block has free hot water to the pre-set showers and the washbasins in private cabins, British WCs and a good unit for the disabled. A smaller separate block has toilets only. Dishwashing is under cover and there is a laundry room. Attractive, heated swimming and paddling pools (from 1/6) with a sun terrace, are located near the bar. There is an excellent takeaway menu and a shop (both from 15/6). Further facilities include 3 tennis courts, bicycle hire, children's play area and field for ball games. Entertainment is organised during peak season featuring traditional Breton music at times and weekly discos. Gate locked 22.00-07.00 hrs. Mobile homes and tents to hire.

Directions: From D168 Ploubalay-Plancoet road turn onto D786 towards Matignon and St. Cast. Site is very well signed on left 5 km. before Matignon.

Alan Rogers' discount Less 5% outside July/Aug

Charges 1996:
-- Per pitch incl. water and drainage Ffr 38.00 - 55.00; adult 20.00 - 24.00; child (under 7) 8.00 - 12.00; extra car 5.00 - 10-00; dog 6.00 - 10.00; electricity (6A) 15.00.
-- Credit cards accepted.
Open:
1 May -30 September.
Address:
22380 St Cast le Guildo.
Tel:
96.41.10.56.
FAX: 96.41.03.72.
Reservations:
Made with deposit Ffr 200 and fee 100 (min. 1 week July/Aug).

2208 Castel Camping Le Ranolien, Ploumenac'h, nr Perros Guirec

Good quality site in outstanding location on the `Côtes de Granit Rose'.

Le Ranolien has been attractively developed around a former Breton farm - everything here is either made from, on or around the often massive pink rocks. The original buildings are sympathetically converted into site facilities and there is an imaginative swimming pool complex with terraces, and with water cascading over the boulders. The site is on the coast, with beaches and coves within walking distance and there are spectacular views from many pitches. The 550 pitches are of a variety of sizes and types, mostly large and flat - some are formally arranged in rows with hedge separators, but most are either on open ground or under trees, amongst large boulders. With a wide variety of static holiday caravans and tour operator tents spread around the site, there are 242 pitches for tourists, most with electricity and there are some special pitches for motorhomes with water and drainage also.

The main toilet block, heated in cool weather, is supplemented by several other more open blocks around the site. The facilities include washbasins in cabins, mostly British WCs and good showers; hot water everywhere is free. Dishwashing facilities are mostly in the open and laundry facilities are provided. A large, busy site, with several tour operators present, there is a range of facilities open over a fairly long season, including a restaurant, crêperie, attractive bar and a supermarket and gift shop (all 1/5-22/9). Amenities include minigolf, tennis, table tennis, a games room and a small children's play area. Plans for 1996 include a covered swimming pool (9 x 22 m). Mobile homes for hire. Reservation is necessary for high season, but outside July/Aug. one should usually find a quiet corner.

Directions: From Lannion take D788 to Perros Guirec. Follow signs to `Centre Ville' past main harbour and then signs to Ploumenac'h, La Clarté. Pass through village of La Clarté and around sharp left hand bend. Site is immediately on the right.

Charges 1996:
-- Per pitch incl. 2 persons Ffr 75.00 - 130.00; extra person 35.00 - 45.00; child (under 7 yrs) 20.00; pitch with electricity, plus 20.00, with electricity and water 35.00, with drainage also 45.00; extra car 15.00; dog 10.00; local tax (over 18 yrs) 1.00.
-- Cedit cards accepted.
Open:
1 February - 15 November.
Address:
Ploumenac'h, 22700 Perros Guirec.
Tel:
96.91.43.58.
FAX: 96.91.41.90.
Reservations:
Made with deposit (Ffr 400) and fee (100).

2210 Camping L'Abri Cotier, Etables-sur-Mer

Small, tranquil, family run site 500 m. from sandy beach.

Owned and personally run by Britons Kate and and Peter Sutton, this site is arranged in two sections, separated by a small country lane. Pitches are marked out on level grass, divided by mature trees and shrubs. Some are in a charming ancient walled area with a quaint, old-world atmosphere. The second section has an orchard setting. The proud owners have created and nurtured a friendly atmosphere. In total there are 130 pitches, 100 with electrical connections (2/4 or 6/10A); 4 holiday caravans are available for hire. Excellent sanitary facilities in good modern blocks which are heated in low season, were all spotlessly clean when we visited. They include British WCs, free controllable hot showers, washbasins both open and in private cabins, washing up under cover, laundry room, 2 units for the disabled with shower, basin and toilet. Baby bath and shower. The site boasts a heated swimming pool with children's pool and outdoor jacuzzi. An attractive bar is adjoined by a shaded terraced area, with a children's play area close by, set under a weeping willow tree. There is a well stocked shop with fresh produce, and a takeaway service. Other facilities include a games room with billiards, darts, pinball, table tennis and animation is organised during peak season. Bicycle hire. Barbecues permitted. No tour operators. Gates locked at 11 pm.

Directions: Take the D786 off the N12 after St Brieuc; site is well signed before St Quay Portrieux.

Alan Rogers' discount
Fr.1.00 off person charge

Charges 1996:
-- Per pitch Ffr. 35.00 - 38.00; person 24.00 - 26.00; child (1-7 yrs) 14.00 - 16.00; electricity 4A 16.00, 6A 19.00; extra car, boat or small tent 10.00.
Open:
6 May - 20 September.
Address:
Ville Rouxel, 22680 Etables-sur-Mer.
Tel:
96.70.61.57.
FAX: 96.70.65.23.
Reservations:
Made with deposit (Ffr 100 for 1 week, 200 for 2); sterling cheque acceptable (£15 or £25).

2211 Camping Fleur de Bretagne, Kerandouaron, Rostrenen

Small, peaceful, family run site centrally situated for north and south Brittany ports.

Neil and Jill Eardley only opened this natural, informal 12 acre site in June 1992. It offers 100 unmarked pitches, 24 with 4 or 10A electricity, in attractive terraced fields of varying sizes, separated by hedgerows. There is a small lake alongside a wooded area at the lower end of the site. The traditional old farmhouse has been converted to house a bar (hot and cold bar snacks available) with a terrace and beer garden, takeaway and games room for pool and table tennis. Two tiled sanitary blocks have British toilets and free hot water to pre-set showers, with large dressing area, and the washbasins (some in private cabins). Hair dryers are provided and there are 2 units for the disabled with toilet, basin and shower. Small laundry and under cover washing up. An unheated open air swimming pool has a small sun terrace. Good size children's playing field with swings and volleyball net. The town is just 1½ km. away. Barbecues allowed. No noise after 10 pm.

Directions: Rostrenen is on the N164; site is south on D764 (Pontivy) road, signed on left after 1 km.

Alan Rogers' discount
Less 10% for stays over 3 days

Charges 1996:
-- Per pitch Ffr 27.00; adult 16.00; child (4-13 yrs) 9.00; car 7.00; m/cycle 4.00; electricity 15.00; local tax 1.00.
Open:
End March - end October.
Address:
Kerandouaron, 22110 Rostrenen.
Tel:
96.29.16.45.
Reservations:
Write or phone.

2220M Camping Municipal Le Bocage, Jugon les Lacs

This well kept, spacious site offers 146 good size pitches, all with electrical connections, set on gently sloping grass and divided by shrubs and bushes, with mature trees providing shade. Some wooden chalets and caravans are intermingled with the touring pitches. Two sanitary blocks are somewhat old fashioned, but adequate. British and Turkish WCs, some washbasins in private cabins and free hot showers. A smaller block in the swimming pool complex has Turkish toilets only and facilities for the disabled. On site facilities include a medium sized pool (July/Aug) with children's section and sunbathing patio, also open to the public. Small shop with basics only (small supermarket in village, 1 km). Bar, tennis court, football pitch and children's play area. Washing machine. Animation and activity programmes organised in July/Aug. Sailing school 200 m. and horse riding 2 km. Mobile homes for hire. Used by tour operators (5%).

Directions: From the N176 (E401) Lamballe-Dinan road, approx. 15 km. from Lamballe take turning for Jugon les Lacs. Site is signed shortly after.

Charges 1995:
-- Per adult 13.00; child (under 10 yrs) 7.00; pitch 16.00; electricity 13.00.
-- Low season less 10%.
-- Credit cards accepted.
Open:
1 May - 30 September.
Address:
22270 Jugon les Lacs.
Tel:
96.31.60.16 (when closed: 96.31.61.62).
Reservations:
Contact site.

2305M Camping Municipal du Plan d'Eau de Courtille, Gueret

A small site on gently sloping ground set in a valley beside a lake, about 3 km. from the centre of Gueret itself, this site offers few facilities but there is a restaurant within walking distance and it is possible to swim from the small beaches around the lake. The 70 pitches, all with electrical connections (3 or 10A), are arranged in six circular clusters around a modern purpose built sanitary block. They are all of a reasonable size, on grass, albeit slightly sloping. The sanitary facilities are very modern.

Directions: Site is well signed from the town centre and is beside the Etang de Courtille, southwest of the town.

Charges 1994:
-- Per pitch Ffr. 32.00; person (over 7 yrs) 11.00; child (2-7 yrs) 5.00; vehicle 5.00; animal 5.00; electricity 3A 9.00, 10A 17.00.
Open:
1 June - 30 September.
Address:
23000 Gueret.
Tel:
55.81.92.24 or 55.52.99.50.
Reservations:
Probably unnecessary, but details from site.

2402 Camping Les Granges, Grolejac, nr Sarlat

Well shaded site with pool close to Dordogne.

Les Granges is situated on undulating ground in woodland. Pitches are marked and numbered on level terraces which are mostly blessed with good shade from mature trees and shrubs; most have electricity. Sanitary blocks are of a high standard, with good hot showers and clean toilets. There are toilet and shower facilities for the disabled. The local doctor will call if needed. There is a moderately sized swimming pool and larger shallow pool. Canoes and bicycles can be hired and there are table tennis, volleyball, minigolf and children's play facilities. An enclosed bar/restaurant is supplemented by an attractive new terrace where dancing and other entertainment are organised in high season. Close to this is a snack bar which also provides takeaway food. There are shops and restaurants in the nearby town of Grolejac and the hypermarkets of Sarlat are not far. The site is popular with tour operators (35%), but there is a sensible balance and most `animation' is organised by the site. Les Granges could provide a good base for touring the Dordogne area and the present French owners have created an ambience that will assist in ensuring a pleasant stay.

Directions: Site is signed in the village of Grolejac on the D704 Sarlat-Gourdon road, 300 m. south of Grolejac bridge.

Charges 1995:
-- Per unit incl. 4 persons Ffr. 157.00; extra person 25.00 (child under 2 free); special pitches 25.00 extra; electricity 16.00. -- 20% less on unit rates outside 15/6-1/9.
Open:
1 May - 25 September.
Address:
Grolejac, 24250 Domme.
Tel:
53.28.11.15.
FAX: 53.28.57.13.
Reservations:
Made for exact dates with deposit and fee.

2400 Camping La Tuilière, St Remy-sur-Lidoire

Traditional French site with small pool and acres of space.

St Remy is situated in the Western Dordogne, not far from Ste Foy la Grande, and well positioned to visit the wine areas of St Emilion, Pomerol and Bergerac. It is a spacious site, with pitches laid out on a gently sloping hillside - there are flat areas on most pitches and access to electrical hook-ups (the owners will help with extension cables if needed). The reception building houses a small shop and a bar/restaurant with takeaway. Outside is a terrace which overlooks a little swimming pool. A good children's playground is close to the pool, as is a tennis court, the surface of which is in some need of repair, but it is free! The toilet block is small but adequate since the site is rarely overcrowded. A walk down the hill leads to a small lake which can be used for fishing or inflatables. Sports include minigolf, table tennis and pool. Nearby hypermarkets in St Foy, and fresh bread in the mornings from the bar. Very much a flavour of camping in France a few years ago, before typical site facilities (and prices) multiplied. Whilst not the most well appointed site in the region, there is enough here to keep families occupied, and plenty of peace and quiet.

Directions: Take D706 from Montpon-Ménestérol to St Foy-la Grande. St Remy is 8 km. south of Montpon and site is on a junction just past the village.

Charges 1995:
-- Per pitch Ffr. 24.00; person 18.00; child (under 7 yrs) 10.00; animal 5.00; electricity 10.00. -- 20% discount outside the main season
Open:
15 April - 15 September
Address:
St Remy-sur-Lidoire, 24700 Montpon-Ménestérol.
Tel:
53.82.47.29.
Reservations:
Made with Ffr. 65 deposit.

2401 Castel Camping Château Le Verdoyer, Champs Romain

Dutch owned site developed in park of restored Château le Verdoyer, 60 km. south of Limoges.

Le Verdoyer is situated in this lesser known area of the Dordogne sometimes referred to as the Périgord Vert, with its green forests and small lakes. The 30 acre estate has two lakes, one in front of the Château for fishing and one accessed by a footpath, with sandy beach and safe swimming area where canoeing and windsurfing for beginners are also possible. There are now 150 marked, level, terraced pitches (ground a little rocky). They are of good size (100-150 sq.m) and all have electricity, with a choice of wooded area or open field, where hedges have been planted and have grown well; 100 are 'confort' pitches with more planned. There is a swimming pool complex with two pools (25 x 10 m. and 10 x 7 m.) and paddling pool for children. In July and August activities are organised for children aged 5-13 years, with a free crêche for 1-5 year olds.

The modern toilet block housed in the old barn buildings is good with free hot water, showers with dividers and hooks, washbasin in cabins and British WCs. There is another equally good, well appointed block opened in 1993. Both blocks have facilities for the disabled, baby baths and hot water also for dishwashing. Serviced launderette. Fridges can be rented. Motorcaravan service point. Multi-purpose shop. Bar with TV and good value bistro for evening meals, both recently renovated, and takeaway facilities in courtyard area. All weather tennis court, volleyball and badminton facilities. Table tennis, minigolf and mountain bike hire also. Children's play areas. Small library. Barbeques. Bungalows and mobile homes to rent. The Château itself also has rooms to let and a public restaurant. Used by a Dutch tour operator (10%).

Directions: Site is 2 km. from the Limoges-Chalus-Nontron road, 20 km. south of Chalus and is well signed from the main road.

Charges 1996:
-- Per person Ffr. 31.00; child (2 -7 yrs) 21.00; pitch and car 46.00; second car on pitch 21.00 (free in car park); electricity (5A) 15.00; animal 12.00.
-- Less 15% outside Jul/ Aug. plus 7th night free.
-- Credit cards accepted.

Open:
1 May - 30 September.

Address:
24470 Champs Romain.

Tel:
53.56.94.66.
FAX: 53.56.38.70.

Reservations:
Write to site.

Alan Rogers' discount
Further 3-5% discounts

2404 Castel Camping Le Moulin du Roch, Sarlat

Family managed site in remote situation midway between Sarlat and Les Eyzies.

Most of the 195 separated pitches at Moulin du Roch are in rows backing onto fences but there are also levelled places in woodland with shade. Many pitches have electrical connections, and some pitches have water and drainage also. The toilet blocks are of very good quality and a well equipped washing area. On the site is a small/medium swimming pool, available from April if conditions permit, but not heated. There is a small shop (from 1/5) and the site has recently completed a new large restaurant and bar and an excellent takeaway (from 12/5). Children's playground. Table tennis. Tennis. Boules. Bicycle hire. Mobile homes to let for long stays. The site becomes full for most of July/Aug. and many of the pitches are taken by British tour operators (40%) or clubs. In high season entertainments and sporting activities, including canoe trips and horse riding, are organised by the site (not tour operators). Tennis and bicycle hire all season. A friendly management makes visitors very welcome.

Directions: Site is 10 km. from Sarlat on the D47 road to Les Eyzies.

Charges 1996:
-- Per pitch incl. 2 persons Ffr. 70.00 - 119.00, with electricity 87.00 - 136.00, full services 106.00 - 155.00; extra person (over 4 yrs) 20.00 - 35.00; local tax 1.00.

Open:
6 April - 15 September.

Address:
Rte. de Eyzies, 24200 Sarlat en Perigord.

Tel:
53.59.20.27.
FAX: 53.29.44.65.

Reservations:
Accepted from 1/1-31/5 (for 1 week min. in July/Aug) with deposit and fee (Ffr. 120).

2405 Castel Camping Les Hauts de Ratebout, Belvès, nr Sarlat

Good family site with pool, on a hill away from habitations southwest of Sarlat.

Not a particularly large site, this one has some 200 separated pitches, varying in size from 80 - 130 sq.m. and on fairly flat or terraced ground. It is in a fine, hill top situation with different aspects. Almost all the pitches have electricity and 155 are fully plumbed. On site is an outdoor, unheated swimming pool (200 sq.m.), a shallower one (100 sq.m.), a small children's pool and a new heated indoor pool. Amenities, including the pools, are available all season. The four modern toilet blocks have British WCs, washbasins in private cabins with free hot water and free hot showers. Facilities for the handicapped. Water taps abound. Self-service shop with takeaway service. A pleasant restaurant and bar area (from 1/6) opens to the pool-side terrace. 2 tennis courts. General room with library, pool, football table, TV. Sports facilities include volleyball, table tennis, and tennis. Adventure playground. Washing machine and dryer. Many organised activities in season, particularly sports for children. Used by tour operators (30%). A site more suitable for families with children under 16 years.

Directions: From Belvès, just off the D710 road 60 km. south of Périgueux, proceed 2 km. on D710 then left on D54 at camp sign and follow through to site.

Charges 1996:
-- Per person Ffr 27.80 - 37.00; child (under 8) 19.50 - 26.00; pitch 39.00 - 52.00; electricity (6A) 18.00.
-- Credit cards accepted.
Open:
1 May - 21 September.
Address:
Ste. Foy de Belvès, 24170 Belvès.
Tel:
53.29.02.10.
FAX: 53.29.08.28.
Reservations:
Made for a few days or more, with deposit Ffr. 420 per week (or 60 per day) and fee (100).

2406 Camping Le Paradis, St. Léon-sur-Vézère, Montignac, nr Sarlat

Exceptionally attractive riverside site halfway between Les Eyzies and Montignac.

This site is well placed for exploring the Dordogne and its prehistoric grottos and other sites. Le Paradis is very well kept and is laid out with mature shrubs and bushes of different types. It has 200 individual pitches of good size on flat grass, divided by trees and shrubs, all with electricity, water and drainaway; some special pitches for motorhomes. The two toilet blocks are of very high quality, with 2 baby baths in each ladies'; free pre-set hot showers with pushbutton. Good swimming pool complex, heated in low season, with one deep swimmers' pool (25 x 10 m.), another shallower one (17 x 7 m.), plus a paddling pool. Self-service shop. Restaurant with choice of menu and also a comprehensive takeaway service. Canoeing on Vézère river from attractive steps constructed on the riverside; also organised trips. 2 tennis courts. Children's playground. BMX track. Washing machines and dryers. A good quota of British clients, many through tour operators (25%), but organised games, competitions and evening events are run by the site, who try to maintain a French flavour. This is a site of real quality which we thoroughly recommend.

Directions: Site is beside the D706 road 10 km. north of Les Eyzies near the village of St Léon-sur-Vézère.

Charges 1995:
-- Per person Ffr. 31.00; child under 4 yrs free; pitch 49.50; electricity (6A) 16.00.
-- Less 10-25% outside main season.
-- Credit cards accepted.
Open:
30 March - 19 October.
Address:
St. Léon-sur-Vézère, 24290 Montignac.
Tel:
53.50.72.64.
FAX: 53.50.75.90.
Reservations:
Any length with deposit and Ffr. 100 fee.

2407 Camping Lestaubière, Pont St Mamet, nr Bergerac

Small country site with swimming pool, mid-way between Bergerac and Périgueux.

Having direct access from the main N21 (though screened from it by woodland), one thinks first of this as a useful transit site but in fact most people stay for a while. It takes only 66 units, mostly on fairly flat, shaded woodland ground at the top of site, some on more sloping open meadow with views. Pitches are marked and all have electrical connections. A swimming pool and paddling pool encourage longer stays, as does the small lake with diving platform and beach. The two toilet blocks have British WCs, washbasins with free hot water (in private cabins in the larger block); they should be large enough. A large washing room houses ample dishwashing and laundry sinks - there are also baby baths. There is a general room with bar and separate room for young with amusement machines, reached via a pleasant shaded patio terrace under vines and chestnuts. Small shop. Occasional organized activities. Good children's play equipment. Volleyball. Boules. Tennis, fishing and riding near. Many British and Dutch visitors. It becomes full in July/Aug. No tour operators. Good English spoken.

Directions: Site is 1 km. north of Pont St. Mamet on N21.

Charges 1996:
-- Per person Ffr. 25.00; child (under 7) 17.00; pitch 27.00; electricity (3A) 15.00.
Open:
15 May - 7 September.
Address:
Pont St. Mamet, 24140 Douville.
Tel:
53.82.98.15.
Reservations:
Exact dates (min. 1 week) without deposit to guarantee admission.

2408 Le Moulin de David, Gaugeac, Monpazier

Secluded valley site with pool, on southwest of the Dordogne.

Owned and run by a French family who continually seek to improve it, this pleasant little site is one for those who enjoy peace, away from the hustle and bustle of larger sites closer to the main Dordogne attractions, yet it is sufficiently close for them to be accessible. Set in 14 ha. of wooded countryside, it has 100 electric pitches, split into 2 sections; 35 below the central reception complex, in a shaded situation, and 65 above on partly terraced ground with varying degrees of shade. Spacing is good and there is no crowding. The site is attractively planted with a pleasing variety of shrubs and trees. The two sanitary blocks (one in each part) are reasonably good, with showers, washbasins in cabins, baby bath room and a washroom for the disabled in the lower block. Dishwashing and laundry sinks are adequate and there is a laundry room. The reception block embraces a restaurant (doubles as games and TV room), bar with shaded patio and takeaway. Good shop. Two swimming pools, one for small children, the other for adults and older children with water toboggan; also a concrete sun terrace. Between these and the upper site is a children's play area and a small lake. Some organised events and games. Boules. Half-court tennis. Table tennis (own bats). Volleyball. Library. Trampoline. Bicycle hire. Money exchange. Tents, mobile homes and caravans for hire; used by a tour operator (18%). Delightful wooded walk via long distance footpath (GR 36) to Biron Château, about 2-3 km distance. The bastide town of Montpazier is also walkable.

Directions: Site is just south off the Monpazier-Villeréal road (D2), about 2 km. west of Monpazier.

Charges 1996:
-- Per pitch Ffr. 44.00; person 32.50; child (under 2 yrs) free; electricity 3A 17.00, 5A 21.00.
-- Less 35-50% outside high season.
Open:
11 May - 15 September.
Address:
Gaugeac, 24540 Monpazier.
Tel:
53.22.65.25.
FAX: 53.22.99.76.
Reservations:
Advisable for Jul/Aug. with Ffr. 250 deposit plus fee (85).

Alan Rogers' discount
Less 10% in low season

2411 Camping-Caravaning Aqua Viva, Carsac, nr Sarlat

Clean site with good pool complex in heart of the Perigord Noir.

This site is divided into two sections separated by the access road. One side is very quiet and spacious, with pitches (some very large) and chalets terraced in woodland. The other half contains pitches on flat grass and has an excellent main pool, children's pool, small lake (for inflatables and canoes) with a kiosk for ices, etc, table tennis tables and a high quality minigolf course. Canoe lessons and competitions in the lake and guided trips on the Dordogne are organised by the site, as are many other sporting activities. Each part of the site has very modern and spotlessly clean toilet blocks, with facilities for the disabled, laundry and baby areas. Between the two sections is the reception area, with a small reasonably priced restaurant, a bar and a terrace where evening entertainment is arranged in season. There is a small shop and takeaway food is available. The site is ideally situated for visits to Rocamadour and Padirac, as well as the many places of interest of the Dordogne region. It is also close to Sarlat for markets and hypermarkets. The site is very popular with families, especially those with pre-teen and younger teenage children.

Directions: Site is 6 km. from Sarlat on the D704 road from Sarlat to Souillac.

Charges 1995:
-- Per pitch Ffr 18.00 - 41.00; adult 15.00 - 29.00; child 7.00 - 21.00; electricity 3A 11.00, 6A 16.00, 10A 21.00; local tax 1.00.
Open:
Easter - 30 September.
Address:
Carsac, 24200 Sarlat.
Tel:
53.59.21.09.
FAX: 53.29.36.37.
Reservations:
With deposit (Ffr 35 per day) and fee (100).

24 Dordogne

2409 Camping Soleil Plage, Vitrac, nr Sarlat

Spacious site with enviable location beside the Dordogne.

The site is situated in one of the most attractive sections of the Dordogne Valley, right on the riverside. It is divided into two sections - one section of 56 pitches has its own toilet block and lies adjacent to the reception, bar, shop and restaurant complex, which is housed in a renovated Perigourdine farmhouse. It is also close to a small sandy river bank and canoe station, from which canoes and kayaks can be hired for down-river trips or transport up-river for a paddle back to the site. Near the reception area is a swimming pool, paddling pool, tennis court and minigolf course.

The friendly bar provides an excellent takeaway menu which can be eaten there or on the terrace, and the attractive refurbished restaurant serves excellent Peregourdine menus. The larger section of the site (124 pitches) is about 250 m. from the reception area, and offers river bathing from a sizeable pebble bank. All pitches are bounded by hedges and are of good size, and in this section there are a few giant pitches for large families. Open air table tennis tables, a volleyball court and a children's playground occupy part of a large central recreation space. Sanitary facilities are in two modern blocks. Washing machine. TV room. The site is becoming increasingly popular, though in late August it begins to empty, and reservations are essential for July/Aug. Used by tour operators (35%).

Directions: Site is 8 km south of Sarlat. Take the D704 and it is signed from Montfort castle. Coming from the west on the D703, take the first right turn 1-2 km. after the bridge at Vitrac-Port, and follow the signs.

Charges 1996:
-- Per person Ffr. 31.00; child (under 10 yrs) 20.00; pitch 48.00, with full services 78.00; local tax 1.00 (over 10s) in high season; dog 10.00; electricity (10A) 18.00.
-- Less 20% outside 20/6-1/9.
-- Credit cards accepted.
Open:
12 May - 20 September.
Address:
Vitrac, 24200 Sarlat.
Tel:
53.28.33.33.
FAX: 53.29.36.87.
Reservations:
Made for exact dates: min. 1 week with deposit and fee; send for booking form.

2410 Camping-Caravaning Le Moulinal, Biron

Spacious, attractive site with lake, developed round former watermill of Château Biron.

Not only does Le Moulinal provide a good base for exploring the southern Dordogne, but it has extensive wooded grounds to explore with picnic areas. There are 200 pitches all with electricity and of at least 100 sq.m. They are level, grassy and well drained with views over the lake. The sanitary facilities have been built to harmonise with the surroundings and provide mostly British toilets, washbasins, some in cabins, and hot showers. Good supply of hot water for washing up sinks and laundry with 2 washing machines and dryer. Facilities for the handicapped and babies.

The 5-acre lake with sandy beach is suitable for swimming and boating (canoes available) and fishing. Shop. Bar/restaurant serving good meals (including 4 course `menu enfant'!) open mid-May - end Sept, plus a snack bar/takeaway on the other side of the lake. A rustic children's play area on grass overlooks the lake. Leisure facilities include tennis, volleyball, table tennis, archery, fishing, canoeing, handicrafts. Excursions organised on foot, on horseback or by bicycle and accompanied if wished and entertainment in high season. There is a new, large, heated swimming pool with jacuzzi and children's pool. The site is popular with tour operators (35%) and is now run as a `Club de Vacances' - all visitors are required to pay a small membership charge in return for access to a wide variety of activities. Tents, new chalets, bungalows and caravans for hire.

Directions: Using the D104 Villeréal-Monpazier road, 9 km from Villeréal, take the D53 south to Biron (3 km). Continue to follow the D53 to Lacapelle Biron (4½ km - the D53 becomes the D150 on crossing the regional boundary before reaching Lacapelle Biron). Site is signed to west from Lacapelle Biron on the D255. From D911 Fumel-Villeneuve road take D162 and after 6½ km, turn right at sign for Lacapelle Biron.

Charges 1995:
-- Per pitch incl. 2 persons: normal Ffr. 60.00 - 128.00, near lake 70.00 - 139.00. with water and drainage 75.00 - 150.00; extra person (over 7 yrs) 15.00 - 37.00; child (2-7 yrs) free - 31.00; extra tent or car 5.00 - 7.00; animal 6.00 - 10.00; electricity 3A 20.00, 6A 27.00.
-- Credit cards accepted.
Open:
11 May - 15 September, with all services.
Address:
24540 Biron.
Tel:
53.40.84.60.
FAX: 53.40.81.49.
Reservations:
Made with deposit (Ffr 250) and for high season, fee (150).

2412 Camping La Palombière, Ste. Nathalène, nr Sarlat

Clean site with good recreational facilities east of Sarlat.

This is a spacious site in a peaceful valley with quiet, well shaded woodland pitches hedged by trees and bushes. The ground is steep but is terraced and accessible. Two very clean modern toilet blocks are provided with laundry and facilities for babies and the disabled. A large recreational area contains a children's play area, small football pitch, tennis and volleyball courts. Boules pitches are terraced at the edge of the field and a minigolf course is set on a higher level by the entrance. The good sized main pool and children's pool are flanked by a raised terrace from which parents can keep an eye on youngsters. Above this again is a larger terrace serving the reception, bar and restaurant complex, from which a good range of meals is available (from 15/5). Well stocked shop, including meat, fresh milk and newspapers. From reception, bicycles can be hired, and canoe trips reserved. The site organises sports competitions and evening activities in season, including talent shows, a weekly disco, cabaret and even Giant Scrabble! This is an ideal site for families where children are at an age where they need a wide range of activities, but it nevertheless preserves a relaxed ambience and general tranquillity. Popular with tour operators (55%).

Charges 1996:
-- Per pitch: simple Ffr 46.50; adult 32.00, plus local tax 1.50; child (under 7 yrs) 22.50.
-- Less 5-25% outside July/Aug.
-- Credit cards accepted.
Open:
1 May - 20 September.
Address:
Ste. Nathalène,
24200 Sarlat.
Tel:
53.59.42.34.
FAX: 53.28.45.40.
Reservations:
Made with deposit and fee - contact site.

Directions: Take the D47 east from Sarlat towards St Nathalène. Site is signed from the main road, just before the village.

2413 Camping Les Grottes de Roffey, Ste. Nathalène, nr Sarlat

Well organised site with good pool, restaurant and shop.

This site is situated some 5 km. east of Sarlat. Clearly marked pitches are set on very well kept grass terraces, with good views across an attractive valley. Some have good shade, although others are more open and all have electricity. There are two toilet blocks with modern facilities which were clean when seen. A very good pool complex, with two deep pools, a fountain and a children's pool, is complemented by a concrete play space and children's play area. All these are close to the main reception, bar, restaurant (indoor and with terrace) and shop area, located within converted farm buildings surrounding a courtyard. We were very impressed with the shop, well stocked with a variety of goods, and with a tempting home-made charcuterie section and plenty of ideas for the barbecue. The restaurant menus were imaginative and sensibly priced, and takeaway food is available. The site is conveniently located for Sarlat and all Dordogne attractions and is a pleasant place to stay in its own right. It caters well for families with younger children.

Charges 1996:
-- Per pitch Ffr 44.00; adult 34.00; child (2-7 yrs) 24.00; electricity 14.00; local tax (15/6-1/9) 1.00.
-- Less 15-40% outside 15/6 - 31/8.
-- Credit cards accepted.
Open:
Easter - 30 September.
Address:
Ste. Nathalène,
24200 Sarlat.
Tel:
53.59.15.61.
FAX: 53.31.09.11.
Reservations:
Contact site.

Directions: Site is 5 km. east of Sarlat on the D47 Sarlat - Souillac road.

2414 Camping Bel Ombrage, St Cybranet, nr Cénac

Clean site with good pool near Dordogne.

Bel Ombrage sits in a pretty location by the little River Céou, with a beach onto a backwater which is safe and clean for bathing. There are 180 well shaded, flat grass pitches of good size, marked up by trees and bushes. Two very modern toilet blocks are kept clean, with laundry, disabled and baby facilities. The site boasts a very good pool complex, but lacks a bar or restaurant, though soft drinks and ice-creams are sold by the pool and a bread van calls each morning. It is a short walk to the village of St Cybranet, where there are restaurants and a well stocked store. Tennis courts are close by and canoeing and other excursions can be booked at reception. Bel Ombrage is very close to Domme and Castelnaud, and would make an ideal base for touring the Dordogne area.

Directions: Take the D57 from Vézac towards Cénac. After St Cybranet, the site is a short distance on the left.

Charges 1996:
-- Per pitch Ffr. 38.00; adult 25.00; child (under 7 yrs) 14.00; electricity 16.00.
Open:
1 June - 5 September.
Address:
24250 St Cybranet.
Tel:
53.28.34.14.
FAX: 53.59.64.64.
Reservations:
Write to site.

2416 Camping Le Grand Dague, Atur, Périgueux

Good quality site with pool on the outskirts of Perigueux.

Having negotiated the narrow access road, Le Grand Dague is found to be a very spacious, clean and pretty site. There are some 93 good sized, level pitches, 60 of which are for tourists, and all have electricity (6A). The sanitary facilities are excellent and comprise four blocks built together in the middle of the site, all of which are open in summer, but in colder months only one does (it is heated and has insulated doors on cubicles). There are two toilets for the disabled and a baby room. The main site building houses the reception area and a small shop which provides essentials (from 20/5). The bar and restaurant area has been tastefully extended by the Dutch owners into what was once a cow barn; snacks, a takeaway service and an appetising restaurant menu make the most of this provision (also from 20/5). Sports facilities on site include football, volleyball, badminton, petanque, minigolf and table tennis. A small number of mobile homes is available for rent along with some attractive chalets. The site is approx. 6 km. from Périgueux and close to hypermarkets and tennis. No tour operators.

Directions: Site is signed from the N89 south of Périgueux.

Charges 1996:
-- Per pitch Ffr. 40.00; adult 31.00; child (0-7 yrs) 20.00; electricity 15.00.
-- Less 5-25% outside high season.
Open:
Easter - 30 September.
Address:
24750 Atur.
Tel:
53.04.21.01.
FAX: 53.04.22.01.
Reservations:
Advised in high season.

Alan Rogers' discount
Extra 5% low season discount

2417 Camping Port de Limieul, Limieul

Delighful site at the confluence of Dordogne and Vézère.

Situated on the banks of the Dordogne, opposite the picturesque village of Limieul, this site exuded a peaceful and relaxed ambience. There are 90 pitches, marked and numbered, some very spacious. All have electrical connections. The young French owners have been steadily developing first class facilities, including two very well appointed sanitary blocks and a good sized pool. The reception area is contained in a building which also houses a friendly bar and restaurant with snack and new takeaway facilities (all 28/5-9/9). All the buildings are in Perigourdine style and surrounded with flowers and shrubs - it is a very pretty site. Sports facilities include minigolf, badminton, football, boules and volleyball. The last of these is set up on a large open grassy area between the trees on the river bank and the camping area, which not only satisfies a planning condition that tents should not impinge on the view from the village, but adds to the feeling of space and provides an additional recreation and picnic area. Mountain bikes and canoes can be hired - the latter are launched from a pebble beach exclusive to the site. This is an ideal location for visiting the west central part of the Dordogne département, and is recommended for long stays. Used by tour operators (30%).

Directions: Take D51 road from Le Buisson towards Le Bugue. Road branches left to Limieul after about 3 km. and the site is then signed.

Charges 1996:
-- Per pitch incl. 2 persons Ffr. 96.00; extra person 25.00; child (0-10 yrs) 18.00; electricity (5A) 20.00; local tax 2.00.
-- Credit cards accepted.
Open:
1 May - 30 September.
Address:
24480 Alles-sur-Dordogne.
Tel:
53.63.29.76.
FAX: 53.63.04.19.
Reservations:
Advised in high season.

Alan Rogers' discount
Less 20% in low seasons

2415 Camping Les Deux Vallées, Beynac, Vézac

Developing woodland site in the heart of the Dordogne.

This site is enviably situated almost under the shadow of Beynac Castle. There are just over 100 flat, marked touring pitches, all of good size, and some generous, divided by trees and shrubs, all with electricity (6A). There is plenty of shade and the general feel is of unspoilt but well managed woodland. The main modern toilet block gives ample provision, with good access for the handicapped. A second smaller block, which is heated for off-season use, has been added more recently. A good sized pool (1.6 m. deep) and children's pool, recently enlarged and refurbished provide on-site swimming facilities, and it is a short distance to the Dordogne for bathing or canoeing. A small lake, with island and tree-house, is available for fishing or just sitting beside, and there are facilities for volleyball, boules, table tennis, table football and an intriguing outdoor pool game. The site owners have introduced French courses (in low seasons) and quiz nights are also a regular feature in the main season. The bar/restaurant serves good value snacks and more ambitious meals to take away, eat inside or on the terrace. Another surprise is English breakfast! The site is being steadily upgraded by its British/Dutch owners, who assure a very friendly welcome. Some tour operator pitches (10%).

Directions: Take the D703 from Bergerac, go through Beynac and, just past the village, turn left towards Sarlat on the D57/D49. Shortly after, turn left and the site is signed from here on.

Charges 1996:
-- Per pitch Ffr. 32.00; adult 24.00; child (4-7 yrs) 15.00, free under 3; electricity 6A 16.00. 10A 20.00; dog 6.00; plus local tax.
-- Less 20-50% outside 6/7-24/8.
-- Credit cards accepted.
Open:
1 April - 15 October.
Address:
24220 Vézac.
Tel:
53.29.53.55.
FAX: 53.31.09.81.
Reservations:
Advised for July and August.

2420M Camping Municipal de la Plage, St Aulaye

Beside the River Dronne, which runs round three of its sides, this prettily situated site shares a river beach with the village community, with bar/snacks and a children's playground. Only open for a short season, the site has 65 pitches marked with small hedges, with shade on those near the river. Sanitary facilities are clean. St Aulaye is located quite close to Bordeaux and Bergerac vineyards.

Directions: Take the D5 from Riberac to La Roche-Chalais. St Aulaye is 19 km. along the road and the site is just after the village.

Charges 1996:
-- Per pitch incl. 2 persons Ffr. 45.00; extra person 10.00; child (under 7) 8.00; electricity 5A 12.00.
Open:
29 June - 31 August.
Address:
24410 St Aulaye.
Tel:
La Mairie: 53.90.62.20.
FAX: 53.90.59.89.
Reservations:
Advised for July/Aug.

2500 Castel Camping Caravaning Le Val de Bonnal, Rougemont

Well managed, attractive site in large country estate.

This is an impressive site, harmoniously designed in keeping with the surrounding countryside, well away from main roads and other intrusions. Having said that the site itself is very busy, with a wide range of activities and amenities. The pitches, all of a good size and with electricity (5A), are separated by a mixture of trees and bushes, carefully landscaped. Some of the newer pitches are less secluded, but the ambience generally is peaceful despite the size of the site (200 pitches in 37 acres) and its deserved popularity. The four toilet blocks, very clean when visited, provide free hot showers (some with separators), washbasins in private cabins and British WCs. There are separate washing up blocks, with sinks and free hot water, and washing machines, ironing boards and sinks for hand washing clothes. Amenities include a riverside restaurant, snack bar/takeaway, bar, terrace, shop (all 20/6-10/9), situated in sympathetically converted former farm buildings, well equipped children's play areas, and a range of sport facilities including table tennis, boules, bicycle hire, etc, but the main attraction is the variety of watersports on the 3 large lakes and nearby river. These include swimming, pedaloes, and fishing as well as water skiing, windsurfing and canoeing. In fact, the range of activities available at this site is almost inexhaustible, not to say exhausting - you can even go hot air ballooning! There are also 150 hectares to walk in and it is ideally placed for day trips to Switzerland. Used by tour operators (38%).

Directions: From Vesoul take the D9 towards Villersexel. After approx. 20 km. turn right in the village of Esprels at sign for Val de Bonnal. Follow for 3½ km. and site is on the left.

Charges 1996:
-- Per pitch with electricity, incl. 3 persons Ffr. 165.00, extra person 30.00; child (2-7 yrs) 15.00; local tax 1.50 per day.
Open:
8 May - 15 September.
Address:
Bonnal, 25680 Rougemont.
Tel:
81.86.90.87.
Reservations:
Only made for pitches with electricity. Contact site.

2505M Camping Municipal de Saint Point-Lac, Saint Point-Lac

A good example of a municipal camp in which the village takes a pride, this site is on the banks of a small lake. There are good views to the distant hills, although at the time of our visit this was slightly marred by large mounds of earth by the shore. The 80 level, numbered pitches are on grass and all have electricity (3A). There is a good central sanitary block with British style WCs and free hot water in washbasins, showers and sinks. The village shop and (good) restaurant are an easy 200 m. walk from the site entrance. It is worth making a detour from the Pontarlier - Vallorbe road or for a longer stay.

Directions: From the north, take the D437 south of Pontarlier and keep on the west side of the lake to the second village (Saint Point-Lac); from the south exit the N57 at Les Hopitaux-Neufs and turn west to lake.

Charges guide:
-- Per pitch incl. 2 persons Ffr. 46.00 - 52.00, incl. 3 services 55.00 - 76.00; extra person 13.00 - 15.00; child (4-10) 6.00 - 7.00.
Open:
1 May - 30 September.
Address:
25160 Saint Point-Lac.
Tel:
Site: 81.69.61.64.
Mairie: 81.69.62.08.
Reservations:
Made with deposit (Ffr. 300) and fee (50).

2602 Castel Camping du Château de Sénaud, Albon, nr Tournon
Pleasant site convenient for the autoroute or a longer stay.

Château du Sénaud, near the N7 south of Vienne, makes a useful stopover on the way south, but one could enjoy a longer stay to explore the surrounding villages and mountains. It has a fair number of permanent caravans used at weekends, but there are also some 140 pitches in tourist parts, some with shade, some with views across the Rhône valley, and electrical connections are available. There is a swimming pool, (from June, depending on the weather) and a tennis court. Four sanitary blocks have constant hot water in basins, showers and sinks, British and continental toilets and washbasins in private cabins, some en-suite with shower in one block. Washing machine. Provision shop (late June - mid-Sept). Bar, takeaway (from 15/6) and good value small restaurant with simple menu (pizzas on Tues and Sat). Table tennis. Bowling alley. Minigolf. Golf course adjacent. Walks. Possibly some noise from the autoroute.

Directions: Leave autoroute at Chanas exit, proceed south along N7 for 8 km. then east near Le Creux de la Thine to site. From south you should leave autoroute at Tain-Tournon exit and proceed north, approaching site on D122 through St Vallier then take D172 towards Anneyron to site entrance.

Charges 1995:
-- Per person Ffr. 22.00; child (under 7) 12.00; pitch 31.00; dog 6.00; visitor 10.00; electricity 18.00.
Open:
1 March - 31 October.
Address:
26140 Albon.
Tel:
75.03.11.31.
FAX: 75.03.08.06.
Reservations:
Made with deposit for min. 3 nights.

Camping - Caravanning
"Château de Senaud"
ALBON (Drôme)
Your night stop or holiday centre in the Rhone Valley

The famous Senaud castle, between Lyon and Valence, has been placed at the disposal of campers and caravanners by the Comtesse d'Armagnac.

In the huge century-old park you can go for wonderful walks. There is a swimming pool for your relaxation, a tennis court, fishing in the lake. The sanitary installations are modern, of course, with showers and hot water.

Only 2 km. from the RN7, the Château de Senaud offers you complete quiet and repose and very good amenities

LARGE NEW PART OF CAMP RESERVED FOR FOREIGN TOURISTS

2605M Camping Municipal de L'Epervière, Valence
A useful overnight stop at Valence, close to A7 and N7 roads, this site is an unusual municipal, run as a holiday/conference centre and looks as though it has been a former school or college. Providing some 150 pitches of moderate size with many electrical connections (6 or 10A), the site consists of two areas - one quite heavily wooded with informal, irregular shaped pitches, and one more formally arranged on more open ground with some hardstandings and hedging. The site is situated beside the Rhône, within about 5 minutes drive of the city centre. There is a restaurant and excellent value self-service snack-bar in the adjacent conference/training centre/holiday club (which also houses the reception), plus a small outdoor swimming pool and shop, open during the summer only. Sanitary facilities in two blocks are utilitarian rather than luxurious, but are a satisfactory provision.

Directions: From autoroute take exit for Valence Sud and immediately on leaving toll booth, turn right following camp signs `Epervière' carefully (you turn back on yourself across the autoroute).

Charges guide:
-- Per unit incl. 2 persons Ffr. 53.00 - 67.00, 1 person 35.00 - 44.00; child (5-12 yrs) 11.00 - 13.00; electricity 6A 16.00, 10A 28.00.
-- Higher price for first night in high season.
Open:
All year.
Address:
Chemin de L'Epervière, 26000 Valence.
Tel:
75.42.32.00
FAX: 75.56.20.67.
Reservations:
Contact site.

2603 Camping Le Grand Lierne, Chabeuil, nr Valence

Conveniently and attractively situated family site on the route south.

In addition to its obvious attraction as an overnight stop, fairly convenient to the A7 autoroute, this site provides a pleasant base to explore this little known area between the Ardèche and the Vercors mountains and the Côte du Rhône wine area . The site has 134 marked pitches, mainly separated by hedges or oak trees, with good shade, on flat grass and all with electricity (4-10A). There is a feeling of spaciousness and there are good views to the mountains on either side of the valley. A varied entertainment programme has a particular emphasis on activities for children, with various excursions, both organised and informal. A disco for teenagers is organised by the owner's sons but is well managed to avoid noise. Two heated swimming pools, one covered in low season (no bermuda shorts allowed in pool), a children's pool and a new 50 m. water slide. A bar/snack bar with terrace provides both `eating in' and takeaway (all season). Two modern sanitary blocks provide hot showers, seatless WCs and washbasins in private cabins. Facilities for the handicapped and a small WC for children. Partly under cover dishwashing area (H&C). Washing machines and dryer (fairly expensive and no outdoor lines permitted). Other amenities include a shop, tennis, children's playgrounds and trampoline, minigolf, table tennis, volleyball, a football field, small climbing wall and bicycles for hire. Organised games and entertainment for children in high season. Library. Bureau de change. Fridge rental. Golf, archery, riding and hang gliding near. American motorhomes not accepted. Bungalows, chalets and tents for hire. No pets allowed. Barbecues allowed on special areas. The site is used by an international tour operator (12%). The owners wish to keep a balance between nationalities and are also keen to encourage rallies and will arrange visit programmes. English spoken.

Directions: Site is signed in Chabeuil about 11 km. east of Valence (18 km. from autoroute). It is best to approach Chabeuil from the south side of Valence via the Valence ring road, thence onto the D68 to Chabeuil itself.

Charges 1996:
-- Per unit, incl. 2 persons and electricity (4A) Ffr 105.00 - 140.00; extra person 30.00; child (under 7 yrs) free - 20.00; electricity (10A) 20.00; refrigerator rental 24.00; local tax 1.00 per person.
-- Credit cards accepted.

Open:
Sat. before Easter - 25 September with all services.

Address:
BP.8, 26120 Chabeuil.

Tel:
75.59.83.14.
FAX: 75.59.87.95.

Reservations:
Accepted with deposit (Ffr. 600) and fee (170).

Alan Rogers' discount
Less 15% outside 20 June 20 Aug.

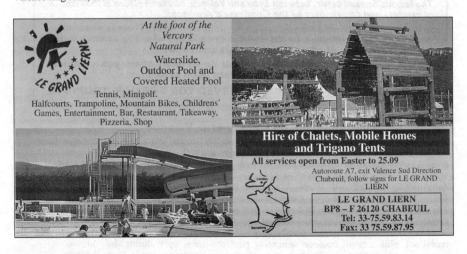

At the foot of the Vercors Natural Park

Waterslide, Outdoor Pool and Covered Heated Pool

Tennis, Minigolf. Halfcourts, Trampoline, Mountain Bikes, Childrens' Games, Entertainment, Bar, Restaurant, Takeaway, Pizzeria, Shop

Hire of Chalets, Mobile Homes and Trigano Tents

All services open from Easter to 25.09

Autoroute A7, exit Valence Sud Direction Chabeuil, follow signs for LE GRAND LIERN

LE GRAND LIERN
BP8 – F 26120 CHABEUIL
Tel: 33-75.59.83.14
Fax: 33 75.59.87.95

A list of the Départements of France and a map showing their location is on pages 214 and 215

2604 Camping-Caravaning Le Couspeau, Le Poet Célard

Lovely small site in little known area, near the village of Bourdeaux.

This small and peaceful site, which enjoys a very relaxed atmosphere, is on a hillside about 4 km. from the small town of Bourdeaux. Approach roads are quite twisty and the pitches, which are uniformly large and well shaded, are divided by the undulating terrain. All 50 pitches have electricity and a number have hardstanding. The views from all pitches, across the valley, are quite lovely. Access roads are a mixture of tarmac, gravel and grass. Two, well placed toilet blocks (extremely clean but not luxurious) are more than adequate for the site which was full at the time of our visit. Each contains 4 showers, washbasins and toilets. Dishwashing facilities are under cover. Facilities for washing clothes are available with washing machines in the toilet blocks. The main swimming pool is very clean and of a good size and there is also a covered pool and a toddlers' pool. The pool area is attractively laid out with ample space for sunbathing and a good supply of sun loungers and chairs at the pool-side. Swimming trunks (not shorts) must be worn, Other sports and leisure facilities include tennis, minigolf, archery, table tennis, and the ubiquitous 'boules'. The exceptionally friendly owners adopt a watchful but low key approach and arrange special meals, walks in the locality, discos and musical events. Play area for small children, not supervised but in view of the pool. Friendly bar and reasonably priced restaurant with takeaway. Small shop on site but a wider range of shops can be found in Bourdeaux. The countryside around is enchanting and ideal for walking or short drives. Further afield for day excursions, are Valence, Montelimar, Nyons, the Drôme Valley and the Vercors Massif.

Charges guide:
-- Per unit incl. 2 persons Ffr 90.00 - 94.00; extra person 25.00; child (under 7 yrs) 18.00; electricity (3A) 14.00; animal 6.00.
Open:
1 May - 30 September.
Address:
26460 Le Poet Célard.
Tel:
75.53.30.14.
FAX: 75.53.37.23.
Reservations:
Advised for July/Aug. and made with deposit (Ffr. 500) and fee (100).

Directions: From Crest take D538 (signed Bourdeaux) and turn right onto D328B (signed Le Poet Célard). At T-junction turn right onto D328 towards the village then turn left onto D328A and, after a short distance, the site is on left.

2606M Camping Municipal St Nazaire-en-Royans, nr Romans

The pretty village of St Nazaire en Royans is on the western perimeter of the Parc Regional du Vercors, on the route between Romans and Grenoble, and is distinguished by its impressive bridge straddling the Isère river. The municipal site is 500 m. from the village, fronted by the municipal tennis courts and boules area. With a well laid out, tidy and organised appearance, the site's 75 grass pitches, all with electricity (3 or 6A) are of a good size, numbered and separated by hedges. Some, towards the bottom left, overlook the river and lots of trees give shade. The sanitary block is basic but in good condition and clean, with continental and British style WCs, washbasins with some private, curtained cabins, facilities for the disabled. Dishwashing and laundry sinks, plus a washing machine. Children's play area on grass. A convenient base for exploring this not so well known, but scenically magnificent area.

Charges 1995:
-- Per unit incl. 2 persons Ffr. 40.00; extra person 15.00; child (0-6) 9.00; electricity (3A) 15.00, (6A) 20.00.
Open:
1 May - 30 September.
Address:
26190 St Nazaire-en-Royans.
Tel:
75.48.41.18 or Mairie: 75.48.40.63.
Reservations:
Contact site.

Directions: From Romans-s-Isère take N532 for 18 km. to St Nazaire-en-Royans. Site is clearly signed in village on the D76 (500 m).

2701 Camping-Caravaning Le Vert Bocage, Verneuil-sur-Avre

Pleasant site for night stop en-route south, or for visiting Paris.

Situated in attractive countryside, this site is conveniently beside the N26, about 700 m. from the town of Verneuil, some 50 km. northwest of Chartres. There is a nearby railway station with fast trains to Paris (1 hour). The site is small but provides good facilities in terms of 65 large, level pitches on grass, many separated by hedges and all with electricity (amps as required). The single, tiled sanitary block provides free hot showers, washbasins with hot and cold water, British WCs and dishwashing facilities (H&C) under cover. It is clean and well maintained. Children's playground. Good restaurant in town (1 km). Fishing, swimming pool, tennis near. Apartments and caravans to let.

Charges 1995:
-- Per adult Ffr. 25.00; child 12.50; pitch 21.00; electricity 26.00.
Open:
All year.
Address:
Ave. Edmond-Demolins 27130 Verneuil-s-Avre.
Tel:
32.32.26.79
Reservations:
Write to site.

Directions: Site is by N26 road at Verneuil, about 50 km. northwest of Chartres.

2801 Camping du Parc de Loisirs, Cloyes-sur-le-Loir, Châteaudun

Pleasant staging post on the N10 south of Châteaudun

This site, conveniently but quietly situated near to the old N10, has been improved and makes a good stop-over for a night or maybe a bit longer - some of the Loire châteaux are not all that far. The site is now in three parts: a permanent section (about 50%), a longer-stay tourist section consisting entirely of individual `special' pitches with electricity, water and drainaway, and an overnight area, with electricity, but where pitches are not marked and units can be packed rather close. Two sanitary blocks serve the site well; one is modern and well appointed, with private cabins and pushbutton showers; the second, by the reception, is older, but has recently been refurbished and includes facilities for the disabled.

The `Parc de Loisirs' itself, also open to the general public on payment, but free of charge to campers, consists of a large children's playground, with inflatable castle, a swimming pool, water chute and splash pool (1/6-31/8), minigolf, tennis, pedaloes, canoes and boats and pony rides (open daily in July/Aug, Sundays May-Sept). Small shop (July/Aug). Washing machine. Spacious restaurant and bar, with upper dining room and terrace, open high season and some weekends.

Directions: Site is well signed in Cloyes, 12 km. south of Châteaudun, on N10.

Charges 1995:
-- Per person Ffr. 25.00; child (under 7) 15.00; pitch and car 35.00; electricity (5A) 20.00. Individual pitches cost more.
-- Credit cards accepted.

Open:
15 March - 15 Nov.

Address:
B.P. 8, 28220 Cloyes-sur-le-Loir.

Tel:
37.98.50.53.
FAX: 37.98.33.84.

Reservations:
Made for min. 1 week for individual pitches with deposit and fee.

Camping Parc de Loisirs

CLOYES-SUR-LOIRE

FREE Attractions:
Pedalos – Minigolf
Ponies – Swimming Pool
Waterslide
Canoes – Games
Ping-pong...

2810M Camping Municipal de Montjouvin, Illiers-Combray

This well kept site is quiet, very green and offers 89 grass pitches on a slope in most areas, with 5A electrical connections available. Tall trees surround the camping areas and there is plenty of shade, peace and quiet. The two large sanitary blocks are fully tiled with British style WCs and showers with free hot water and dressing areas, some washbasins in private cabins and the usual under cover laundry and dishwashing sinks. There are good facilities for the disabled including telephone booths and, although the site is on a slope, it could possibly be acceptable for wheel chairs. All restaurant, shop and bar amenities are to be found in the town itself (1 km). An outdoor municipal swimming pool (unheated) alongside the site is free for campers staying for 4 days or over. There are boules pitches, two children's playgrounds and table tennis on site, but no other sporting facilities or other organised activities. This is a site really for those who want peace and quiet or a convenient overnight stop.

Directions: Site is on the D921 road from Illiers-Combray to Le Mans.

Charges guide:
-- Per pitch Ffr. 15.00; adult 11.00; child (under 7 yrs) 5.50; electricity 14.00.

Open:
1 April - 31 October.

Address:
Rte. de Brou, 28120 Illiers-Combray.

Tel:
37.24.03.04 (site)
37.24.00.05 (Mairie).

Reservations:
Contact site.

ALAN ROGERS GOOD CAMPS GUIDE, FRANCE 1996
DISCOUNT CARD, Valid 1 Jan - 31 Dec 1996

ME:
DRESS:
GNATURE:

PART 1   CAMPSITE DISCOUNT VOUCHER, Valid 1st Jan - 31st Dec 1996

his voucher entitles the holder to the discounts shown against the relevant individual Campsite Report in this Guide. This ortion of the voucher should be retained by the holder, but made available for inspection at the campsite(s) concerned when ooking-in and/or on departure.

AME of voucher holder:
DDRESS:
SIGNATURE:

VOUCHER NUMBER

00068

F96

PART 2   Travel, Breakdown, Caravan & Motorcaravan Insurance Discount Voucher, Valid 1st Jan - 31st Dec 1996

his portion entitles the holder to a discount of 10% on the Travel & Breakdown Insurance arrangements detailed on pages 6/17 of this guide, and/or a discount of 5% on the annual caravan or motorcaravan insurances arranged through Bakers f Cheltenham, and advertised on pages 207/208 of this guide.

or travel/breakdown insurance please complete the relevant proposal form, and send it together with this voucher and the ppropriate premium to Deneway Guides & Travel Ltd., Chesil Lodge, West Bexington, Dorchester DT2 9DG. For short-otice requirements ONLY (ie within 7 days of departure) please telephone 01308 897809, quoting this voucher number, nd your credit card details. Alternatively Fax details to 01308 898017.

or caravan or motorcaravan insurance, please complete the forms on pages 207/208 and send it to BAKERS OF HELTENHAM at the address shown on pages 207/208, quoting this discount voucher number.

VOUCHER NUMBER

00068

F96

AME of voucher holder:
DDRESS:
SIGNATURE:

PART 3   BRITTANY FERRIES DISCOUNT VOUCHER   Brittany Ferries

his voucher entitles the holder to the following reductions with Brittany Ferries for "D" & "E" rate sailings on all their routes etween BRITAIN & FRANCE between 1st January 1996 to 31st December 1996.

eductions: For caravans and trailer tents - a discount of 50% off the published brochure tariff. For motorcaravans no verheight supplement will be charged (ie they will be carried at the standard rate as for motor cars - on "D" & "E" sailings only)

onditions of use: (1) Travel must actually take place within the period 1st Jan - 31st Dec 1996. (2) Any application for a refund must be accompanied by e unused portion of the ticket, and made through the issuing office within six months of the expiry date of the ticket. No replacement discount voucher will e supplied, nor cash refunded against the value of the voucher. (3) Only one discount voucher per booking will be permitted, and the voucher may not be changed for cash. (4) Brittany Ferries reserves the right not to accept any discount voucher where fraudulent use is suspected. (5) All other conditions are s published in the Brittany Ferries brochure at the time of booking.

ow to book: For telephone bookings: Telephone Brittany Ferries direct on 0990 360360 and quote the Alan Rogers Good amps Guide Special Discount Offer, and this voucher number. The booking will be made initially at the full brochure tariff. his portion of the voucher should be sent immediately to Brittany Ferries Plymouth office, for the attention of the eservations Manager. On receipt of the voucher Brittany Ferries will then allocate the appropriate discount, which will be hown on your official confirmation document. A similar procedure should be adopted if booking through a travel agent. order for the discount to be applied the Special Offer MUST be requested AT THE TIME OF BOOKING, and this section f the voucher sent to Brittany Ferries immediately.

AME of voucher holder:
DDRESS:
SIGNATURE:

VOUCHER NUMBER

00068

F96

2811M Camping Municipal de Bonneval, Bonneval, nr Chartres

On the outskirts of Bonneval and within walking distance of the town centre, this site offers good facilities in peaceful surroundings near the river (said to be good for fishing, but not swimming or boating). The site has thick cover from trees in most parts with some pitches entirely hidden for those who like lots of privacy. Otherwise, the pitches are marked on grass in clearings, the majority fairly flat. All 122 have 6A electricity, some hardstanding. Sanitary facilities consist of one large block and three smaller units with just toilets and washbasins. The large block has free hot showers (with chain), British style WCs and facilities for the disabled. Laundry room. No bar, restaurant or shop on the site, but all are to be found in Bonneval itself or, when open, in the municipal swimming pool and tennis complex adjacent (reduced rates for campers).

Directions: Site is signed from Bonneval town centre on the N10 from Châteaudun to Chartres (on Rte de Vouvray).

Charges guide:
-- Per pitch incl. 1 person Ffr. 21.90, with electricity 31.85; 2 persons 31.85 or 43.80.
-- Plus VAT.
Open:
All year.
Address:
28800 Bonneval.
Tel:
37.47.54.01.
Reservations:
Contact site.

2900 Camping Les Mouettes, Carantec, nr Roscoff

Sheltered site in attractive bay, near to Roscoff ferry port.

Les Mouettes is less than 15 km. from the ferry port so is ideal for a short stay when heading to or from home. However, the area has plenty to offer for longer holidays for those who do not wish to drive far, with beautiful bays and many places of interest within easy reach. The site is comfortable and peaceful in a wooded setting with many attractive trees and shrubs, and there is access to a small beach at the front of the site. The 273 pitches, mostly of good size, are arranged in named groups, with electricity throughout (6A). The four sanitary blocks (unisex) are clean with free hot water to all facilities, with washbasins in cabins, mainly British WCs and a good supply of showers, all arranged in long rows. Baby bathrooms and facilities for the disabled. The centrally located bar has a terrace overlooking the heated swimming pool, water slide pool and children's pool. Discos and other entertainment are organised in the main season. Takeaway and shop. Volleyball. Minigolf. Table tennis. Games/TV rooms. Archery (July/Aug.) Children's play area. Small fenced fishing lake. Bureau de change. Laundry facilities. Mobile homes to rent. Used by British tour operators.

Directions: From the D58 Roscoff - Morlaix road, turn to Carantec. Site is 1 km. before the town, signed to the left.

Charges 1995:
-- Per pitch Ffr 75.00; person 27.00; child (under 15 yrs) 17.00; local tax 1.00; electricity 18.00.
-- Less 20% in low season, excl. electricity.
Open:
29 April - 25 September
Address:
29660 Carantec.
Tel:
98.67.02.46.
FAX: 98.78.31.46.
Reservations:
Write to site with deposit (Ffr. 200) and fee (120).

2903 Camping du Letty, Bénodet, nr Quimper

Family run site with high quality amenities and access to small beach.

Du Letty is personally run by the owner and is a select site built around a former farm, with excellent facilities. On the edge of the popular resort of Bénodet, it is not far on foot to the main beaches, but there is direct access from the site to an attractive small, sandy beach at the mouth of the river (safe bathing depends on the tides). There are over 500 pitches here, although the site does not appear large as they are arranged in small groups enclosed by neat, high hedges and trees. There is plenty of well kept, grassy space and almost all pitches have electrical connections, water and drainage. Sanitary facilities in seven modern blocks are of very good quality with washbasins in large cabins, controllable hot showers and bathrooms, both on payment. Baby rooms (3) and, in one block, facilities for the disabled. No swimming pool, but there is a fitness room, saunas, solarium, jacuzzi and tennis courts. Beautifully furnished library/reading room, hairdressing room, small launderette, games lounge with billiards and card tables, and attractive bar with satellite TV are also located in the converted farm buildings. Snack bar and takeaway. Activities and entertainment in high season. Children's play area. Basketball and volleyball. Motorcaravan and boat service point. Only 23 tour operator pitches. Reservations are not accepted but there is said to be usually space, although the site is only open over a short season.

Directions: From the D44 Bénodet - Fouesnant, follow signs to Fouesnant, then `Toutes Directions' sign - site sign follows very soon afterwards.

Charges 1996:
-- Per adult Ffr. 23.00; child (under 7 yrs) 11.50; pitch 36.00; car 11.00; m/cycle 8.00; electricity (1, 2, 5 or 10A) 10.00 - 26.00; water connection 5.00; local tax 2.00.
Open:
15 June - 6 September.
Address:
29950 Bénodet.
Tel:
98.57.04.69.
FAX: 98.66.22.56.
Reservations:
Not made.

LE VORLEN ★★★

F 29170 FOUESNANT
200 yds from a beautiful sandy beach which stretches for 2
miles and faces south.

In green and quiet surroundings - Heated Swimming Pool
Paddling Pool - Mobile Homes for Hire.

Nearby:

Large supermarkets - boat trips -
sailing school - tennis - riding -
many holiday trips

00 33 9894 97 36
(We speak English)

2901 Castel Camping Ty Nadan, Arzano, nr Quimperlé

Country site beside the River Ellé, with swimming pool.

Ty Nadan is situated deep in the countryside in the grounds of a country house,
some 18 km. from the sea. It offers 220 individual pitches (160 with electricity).
They are of good size on fairly flat grass, some on the banks of the river. The
two toilet blocks are of an unusual design with access from different levels and
are of fair quality (a reader reports maintainance is variable). They have mixed
British and continental WCs, and free hot water in the washbasins (in private
cabins), sinks and showers (with single pushbutton). Access for the disabled may
be a little difficult, although there are facilities in one block. Dishwashing
facilities are in the ladies' block (!) Laundry room with washing machines and
dryers. There are plenty of activities for young people here, including a heated
swimming pool (17 x 8 m. - caps compulsory) and children's paddling pool,
tennis courts and a restaurant, takeaway and bar. Table tennis. Trampolines.
Bicycles, skateboards, roller skates, boats for hire. Canoeing. Riding. Small
roller-skating rink. BMX track. Archery. Many organised activities for children
during season, particularly sports, exercises, excursions and guided canoe trips
and mountain bike tours. Across the road, by the attractive house and garden, is
minigolf, and in converted Breton outbuildings, a TV room and delightful
crêperie. Chalets for hire. Used by tour operators (10%).

Directions: Make for Arzano which is northeast
of Quimperlé on Pontivy road and turn off D22
just west of village at camp sign.

see advert in next
colour section

Charges 1996:
-- Per person Ffr. 26.00;
child (under 7) 18.00;
pitch 50.00; electricity
(6A) 14.00;
water/drainage 14.00;
dog 8.00.
-- Less 15-20% outside
July/Aug.
-- Credit cards accepted.
Open:
1 May - 7 September.
Address:
Rte d'Arzano,
29310 Locunolé.
Tel:
98.71.75.47.
FAX: 98.71.77.31.
Reservations:
Made for exact dates
with deposit (Ffr. 200)
and fee (100).

**Alan Rogers'
discount**
Less 5% on
pitch fee

2902 Camping International du Saint-Laurent, La Forêt-Fouesnant

Shady, attractively situated seaside site with various amenities, near Concarneau.

St. Laurent is a well established site, by the sea on a sheltered wooded slope at
the mouth of an estuary, with attractive views. There is direct access to two
small strips of beach, but at low tide the sea recedes from the estuary leaving a
large expanse of sand, mostly wet, and rocks. The best beach is about 800 m.
The site has a jetty in the estuary. The 280 pitches for tents or caravans are on
levelled terraces, under tall trees. They are divided into individual numbered
plots, not over-large. Many electrical connections. The sanitary installations are
in three tiled blocks of satisfactory quality with free hot showers, British and
continental WCs; washbasins, some in private cabins. Interesting sea water
swimming pools (good for crabbing!) have been replaced with a conventional
pool, children's pool and whirlpool. Torches are needed. Supermarket. Bar/snack
bar (mid-June-Sept) with takeaway (July/Aug). Volleyball, basketball. Small
children's playground. Two tennis courts. Table tennis. Golf 1 km. Washing
machines. Exchange facilities. Used by tour operators (40%).

Directions: Approach from Quimperlé either via N783 and Concarneau or via
Rosporden and D70; from Quimper via N783. Follow signs for Fouesnant but
turn left to Kerleven and camp before reaching town.

Charges 1995:
-- Per unit incl. 2
persons, and 3 services
Ffr. 75.00 - 125.00;
extra person over 7 yrs
15.00 - 25.00, under 7
7.20 - 12.00.
Open:
1 April - 30 September.
Address:
Kerleven, 29170
La Forêt-Fouesnant.
Tel:
98.56.97.65 or low
season 98.90.27.91.
FAX: 98.56.92.51.
Reservations:
Advised for July/Aug.
and made with deposit
(Ffr. 500) and fee (100).

2904 Camping Le Vorlen, Beg Meil, nr Quimper

Large, informal family site with pool, adjacent to sandy beach - family managed.

This spacious, unsophisticated site is on 24 acres of level ground in a rural setting and caters for a wide variety of tastes with good sized pitches providing a choice of sun or shade within a number of small 'bays' or meadows, which create an impression of tranquillity unusual in such a large site. Because of its size the site is seldom fully booked. The atmosphere is pleasantly cosmopolitan and the situation provides easy access (about 200 m.) to a long sandy south facing beach. Two thirds of the 600 pitches have electricity. There are two modern toilet blocks with ample showers, free hot water, individual wash cabins, British toilets, and numerous sinks for washing up. In the two original blocks, in the older part of the site near the entrance, the showers and basins have been modernised and baby baths provided (one unit for the handicapped). They have British style WCs, all with external entry. A swimming pool (open 20/6-10/9) and paddling pool have been built at the newer, opposite end of the site from reception. Mini market and takeaway (27/6-1/9). Launderette. Children's play area. Bar in season just outside site entrance with some regional music. English spoken in high season. No tour operators; 30 mobile homes for hire.

Directions: Follow signs to Beg Meil village; site is signed from there.

Charges 1995:
-- Per person Ffr. 21.00; child (under 7) 12.00; pitch 40.00; vehicle 8.00; electricity 12.00.
-- Less 20% outside 29/6-1/9.
Open:
1 May - 20 September
Address:
29170 Fouesnant, Beg Meil.
Tel:
98.94.97.36.
FAX: 98.94.97.23.
Reservations:
Write with deposit of Ffr. 250 (Eurocheque or credit card).

2905 Castel Camping L'Orangerie de la Lanniron, Quimper

Quiet site in the grounds of a riverside and parkland estate, 15 km. from the sea.

This is a peaceful, family site in an attractive, 15th century country estate on the banks of the Odet river. It is just south of Quimper, about 15 km. from the sea and beaches at Bénodet. The original outbuildings have been attractively converted around a walled courtyard which includes a heated swimming pool (144 sq.m.) with children's pool and a small play area. There are 199 grassy pitches on fairly flat ground laid out in rows alongside access roads; most with electricity and 32 with three services. The original sanitary block, on one side of the courtyard, is good, with free hot water. A second modern block serves the newer pitches at the other side of the site. They have facilities for the disabled and babies. Bar, snacks and takeaway, and restaurant in the beautiful XVIIth century Orangerie with attractive views across the gardens (reasonably priced and with children's menu). Karaoke is organised in season. General reading room. Games rooms. Billiards room. Golf driving range. Tennis court. Minigolf. Table tennis. Fishing. Archery. Bicycle hire. Children's adventure playground. Animation is provided with a large room for indoor activities; also canoeing and outdoor activities. TV/video room (cable and satellite). Shop. Washing and drying machines. Rooms in the château and 3 cottages in the park to let. The historic town of Quimper, with some attractive old areas, is under 3 km. and a hypermarket is 1 km. Site used by tour operators (<40%). Mobile homes for hire.

Directions: From Quimper follow 'Quimper Sud' signs, then 'Toutes Directions' and general camping signs, finally signs for Lanniron.

Charges 1996:
-- Per person Ffr. 26.00; child (2-6 yrs) 16.00; car 16.00; normal pitch (100 sq.m.) 46.00, with electricity 66.00, special pitch (140 sq.m. with water and electricity) 81.00, (140 sq.m. with 3 services) 86.00; animal 16.00.
-- Low season less 10%.
-- Credit cards accepted.
Open:
1 May - 15 September.
Address:
Château de Lanniron, 29000 Quimper.
Tel:
98.90.62.02.
FAX: 98.90.84.31.
Reservations:
Made with deposit (Ffr. 400) and fee (100).

29 Finistère

2906 Camping Caravaning Le Pil Koad, Poullan-sur-Mer, nr Douarnenez

Family run, small site just back from the sea in Finistère.

Pil Koad provides 200 pitches on fairly flat ground, marked out by separating hedges and of quite good, though varying, size and shape. Nearly all have electrical connections (10A). Trees provide shade in some areas. There are two toilet blocks, in modern style with British WCs (a few continental) and washbasins partly in private cabins but mostly not. Free, preset hot water in these and in the showers, which have pushbuttons. The site is 6 km. from Douarnenez, 5 km. from the nearest sandy beach. There is a heated swimming pool and paddling pool by the bar with attractive sunbathing patio, a tennis court and a large room for entertainment. Small shop (18/5-7/9). Two bars (from 1/6) with takeaway at times (restaurants in the village) and entertainment (discos, cabarets) in July/Aug. Table tennis. Minigolf. Volleyball. Mountain bike hire with weekly outings. Clubs are arranged for children in season (2/7-3/9). An obligatory daily charge is made for activities. Children's playground. Laundry. Mobile homes and chalets to rent. Used by British tour operators (10%).

Directions: Site is 500 m. from centre of Poullan on road to Douarnenez. From Douarnenez take circular bypass route towards Audierne; if you see road for Poullan at roundabout, take it, otherwise camp sign at Poullan turn from D765.

Charges 1996:
-- Per pitch Ffr. 70.00; extra person (over 7 yrs) 28.00; child (2-7) 16.00; electricity (10A) 22.00; local tax 1.00.
-- Low season less 40%.
-- Credit cards accepted.

Open:
8 April - 15 September

Address:
Poullan, 29100 Douarnenez.

Tel:
98.74.26.39.
FAX: 98.74.55.97.

Reservations:
Made for min. 1 week with deposit (Ffr. 300) and fee (120).

2907 Camping International de Kervel, Plonévez, nr Douarnenez

Pleasant spacious site close to sea near Douarnenez.

This site has developed well and is certainly worth considering for holidays in this area. It lies about 800 m. from the sandy Kervel beach and the resort of Douarnenez with its harbour is about 10 km. The site has 330 numbered pitches of good size on flat or very slightly sloping grass. They are mainly in small groups of 6 or so, in enclosures with plenty of grassy space and surrounded by tall hedges and trees. All pitches have electricity, some water and drainaway also. Many pitches are occupied by hire caravans and tents belonging to British operators but the design of the site gives reasonable privacy. The sanitary installations consist of two modern blocks, the newer being a particularly large one with facilities for the disabled and babies. British toilets, washbasins, mainly in private cabins; controllable showers. Amenities include heated swimming pools with water slide and children's pool. Well stocked shop (from late May). Spacious bar. Takeaway hot food. Tennis and minigolf (free). Games room, table tennis, bar billiards, pin-tables. Two children's playgrounds. Washing machine and dryer. Bicycle hire. Mobile homes and tents to hire.

Directions: Turn off D107 towards Kervel 8 km. east of Douarnenez and west of Locronan and follow signs to camp.

Charges 1996:
-- Per person Ffr. 25.00; child (1-10 yrs) 15.00; local tax 1.00; pitch 75.00; electricity (3A) 13.00; water 20.00.
-- Low season less 40%.
-- Credit cards accepted.

Open:
10 May - 15 September.

Address:
29550 Plonévez-Porzay.

Tel:
98.92.51.54.
FAX: 98.92.54.96.

Reservations:
Made with deposit (Ffr 300 per week) and fee (120); min. 1 week.

2908 Camping Le Panoramic, Telgruc-sur-Mer, nr Châteaulin

Family site in west Brittany, quite close to a good beach.

This medium sized site is on quite a steep hillside, with fine views along the coast. It is well tended and personally run by the owner. The 220 pitches are arranged on flat terraces, mostly in small groups with hedges and 20 pitches have services for motorhomes. A good sandy beach is around 700 m. downhill by road, a bit less on foot. The main site has a single well kept toilet block (so some up-and-down walking needed). Another very good one is opened for the main season, in an annexe across the road where there is also a heated swimming pool, child's pool and whirlpool (open 20/5-7/9). Mainly seatless WCs, some Turkish style, washbasins in cubicles with free hot water and hot showers. Facilities for the handicapped and also baby baths. Hot water for clothes and dish washing. Water points around. Small shop (20/5-7/9). Bar/restaurant with takeaway (15/6-31/8). Tennis, volleyball. Children's playground. Games room and children's club in season. Washing machines and dryers. Bicycle hire. Barbecue area. Mobile homes for hire. Used by a tour operator (10%).

Directions: From Telgruc town centre, take road with signs to camp and Trez-Bollec-Plage and continue to site on right.

Charges 1996:
-- Per person Ffr. 23.00; child (under 7) 12.00; pitch 50.00; car 10.00; m/cycle 8.00; electricity (6A) 20.00, (10A) 28.00; water 15.00.
-- Low season less 20%.

Open:
15 May - 15 September.

Address:
Rte de la Plage, 29560 Telgruc-sur-Mer.

Tel:
98.27.78.41.
FAX: 98.27.36.10.

Reservations:
Made for any period with deposit.

2909 Camping Le Raguénèz Plage, Névez, nr Pont-Aven

Well regulated, attractive site in small seaside village, with beach access.

This site is personally run by the owner who takes great pride in her site. She has planted many attractive shrubs and trees and all is kept very clean and neat. A sandy beach can be reached by footpath (300 m.) and there is a sailing school and small fishing port adjacent to the site. The 287 pitches all have electrical connections and are of good size, on flat grass, arranged in rows on either side of asphalt access roads, separated by hedges and trees. The sanitary facilities are in three well designed blocks of different size and are of very good quality. They provide British WCs, pre-set hot showers, washbasins in private cabins, plus free hairdryers and include good baby bathrooms and excellent facilities for the disabled. Hot water is free throughout. The site has a sauna and new heated swimming pool with terrace (from 1//5). Table tennis, volleyball, games room and animation are offered for children. A small bar and restaurant (open from 15/6) have an outside terrace, again with lots of flowers; breakfast is served here. Takeaway. Small shop (from 15/5, supermarket 5 km.). Good children's play areas. Reading, TV rooms and films. Laundry. Exchange facilities. Fishing and watersports near. Used by British tour operators (20%). Mobile homes for hire.

Directions: From the D783 Concarneau - Pont-Aven road go south to Névez. Site is signed from there, 5 km. on Raguénèz-Plage road.

Charges 1995:
-- Per unit incl. 2 persons Ffr. 99.00; extra adult 25.00; child (under 7 yrs) 13.00; electricity (2A) 15.00, (6A) 20.00; dog 8.00.
-- Low season less 20%.
Open:
1 April - 1 October.
Address:
Rue des Iles,
29920 Névez.
Tel:
98.06.80.69.
FAX: 98.06.89.05.
Reservations:
Recommended in high season; min. 7 days for July/Aug. Write with deposit (Ffr. 300).

2910 Camping du Manoir de Pen-ar-Steir, La Forêt-Fouesnant

Charming, small site for a quiet stay, with few on-site amenities.

Manoir de Pen-ar-Steir will appeal to those who prefer a quiet place to stay without lots of amenities and entertainment on the site. It is arranged on terraces up the steep sides of a valley in the grounds of an old Breton house and has a picturesque, garden-like quality, with lots of well tended trees and flowers, including a pond and stream. There are some steep slopes to reach most of the pitches, but they are all on flat, grassy, terraces with hedges around them. They are of reasonable size and all have electricity. Two main sanitary blocks, of a slightly older style but reasonable standard, have mixed British and continental toilets and cabins with basin and shower, plus washbasins in rows. The provision should be adequate. There are also a few facilities of an excellent, modern standard, including facilities for the disabled and heated in a small block behind the house. Washing machines and dryer are also there. The site has a tennis court and minigolf, plus children's playground on site but no bar, restaurant or shop (baker 50 m.), however the facilities of the town and nearby resorts are easily reached. Some site owned mobile homes and one British tour operator.

Directions: Signed on northeast edge of Forêt-Fouesnant, on D44 to Quimper.

Charges guide:
-- Per adult Ffr 22.00; child (under 7 yrs) 13.00; pitch/car 38.00; electricity 12.00; dog 4.00.
Open:
All year.
Address:
29133
La Forêt-Fouesnant.
Tel:
98.56.97.75.
FAX: 98.51.40.34.
Reservations:
Write to site for details.

2920M Camping Municipal du Bois de Pleuven, Saint Yvi

Set in forest surroundings, this large site has 280 pitches of varying size, most with electricity. They are very spacious and some provide a good degree of privacy. The two sanitary blocks have free hot water. On site facilities include 3 swimming pools, 1 large with 2 smaller ones, tennis courts, a football pitch, 2 children's play areas, a TV room with satellite, bar and takeaway, minigolf and washing machines. There is a small charge for some of the amenities. Chalets, caravans and mobile homes for hire. The site is situated between Concarneau and Quimper, 5 minutes from the coast.

Directions: From Quimper on D783 (Quimper - Concarneau) road, take left turn signed Pleuven (approx. 13 km. from Quimper). Continue along this road to camp site sign. Note: there is a convalescent home with the same name, approx. 50 m. along from the site.

Charges guide:
-- Per pitch Ffr. 19.50; adult 11.00; child (under 7 yrs) car 6.00; m/cycle 3.20; electricity 12.00.
Open:
All year.
Address:
29140 Saint Yvi.
Tel:
98.94.70.47.
FAX: 98.94.76.92.
Reservations:
Contact site.

29 Finistère

2911 Grand Camping de la Plage, Le Guilvenec, nr Pont l'Abbé

Friendly site, ideal for families, with access to good sandy beach.

Grand Camping is located on the edge of a long sandy beach between the fishing town of Le Guilvenec and the watersports beaches of Penmarc'h on the southwest tip of Brittany. This spacious site is surrounded by tall trees, which provide shelter, and is made up of several flat, sandy meadows. The 410 pitches are arranged on either side of sandy access roads, mostly not separated but all numbered. There is not much shade. Electricity is available on most pitches (2, 5 or 10A) and there is a motorcaravan service point opposite the entrance to the site. The 5 excellent sanitary blocks are of differing designs, but all provide modern, bright facilities including large, free, controllable showers, washbasins in cabins, British WCs and good facilities for children. Toilet for the disabled. As well as the obvious attractions of the beach, the site offers a heated swimming pool and child's pool, tennis courts and many other leisure facilities including volleyball, basketball, minigolf, golf practice, badminton, petanque, table tennis, giant chess/draughts, a sauna and bicycle hire. Fishing, watersports, riding near. Children's play area. TV room. There is a bright, airy and well furnished bar, with a crêperie and terrace overlooking the pool (all from 13/5). Takeaway. Laundry. Exchange facilities. Barbecues permitted. Entertainment is organised in season for adults and children. There is plenty to occupy one at this friendly site but the bustling fishing harbour at Le Guilvenec and the watersports of Penmarc'h and Pointe de la Torche are within easy travelling distance. Gates locked 22.30-06.30 hrs. Used by British tour operators (10%).

Charges 1996:
-- Per adult Ffr 20.00 - 29.00; child (under 7 yrs) 10.00 - 15.00; pitch incl. car 50.00 - 96.00; electricity 2A 10.00, 5A 16.00; local tax 1.00.
-- Credit cards accepted.
Open: 1 May - 30 September.
Address: Rue de Men-Meur, BP.9, 29730 Le Guilvenec.
Tel: 98.58.61.90; when closed: 98.58.14.14. FAX: 98.58.89.06.
Reservations: Recommended and accepted until 15/6 with deposit (Ffr. 300) and fee (120).

Directions: From Pont l'Abbé, take D785 road to Penmarc'h. Site is signed from there or from the D57 to Le Guilvenec, on the coast road between the two towns.

2912 Camping Manoir de Kerlut, Plobannalec, nr Pont l'Abbé

Developing site in grounds of manor house on river estuary.

Manoir de Kerlut is situated on the banks of a river estuary, 2 km. from the beaches of Lesconil and not far from the fishing and watersports opportunities offered by the southwest coast of Brittany. There are pleasant walks in the park and along the river bank. This new site, with strikingly modern buildings, has been constructed on flat grass near the house and was opened in 1990. It provides 240 pitches, all with electrical connections (5/6A), many with water and drainage also and has hardstandings available on 10 or so pitches. One area is rather open with separating hedges planted, the other part being amongst mature bushes and some trees which provide shade. Site amenities are of good quality, with a large modern bar with entertainment in season, and two heated swimming pools with children's pool. Well stocked small shop. Takeaway. Sauna, solarium and small gym. Tennis, volleyball, badminton, petanque. Children's play area. Games room. Bicycle hire. Exchange facilities. Laundry equipment. The sanitary facilities, in two very good blocks, provide controllable hot showers, washbasins all in cabins and British WCs. Facilities for babies and for the disabled are also provided and hot water throughout is free. Mobile homes to rent. The site is used by British tour operators (10%).

Charges 1996:
-- Per person 20.00 - 29.00; child (under 7 yrs) 10.00 - 15.00; pitch incl. car 50.00 - 96.00; electricity 2A 10.00, 5A 16.00.
-- Credit cards accepted.
Open: 14 May - 15 September.
Address: 29740 Plobannalec-Lesconil.
Tel: 98.82.23.89 FAX: 98.58.89.06.
Reservations: Write with deposit (Ffr. 300) and fee (120).

Directions: From Pont l'Abbé, on the D785, take the D102 road to Lesconil. Site is signed to the left, shortly after the village of Plobannalec.

see advert in next colour section

Thinking of travelling further afield on the continent?
Remember the GOOD CAMPS GUIDE - EUROPE

2913 Camping des Abers, Landeda

Attractively situated, family run site in western Brittany.

This 12 acre site is beautifully situated almost at the tip of the Ste. Marguerite peninsular, on the south shore of L'Aber Wrac'h. There are 200 pitches spread over some ten quite distinct areas, partly shaded and sheltered by mature trees. These areas have been landscaped and terraced where appropriate, on different levels to avoid any regimentation or crowding. All are easily accessed by good internal roads. Electrical points are available, with some special pitches for motorcaravans. Modern toilet blocks placed at strategic points, are clean and bright with cubicled washbasins, good showers (on payment), dishwashing sinks and fully equipped laundry. Facilities for the disabled and for babies have been added in a new block. Mini-market (July/Aug) and a van with organic vegetables daily. The site offers good takeaway dishes or there is an excellent restaurant almost next door. A splendid beach reached direct from the site has good bathing (high tide) or fishing, sailing and watersports and miles of superb coastal walks. Covered table tennis, good adventure playground, trampoline, TV room and new indoor games room. Live music twice weekly in high season. Fishing, watersports, tennis and riding close. 4 mobile homes for rent. Gates locked 22.30-07.00 hrs. Monsieur Le Cuff provides a friendly welcome.

Charges 1996:
-- Per person Ffr. 16.00; child (1-7 yrs) 8.00; pitch 24.00; car 6.00; electricity 11.00; dog 5.00.
-- Less 20% outside July/Aug.
Open:
1 May - 30 September.
Address:
29214 Landeda.
Tel:
98.04.93.35.
FAX: 98.04.84.35.
Reservations:
Write to site.

Directions: Cross Aber Wrac'h by D13 or D113, then from Lannilis follow signs for Ste. Marguerite and `camping'.

3002 La Petite Camargue, Aigues Mortes

Impressive site with large swimming pool on the edge of the Camargue.

This is a large site (480 pitches) with a huge swimming pool complex and other amenities to match, conveniently situated beside one of the main routes across the famous Camargue. Its convenience and position alongside this busy road is its one major drawback. It offers a variety of good sized pitches, regulalry laid out, with varying amounts of shade. The majority are set well back from the road. The swimming pool and adjacent bar/restaurant, shops, etc. are situated between the pitches and the road and are attractively designed, providing a wide range of facilities and activities. The several sanitary blocks are all of relatively old construction but have been refurbished to provide adequate, if not marvellous, facilities including a number of unusual combined showers and washbasins `en-suite' and British WCs.   Not only is the site conveniently situated for visiting the Camargue, it is also not far from the sea and beaches (3 km.) and other sport facilities and activities. Horse riding at the adjoining large riding stables. Children's play area. Tennis (charged July/Aug). Table tennis. Laundry facilities. Entertainment and activity programme and disco. Free bus service to beach (July/Aug). Mobile homes to let.

Charges 1996:
-- Per unit with 1 or 2 persons: standard pitch Ffr. 73.00 - 138.00, with electricity 90.00 - 160.00; extra person (over 4 yrs) 26.00; local tax 1.00; second tent or car 27.00; animal 13.00.
Open:
27 April - 21 September
Address:
30220 Aigues-Mortes
Tel:
66.53.84.77 or 66.53.86.56.
FAX: 66.53.83.48.
Reservations:
Write to site for details.

Directions: Site is just north of the Carrefore du Mole where the D62, the D979 and the road to Aigues-Mortes intersect, about 8 km. from Le Grau-du-Roi.

3003 Camping Abri de Camargue, Le Grau-du-Roi, nr Montpellier

Pleasant site with both indoor and outdoor swimming pools.

This is a well organized and agreeable site, which has two free swimming pools, one 250 sq.m. and a smaller, indoor heated one (12 x 6 m.) which is overlooked by the restaurant/bar (with heating and air conditioning) and sheltered terrace. The 300 flat pitches are said to average 100 sq.m., but there is some variation in size, and electricity and water are available on most. The site is now well shaded, with trees and flowering bushes quite luxuriant in parts. The six toilet blocks have British WCs, washbasins with free hot water in private cabins, and free hot water also in the adjustable showers and sinks. They may come under pressure when the site is full. There are facilities for dishwashing and laundry. The site is 800 m. from the nearest beach at Port Camargue and 2 km. from the one at L'Espiguette (in July and Aug. a free bus to L'Espiguette beach stops outside). There is a summer fair within walking distance which can be noisy until late. Le Grau-du-Roi is 1½ km. and the old town of Aigues-Mortes 9. TV room. Bar, restaurant, takeaway and shop. Children's playground. Petanque. Very good security. All facilities open or available when site is open. Tennis 800 m. Caravans and mobile homes for short or long let. Used by tour operators (15%). English spoken. Motorhome service point. Telephones.

Directions: There is now a road bypassing Le Grau-du-Roi from west as well as the approach from Aigues-Mortes. Turn left at sign to `Port Camargue' and `Campings' just northeast of Grau-du-Roi. At next crossroads go left again towards `Phare de l'Espiguette/Rive Gauche' and after 200 m. you come to site on right. If approaching via the D979 from north, turn onto D62 and D62A towards La Grande Motte at junction north of Aigues-Mortes.

Charges 1996:
-- Per unit incl. 1-6 persons and electricity Ffr 115.00 - 250.00, acc. to season.
-- Credit cards accepted

Open:
3 April - 23 October.

Address:
320 Rte. du Phare de l'Espiguette,
Port Camargue,
30240 Le Grau-du-Roi.

Tel:
66.51.54.83.
FAX: 66.51.76.42.

Reservations:
Only required for very high season (10/7-20/8) and made for min. 1 week. (Site will be happy to help with any length of stay - phone and talk to them).

3005 Camping L'Eden, le Grau-du-Roi, nr Montpellier

Good modern site close to beaches and Camargue, with swimming pool.

The Eden is a good example of a modern, purpose built 4-star site. It is on flat ground about 500 m. from a sandy beach, with 400 individual hedged pitches. The flowering shrubs and trees make it cool and very pretty. Shade is available on many of the pitches and electricity on most. Reservation is advisable for the main season. The five modern sanitary blocks are attractively designed and tiled blue or pink as appropriate! They have free hot water everywhere; toilets as so often in France are in shorter supply than washbasins, which are in cubicles or private cabins; free pre-set hot showers, some en-suite with washbasins. Unit with baby bath and full facilities for the disabled. There is a swimming pool (18 x 8 m.) with water chute and children's pool on site (from early May). Supermarket, boutique, bar and restaurant with takeaway (all open all season). TV room and meeting room. Half court tennis. Minigolf. Archery. Table tennis. New fitness centre with sauna and solarium. Sports area with volleyball and basketball. All activities on site are free. In high season organised events, sports, excursions, entertainment, etc. Mini club for children (23/6-1/9). Marina, with sailing lessons, and riding, tennis nearby. Bicycle hire. Laundry facilities. Free bus service to beach in main season. Some tour operators.

Directions: There is now a road bypassing Le Grau-du-Roi from the west, which is easier if towing a caravan, as well as the approach from Aigues-Mortes. Turn left at sign to `Port Camargue' and `Campings' just northeast of Grau-du-Roi and follow signs for `Phare de l'Espiguette' and after 200 m. right at second sign for l'Eden. **Note:** It is not the site with entrance where you turn; for l'Eden go hard right onto access road and a further 200 m. around corner to site on left (it is a busy access).

Charges 1995:
-- Per pitch incl. 2 persons: simple (small tents) Ffr. 111.00 - 152.00, with electricity and water 109.00 - 170.00, with drainage 128.00 - 193.00; extra person 10.00 - 30.00; extra car, small boat 20.00; extra small tent 15.00; local tax 1.00.
-- Less 20% for a 2 week stay outside 1/7-26/8 or 5% for 3 weeks in high season.
-- Credit cards accepted.

Open:
31 March - 4 October.

Address:
Port Camargue,
30240 Le Grau-du-Roi.

Tel:
66.51.49.81.
FAX: 66.53.13.20.

Reservations:
Sat.-Sat. high season only with deposit and fee. Write between 1/1 and 15/5.

HOTEL de PLEIN AIR L'EDEN ★★★★

Port-Camargue
30240 Le Grau du Roi
Tel 66 51 49 81

Shady pitches in a green environment only 500m from the beach.

Entertainment and activities throughout July and August with:
Shows, dancing, clowns, magicians, tea dances competitions and sports tournaments . . .

A team of `animateurs' will help you to discover all our free activities:
Fitness centre, UVA, swimming pools, sauna, mini golf half-court tennis, mini-club (open 23/6-1/09), archery table tennis etc . . .

3007 Camping-Caravaning Le Fief, Anduze

Rather unusual, unpretentious, family oriented site in the Cevennes.

Well situated for exploring this little known area, Le Fief has its pitches in three distinct areas - the first, with large separated pitches on level grass with good shade, the second, rather similar, but with somewhat smaller pitches (in both cases with 6A electricity throughout) and the third with pitches of varying size and shape, informally arranged in woodland, some with some without electricity. A good range of facilities includes a swimming pool, bar and open-air café/ restaurant and takeaway in main season, a fishing lake and with direct access to the river (about 200 m). This is an unpretentious site with the emphasis on family camping and competitive prices, with the possibility of a range of activities and excursions into the surrounding area. The two sanitary blocks are of a very acceptable standard with modern fittings including free hot showers, washbasins in private cabins, British and Turkish WCs, washing machine and open-air dishwashing sinks.

Directions: Following N110 southwards from Alès, follow signs for Anduze at St. Christol-lès-Alès. After 300 m. turn left towards Lézan, after 6 km. turn right at roundabout (after bridge) towards Atuech and site is signed on the right after approx. 1 km. From the south, leave the N110 at signs for Atuech and Lézan.

Charges 1995:
-- Per unit incl. 1 or 2 persons Ffr. 45.00 - 75.00; extra person 10.00 - 16.00; child (under 7 yrs) 5.00 - 8.00; dog 3.00 - 5.00; electricity 15.00.
Open:
Easter/1April - end Sept.
Address:
Massillargues-Atuech, 30140 Anduze.
Tel:
66.61.81.71.
Reservations:
Contact site.

N3010 Domaine de la Sablière, Saint-Privat-de-Champclos, nr Barjac

Spectacularly situated naturist site in the Cèze Gorges.

This site, occupying a much larger area than its 300 pitches might suggest, enjoys a spectacular situation and offers a wide variety of facilities, all within a really peaceful, wooded and dramatic setting. Pitches are grouped in three areas - `Mesange', at the bottom of the gorge, mainly for tents, alongside the river (good for swimming and canoeing), at various points close to the main access road, which is well surfaced but steep and winding, and in a newer area, `Pinson', near the top of the hill, the whole side of which forms part of the site. The pitches themselves are mainly flat on terracing with many of good size, with 3 or 6A electricity. There is a further area, `Fauvette', along the river for caravans. During high season cars are banned in some of the areas by the river but parking is provided some 100-200 m. away. All pitches are attractively situated among a variety of trees and shrubs. There are six good sanitary blocks with excellent free hot showers in typical open plan, naturist site style and washbasins (cold water). Washing up and laundry sinks are also open plan. Toilets are mainly the seatless type. Laundry has 2 washing machines and a dryer. An open air, covered restaurant (1/5-30/9) provides good value waiter service meals in an attractive setting and a takeaway service. A useful small café/crêperie has been added in the Fauvette area. A supermarket (28/3-30/9), charcuterie, bureau de change and swimming pool complex, dynamited out of the hillside and built in local style and materials, complete the facilties. The complex provides two large pools and a children's pool, sunbathing terraces, bar, sauna, TV room and a disco (about halfway up the hill).

This is essentially a family run and family oriented site. The owner/manager, Gaby Cespedes, and her team, provide a personal touch that is unusual in a large site and this no doubt contributes to the relaxed and very informal atmosphere. First time naturists would probably find this a gentle introduction into naturism without any pressure. Activities available at La Sablière are varied and numerous and include walking, climbing, swimming, canoeing, fitness track, fishing, archery, canoeing, tennis, minigolf, volleyball, badminton, boules (including special floodlit area), table tennis, pottery lessons, silk painting, bindery, yoga, etc. not forgetting the Indian Village! Activity and entertainment programme for adults and children (28/6-31/8). Mobile homes, caravans, chalets and tents to hire. You must expect some fairly steep walking between pitches, swimming pool complex, restaurant and supermarket and a torch would also be handy.

Directions: From Barjac take D901 for 3 km. Site is signed just before St. Privat-de-Champclos and is approx. 3 km. on narrow roads following signs.

Charges 1995:
-- Per regular pitch incl. 2 persons Ffr. 80.00 - 112.00, acc. to season; extra adult 15.00 - 27.00; child (under 8 yrs) 10.00 - 18.00; pet (not accepted in peak season) 10.00 - 18.00; extra car free - 15.00; leisure card (for activities) free - 6.00; electricity 6A 22.00; local tax (over 16 yrs) 1.00.
Open:
1 April - 9 October.
Address:
Saint-Privat-de-Champclos, 30430 Barjac.
Tel:
66.24.51.16 or 66.24.55.72.
FAX: 66.24.58.69.
Reservations:
Made with deposit (Ffr. 250 per week booked) and fee (110).

3006 Domaine des Fumades, Les Fumades, Allègre, nr Alès

Attractive, medium sized site with many activities and near thermal springs.

This is a very pretty site with large pitches (all with electricity) on flat grass, attractively laid out in bays amongst a wide variety of trees. There is less shade in the newer area at the top of the site. Located in the Cevennes, it is conveniently situated for excursions into the Ardèche, Provence, and the Camargue and within easy reach of the Mediterranean beaches. It has an extensive, varied activity and entertainment programme with a very attractive pool complex with two swimming pools and a children's pool, surrounded by terracing which provides ample sunbathing facilities. The pleasant restaurant and terrace is located in the attractive original Provencal style buildings, which also house the bar, takeaway, reception, shop and a small sanitary block serving the pool area. The two main sanitary blocks are central and provide free hot showers in cubicles with separators, including some with washbasin also, mainly British WCs, washbasins in cabins, baby baths, facilities for the disabled. Washing up and laundry facilities. Minigolf. Volleyball. Petanque. Children's playground. Library. American motorhomes are not accepted. Apartments, chalets and caravans for hire. One British and one Dutch tour operator use the site.

Directions: From Alès take the D16 through Salindres, continue towards Allègre until you see signs for Fumades (and the thermal springs) on the right.

Charges 1995:
-- Per pitch Ffr 42.00 - 63.00; person 17.00 - 26.00; child (0-7 yrs) 10.00 - 11.00; local tax 1.00; electricity (2A) 11.00 or (4A) 19.00; animal 10.00.
Open:
15 May - 30 September.
Address:
Les Fumades, 30500 Allègre.
Tel:
66.24.80.78.
FAX: 66.24.82.42.
Reservations:
Made with deposit (Ffr 700) and fee (120).

3002 Camping Le Mas de Reilhe, Crespian, nr Nîmes

Well established, small site with pool in southern hinterland between Alès and Sommiéres.

Although Crespian is within fairly easy reach of some of the well known places in the sunny south - about 25 km. from Nîmes and 40 km. from the sea at La Grande Motte, it is a little away from the usual through routes and might suit you if you want a quiet base in the countryside from which to make excursions. It has a swimming pool (open about early June - mid-Sept.) and child's pool and there are walks directly from the site. There are about 90 numbered pitches, most on flat grassy ground and hedged, with electricity, water and drainaway. Others, especially suitable for tents, are on levelled plots on a wooded hillside with a good tarmac access road and superb views. The three small sanitary units are quite satisfactory with British WCs, washbasins mainly in private cabins with hot water, and free hot showers at pre-set temperature. Small shop (others a short walk) and hot food service to take away or eat on the spot from 1/6. Volleyball. Pétanque. Table tennis. Tennis and fishing near. Some entertainment for children in high season. Barbeque areas. Although a peaceful site, it has a little bar for evening socialising. The site is now under new ownership - comments welcome.

Directions: Site is by N110 road just on southern edge of Crespian; watch carefully for the entrance.

Charges 1995:
-- Per person Ffr. 30.00; child (under 7 yrs) 15.00; pitch 50.00; supplement for 150 sq.m. pitch 25.00; dog 8.00; electricity (6 or 10A) 20.00.
Open:
15 May - 15 September.
Address:
30260 Crespian.
Tel:
66.77.82.12.
Fax: as phone.
Reservations:
Made with deposit and fee - contact site for details.

3001M Camping-Caravaning Domaine de la Bastide, Nîmes

This municipally owned but privately managed site has 230 large, hedged pitches on flat ground, 150 marked for caravans in circular groups with electricity (3, 6 or 16A), water and drainaway, and the others for tents. The site has a spacious feel with flowering shrubs and you should always be able to find a pitch. The copious sanitary installations consist of three blocks, one of which can be heated, with British WCs, washbasins in private cabins with shelf, most but not all with hot water, and free hot showers with single push-button at pre-set temperature (some with washbasins). Full facilities are provided for the disabled. Self-service shop. Public restaurant/bar with takeaway, open all year and catering for routiers-type lunches. Children's playground. Washing machines. Four neat studios and some caravans for hire (booking necessary). Tennis courts opposite, swimming pool, riding and golf nearby.

Directions: Site is 5 km. south of city centre on D135 road towards Aubord; well signed from junctions on ring road.

Charges 1996:
-- Per caravan incl. car, electricity (3A) Ffr 49.00 (1 person) - 142.00 (6); tent 33.50 (1 person) - 136.00 (6); extra person 21.00.
-- Credit cards accepted.
Open:
All year.
Address:
30900 Nîmes.
Tel:
66.38.09.21.
Reservations:
Contact site.

3015M Camping Municipal de la Laune, Villeneuve lès Avignon, Avignon

Ideally situated for those wishing to visit the historic city of Avignon but preferring to stay in a quieter area, this site will be an attractive proposition. With some of the biggest pitches we have ever seen, on well shaded, flat grass, this will appeal to those with larger units or those who appreciate space around them. The 127 pitches are marked and divided by hedges or trees and around 65% have 6-8A electrical connections, the rest being mainly intended for tents. The two sanitary blocks are modern, well maintained and offer British and Turkish WCs, roomy hot showers with divider, mirror, hooks, etc. and washbasins in private cabins, all tiled throughout. Dishwashing and laundry sinks, but at present no washing machine, although one is promised. There is a municipal swimming pool, tennis courts, horse riding, shops and restaurants close by, although the site has its own small snack bar and shop for essentials. Other on-site facilities include a TV lounge and a children's play area.

Directions: Take Nîmes road, N100, out of Avignon towards Bagnoles-sur-Cèze and turn right after the bridge over the Rhône. Take left road beside the river (D980) towards Roquemaure, then pick up signs for Municipal Camping.

Charges guide:
-- Per person Ffr. 19.00; child (3-7 yrs) 9.00; vehicle 11.00; caravan or large tent 17.00; motorcaravan 26.00; electricity 15.00.
Open:
1 April - 30 September.
Address:
Chemin Saint-Honoré, 30400 Villeneuve lès Avignon.
Tel:
90.25.76.06 (Office de Tourisme: 90.25.61.33. FAX: 90.25.91.55.
Reservations:
Recommended for July/Aug. and made with Ffr. 120 deposit.

3105M Camping Municipal Bélvèdere des Pyrénées, Saint Gaudens

This is a well organised, neat site with views to the Pyrénées, within walking distance of town. There are 96 pitches of average size on fairly level grass, most with electricity (4 or 6A) and partially separated by shrubs and trees, and also some small pitches for tents. A new, tiled sanitary block has large showers, (without shelf or divider), washbasins in private cabins, British type WCs, good dishwashing and laundry facilities; not all as clean as we would wish, but site was very full when visited in late July and very busy.

Directions: Site is west of the town off the RN117 road, signed from a small roundabout.

Charges guide:
-- Per person Ffr. 15.00; child (under 7 yrs) 7.00; pitch 18.00; electricity 4A 13.00, 6A 23.00.
Open:
All year.
Address:
31800 St Gaudens.
Tel:
61.89.15.78.
Reservations:
Contact site.

3203 Camping Château Le Haget, Montesquiou

Mature site in parkland setting on Pilgrims Route to Santiago.

Charm and a certain, if slightly faded, elegance seem to characterize this site which is situated in the grounds of a romantic-looking, restored château. The grounds contain a wide variety of mature trees, some of them immensely tall and impressive, as well as many of the more old fashioned and fragrant rose bushes. There are 100 good sized pitches on fairly level grass, about half with electricity. Although there are many big trees and shrubs, the site is not oppressive and shade varies. A secluded, hedged swimming pool with sunbathing area and separate, quite large children's pool, children's play area, table tennis, bicycle hire, occasional discos in the former stables and an `animation' programme provide entertainment for youngsters. The owners (who are Dutch although the site has a distinctly French atmosphere) arrange excursions to destinations such as the Pyrénées, Armagnac châteaux (including tastings!), etc. Sanitary facilities are perhaps unique in having the showers upstairs - the actual facilities including hot showers, washbasins, some continental style WCs, washing up sinks and washing machine, are mainly housed in wooden cabins within the large, old buildings, one of which was the original Orangerie. They are certainly not of the latest design but seem to operate satisfactorily and were very clean when seen in July. Small bar/restaurant serving a `menu of the day' in another of the original outbuildings. Tennis 2 km. Rooms, caravans, tents and chalets to hire.

Directions: From Auch take the road to Bayonne (124). After about 3 km. turn left on the D943 - Route des Bastides et Castelnaux. At Montesquoiu pass the village and turn left at camp site sign.

Charges guide:
-- Per person Ffr. 25.00; child (under 7 yrs) 15.00; pitch 35.00; car by unit 10.00; car in parking place 6.00; electricity (6A) 12.50; drainage 10.00; dog 6.00.
-- Less 25% outside 15/6-31/8.
Open:
15 May - 15 September
Address:
32320 Montesquiou.
Tel:
62.70.95.80.
FAX: 62.70.94.83.
Reservations:
Write to site for details.

3201 Le Camp de Florence, La Romieu

Pleasant site in undulating countryside of woods and fields of wheat and sunflowers.

A warm welcome awaits visitors to the Camp de Florence from its Dutch owners who have sympathetically converted the old farmhouse buildings to provide facilities for the site. There are now 139 pitches of 100 sq.m. plus, most with electricity, 3 with hardstanding and terraced where necessary, arranged around a large field (full of sunflowers when we visited), giving a feeling of spaciousness. The older pitches near the main buildings have good shade but it gets progressively less the newer the pitch. However, 25 of these are fully serviced and shade will develop. There are two toilet blocks, mixed male and female and one heated for winter use. They have British toilets, free hot water, showers with hooks, stools, and washbasins, some in cabins; they should suffice. Washing machine and dryer. A restaurant, for visitors as well as campers, provides a range of food plus a good value à la carte menu. It is only open at limited times in winter. The site also provides a swimming pool (open 15/5-30/9) built with a beach effect so one can walk in on 3 sides, a paddling pool, children's adventure play area, games area and pets area typical of Dutch owned sites. Barbecues are permitted. Takeaway. Games room. Tennis. Table tennis. Petanque. Volleyball. Clay pigeon shooting. Video shows. Discos. Picnics. Musical evenings. Excursions. Exchange facility. Shop in nearby village (bread available on site in season). The 13th century village of La Romieu is on the Santiago de Compostela pilgrim route and the collegiate church is well worth a visit (the views are magnificent from the top of the tower), as is the local arboretum, the biggest collection of trees in the Midi-Pyrénées. The Pyrénées are 2 hrs. drive, the Atlantic coast a similar distance. Fishing, riding, bicycle hire are all available nearby for those seeking a quiet holiday. Mobile homes and chalets for hire.

Charges 1996:
-- Per unit Ffr. 43.00, with water and drainage 54.00; person 21.00 - 32.00; child 0-3 yrs 8.00 - 11.00, 4-7 yrs 15.00 - 22.00; electricity 3A 15.00, 6A 20.00; dog 9.00.
-- Special prices for winter, groups, rallies.
-- Credit cards accepted.
Open:
All year.
Address:
32480 La Romieu.
Tel:
62.28.15.58.
FAX: 62.28.20.04.
Reservations:
Write or phone for information (English spoken).

Directions: Site is signed on the D931 Agen-Condom road 3 km. before Condom in the direction of La Romieu (D41).

LE CAMP DE FLORENCE 32480, LA ROMIEU, GERS
SUN ★ COMFORT ★ NATURE ★ WATER

The Gers – A county waiting to be discovered, an unspoilt landscape of rolling hills, sunflowers and historic fortified villages and castles. Peace, tranquility, the home of Armagnac, Fois Gras and Magret Duck. A four star campsite with bungalows, mobile homes and trigano tents for hire.

Tel 62 28 15 58   Fax 62 28 20 04

3205M Camping Municipal Julie Moignard, Masseube

Quiet and spacious, this site has free access to a large double swimming pool complex to suit all swimming needs. It has 150 flat pitches which are delineated by trees but not numbered. Sanitary facilities are a mixed bag - old, but clean. Hot showers and good new toilets plus a few old `calf-stretchers'. There is also a full sized football pitch adjacent to the site, table tennis room, boules area and shops within walking or cycling distance.

Charges guide:
-- Per pitch incl. 4 persons Ffr. 70.00; extra person 15.00; electricity (5A) 11.00.
Open:
1 July - 15 September.
Address:
32140 Masseube.
Tel:
62.66.00.09 or 62.66.01.75 (July/Aug).
Reservations:
Advised - contact site.

Directions: Take the D929 south from Auch and Masseube is 25 km. along this road. Turn left in the centre of the town and the site is 250 m. on the left.

N3204 Centre Naturiste Deveze, Gaudonville, nr Saint-Clar

Relaxed, well equipped naturist site in beautiful Gers countryside.

This is a well established and very pleasant site in 50 acres of lovely country-side. The 120 pitches, the majority with electricity and many terraced, are in several different areas. Most of the older ones are separated by mature hedges and trees, the newer ones with shrubs - the amount of shade available varies from area to area and some pitches are flatter than others. In many respects this site would be an excellent introduction to naturist camping, being quite 'laid-back' in terms of rules and regulations, but offering a wide range of activities for those that want them without any pressure to join in if you don't want to! Deveze has an attractive swimming pool complex with two pools and a children's pool and its own 4 acre lake for fishing (free) and woodland area. Other activities available include tennis, volleyball, boules, a children's play area, boating, badminton, archery, film shows and a small gym for working out. There is a small outdoor restaurant and takeaway, with quite a varied menu, and a well stocked shop. Two TV rooms, one satellite and one French. Sanitary facilities are in three blocks and include hot showers (communal), washbasins (cold water only, but hot tap nearby), British type WCs, hairdryers, all fitted out to a high standard and very well maintained. The ambience at Deveze is warm and friendly with the centrepiece bar and terrace in the original farm buildings somewhat reminiscent of an English country pub. Campers are encouraged to provide their own entertainment and we thoroughly enjoyed one of their shows on the outdoor stage. Mobile homes, bungalows and caravans for hire.

Charges guide:
-- Per adult alone Ffr. 38.30, with family 34.70; child 3-10 yrs 15.10, over 10 yrs 18.50; electricity 2A 11.40, 6A 22.80; dog 6.80.
-- Less 20% outside 20/6-20/9, except electricity.

Open:
All year (limited facilities Oct-May).

Address:
Gaudonville, 32380 Saint-Clar.

Tel:
62.66.43.86. FAX: 62.66.42.02.

Reservations:
Made with deposit. For further information phone (01522) 687447 (UK).

Directions: From Agen or Auch use the N21 to Lectoure and the D7 to St Clar. From St Clar take the D13 (site signed) to Gaudonville. From Montauban take the D928 southwest then the D77 at Beaumont de Lomagne for Gaudonville.

3301 Camping de la Dune, Pyla-sur-Mer, nr Arcachon

Busy site with pool and other amenities separated from sea by well known giant dune.

La Dune is a good example of a busy French family site. It is an informal, friendly, lively site and although the amenities are not luxurious, they are comprehensive and serve their purpose. From its situation at the foot of the enormous dune you can reach the beach either by climbing over the dune (a ladder goes up nearly to the top) or driving round, or you can use the free medium-size swimming pool at the far side of the site. The marked out pitches, some terraced but level, vary somewhat in size but nearly all are hedged and have shade from pine trees. Nearly half are caravan pitches with electricity, water and drainaway. Some of the roads on the site are quite narrow and parts are quite sandy. There are now three new, modern sanitary blocks and one small one, in addition to the existing one which has been refurbished to make roomy showers and washbasins en-suite. They should be a good provision with WCs of different types, individual basins with many in private cabins (with H&C) and a good supply of pre-set hot showers. Several small shops of different types. Pleasant little bar and restaurant which can get busy and noisy at times (opens June, all other facilities are all season), with takeaway also. Purpose built barbecue (individual ones not allowed). Fridges for hire. Riding. Open-air theatre. Organised sports, tournaments etc. mid-June to end Aug. Special children's playground with mini-club. Motorcaravan service point. Mobile homes and chalets for hire. English spoken in season. No tour operators.

Charges 1995:
-- Per unit incl. 2 persons: with tent Ffr 70.00 - 105.00; with caravan incl. electricity and water 90.00 - 125.00; extra person 20.00 - 30.00; extra child (under 7) 15.00 - 20.00; extra car 15.00 - 25.00; dog 5.00 - 15.00; local tax (over 18s) 1.10.
-- Credit cards accepted.

Open:
1 May - 30 September.

Address:
Rte. de Biscarrosse, Pyla sur Mer, 33260 La Teste.

Tel:
56.22.72.17. FAX: as phone.

Reservations:
Made for min. 1 week with 25% deposit and fee (Ffr. 120).

Directions: There is now a new road (D259) signed from the N250 to Biscarrosse and Dune du Pilat, just before La Teste, which avoids Pyla-sur-Mer. At end of new road turn right at roundabout onto D218 coast road. La Dune is second site on right.

3302 Camping de Fontaine-Vieille, Andernos-les-Bains, nr Arcachon

Large site on east side of Bassin d'Arcachon with swimming pool and frontage to Bassin.

Fontaine-Vieille is a large well established site with over 840 pitches on flat grassy ground, some with lovely views, in the residential area of the small town of Andernos. The site stretches along the edge of the Bassin d'Arcachon under light woodland. Pitches are individual ones marked by stones in the ground or newly planted trees, 540 with electricity. The several sanitary blocks, of rather unusual design, provide an adequate number of hot showers (perhaps on the small side), washbasins, some in private cabins and an increasing proportion of British WCs. Facilities for the handicapped and children. All the blocks are being refurbished (on a rota basis) to a high standard in terms of fittings and maintenance and cleaning when seen in July appeared to be very good.

A beach runs along the Bassin which can be used for boating when the tide is in. When it is out, it is sand and mud but they claim that bathing in the channels is still possible. On site there is also an unheated 15 x 12 m. swimming pool open all season, plus paddling pool (charged for - Ffr. 80 leisure card for entire stay). Self-service shop (from 1/6), bar with terrace and restaurant with takeaway also (all 15/6-31/8) - town shops, etc. near. Communal barbecue. 4 tennis courts. TV room. 2 children's play areas for little one, adventure area for older ones. Minigolf. Washing machines. Boats, sailboards and bicycles for hire. Organised sports. As good a value site as you will find round the Bassin. No tour operators when seen but mobile homes, chalets and bungalows to rent.

Directions: Turn off D3 at southern end of Andernos towards Bassin at camp sign.

Charges 1996:
-- Per unit with 2 persons Ffr. 60.00 - 80.00, with electricity (5A) 75.00 - 100.00, with water and drainage 85.00 - 120.00; extra person 12.00 -16.00; child (2-7 yrs) 10.00 - 13.00; extra tent or car 5.00 - 7.00; animal 5.00 - 7.00; local tax 1.10.
-- Credit cards accepted.
Open:
4 May - 22 September.
Address:
4 Bvd. Colonel Wurz, 33510 Andernos-les-Bains.
Tel:
56.82.01.67.
FAX: 56.82.09.81.
Reservations:
Any length with deposit (Ffr. 500) and fee (120).

☆ ☆ ☆

CAMPING CARAVANNING
FONTAINE VIELLE

4, Boulevard du Colonel Wurtz
33510 ANDERNOS-LES-BAINS
Téléphone: 56 82 01 67

On the edge of the beach, in the Arcachon Basin, in the heart of a pine and oak forest. Swimming pool. Mobile homes and chalets for hire/to rent. Ask for a Free Brochure.

3320M Camping Municipal de l'Eyre, Mios

This is a well kept site with 107 pitches and good basic facilities, close to Bordeaux, Arcachon and the Dune de Pilat. It abuts an extensive sports complex and has access to a large pool, with shops and restaurants in the village. Pitches are marked out on flat ground and many are well shaded. Reservation is advised mid-July to mid-August.

Directions: Mios is on the D3 Biganos - Belin road. Site is in the centre of the town on the west side of the road.

Charges 1995:
-- Per unit incl. 2 persons Ffr. 65.00; extra person 20.00; child (under 8 yrs) 10.00; electricity: (5A) 15.00.
Open:
All year.
Address:
B.P. 14, 33380 Mios.
Tel:
56.26.42.04.
Reservations:
Contact site.

3303 Airotel de l'Océan, Lacanau-Océan, nr Bordeaux

Pinewood site with swimming pools close to Atlantic beach.

This site has some 550 pitches, all under the tall trees of a pinewood and on very sandy soil - caravans often have to be installed by tractor. Plots are numbered and marked and some are now separated by newly planted hedges, mostly on a slight slope in either direction. There are 400 electrical connections available. The six toilet blocks are in modern style with washbasins in private cabins with free hot water and free controllable hot showers with two taps; the hot water supply is claimed to be particularly good here. Toilets are in four separate blocks with mostly British WCs. The total provision and maintenance are probably adequate, if somewhat hard pressed in high season. Facilities for the disabled. The sandy beach, partly naturist, is 800 m. away, the first half easy but the second part quite heavy going over the dunes. On site are two swimming pools, one heated with water toboggan and children's games. Supermarket, general shop and bar/restaurant (15/5-15/9). Takeaway. Tennis. Table tennis. Children's playground. TV room. Disco. Amusement machines. Washing machines. Used by tour operators (15%), plus large caravans and bungalows for hire. Special barbecue area. Lacanau-Océan has many weekend visitors from Bordeaux.

Directions: Site is on the north side of Lacanau-Océan; follow signs in town.

Charges 1996:
-- Per unit incl. 2 persons: tent Ffr. 135.00, with electricity 150.00; caravan or trailer tent 140.00 - 160.00; extra person 28.00; extra car or tent 22.00; local tax 2.20.
-- Less in low seasons.
-- Credit cards accepted.
Open:
1 May - 30 September.
Address:
33680 Lacanau-Océan.
Tel:
56.03.24.45.
FAX: 57.70.01.87.
Reservations:
Made for Sat. to Sat. with deposit (Ffr. 500) and booking fee (120).

A fine 4-star camp on the AQUITAINE COAST

AIROTEL DE L'OCÉAN

33680 LACANAU-OCÉAN   Tel: 56 03 24 45   Fax: 57 70 01 87

Aquatic Space - Tennis - Shopping Centre - Disco

30% reduction on camp charges outside 15 June to 31 August or

30% for min. 2 weeks outside 1 July - 25 August booked in advance.

Caravans, Mobile Homes, Bungalows and Trigano Tents for hire

3304 Camping-Caravaning Int. Les Viviers, Claouey, nr Arcachon

Large site on the peninsular of Cap Ferret, with frontage to the Bassin d'Arcachon.

Les Viviers is a pleasant pinewood site covering a large area, divided by sea water channels and lakes which have been developed to form a positive feature of the site. Sluice gates allow the water level to be maintained so that bathing from the sandy beach, fishing and use of non-powered boats is possible within the site (swimming instructor/lifeguard). There are 980 numbered pitches, some in more open situation than others, level and grassy (sandy), with pinewood shade and electricicty in all parts. There are twelve toilet blocks, the largest four of which have recently been completely and stylishly rebuilt to a high standard and the others refurbished. They have British WCs, washbasins with shelf and mirror (some in cabins) and have free hot water in these and the showers and sinks. A commercial area near the entrance provides shops, restaurant, bar, takeaway and other facilities (from 15/6), with a little train (Petit TGV), a feature of the site, running in the high season. General room. Cinema. Crêperie. Disco. Minigolf. Children's play area. Sports organiser (from 1/7). Bicycle hire. Motorcaravan service point. Washing machines and dryers. The Atlantic beaches are only ten minutes run away so, with the Bassin d'Arcachon (tidal), there are good facilities for all watersports activities. A few tour operator pitches (5%).

Directions: Site entrance is on D106 road 1 km. south of Claouey.

Charges 1996:
-- Per unit, with up to 3 persons Ffr. 145.00, if booked - 160.00, if not, tent, 135.00 or 150.00; extra person (over 2 yrs) 21.00; local tax (over 7 yrs) 1.10; extra car or boat 22.00; dog 13.00; electricity (6A) 21.00.
Open:
1 May - 30 September.
Address:
Claouey,
33950 Lège-Cap Ferret.
Tel:
56.60.70.04.
FAX: 56.60.76.14.
Reservations:
Min. 1 week with deposit and fee.

3305 Camping Les Ourmes, Hourtin

Conveniently situated site close to lake, providing good value.

Situated only 500 m. from the largest fresh water lake in France, only 10 minutes drive from the beach and with its own pool, this is essentially a holiday site. Pitches, marked but in most cases not actually separated, are situated amongst tall pine trees giving good shade. There are 300 pitches in total, some with electricity. There is a medium sized swimming pool (15/5-10/9) with paved sunbathing area and separate large 'leisure' area including a children's play area, volleyball and basketball courts and table tennis tables (under cover). There is an evening entertainment programme, TV room, games room, bar/snack bar serving snacks and takeaway meals (10/6-10/9) and a shop (1/6-15/9). Watersports are possible on the lake. Sanitary facilities in three purpose built blocks are of a good standard with free hot showers (with hooks, shelf, but no separated dressing area), some washbasins in cabins and British type WCs. This site had a busy, cosmopolitan feel, with visitors of many different nationalities when we visited but no tour operators. Although not the most luxurious site in the area, it seems to offer good value.

Directions: Follow Route du Lac from the town centre and site is signed.

Charges 1996:
-- Per unit incl. 2 persons Ffr. 94.00; extra person (over 2 yrs) 16.00; extra small tent or extra car 10.00; dog 10.00; electricity 6A 18.00; local tax (over 10 yrs) 1.10 - 3.30.
Open:
1 April - 30 September.
Address:
Av. du Lac, 33990 Hourtin.
Tel:
56.09.12.76.
FAX: 56.09.23.90.
Reservations:
Necessary in high season.

CAMPING–CARAVANING **LES OURMES** ★ ★ ★

AVENUE DU LAC   33990 HOURTIN
Tel 56 09 12 76   Fax 56 09 23 90

Swimming pool – Snack Bar – Bar – Laundry – Sports field (1ha.)

IN HIGH SEASON:

- Sports competitions for children and adults
- Evening entertainment 2 or 3 times a week
- Guided tours to the Châteaux of the Médoc

3307 Camping-Caravaning L'Amelie Plage, Soulac-sur-Mer

Relaxed, wooded site south of Royan with direct access to the beach.

Amelie is a large family site in pine woods bordering a wide sandy beach where bathing is supervised only in season, but is said not to be dangerous. A popular site with continentals, there are no British tour operators. It is divided into two sections providing a total of 527 pitches of about 100 sq.m. The main section with the shop and bar provides a wide choice of pitches due to the undulating nature of the site. Some are on level ground, others on terraces and all are well shaded and fairly accessible (access roads are windy and narrow in some places). The newer section, bordering the beach, has more sun and rather more sandy pitches. The five toilet blocks are of reasonable standard but could be under pressure at peak times. Continental style toilets, rather less in total compared to showers and basins. The cabins with basins are rather small but adequate, chain operated warm showers. Well stocked self service shop. Pizzeria, snackbar and restaurant with takeaway. Entertainment in season. Children's play area. Table tennis. Boules. Barbecue area. Telephones. Well equipped laundry van near reception. Riding and tennis nearby. Caravans for hire.

Directions: Site is 4½ km from Soulac-sur-Mer in the village of L'Amelie Plage and signposted from the D101. There is a short stretch of poorly made up road before reception.

Charges 1995:
-- Per unit incl. 2 persons Ffr 79.00; extra person 14.00; extra tent or car 10.00; visitor 10.00; electricity (4A) 18.00, (6A) 21.00, (10A) 24.00; local tax 1.10 (over 10s).
-- Low season less 15%.
Open:
Easter - October.
Address:
33780 Soulac-sur-Mer.
Tel:
56.09.87.27 or 56.09.85.26.
FAX: 56.73.64.26.
Reservations:
Made with deposit (Ffr. 340) and fee (60).

3306 Camping Palace, Soulac-sur-Mer, nr Royan

Large uncrowded site close to beach, south of Royan.

This big, flat site has good-sized individual pitches regularly laid out. Those for tents are on very sandy ground, but those for caravans are on hardstandings, all amongst tall pines providing good shade with electricity available. Reservations are made for all and would be needed to make sure of finding a place in the main season. There are twelve small, separate toilet blocks with facilities in private cabins, British WCs, free pre-set hot showers and facilities for the disabled in one new block. English is spoken. It is a more formal site than no. 3307. A wide beach is 400 m. from the site gates and bathing, said not to be dangerous in normal conditions, is controlled by the site's lifeguards. However, the site now has its own swimming pool, also with lifeguards, which is attractively set in a part grass, part tiled area with its own shower facilities, etc. Shops (1/6-10/9). Restaurant (15/6-10/9). Bar with dancing and concerts. Tennis. Supervised children's playground with paddling pool. Programme of sports, entertainments and excursions in July/Aug. Washing machines. Treatment room and doctor will call. A few tour operator pitches (5%); mobile homes for hire.

Directions: Site is well signed 1 km. south of Soulac. The shortest and simplest way is via ferry from Royan across the Gironde estuary to Pointe de Grave, but this is unreasonably expensive with a caravan. Alternatively go via Bordeaux.

Charges 1996:
-- Per person (over 3 yrs) Ffr. 18.00 - 24.00; local tax1.50 - 1.85; caravan incl. electricty, water 50.00 - 67.00, drainage 52.00 - 69.00; tent 34.00 - 45.00.
-- Credit cards accepted.
Open:
1 April - 30 September.
Address:
B.P. 33, Bd. Marsan de Montbrun, 33780 Soulac-sur-Mer.
Tel:
56.09.80.22.
FAX: 56.09.84.23.
Reservations:
Made for min. 1 week with deposit.

3308 Camping de la Barbanne, St Emilion, nr Libourne

Satisfactory, friendly site in fine wine region 40 km. east of Bordeaux, with pools.

La Barbanne has some 160 unmarked pitches on flat grass. The older parts of the site nearest the lake have tarred access roads, good shade, electricity and generally pleasant surroundings; newer parts are on a more open area with very young trees and gravel access roads. Electrical connections should be extended to all pitches by 1996. With little shade in the newer area, the older section fills up quickly in the main season. The site has two toilet blocks. The original block, in the older part of the site, was refurbished in 1994 and is in constant use. The other, more modern, block is at one end of the newer meadow and is opened in high season. Both provide British WCs, washbasins (some in private cabins) and showers, all with free hot water. Small swimming pool plus water slide pool (June-Sept). Small shop. Grill room/bar plus takeaway (July/Aug). Two tennis courts, volleyball, table tennis, bicycle hire and minigolf. Fishing in lake on site. Some mobile homes for hire. Used by tour operators (30%).

Directions: Site is 3 km. north of St Emilion on Lussac road. St Emilion bars caravans so use D243 from Libourne or from Castillon on D936 via D130/D243.

Charges 1996:
-- Per adult Ffr. 20.00 - 21.00; child (under 7) 12.00; pitch 30.00 - 35.00; electricity (6A) 15.00.
Open:
1 April - 30 September.
Address:
33330 St. Emilion.
Tel:
57.24.75.80.
Reservations:
Made for min. 4 days without deposit.

3401 Camping Lous Pibols, La Grande Motte, nr Montpellier

Site with good installations, close to sea and yachting resort.

La Grande Motte, 7 km. west of Le Grau-du-Roi, has been turned into a very large yachting marina. Camping Lous Pibols, on the edge of the resort, is neatly laid out and has first class sanitary installations with British toilets, individual basins in private cabins with shelf and mirror, free hot water for showers and for washing up and clothes sinks. Except for a small section for short visits, the camp is divided into marked-out and numbered pitches of fair size (100 sq.m.), mostly well shaded and on firm ground with sandy topsoil (there are tarred access roads with flat and easy access). Electricity is available on caravan pitches. From late June to late August early arrival may be needed to find a place. The beach here is 300 m. from the camp (you can also take the car and park alongside). It is a long sandy one, with gentle slope and safe bathing, though the loose sand may blow about at times. Self-service shop, restaurant/bar and takeaway (May-Aug). TV room. Table tennis. Washing machines. Children's playground. Swimming pool (open 15/6-1/9) with paved sunbathing terrace and a snack bar on site. Doctor calls. Mobile homes for hire.

Directions: Site is well signed at La Grande Motte.

Charges 1995:
– Per pitch incl. up to 3 persons, with electricity, water and drainaway Ffr. 169.00, extra person 29.00; local tax 1.00.
– Less 20% outside 1/7-1/9.
Open:
1 April - 30 September.
Address:
34280 La Grande Motte.
Tel:
67.56.50.08.
Reservations:
Not made.

3403 Camping International Le Napoleon, Vias Plage

Smaller family site bordering the Mediterranean at Vias Plage.

The town of Vias is in the wine-growing area of the Midi, an area which includes the Camargue, Beziers and popular modern resorts such as Cap d'Agde. The single street that leads to Vias Plage is hectic to say the least in season, but once through the new security barrier and entrance to Le Napoleon, the contrast is sublime! - tranquillity, yet still only a few yards from the beach and other attractions. Not that the site itself lacks vibrancy, with its own pool (open from 15 June), bar and extensive entertainment programme, but thoughtful planning and design ensure that the camping area is quiet, with good shade from the many tall trees. The 200 partially hedged pitches, most with electricity, vary in size from 80-100 sq.m. and two of the three sanitary blocks have been refurbished to a high standard, including British WCs, washbasins in private cabins, baby bath, laundry and facilities for the handicapped, all well maintained when seen in peak season. The site has its own well stocked supermarket and there are plenty of other shops, restaurants, etc. all immediately adjacent. Activities and facilities include volleyball, bicycle hire, boules and TV. Chalets, mobile homes and apartments to let.

Directions: From Vias town, take the D137 towards Farinette beach. Site is on the right near the beach.

Charges 1995:
– Per pitch incl. 1 or 2 persons and electricity Ffr. 90.00 - 126.00, full services 118.00 - 168.00; extra person 18.00 - 27.00; extra tent 12.00 - 16.00; local tax 1.65, 0.85 per child.
Open:
Easter - 30 September.
Address:
Farinette Plage, 34450 Vias sur Mer.
Tel:
67.21.64.37.
FAX: 67.21.75.30.
Reservations:
Taken from 1 Jan. with deposit (Ffr. 500) and fee incl. cancellation insurance (170).

3404 Camping Lou Village, Valras-Plage, nr Beziers

Good value site with direct access to beach and bathing lagoon.

Valras is perhaps smarter and is certainly larger than nearby Vias but, although there are several campsites, our choice of Lou Village has been influenced by several factors - direct access to the beach, a rather unusual lagoon for bathing (with lifeguard) and in another part windsurfing, a new swimming pool with quite elegant terrace bar/restaurant (serving a wide range of meals), and cost. Prices at Lou Village are quite competitive and may provide better value than other sites in the area. Like all the better sites in the area, Lou Village becomes crowded in the high season.

The pitches further inland are partly separated by tall trees which provide good shade. Nearer the beach the pitches are smaller, many separated by bushes, bamboo hedges, etc. The site has many attractive features and a pleasant, relaxed atmosphere. It is let down somewhat by the sanitary blocks, which provide a few continental style WCs, although mostly Turkish, free hot showers in cabins without separators. They do have about half the washbasins in private cabins. Considering the heavy use of a beach site, the maintenance (in July) seems satisfactory. Takeaway. Shop. Tennis. Volleyball. Boules. Minigolf. Football field. Children's playground. Bathing and wind- surfing (with school) lagoons. Entertainment and organised activities, with lots to do on and off the site. English spoken. A few tour operator pitches (5%), plus mobile homes and tents for hire.

Directions: Site is south of Beziers. From autoroute, take Beziers-Ouest exit for La Yole and Valras Plage. Continue for 13-14 km. Sign to Lou Village is just past Camping de la Yole before the built up area of Valras Plage.

Charges 1995:
-- Per unit incl 2 persons Ffr. 115.00, 3 persons 130.00, 4 persons 145.00; extra person (over 7 yrs) 16.00 (under 4 free); extra car 13.00; electricity 17.00; dog 15.00; local tax 1.70 (over 4 yrs).
-- Less 30% outside July/Aug.
-- Credit cards accepted.

Open:
1 May - 20 September.

Address:
B.P. 30,
34350 Valras-Plage.

Tel:
67.37.33.79.
FAX: 67.37.53.56.

Reservations:
Made with deposit (Ffr. 700).

N3405 Camping Naturiste Le Mas de Lignieres, Cesseras, nr Olonzac

Small, rural site with pool and very large pitches, in the hills of the Minervois.

Only 3 km. from the medieval town of Minerve with its Cathar connections, parts of the site enjoy some marvellous views to the Pyrénées, the Corbières and the coast at Narbonne. It provides 50 large (200 sq.m.) pitches, all with electricity (6A), with 25 designated 'grand-confort' with water and waste water connections also. They are on mainly level grass, separated by small hedges. Some smaller pitches (100 sq.m.) are available for tents, with cars parked elsewhere. There is some shade, although as the site is fairly new, the many trees are mainly young, and there is a variety of flora, including four types of orchid. Within the confines of the site there are some good walks with superb views and, although the camping area is actually quite small, the very large pitches and young trees and hedges give an impression of spaciousness and freedom, creating a very relaxing ambience and a nice introduction to naturist camping. The attractive swimming pool (15/6-30/9) has a paved area for sunbathing and a new children's paddling pool. Tennis, volleyball and boules courts (all free). A small shop sells the usual range of essentials (including fresh bread and croissants to order) plus local specialities. Although at present there is only a bar/snackbar, a restaurant is planned for future years. Sanitary installations are presently being upgraded and expanded and include hot showers in cabins, British WCs, washbasins, washing up and laundry sinks (H&C) and washing machine. Children's playground. Sailing, riding, canoeing, bicycle hire near. Mobile homes and caravans for hire. No dogs allowed.

Directions: From A61 autoroute take Lezignan-Corbières exit, through the town via the D611 to Homps, then via the D190 to Olonzac. Go through the village following the signs to Cesseras, from where the site is signed.

Charges 1995:
-- Per large pitch, incl. 2 persons and electricity, water and drainage Ffr. 108.00; smaller pitch 78.00 (electricity 18.00); extra person 18.00; child (2-7 yrs) 12.00; extra car or tent 11.00.
-- Less 10% outside 1/7-1/9.
-- Credit cards accepted.

Open:
All year.

Address:
Cesseras-en-Minervois,
34210 Olonzac.

Tel:
68.91.24.86.
FAX: as phone.

Reservations:
Made until 25/6 with deposit (25%) and fee (Ffr. 70).

3406 Hotel de Plein Air L'Oliveraie, Laurens

Site with many attractive features at the foot of the Cevennes.

This lively site has a lot to offer in terms of activities, particularly those for youngsters, including plenty of evening entertainment in the high season. Most of the 120 pitches are large (up to 150 sq.m. in some parts). Arranged in rows on two levels, those on the higher level being older and with more shade from mature trees (mainly olives), all have electricity (6 or 10A). The ground is stony. The large leisure area, slightly apart from the pitches, includes a good sized pool and children's pool (open 1/6-30/9), with an attractive paved sunbathing area, tennis court and tennis practice wall, volley- ball, basketball, minigolf, children's play area and adjoining riding stables. Overlooking is a large terrace with a bar/restaurant serving simple grills in the high season. At other times there is an indoor bar, also used as a lounge for films and activities for younger children. There is a small well-stocked shop. The two sanitary blocks, one on either level, have modern fittings, including hot showers with dividers, washbasins in cabins, British WCs, covered dishwashing areas and a washing machine. All were perfectly adequate and clean when seen in high season, but perhaps in need of some 'TLC' in terms of maintenance.

Directions: Signed from D909 Beziers-Bedarieux road, 2 km. north of Laurens.

Charges 1995:
-- Per unit without electricity: 1 or 2 persons Ffr. 36.00 - 54.00, 3 or 4 persons 46.00 - 65.00, 5 or 6 persons 56.00 - 75.00; with electricity 54.00 - 72.00, 64.00 - 83.00 or 74.00 - 93.00.

Open:
All year.

Address:
34480 Laurens.

Tel:
67.90.24.36.
FAX: 67.90.11.20.

Reservations:
Contact site.

3500 Ferme-Camping Le Vieux Chêne, Dol de Bretagne

Attractive, family owned farm site between St Malo and Mont St Michel.

This site has been built around a farmhouse which dates from 1638. It offers 200 good sized pitches on gently sloping grass, most of which have electricity, water tap and light. They are separated by bushes and flowers, with mature trees for shade. A very attractive tenting area (without electricity) is located in the orchard. Two modern, unisex sanitary blocks have British toilets, pre-set showers, washbasins in private cabins, a baby room and facilities for the disabled. There is also an older block, which is rather basic, but was very clean when we visited. Small laundry room. Medium size, heated swimming pool, with children's pool (open 15/5-15/9, no shorts allowed) with lifeguard in attendance during July/Aug. TV room (with satellite), table tennis and pool table. Other facilities include a tennis court, trampolines (no safety matting), crazy golf, giant chess set and a small children's play area on grass alongside the lake, to be fenced for 1996. There is also a bar, café, takeaway (15/6-15/9), small shop (supermarket 3 km. in Dol) and a farm shop with organic produce and delicious home made jams. Fishing is possible in the two lakes. Some entertainment is provided in high season. Madame Trémorin opens the old farm house to campers to look around on demand. Wooden chalets (4) and gites (4) for hire. Used by British and Dutch tour operators (10%).

Directions: Approaching from Avranches on the N175, continue south on the N176 in the direction of Dinan-Dol and take Dol-Est/Baguer-Pican exit. This exit is 3 km. from the site which is signed.

Charges 1996:
-- Per unit Ffr. 38.00 - 46.00; adult 22.00 - 28.00; child (under 7 yrs) 11.00 - 14.00; electricity 16.00.

Open:
Easter - 30 September.

Address:
Baguer-Pican, 35120 Dol de Bretagne

Tel:
99.48.09.55.
FAX: 99.48.13.37.

Reservations:
Contact site.

 Alan Rogers' discount
Less 5% in high season

3503M Camping Municipal de Paron, Fougères

Paron is a neat, green, municipal site with a relaxed atmosphere which makes a useful staging point on the routes from St. Malo, Cherbourg, Le Havre etc. It is modern and has a well kept air. The 90 pitches are all individually marked and of good size, some being separated by rows of bushes and trees. Most are on flat grass with several hardstandings. The good sanitary block has British WCs, washbasins, partly in private cabins, and large showers with hot water between the hours: 7-10 am, 12-2 and 7-10 pm. No shop (baker 500 m.) Tennis and minigolf nearby. American motorhomes not accepted. The site has had good reports from readers. Office open 9-11 am and 5-8 pm.

Directions: Site is 300 m. east of the eastern bypass on minor road D17 to La Chapelle-Janson. Easiest approach is from bypass; some camp signs from town centre but easy to miss.

Charges guide :
-- Per adult Ffr. 12.00; child (under 7 yrs) 6.00; pitch 13.50; car 8.00; electricity 5A 15.00, 10A 18.50.

Open:
1 April - 30 September.

Address:
35300 Fougères.

Reservations:
Write to site.

3502 Castel Camping des Ormes, Epiniac, nr Dol-de-Bretagne

Impressive site on an estate of wooded parklands and lakes, with 18 hole golf course.

This site is in the northern part of Brittany, about 30 km. from the old town of St Malo, in the grounds of the Château des Ormes. It has a pleasant atmosphere, busy in high season but peaceful at other times, with a range of facilities. The 450 pitches are divided into a series of different sections, each with its own distinctive character and offering a choice of terrain - flat or gently sloping, wooded or open. There are electrical connections (3/6A) on 200 pitches. An `Aqua Park' with heated pools, toboggan, waterfalls and jacuzzi (free) overlooks a small lake with pedaloes and canoes for hire. The pools are sheltered by the bar and restaurant buildings, parts of which are developed from the original, 600 year old watermill. A particular feature is an 18 hole golf course; also a golf practice range and a beginners 5 hole course. Shop. Takeaway. Games room. Bar and disco, recently refurbished. Minigolf. Bicycle hire. 2 tennis courts. Fishing. Paintball. Archery. Horse riding on site. Sanitary installations are of a good standard, providing British style WCs, washbasins in private cubicles, pre-set hot water in showers and sinks, at no charge. Ample facilities for the disabled. The site reports the addition of a motel adjacent. A popular site with British visitors and tour operators (45%).

Charges 1996:
-- Per person Ffr. 29.00; child (under 7) 15.00; pitch 87.00; electricity 3A 16.00, 6A 18.00; water and drainage 5.00; animal 5.00.
-- Less 10% outside July/Aug.
Open:
15 May - 15 September.
Address:
35120 Dol-de-Bretagne.
Tel:
99.73.49.59.
FAX: 99.73.49.55.
Reservations:
Made for minimum of 1 week - details from site.

Directions: Access road leads off the main N795 about 7 km. south of Dol-de-Bretagne at Le Pont Melin.

3504 Camping Le P'tit Bois, St. Jouan des Guérêts, nr St. Malo

Busy, well kept site near ferry port and yachting centre of St. Malo.

This flat, grassy, family oriented site is situated on the outskirts of St. Malo, ideal for one night stops or for longer stays in this interesting area. Le P'tit Bois is very neat and clean, with 160 pitches, nearly all with electricity (5A), divided by hedges into groups and separated by shrubs and flowers. Some are under trees giving shade. There is one main sanitary block, a little open in cool weather, but providing good quality facilities with British WCs, washbasins all in cabins with mirrors, shelves and lights and modern, preset showers. Laundry facilities are available (in the ladies' block). Free hot water throughout. There is a bright restaurant, with takeaway food and swimming pools with terrace and water slide. Good children's playground and games room. Small shop. Minigolf. Tennis. Volleyball. Bicycle hire. Service point for motorcaravans. There are many British tour operators here (30%) and site-owned mobile homes, but this does mean that the facilities are open over a long season.

Charges 1995:
-- Per person Ffr. 26.00; child (under 7yrs) 16.00; pitch 70.00; extra car 20.00; electricity (5A) 18.00.
-- Less 20% in May, June and Sept.
Open:
1 May - 15 September.
Address:
35430 St. Jouan-des-Guérêts
Tel:
99.21.14.30.
FAX: 99.81.74.14.
Reservations:
Made on receipt of 30% of total cost (no fee).

Directions: St. Jouan is west off the St. Malo - Rennes road (N137) just outside St. Malo. Site is signed from the N137.

3510M Camping Municipal de la Gacilly, Sixt sur Aff

A small, neat site, with 86 pitches, most with electrical connections and set on flat grass with trees, the river L'Aff runs along the bottom of the site (fenced). The single sanitary block is of satisfactory standard with British WCs, hot showers and with some washbasins in private cabins. No on-site facilities apart from a small children's play area, but the village of Gacilly is within easy walking distance. Known as Le Village des Artisans, it has attractive, small, cobbled streets and terraced squares filled with small art and craft centres and a good selection of bars, crêperies and restaurants. When we visited in early September, the floral arrangements in the village were quite impressive.

Directions: Follow the D873 road from Redon to La Gacilly. At the village turn onto the D777. Site is signed 'municipal' from outskirts of village on the D777.

Charges 1995:
-- Per adult Ffr. 10.50; child (under 7 yrs) 7.50; pitch 7.50; vehicle 7.50; electricity 9.50. + VAT.
Open:
15 June - 15 September.
Address:
35550 Sixt sur Aff.
Tel:
99.08.10.18 or 15.28.
Reservations:
Contact site.

3605M Camping Municipal Les Vieux Chênes, Chaillac

Delightfully peaceful small site on edge of attractive village, this is another little gem - only 40 pitches, on slightly sloping grass, but all with electricity. It is very pretty and very peacefully situated beside a small lake, despite being within easy walking distance of the village centre, where there are shops, bars, cafés and restaurants, etc. The excellent sanitary facilities are modern, insulated for winter use and include hot showers with dividers and hooks, washbasins in private cabins and some British style WCs.

Directions: From the N20, south of Argenton sur Creuse, take the D1 to St Benoit (16 km.) and then west to Chaillac on the D36 (8½ km). Go through the village and turn left by the Mairie. From the south leave the N20 approx. 23 km. north of the N20/N145 junction to St Benoit.

Charges guide:
-- Per person Ffr. 7.00; pitch 10.00; tent 3.00; water 5.00; electricity 7.00 - 15.00 (winter).
Open:
All year.
Address:
36310 Chaillac.
Tel:
54.25.61.39.
Reservations:
Not made.

3606M Camping Municipal du Rochat, Châteauroux

A convenient and attractive site beside L'Indre river, within walking distance of the city, this is a large site close to the city centre and airport (some aircraft noise) with many facilities nearby. The 300 marked and numbered pitches, many with electricity (3, 6 or 10A), are on level grass, some with hardstanding. They are among a variety of trees providing good shade, beside the river. A lake used for angling and for swimming and with small beaches is next door. There are two public swimming pools, one open air, one ultra modern indoor, next to the site. They are unfortunately not free to campers who must pay the normal fee. Sanitary facilities, in three blocks, tend to vary somewhat from block to block, but are generally acceptable. One block even provides hot showers, not just with a divider, but with a sliding glass door between the shower and dressing areas! Some washbasins in private cabins; mostly Turkish type WCs, with relatively few British. Châteauroux and the surrounding area are worth a visit.

Directions: Site is north of the city, part of the Belle Isle leisure complex, and is signed from the city centre. Also signed from the Blois road (D956).

Charges guide:
-- Per person Ffr. 9.00; child (under 7 yrs) 4.50; pitch 8.00; electricity 3A 4.00, 6A 8.00.
Open:
1 April - 31 October.
Address:
Rue du Rochat, 36000 Châteauroux.
Tel:
54.34.26.56.
FAX (Mairie):
54.07.03.11.
Reservations:
Advised for high season. Contact site.

3607M Camping Municipal Les Chênes, Valençay

Les Chênes is an excellent site within walking distance of the town of Valençay, which is noted for its fine château. Behind reception is the town swimming pool (on payment) and a small fishing lake which is overlooked by several pitches. Two large oaks, as the name suggests, occupy a large green area, beyond which are the spacious, level, grass pitches, divided by hedges. A forest borders the site to the left and many trees on site give shade. The sanitary block, beside which is a covered wet weather area for campers, is centrally positioned and of modern design. Facilities are of a high standard and kept very clean with washbasins in cubicles, showers, children's sinks, British style WCs and facilities for the disabled. Table tennis, children's play field and three adjacent tennis courts. An excellent base for exploring the countryside around the Indre.

Directions: Site is 800 m. west of Valençay on the D960.

Charges 1995:
-- Per adult Ffr. 16.00; child (under 10) 8.00; pitch 14.00 - 27.00; electricity 10.00 - 20.00.
Open:
Mid-April - 30 Sept.
Address:
Rte. de Loches, 36600 Valençay.
Tel:
54.00.03.92.
Reservations:
Contact site.

3701 Camping de la Mignardière, Ballan-Miré, nr Tours
Pleasant little site quietly situated just southwest of Tours.

The situation of this little site may appeal to many - only 8 km. from the centre of the city of Tours, yet in a peaceful spot within easy reach of several of the Loire châteaux, notably Azay-le-Rideau, and with various sports amenities on or very close to the site. There are now 150 numbered pitches (30 in a new area) all with electricity and 100 with drainage and water also. They are on flat grass and are of good size. Four modern sanitary blocks have British WCs, free hot water in the washbasins (in private cabins) and the sinks, and premixed hot water in the showers. There is a unit for the disabled, a baby bath in the heated block near to reception and laundry facilities. Amenities on the site include a shop, two new swimming pools with sunbathing terrace, a good tennis court and table tennis. There is a bar and restaurant/crêperie with takeaway. Just outside the site is a small `parc de loisirs' with pony rides, minigolf, small cars, playground and some other amusements. An attractive lake catering particularly for windsurfing is 300 m. away (boards can be hired, or your own put on, but not other boats) with restaurants also, and there is a family fitness run. Barrier gates with card (100 Ffr. deposit), closed 2230 - 0730 hrs. Reservation is essential for most of July/Aug. Some pitches are taken by tour operators (15%). Mobile homes (6) and chalets for hire.

Directions: Site is difficult to find due to new roads and general housing and industrial developments. It lies between, not in, Ballan-Miré and Joué-les-Tours and is signed north off the D751, though the sign is hard to spot. Better to follow the D751 Joué-les-Tours road and signs to `Lac' or Campanile Hotel and pick up camp signs (300 m. northwest of lake) from there.

Charges 1996:
-- Per unit incl. 2 persons Ffr. 86.00 - 100.00, comfort pitch with electricity, water and drainage 120.00 - 140.00; extra person 24.00 - 28.00; child (under 7) 16.00 - 18.00; electricity (6A) 18.00; dog 10.00.
-- Credit cards accepted.

Open:
27 April - 29 Sept.

Address:
37510 Ballan-Miré.

Tel:
47.73.31.00.
FAX: 47.73.31.01.

Reservations:
Any length with deposit (Ffr. 260) and fee (90).

 Alan Rogers' discount
10% discount

Camping ★★★★
DE LA MIGNARDIERE
37510 Ballan-Miré
Tel: 47 73 31 00 Fax: 47 73 31 01

All the comforts of a 4 star camp with a wide range of activities for enjoyment and relaxation of adults and children; swimming pool and tennis on site, water sports lake, ponies and minigolf very close, the Loire châteaux and all the attractions of Tours.

6 Mobile Homes and 8 Chalets for hire
From autoroute take exit for Chambray-les-Tours.

3711M Camping Municipal Les Isles, Veretz, nr Tours

Les Isles is a select, pretty site on the bank of the River Cher with views through tall elm trees to the Château of Veretz. With 64 pitches, all with at least 6A electricity, the site is just outside the town of Veretz, where can be found shops, bars, restaurants, etc. An outdoor swimming pool (open July/Aug.) is 5 km. away. Bread and croissants can be ordered from reception in high season and the nearest supermarket is 500 m. The large, modern sanitary block includes free hot showers, British style WCs, dishwashing under cover and a washing machine. Children's playground and table tennis. Tranquil and beautiful, Les Isles is run by a family who live in a caravan on the site and are justly proud of it. English spoken.

Directions: Site is at Veretz, via the N76 road, 10 km. southeast of Tours (much better than the municipal at St. Avertin en-route).

Charges 1995:
-- Per pitch Ffr. 10.00; adult 10.00; child (under 7 yrs) 5.00; car 8.00; electricity 6A 11.00, 16A 16.00; visitor 5.00.

Open:
1 June - 30 September.

Address:
37270 Veretz.

Tel:
47.50.50.48.
FAX: 47.50.30.12 (Mairie).

Reservations:
Contact site.

 Alan Rogers' discount
10-15% discounts

3703 Camping Le Moulin Fort, Chenonceaux

Tidy riverside site with pool close to Château.

Le Moulin Fort is situated on the banks of the river Cher, on flat grass with some 100 pitches marked out by shrubs and trees. The two toilet blocks are well appointed and clean when seen. There is a small swimming pool and paddling pool (from 3 June) and canoes can be hired from a little river beach, from which fishing is also possible. The reception houses a compact terrace bar, also providing takeaway meals, open in high season at lunchtime but shut after 8 pm. in the evening. A few provisions, including bread, can be purchased at reception, but there is a supermarket across the bridge in Chisseaux. The site is less than 2 km. from one of the most beautiful Châteaux, and in season there is a 'son et lumiere' spectacle every evening. It is a good touring base for this and other sights, as well as an ideal location for a short stay en-route to the Auvergne or points further south. Used by tour operators (8%).

Directions: Take the D40 Tours - Chenonceaux road, go through village. After 2 km. turn right on D80 to cross river at Chisseaux. Site is on left just after bridge.

Charges 1996:
-- Per pitch incl. 2 persons Ffr. 88.00; extra adult 25.00; child (under 6 yrs) 19.00; dog 7.00; electricity (6A) 22.00.
Open:
1 May - 15 September.
Address:
37150 Chenonceaux
Tel:
47.23.86.22.
FAX: 47.23.80.93.
Reservations:
Write to site.

3710M Camping Municipal de Pincemaille, Rille

In a woodland park, beside Lake Rille and a sailing school, about 3 km. from the village of Rille itself and some 37 km. west of Tours, this site is very conducive to a longer stay. In a peaceful forest and lakeland environment, the windsurfing school alongside complements the site. It is available for both beginners and for those taking their own equipment, with professional instruction available and equipment hire possible too. The campsite offers some 100 pitches, many with electricity, with varying degrees of sun or shade, either near to the lake or in more wooded surroundings. The central, modern sanitary block has good facilities including hot showers with changing cubicles, washbasins in private cabins, continental style WCs and dishwashing and laundry sinks under cover. There is a small snack bar on site for takeaway meals and a more upmarket restaurant nearby. The 'train historique' (mostly steam engines) operates from a stop only 100 m. from the site and offers an interesting route into Rille through woods and bushes beside the lake. Generally this is a relaxing and tranquil situation, but with plenty of activity for those that want it.

Directions: Site is 2½ km. from Rille on the D58. Turn off at sign for Ecole de Voille and site is adjacent.

Charges guide:
-- Per adult Ffr. 15.00; child (2-10 yrs) 10.00; pitch 12.00; vehicle 6.00; electricity 14.00; animal 3.00; local tax 1.00.
Open:
1 May - 30 September.
Address:
37340 Rille.
Tel:
47.24.62.97 (Site) or 47.24.64.68 (Mairie).
Reservations:
Possible through La Mairie.

3801 Le Coin Tranquille, Les Abrets

Family run site with swimming pool and restaurant, in peaceful surroundings.

Le Coin Tranquille is set in peaceful surroundings of the Dauphiny countryside in the northeast corner of the département of Isère, north of Grenoble and east of Lyon. It is well situated in relation to the Chartreuse Massif, the Savoy regions and the Alps. A pleasant and friendly site, it has 136 pitches available for tourists (all with electrical connections) on grass and separated by hedges. Amenities include a swimming pool (18 x 10 m.), paddling pool (May-Sept) and an excellent restaurant which is open all year, also used by locals, with a reasonably priced menu and takeaway service. A new, large, excellent sanitary block in the centre of the camp has private washing cabins and special facilities for children and the disabled. Two other blocks on the edge of the site have been refurbished. There is a shop, laundry/ironing facilities, two children's play areas on grass and a TV/video room with balcony, games room and quiet lounge. During high season there are programmes of supervised games for children and a weekly programme for adults which includes live music - sometimes folk-lore, which continues until midnight. This is a popular site where you may be tempted to remain in camp enjoying the views and amenities or venture further to explore the many interests of this region. Used by tour operators (12%).

Directions: Site is northeast of Les Abrets. From the town take the N6 towards Chambery, turning left after about 2 km. where the camp is signed.

Charges 1996:
-- Per pitch incl. 2 persons Ffr. 75.00 - 112.00; extra adult 22.00 - 30.00; child (2-7 yrs) 12.00 - 19.00; extra vehicle 12.00 - 19.00; electricity 2A 8.00, 3A 12.00 or 6A 19.00.
Open:
1 April - 31 October.
Address:
38490 Les Abrets en Dauphine.
Tel:
76.32.13.48.
FAX: 76.37.40.67.
Reservations:
Write to site with deposit (Ffr. 600) and fee (50).

3803 Camping La Cascade, Bourg d'Oisans, nr Grenoble

Small site amongst the mountains, with heated sanitary facilities.

Although very much among the mountains, with the ski resorts of Alpe d'Huez and Les Deux Alpes close at hand, Bourg d'Oisans, which is in the Romanche valley at 725 m. above sea level, presents no access problems at all for caravanners. You simply drive from Grenoble along the wide N91 Briancon road with no passes or steep gradients. La Cascade is close to, and within sight and sound of, the waterfall from which it takes its name. It has about 130 individual pitches of varying but quite adequate size on mainly flat ground and with 6/15A electricity. The two heated sanitary blocks are of top quality with mainly British toilets, washbasins in private cabins with light, mirror, free hot water; good free hot showers, fully controllable. The heated municipal swimming pool is very close but the site has its own pool from late May. Shop, bar and snack bar (15/6-15/9). Children's playground. General room with TV. Animation some evenings. Games/TV room. Table tennis. Volleyball. Boules. Washing machine. Chalets and caravans for hire.

Directions: Site is about 400 m. along the road towards Alpe d'Huez which leads off from the N91 just east of Bourg d'Oisans.

Charges 1995:
-- Per unit incl. 1 person Ffr. 68.00 - 90.00, 2 persons 76.00 - 106.00; local tax (15/6-31/8) 1.00; electricity (6A) 15.00 (more in winter - 25.00 - 30.00).
Open: 15 December - 30 Sept.
Address: Rte. de l'Alpe-d'Huez, 38520 Bourg d'Oisans.
Tel: 76.80.02.42. FAX: 76.80.22.63.
Reservations: Essential for July/Aug; made for any length with deposit and fee.

3804 Camping La Rencontre du Soleil, Bourg d'Oisans, nr Grenoble

Small, friendly site in mountain area.

Situated almost opposite Camping La Cascade, this site is somewhat smaller with 80 enlarged pitches. There is little to choose between them. Rencontre de Soleil is an informal and friendly site, again with individual, mainly flat pitches of varying size. It has a good heated toilet block with British toilets, basins with free hot water, shelf and mirror, mostly in private cabins, and preset free hot showers; it should be large enough. Torches required at night. New bar with terrace. No shop; supermarket 1½ km. in town. Self-service restaurant (from 1/6), with takeaway also. Pizzeria. Tennis. General room for sitting and TV with children's play room adjoining. Drying room. Swimming pool. Bourg d'Oisans is situated at the foot of France's largest National Park - Le Parc des Ecrins. A haven for cycling enthusiasts, it is at the centre of the staging points for the Tour de France.

Directions: Site is almost opposite no. 3803 on the Alpe d'Huez road from the N91, just east of the town.

Charges 1996:
-- Per unit incl. 2 persons Ffr. 84.00 - 128.00; extra person 28.00; child (under 5) 18.00; electricity 2A 17.00, 6A 22.00, 10A 25.00; local tax 2.00.
-- Credit cards accepted.
Open: 16 May - 16 September.
Address: Rte de l'Alpe-d'Huez, 38520 Bourg d'Oisans.
Tel: 76.79.12.22. FAX: 76.80.26.37.
Reservations: Min. 1 week with deposit and fee; essential in peak season.

3802M Camping Municipal Porte de Chartreuse, Voiron

A neat, modern little municipal site, this is quite satisfactory for overnight or a short stay. With less than 100 pitches, most with electricity, on flat grassy strips divided by access roads, the site becomes full each evening in high season, but they try to find room for all, which may mean squeezing a little close during this period. The two toilet blocks are both small but maybe just large enough; toilets of mixed type, washbasins in cabins, hot showers on payment and facilities for the disabled. One block has recently been renovated and can be heated. No shop but others 500 m. Some mobile traders call. Snack bar planned. Games room. Children's playground.

Directions: Site is in northern part of the town beside the N75 road to Bourg and Lyon (perhaps some road noise).

Charges 1996:
-- Per adult 20.00; child (under 12) 12.00; tent 12.00 - 16.00; caravan 20.00; motor caravan 26.00; electricity 16.00.
Open: All year.
Address: 33 Ave. du 8 Mai 1945, 38500 Voiron.
Tel: 76.05.14.20.
Reservations: Made with deposit (Ffr. 200) and fee (60).

3805 Camping-Caravaning Le Temps Libre, Bougé Chambalud, nr Vienne

Unusual, rural site, not far from the A7 autoroute.

This is a rather pretty site with 70 tourist pitches, but with a further 85 for a variety of permanent caravans used at weekends or long stay units in a separate area. The pitches all offer electricity (9A), but in some cases with long cables needed. Shade in most places. The site has a lot by way of on-site activities, including four swimming pools, two of which have large water slides, four tennis courts, minigolf, numerous boules courts, volleyball, basketball, a climbing wall and fishing and some boating activities on a small lake. Open air theatre and full animation programme. There is a bar, a restaurant with terrace, takeaway and snacks, and a small shop for basics. The original toilet block under the bar/restaurant is a little dark and old fashioned, with mainly Turkish style toilets. The other block near the pool is more cheerful, providing all necessary facilities. The site has an essentially French atmosphere with lots going on in an area often passed by. It is worth considering by anyone looking for something a little different, without paying the earth. Used by a UK tour operator.

Directions: From A7 (exit Chanas) or N7, take D519 towards Grenoble for 7 km. to Bougé Chambalud from where site signed to right (sharp turn in village).

Charges 1996:
-- Per pitch and vehicle Ffr. 35.00; person 30.00; child (2-4 yrs) 15.00; dog 5.00; electricity (9A) 20.00.
Open: 1 April - 30 September.
Address: 38150 Bougé Chambalud.
Tel: 74.84.04.09.
FAX: 74.84.15.71.
Reservations: Contact site.

3806 Camping Les Trois Lacs, Trept, nr Sablonnieres

Country site on edge of three lakes.

In flat, open country in the north of Dauphine, Trois Lacs is a pleasant relaxing base to enjoy either the countryside, the historic places of the region or the programme of leisure activities provided by the camp. The land around the lakes has been well landscaped with smooth lawns and a variety of shrubs and trees, and the camping area is on one side of the largest lake with tall trees on one side and views of distant mountains. The good sized pitches are in pairs on either side of hard access roads separated by low hedges, but there is little shade. The good quality sanitary block is in the centre of the camping area with British WCs and hot water in the basins, sinks and showers. Laundry room. The attractive bar/restaurant near reception serves drinks and simple snacks and there are other snack bars around the lakes. A mobile shop calls and there are other shops at Trept (2 km). Well away from the camping area is a large building, open on one side, for roller skating and entertainment which is provided in July/Aug. This includes two discos for teenagers and one for older people each week. Two small children's playgrounds and a games area. The smallest lake is kept for fishing and the others for boating and watersports with one section for swimming having a water slide. Other activities include walking, riding, mountain biking, tennis and minigolf

Directions: Leave the N75 Grenoble-Bourg-en-Bresse road at Morestel and travel west on D517 when site will be found between Sablonnieres and Trept.

Charges 1995:
-- Per person Ffr. 25.00, under 10 yrs 18.00; pitch 25.00; car 5.00; animal 8.00; electricity 14.00; guest 25.00.
-- Extra charges made for some activities.
Open: 15 April - 15 September
Address: 38460 Trept.
Tel: 74.92.92.06 or 74.92.81.73. FAX: 74.92.93.35.
Reservations: Made with deposit (Ffr. 450) and fee (50).

3901 La Plage Blanche, Ounans

Attractive riverside site with good amenities.

Situated in open countryside, along the banks of the River Loue, this site has 154 good sized pitches (marked out) on level ground, most with electricity (6A). Trees have been planted which provide some shade. It is possible to swim and play in the river from the site's own beach which has recently been enlarged, and we are told that this is normally safe for children. New sanitary facilities in three unusual blocks have tiled hot showers, separate washing cabins, ample hooks, mirrors etc, and with both continental abd Turkish style WCs. Dishwashing facilities are provided in blocks of 8 sinks. Bar/restaurant with terrace, pizzeria and takeaway (all open for the entire season). River fishing. Launderette. Table tennis. Riding. Bicycle hire. TV room. Children's play area. Caravans for hire and some pitches taken by tour operators (30%).

Directions: Ounans is about 20 km southeast of Dole. Site is best approached from Dole via the D405 to Parcey, thence on the N5 towards Poligny/Pontarlier. After 8 km. at Mont Sous Vaudrey take the D472 in the direction of Pontarlier to Ounans from where site is signed.

Charges 1996:
-- Per person Ffr 22.00 plus local tax 1.00 (over 14s); child (under 7 yrs) 11.00; pitch 26.00; extra car 15.00; dog 5.00; electricity (6A) 16.00.
-- Credit cards accepted.
Open:
1 April - 31 October.
Address:
39380 Ounans.
Tel:
84.37.69.63.
FAX: 84.37.60.21.
Reservations:
Write with 20% deposit (by Eurocheque).

3902 Camping de Surchauffant, La Tour du Meix, nr Orgelet

Comfortable site situated on the shores of Lake Vouglans.

This site is one of a group which includes site no. 3903 but it is much smaller. With only 180 pitches, it may appeal to those who prefer a more informal or intimate atmosphere. It is pleasantly situated above the beaches bordering the Lac de Vouglans, which also offers a variety of watersports activities, boat trips, etc. and is used for swimming, being guarded in high season as it shelves steeply. The pitches are of reasonable size, informally arranged, and most offer electricity; they are divided by hedges, and there is some shade. The sanitary installations are adequate rather than luxurious, with continental style WCs, hot showers and some washbasins in private cabins. Laundry. Amenities include a shop, restaurant and snacks (all 10/6-10/9), other restaurant and shops nearby. Children's games. Watersports on lake. Used by tour operators (12%).

Directions: From Lons le Saunier take the D52 to Orgelet. Site is adjacent to the D470, at La Tour du Meix, about 4 km. east of Orgelet.

Charges 1995:
-- Per unit incl. 2 persons Ffr. 52.00 - 67.00; extra person (over 4 yrs) 12.50 - 16.00; electricity 15.00; plus water and drainage 20.00; local tax 1.00.
-- Credit cards accepted.
Open:
1 May - 19 September.
Address:
39270 La Tour du Meix.
Tel:
84.25.41.08.
FAX: 84.35.56.88.
Reservations:
Contact site for details.

3903 Le Domaine de Chalain, Doucier, nr Lons-le-Saunier

Large lakeside site with many sports and amenities available.

Doucier lies east of Lons-le-Saunier among the wooded hills of the Jura and rather away from the main routes. This large, park-like site is on the edge of the Lac de Chalain surrounded on three sides by woods and some cliffs. Large areas are left for sports and recreation. The lake shelves gently at the edge but then becomes deep quite suddenly; there is a small shallow pool for non-swimmers. Day visitors can be very numerous on fine weekends. The site is divided into two parts, one (nearer the lake) with larger pitches (costing more). You should find room in the other part, but from 5/7-16/8, it is better to reserve to make sure. Over 200 electrical connections; little shade. The ten sanitary blocks, have been improved over the years, with continental and Turkish style WCs, basins with warm water (mainly in private cabins) and free hot showers in separate blocks. Shops, bar and takeaway, all 31/5-31/8. Community room. Tennis. Table tennis. Paddling pool. Minigolf. Pedaloes for hire. Animals and birds in enclosures. Organised activities. Cinema. Disco for the young. Washing machines. Medical centre - doctor calls daily in high season. Used by tour operators.

Directions: Site can only be approached via Doucier: from Switzerland via N5 (from Geneva), then the N78 and D39; from other directions via Lons-le-Saunier or Champagnole.

Charges 1995:
-- Per unit incl. 3 persons: lakeside pitch Ffr. 71.00 - 122.00, others 71.00 - 109.00; electricity 15.00; pitch with 3 services 92.00 - 143.00; extra person (over 4) 13.00 - 18.00; local tax 1.00.
Open:
1 May - 20 September.
Address:
39130 Doucier.
Tel:
84.24.29.00.
FAX: 84.24.94.07.
Reservations:
Min. 7 days with 30% deposit (min. Ffr 400). Sat.-Sat. in high season.

3904 Camping La Pergola, Marigny, Lac de Chalain

Hillside, terraced site overlooking lake.

Bordering on Switzerland and overlooking the sparkling waters of Lac de Chalain, Le Pergola is set amidst the undulating, cultivated countryside of the Jura. Not on a main route, it is worth a detour if seeking the restful peace of the country, although the lake could well become crowded at weekends in the summer. This is a very well appointed camp with 200 level, mainly stony pitches, separated by small conifers and having some shade on numerous terraces with steep steps between, giving good views over the lake. All have electricity, water and drainage. A tall wire fence protects the site from the path which separates it from the lake but there are access points. The entrance is nicely landscaped with flowers and a small waterfall next to the three pools (two are heated) and entertainment area. An excellent new sanitary block has private cabins on the lowest level and four others on different terraces. Good children's play area with children's club. A high season programme includes cycle tours, keep fit and evening entertainment with 2 discos weekly (til midnight). Table tennis and volleyball. Watersports. Shop and large restaurant at entrance, also used by day visitors who use the lake for watersports. Used by three British tour operators. Facilities for the disabled who need to select a lower terrace.

Charges 1995:
-- Per unit incl. 2 persons, electricity and water: lake pitch Ffr. 80.00 - 205.00, standard 80.00 - 150.00; extra person 25.00; child (3-7 yrs) 20.00; baby (0-2 yrs) 10.00; extra car 15.00; local tax 1.00.
Open:
1 May - 30 September.
Address:
39130 Marigny.
Tel:
84.25.70.03.
FAX: 84.25.75.96.
Reservations:
Write with Ffr. 800 deposit and 170 fee.

Directions: Site is 2½ km. north of Doucier on Lake Chalain road D27.

4001 Airotel Le Boudigau, Labenne-Océan, nr Bayonne

Pinewood site close to beach 12 km. north of Bayonne.

Between the Landes and the Basque country, this site is well placed for some interesting excursions as well as being close to a wide sandy beach. This is 500 m. on foot from one side of the camp and rather longer by car (car park available) and includes an area for naturists. The site has a good swimming pool of 16 x 8 m. The 320 pitches are all covered by a pinewood, and of very fair size and numbered, with young shrubs planted to define the pitch area. Although the terrain is basically sandy, most pitches seemed to have a hard core, flat or slightly sloping. About half have electricity. Two identical sanitary blocks in standard modern style have washbasins and toilets, with a further small unit at one end of the site. They have mostly British WCs and washbasins in good cabins with free hot water. There are 40 hot, pre-set showers with pushbutton, few hooks and no shelf in a separate block. Facilities for the disabled are provided. At the entrance to the site, open to all, are a well stocked supermarket, snack bar, restaurant (15/6-10/9), separate bar and a sound-proof disco. Cinema weekly. Washing machines and dryers. TV room. Table tennis. Minigolf. Amusement machines. Petanque. Children's play area. Entertainment in season. Folk music. Bicycle hire. Mobile homes, caravans and bungalows to let.

Charges 1995:
Per unit incl. 2 persons Ffr 40.00, 80.00 or 100.00, acc. to season; extra adult 15.00; local tax: adult 3.30, child (10-18 yrs) 1.65; animal 10.00; extra car 12.00; m/cycle 6.00; electricity (5A) 16.00.
Open:
Late May - late Sept.
Address:
40530 Labenne-Océan.
Tel:
59.45.42.07.
FAX: 59.45.77.76.
Reservations:
Made for any length with deposit (25%) and booking fee (Ffr. 140).

Directions: Turn off N10 at Labenne for Labenne-Océan and site is on right in village. From the north, join N10 via St. Geours de Maremne.

4002 Camping Les Chênes, Dax

Established, well kept and attractive site on outskirts of busy spa town.

Dax is not a place that springs at once to mind as a holiday town but, as well as being a spa, it has a comprehensive cultural programme of events (concerts, special shows, `courses landaises', corridas, etc.) during the season. Pleasantly situated on the edge of the town amid parkland and close to the river, a number of the 250 pitches are occupied by French seasonal caravans or people taking thermal courses. The pitches are of two types: good sized `boxes' with hedges including electricity (5A), water and waste water connections, and others on open ground with electricity, some with hardstanding. Two toilet blocks, one new and modern with British style WCs, the other of standard French design. Washbasins all in cubicles and a good supply of pre-set, free hot showers, facilities for babies and the handicapped. Washing machines and dryers. Boules. Children's playground. Shop with takeaway. Restaurant opposite (El Callejon) with `tapas' a speciality. Fishing, riding and golf near. Beaches 28 km. A very reliable site, particularly suitable for adults (many take the waters) or those with older, more independent youngsters. Mobile homes and bungalows for hire.

Directions: Site is west of town on south side of river, signed after main river bridge and at many junctions in town - Bois de Boulogne (1½ km).

Charges 1995:
-- Per pitch incl. 1 or 2 persons and electricity (5A) Ffr. 77.00 - 95.00, water and drainage also plus 16.00; extra person 18.00; child (under 7) 10.00; local tax 1.10.
-- Credit cards accepted.
Open:
23 March - 31 October.
Address:
40100 Dax.
Tel:
58.90.05.53.
FAX: 58.56.18.77.
Reservations:
Only made for rented accommodation.

4003 Les Pins du Soleil, St. Paul lès Dax, nr Dax

Family oriented site with swimming pool close to spa town of Dax.

This site will appeal to families, particularly those with younger children who prefer to be some way back from the coast within easy reach of shops, cultural activities, etc. and well placed for touring the area. Dax is a busy spa town with many attractions - Les Pins du Soleil is actually at St. Paul lès Dax, some 3 km. from Dax itself. The site has 140 good sized pitches, 100 with electricity and drainage and, although new, the site benefits from being developed in light woodland so there is a fair amount of shade from many small trees. Attractive, medium sized swimming pool with sunbathing area. Modern sanitary facilities include free hot showers with dressing area, washbasins with H&C, British style WCs and facilities for babies and the handicapped. Children's playground. Volleyball. Table tennis. Laundry facilities. Bus to thermal baths. Takeaway, small supermarket and bar on site, but no restaurant (many in Dax). Range of excursions by bus to St Sebastian, Lourdes, etc. English spoken. Mobile homes and chalets to rent (including one designed for the disabled).

Directions: From west on N124, avoid bypass and follow signs for Dax and St. Paul. Almost immediately turn right onto D495 and follow signs. Site is a little further along on the left. Also well signed from town centre, north of the river.

Charges 1995:
-- Per pitch incl. 2 persons no electricity Ffr. 65.00 - 88.00, with electricity (4A), water and drainage 90.00 - 120.00; extra person 25.00; child (under 7) 12.00; local tax 1.10.
Open:
8 April - 28 October.
Address:
40990 St. Paul lès Dax.
Tel:
58.91.37.91.
FAX: 58.91.00.24.
Reservations:
Made with 25% deposit and fee (Ffr. 60).

4007 Camping Lous Seurrots, Contis-Plage, nr Mimizan

Large and shady site close to beach to south of Mimizan.

This site is very close to the sea with a frontage overlooking an estuary, but a walk or drive of about 500 m. to the sandy Atlantic beach. There are now some 700 pitches, mostly in a pinewood on sandy, undulating ground, numbered and roughly marked out and the majority with good shade. Electrical connections are available over 80% of the area. Three new, modern sanitary blocks and three renovated ones make a good provision. They have washbasins in cabins (some en-suite toilets and basins), controllable hot showers, facilities for baby changing and the handicapped and washing machines A super new swimming pool complex (1/6-15/9), is terraced and landscaped and provides three pools and a jacuzzi. There is also a new open air auditorium for evening animation for children and adults (July/Aug). Self-service shop (20/5-11/9). Bar/restaurant with takeaway food also (10/6-5/9). Tennis court. Bicycles for hire. No British tour operators. Reservations are made for high season. Chalets and mobile homes to hire.

Directions: Turn off D652 on D41 to Contis-Plage; site is on left as you reach it.

Charges 1996:
-- Per unit incl. 2 persons Ffr. 75.00 - 119.00; extra person 20.00 - 25.00; child (under 7) free - 19.00; electricity (6A) 21.00.
Open:
1 April - 30 September.
Address:
Contis Plage, 40170 St. Julien en Born.
Tel:
58.42.85.82.
FAX: 58.42.49.11.
Reservations:
Made with deposit (Ffr. 300) and fee (100).

4006 Camping Eurosol, St. Girons-Plage, Castets, nr Dax

Well shaded site with swimming pool just back from sea.

Eurosol is 500 m. from a sandy beach with supervised bathing and there are also two swimming pools on site. On undulating ground in a pinewood with numerous tall trees, pitches are marked at the corners but have nothing to separate them and so there is little privacy. On flatter ground are some special caravan pitches with their own water and electrical points. On the site generally, about 300 of the 641 pitches are accessible for caravans (with electricity), so in high season space may be more easily obtainable for tents. Reservation is therefore advisable for caravans especially as only half the site is reserved. There are four main toilet blocks plus two smaller units. They have continental seatless type WCs, washbasins in cabins with free hot water, pre-set free hot showers with pushbutton which runs on a bit and hot water to the sinks - some wear and tear is beginning to show. Motorcaravan service point. Self-service shop. Large bar and snack bar with hot food (including takeaway). Two tennis courts. Games room with table tennis. Minigolf. Comprehensive recreation programme in July/Aug. with several events each day for children and adults both daytime and evening (a lively atmosphere in the evenings). New play area for young children (3-10 yrs). Bureau de change. Fridges for hire. Deposit boxes. Mobile homes for hire. Used by tour operators (7½%).

Directions: Turn off the D42 road at St. Girons towards St. Girons-Plage, and site is on left before coming to beach.

Charges 1995:
-- Per unit incl. 2 persons Ffr 105.00, with electricity 130.00, with water and drainage also 135.00; with 3 or 4 pers. respectively 155.00, 180.00, 185.00; extra person 25.00; local tax 2.00 (child 1.00).
-- Less 20% outside 1/7-25/8.
-- Credit cards accepted.
Open:
1 June - 15 September.
Address:
40560 St. Girons-Plage when open or address in advertisement.
Tel:
58.47.90.14.
FAX: 58.47.76.74.
Reservations:
Min. 1 week with deposit (Ffr. 500) and fee (150), Sun. to Sun. only in high season.

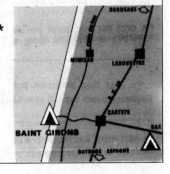
See also 4002 Camping Les Chênes on page 103

40 Landes

4004 Camping La Paillotte, Azur, nr Soustons

Very attractive, good lakeside site with an individual atmosphere.

La Paillotte, in the Landes area of southwest France, is a site with a character of its own. The camp buildings (reception, shop, restaurant, even sanitary blocks) are all Tahitian in style, circular and constructed from local woods with the typical straw roof (and layer of waterproof material underneath). Some are now being replaced but still in character. It lies right by the edge of the Soustons lake, 1½ km. from Azur village, with its own sandy beach. This is particularly suitable for young children because the lake is shallow and slopes extremely gradually. For boating the site has a small private harbour where your own non-powered boat of shallow draught can be kept. Sailing, windsurfing (with lessons) and rowing boats and pedaloes for hire. The Atlantic beaches with their breakers are 10 km. Alternatively the site has two swimming pools. All pitches at La Paillotte are marked out individual ones, usually shady, and new shrubs and trees have been planted. Pitches vary in price according to size, position and whether they are equipped with electricity, water, etc. The circular rustic-style sanitary blocks are rather different from the usual camp site installations, but are modern and fully tiled with British WCs and free hot showers in central enclosed positions, then individual washbasins with free hot water partly enclosed (some toilets and basins en-suite). Separate `mini' facilities for children. Outside are washing-up sinks with hot water. Washing machines and dryers. Self-service shop. Good restaurant with very pleasant terrace overlooking the lake and bar (3/6-31/8). Takeaway. Organised sports, games and activities. `Mini-club' room, again with `mini' equipment. TV room. Table tennis. Amusement room with juke box. Library. Treatment room. Bicycle hire. Mobile homes to let. La Paillotte is an unusual site with its own atmosphere which appeals to many regular clients. Reservation for main season is advisable. Used by tour operators. No dogs.

Charges 1996:
-- Per unit incl. 2 persons: standard pitch Ffr. 87.00 - 150.00; electricity 20.00 - 22.00; water and electricity 30.00 - 42.00; extra person (over 2 yrs) 20.00 - 32.00; local tax (over 10) in July/Aug 1.10.
Open:
25 May - 15 September.
Address:
Azur, 40140 Soustons.
Tel:
58.48.12.12.
FAX: 58.48.10.73.
Reservations:
Made for Sat. to Sat. only 2/7- 27/8, with deposit (Ffr. 250 per week) and fee (160).

see advertisement opposite

Directions: Coming from the north along N10, turn west on D150 at Magescq. From south go via Soustons.

4005 Camping Le Col Vert, Vielle-Saint-Girons, nr Castets

Family holiday centre with long frontage to a good lake for water sports, 5 km. from Atlantic beaches.

This extensive, but natural site (edging a nature reserve), stretches right along the Lac de Léon, a conservation area, for 1 km. on a narrow frontage which makes it particularly suitable for those who want to practise water sports such as sailing and windsurfing. Bathing is also possible; the lake bed shelves gently making it easy for children and the site has a supervised beach, sailboarding courses are arranged and there are some boats and boards for hire. There are two heated pools, both supervised, an open air one with whirl pool and a covered one, with sunbathing areas. The 500 pitches are all flat and covered by light pinewood, most with good shade. They are of around 100 sq.m., only partly separated, some 50 with water and electricity. The four modern toilet blocks, one very large at the far end of the site, are a good supply, with excellent facilities for the handicapped. They have mostly British WCs, washbasins in private cabins or cubicles with free hot water and free hot showers (now in all blocks) with pre-set hot water. There are washing-up sinks mainly with cold water but with hot tap to draw from. There is a range of facilities on site including shops (25/5-10/9), sports area with tennis and volleyball, a fitness centre and workshops, and sauna and solarium. Sailing school (15/6-15/9). A good terraced bar/restaurant is by the lake (open to all 25/6-3/9). Simple hot takeaway food service. Two special areas provided for barbecues. TV room. Table tennis. Amusement machines. Washing machines (4), dryer and dishwasher. Children's playground. Minigolf. Walking and cycle ways in the forest and two jogging tracks. Stables and riding on site. Much `animation' in season: children's games, tournaments, etc. by day and dancing or shows evenings. Deposit boxes. Chalets and mobile homes for hire. Used by tour operators (10%).

Charges 1996:
-- Per pitch incl. 2 persons Ffr. 75.00 - 150.00, acc. to season; extra person 12.00 - 24.00; child (under 7 yrs) 9.00 - 18.00; local tax (high season only) 2.00, child 1.00; electricity (6A) 20.00, (10A) 30.00.
-- Less 20-30% outside 8/7-26/8 (excl. electric)
-- Credit cards accepted.
Open:
Easter - 30 September.
Address:
Lac de Léon, 40560 Vielle-Saint-Girons.
Tel:
58.42.94.06.
FAX: 58.42.91.88.
Reservations:
Any length with £27 deposit and £20 fee per week booked.

see advertisement opposite

Directions: Roads to lake and site lead off the D652 St. Girons-Léon road at Vielle-St-Girons, clearly signed.

Private beach, swimming pools, bar and restaurant for your enjoyment.
A Mini-club and a Junior-club for children.
A variety of entertainment is organised both daily and in the evenings
for parents.   Chalets and Mobile-Homes for hire.

LA PAILLOTTE LAC DE SOUSTONS   40140 AZUR
Tel.: 58.48.12.12   Fax: 58.48.10.73

EURO-PACT

HOTEL - OPEN AIR CLUB
LE COL VERT

*MINI-CLUB, JUNIOR CLUB, SWIMMING
POOLS (ONE INDOOR), TENNIS, GOLF
AND ORGANISED
ENTERTAINMENT
FOR 7 TO 77
YEAR OLDS*
An exceptional position
on the banks of
Lake Léon
*Chalets, Mobile-homes
and pitches for tents
and caravans for hire.*

DOMAINE DU COL VERT
LAC DE LEON 40560 VIELLE ST-GIRONS
Tel : 58 42 94 06 Fax : 58 42 91 88
Direct access to the beach

EURO-PACT

La Grande Métairie

DES VACANCES UNIQUES

B.P. 85 - 56342 Carnac Cedex - Tél. 97 52 24 01
Bretagne-Sud - France

CASTELS
&CAMPING
CARAVANING
★★★★

CASTELS
& CAMPING
CARAVANING
★★★★

for exceptional fun-filled family holidays

CHÂTEAU DE LEZ-EAUX
★ ★ ★ ★
ST-AUBIN DES PRÉAUX
50380 ST-PAIR-SUR-MER
Tél. 33 51 66 09 - Fax 33 51 92 02

NORMANDIE - FRANCE

CAMPING DE LA DUNE
★★★ NN
MER • SOLEIL • FORET
Tél. 56.22.72.17
Route de Biscarrosse • 33115 PYLA/MER

Le Village Européen

Résidences Hôtelières - Gîtes - Hôtel

Barrage de Pannecière -
58120 Montigny-en-Morvan
Tel. 86 84 79 00 - Fax. 86 84 79 02

4008 Parc Montana Aureilhan, Aureilhan, nr Mimizan

Pleasant, attractively laid out, lakeside site with good sized pitches and pools, 9 km. from sea.

Previously Camping Eurolac, this site is now under the ownership of the Parc Montana group. In a peaceful situation by a lake (with a minor road to cross), it is largely used by families but offers a good choice of activities - bathing or boating in the lake (with sailing school in season), windsurfing (boards for hire), a good riding school on site and organised events for young and old. The Atlantic beaches are 9 km. (for surfing) and there are two butterfly shaped swimming pools and a jacuzzi on the site. The terrain is flat, grassy and park-like, divided into 475 good size, numbered pitches, 280 of which have electricity and water connections and with shade from some mature trees. The six sanitary blocks give a very reasonable provision. The newest ones are of particularly good quality with mostly continental style WCs, washbasins in private cabins and pre-set showers. Hot water is free throughout and can be drawn from tap for washing-up. During the main season various activities and events are organised for both adults and children. Shop (all season), bar/ restaurant (1/5-30/9) and takeaway. General room with TV, bar and some special evenings; dancing twice weekly in season. Tennis courts. Games room. Table tennis. Volleyball. Basketball. Minigolf. Children's playground. Mini-club. Bicycle hire. Treatment room. Washing machines. Chalets, caravans and bungalows to let. Motorcaravan station. No pets taken July/Aug. Some tour operators. A very popular site, the facilities could become stretched in high season. Good English is spoken.

Directions: Turn north off D626 at camp sign 3 km. east of Mimizan-Bourg.

Charges 1995:
-- Per tent or caravan incl. 1 or 2 persons Ffr 66.00 - 110.00, motorcaravan 100.00 - 130.00; extra person 15.00 - 20.00; child under 10 yrs free; extra car free - 12.00; animal 12.00 - 20.00; electricity (6A) 12.00 - 20.00; water connection 10.00.

Open:
1 May - 30 September.

Address:
Aureilhan,
40200 Mimizan.

Tel:
58.09.02.87.
FAX: 58.09.41.89.

Reservations:
Made for any period with 30% deposit and Ffr. 115 fee.

CAMPING PARC MONTANA AUREILHAN ★★★★

Lakeside site with good pitches and swimming pool, only 9km from the Atlantic Ocean. Bar Restaurant.

Open 1st May - 30th Sept

Mobile Homes and Chalets to Hire

**Promenade de l'étang
40200 MIMIZAN
Tel: 58 09 02 87 Fax: 58 09 41 89**

4010 Camping La Rive, Biscarrosse

Landes site with excellent beach on the Lac de Sanguinet.

This site is set in pinewoods, with some 650 pitches, mostly level, of generous size and with electricity. There is generally good shade and the site is normally very quiet (except near the bar/disco area before 11 pm). The seven modern toilet blocks were found to be clean and usually sufficient, but there may be queuing in some parts of the site during the first week of August. The bar serves snacks and takeaway meals and the unpretentious restaurant provides cheap family meals (pizzas, burgers, etc), all from 15 June. The hourglass shaped pool is perfectly adequate (from 25/4), but most campers prefer to use the excellent lake beach. The lake shelves very gently, providing safe swimming for all ages and in another section, an ideal place to learn how to fall off a sailboard! Small craft and dinghies can be launched from the site's own slipway. Facilities for the energetic include a children's playground, two good tennis courts, table tennis and a boules court. Shop (from 15/5). Mobile homes and log cabins for hire. Used by tour operators (20%).

Directions: Take D652 from Sanguinet to Biscarosse, and site is signed on right.

Charges 1996:
- Per pitch incl. 2 persons Ffr. 120.00, with electricity 140.00; extra person (over 3 yrs) 23.00; boat 25.00.
-- Less 30% outside 18/6-27/8.

Open:
1 April - 30 October.

Address:
40600 Biscarosse.

Tel:
58.78.12.33.
FAX: 58.78.12.92.

Reservations:
Advised for July/Aug. - write or fax site.

4009M Camping Lou Broustaricq, Sanguinet, nr Arcachon

This is a good municipal site, if lacking a little in atmosphere, with some 555 individual pitches on flat ground in light woodland, partly shaded by high trees. Some pitches are now separated by newly planted shrubs and trees. Caravan pitches are 110 sq.m. with hardstanding, electricity and water, pitches for tents average 100 sq.m. A path of about 200 m. leads from the camp to the big lake (no cars this way, but access for cars with boats 2 km). The site has seven toilet blocks and one new modern one (heated in winter), with sexes mixed. Generally they have seatless and continental WCs, washbasins in private cabins, free hot water in showers and sinks, a bathroom for the handicapped, facilities for babies and washing machines. This is a very reliable site where there is always a chance of finding space, with the added attraction of a swimming pool complex with sunbathing area. Two good tennis courts, minigolf and table tennis. Children's playground. Commercial centre by entrance includes supermarket and other shops, snack bar and hot takeaway food service, mostly opening mid-June. Area to barbecue. Mobile homes to rent. It is used by an English tour operator.

Directions: Turn to northwest off D46 at camp sign northeast of Sanguinet.

Charges 1995:
-- Per unit incl. 1 or 2 persons: pitch Ffr. 60.00 - 108.00, with electricity 67.00 - 127.00, three services 70.00 - 133.00; extra person 10.00 - 18.00; local tax 2.20

Open:
All year.

Address:
40460 Sanguinet.

Tel:
58.78.62.62.
FAX: 58.82.10.74.

Reservations:
Any length with booking fee (Ffr. 130).

N4012 Domaine Naturiste Arnaoutchot, Vielle-Saint-Girons

Large naturist site with extensive facilities and direct access to beach.

Although `Arna' is a large site with 450 emplacements, its layout in the form of a number of sections, each with its own character, makes it quite relaxing and all very natural. These sections amongst the trees and bushes of the Landes provide a variety of reasonably sized pitches, most with electricity, although the hilly terrain means that only a limited number are flat enough for camping cars. The sanitary facilities include not only the usual naturist site type of blocks with individual British type WCs and communal hot showers, but also a number of tiny blocks with one hot shower, WC and basin each in an individual cabin. Two blocks have been upgraded providing fully tiled, modern facilities. The amenities, situated centrally, are extensive and of excellent quality. They include a heated, indoor swimming pool with whirlpool, outdoor pool (open Easter-20/9) and terraced sunbathing area, sauna, bar/restaurant, pizzeria, a large supermarket (1/5-24/9) and a range of other shops, mainly built of timber in an attractive style. The site has the advantage of direct access to a large, sandy naturist beach, although access from some parts of the site may involve a walk of perhaps 600-700 m. The `Arna Club' provides more than 30 activities and workshops (main season) including riding, archery, golf practice, petanque, tennis, swimming, rambling, cycling, sailing, handicrafts, excursions and special activities for children. TV, video and games rooms. Cinema. Library. Hairdresser. Laundry facilities. Chalets, mobile homes and tents for hire. English spoken. A torch is very useful. No barbecues permitted. Used by a tour operator (5%).

Directions: Site is signed off the D652 road at Vielle-Saint-Girons - follow the D328 for 3-4 km.

Charges 1995:
-- Per pitch incl. 2 persons Ffr 70.00 - 140.00, acc. to season; extra person (over 3 yrs) 17.00 - 36.00; extra car 7.70 - 11.00; animal 7.00 - 10.00; leisure club 2.00 - 5.00; electricity (3A) 18.00, (6A) 30.00; local tax in high season 1.65.
Deposit on arrival for entry pass 100.00.
-- Credit cards accepted.

Open:
Easter - 1 November.

Address:
40560
Vielle-Saint-Girons.

Tel:
58.48.52.87.
FAX: 58.48.57.12.

Reservations:
Made with deposit of £38 and £21 fee.

The sites featured in this Guide are regularly inspected by our team of experienced site assessors, but we welcome your opinions too.
Please see Readers' Reports on page 205

4011 Camping-Caravaning Sen Yan, Mezos

Superb family site set in the Landes forest area.

This exotic site, amongst tall pines, is about 15 km. from the Atlantic coast and just outside the village. There are 250 pitches marked with hedges, 190 of which have electricity (3 or 6A), with ample water points. Some mobile homes and tour operator pitches (5%) are in a separate 'village'. Three toilet blocks with good quality fittings have showers and washbasins in cabins. The newest block is specially suitable for pre- and post-season clients and has a special section for young children and babies. Facilities for the disabled. The reception, bar and pool area is almost tropical with the luxuriant greenery of its banana trees, palm trees and cannas, and its straw sunshades. This attractive area has a terrace for sunbathing, 3 swimming pools, (one indoor), 18 hole minigolf course, tennis, petanque, archery, table tennis, children's games, mountain bike hire, fitness centre (Fr. 100 per week per adult), animation and evening entertainment with a disco twice a week in high season. Barbecue areas provided. Note: not all the facilities are open outside the high season.

Directions: From N10 take exit 14 (Onesse-Laharie), then D38 Bias-Mimizan road. After 13 km. turn south to Mezos from where site is signed.

Charges 1996:
-- Per pitch incl. 2 persons Ffr. 125.00, pitch incl. 2 persons and 3A electricity 135.00; extra person 30.00; child (under 7 yrs) 18.00; 6A electricity 8.00 - 20.00.
-- Credit cards accepted.
Open:
1 June - 30 September.
Address:
40170 Mezos.
Tel:
58.42.62.05.
FAX: 58.42.64.56.
Reservations:
Write with deposit (Ffr. 350) and fee (150).

4013 Camping-Caravaning de la Côte, Messanges, nr Vieux-Boucau

Peaceful family site near the beaches of the Landes.

Formerly Aire Naturelle Les Cheureuils, this family oriented site has been extended to provide 78 large, level pitches which are edged with newly planned trees and shrubs (the first planting was demolished by the native deer). All have electrical connections, some with water and waste facilities also. The few original pitches are amongst pine trees. Surrounded by farmland and pine woods, with the beaches and dunes within walking distance, the site should provide for a peaceful, relaxed stay. Tomatoes, eggs and lettuce are available from the farm in season. The recently constructed, modern sanitary block is built in the traditional Landes style and is of very good quality and well maintained. Facilities are mixed male and female, semi open with controllable hot showers, washbasins in private cabins, British style toilets and provision for the handicapped including ramps. Washing machine. Purpose built reception, bread and drinks provided in high season. Amenities include a barbecue, games room, children's play area, petanque, football, volleyball and table tennis. Mobile home, gite and two caravans to rent. Supermarket nearby, plus the modern resort of Vieux-Boucau.

Directions: Site is signed off the D652, 1½ km. north of Vieux-Boucau.

Charges 1995:
-- Per unit incl. 2 persons Ffr. 48.00; extra person 15.00; child 10.00; electricity (6A) 13.00; dog 5.00; local tax (June-Sept) 1.65.
Open:
1 April - 31 October.
Address:
40660 Messanges.
Tel:
58.48.94.94.
Reservations:
Are made - contact site.

4021M Camping Municipal L'Airal, Soustons

This pleasant site is set in typical Landes countryside near several lakes, just 3 km. from Soustons and 6 km. from the coast. There are 400 pitches, all of over 100 sq.m. Those for vans are in a grassy area with lots of smaller trees and bushes, those for tents in open 'forest' between large mature pines. Both areas offer adequate shade, 270 pitches have electricity (5 or 8A) and there are plenty of water points. Four toilet blocks, with good proximity to the pitches, have showers and washbasins in private cabins with plenty of free hot water. Laundry facilities have washing machines but no dryers, although irons are supplied, and there are good facilities for the handicapped. Amenities include a small (18x18 m.) heated swimming pool and paddling pool for children, 4 tennis courts, table tennis, games for children, minigolf, volleyball, basketball, boules and organised sports and swimming competitions. A large lake (200 m.) offers fishing, canoeing and sailboarding. Room for reading and watching TV, bar/cafe and takeaway food. Small shop. Horse riding available in the area.

Directions: Leave the N10 road for Soustons (D116). From Soustons, take the D652 Vieux-Boucau road and the site is well signed, 6 km. from Vieux-Boucau.

Charges guide:
-- Per adult Ffr. 17.70; child (under 7 yrs) 10.50; pitch 21.00; electricity (5/8A) 12.60 - 14.70.
Open:
1 April - 15 October.
Address:
40140 Soustons.
Tel:
58.41.12.48.
Reservations:
Necessary for July/Aug. and taken January - June with deposit (Ffr. 90).

4020M Camping-Caravaning Municipal Le Grandjean, Linxe

This is a small, quiet, unsophisticated site away from the main summer tourist centres, yet only 1 km. from the village of Linxe and 9 km. from the Atlantic coast. Of almost 3 ha. it has 55 pitches for tents and 45 for caravans or motorcaravans, all marked and numbered; 60 pitches have electricity (4A) and there are adequate water points. No tour operators or mobile homes. Two toilet blocks have British type WCs, well fitted out showers and washbasins in private cabins all with pre-set hot water. Facilities for the disabled. Laundry with washing machines. Games room, children's play area and volleyball pitch. Two barbecue areas. Boules pitch. For information or reservation (in French) contact La Mairie, 40260 Linxe, tel: 58.42.92.27

Charges guide:
-- Per adult Ffr. 14.00; child (under 8 yrs) 6.50; tent 17.50; caravan or motorcaravan 29.50.
Open:
Late June - early Sept.
Address:
40260 Linxe.
Tel:
58.42.90.00.
Reservations:
See text.

Directions: Leave N10 at Castets and take D42 to Linxe where site is signed.

4101 Le Parc du Val de Loire, Mesland, nr Blois

Family owned site with swimming pools, situated between Blois and Tours.

This site is quietly situated away from the main roads and towns, but is nevertheless centrally placed for visits to the châteaux; Chaumont, Amboise and Blois (21 km.) are the nearest in that order. It has 300 pitches of reasonable size, either in light woodland marked out by trees, (30 occupied by British hire tents) or on open meadow with separators. Some 135 pitches have electricity, water and drainaway. The two original toilet blocks are of very fair quality and have British WCs (with external entry), washbasins all in private cabins with free hot water, free pre-set, hot showers, and hot water also in sinks. A third toilet block has been built with modern facilities. Units for the handicapped and new baby bath facilities. On site there are 3 swimming pools, the newest (200 sq.m.) with sunbathing area, and heated all season; also a smaller pool with a very popular water slide, and small children's pool (all mid-May to mid-Sept). Tennis court with floodlighting, and good children's playground enlarged with skate board facilities. Barbecue area - some organised or DIY (free wood). Large shop. Limited takeaway food all season. Bar adjacent to pools, with snack service and TV room. Pizzeria with takeaway. Laundry facilities. Bicycle hire. Table tennis. Minigolf. BMX track. Tennis training wall. Football practise pitch. Basketball. Pony rides and some organised sports and competitions in July/Aug. Wine tasting opportunities each Friday. Local walks on marked footpaths (maps Ffr.2). Mobile homes for hire and some tour operators. Watch for the Rabbit family!

Charges 1996:
-- Per unit incl. 2 persons: standard pitch (100 sq.m.) Ffr. 100.00 - 135.00, large pitch (150 sq.m.) with water and drainage 110.00 - 150.00; extra person 24.00 - 30.00; child (2-7 yrs) 16.00 - 20.00; electricity (6A) 16.00 - 20.00; animal 8.00 - 10.00.
-- Credit cards accepted.
Open:
1 May - 15 September.
Address:
41150 Mesland.
Tel:
54.70.27.18.
FAX: 54.70.21.71.
Reservations:
Made for min. 4 days with deposit and fee (Ffr. 100).

Directions: The village of Mesland is 5 km. northwest of Onzain, accessible from Château-Renault/Amboise exit of the A10 autoroute via D31 to Autrèche, continue 5 km. then left at La Hargardière at camp sign and 8 km. to site.

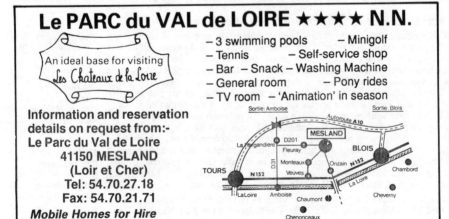

4102 Castels Camping Château de la Grenouillère, Suevres

Comfortable site with good amenities on the N152 midway between Orléans and Tours.

This site is well situated for visiting many of the Loire châteaux and makes a good stopover, but there are also enough attractions on site and locally to make it suitable for a longer stay. It is set in a 28 acre park and the 250 pitches are in three distinct areas. The majority are in a well wooded area, with about 60 in the old orchard and the remainder in open meadow, although all pitches are separated by hedges; 200 of the pitches have electricity (5A) and there is one water point for every 4 pitches. Additionally, there are 15 'grand comfort' pitches with a separate luxury sanitary block in the outbuildings of the château itself. The three other sanitary blocks, one for each area, are modern and well appointed. All the toilets are British with handwashing facilities nearby. Other washbasins are in private cabins with hot water, mirror and shelf. Some showers are pre-set, some controllable and all have dressing area, hooks and shelf. Razor points in the men's and hair dryers are provided. Site facilities include a shop, a well appointed bar, 2 supervised outdoor swimming pools, tennis, squash, minigolf, table tennis, pool, baby foot and video games. Bikes and canoes may be hired in July/August and guided tours are organised once a week. There are washing machines and dryers. The site is popular with tour operators.

Directions: From the A10 coming west from Paris, take Meung exit and N152 in the direction of Blois. Coming east from Tours, take Blois exit and N152 in direction of Orléans. Site is on the north side of the road.

Charges 1995:
-- Per unit incl. 2 persons, standard pitch Ffr. 110.00; extra person 35.00; child (under 5 yrs) 25.00; electricity (5A) 20.00.
-- 'Grand comfort' pitch extra - apply to site.
Open:
15 May - 15 September
Address:
41500 Suevres.
Tel:
54.87.80.37.
FAX: 54.87.84.21.
Reservations:
Made for min. 5 days with Ffr. 400 deposit and Ffr. 100 fee.

4104 Castels Camping Château des Marais, Muides s. Loire, nr Chambord

Impressive site with excellent facilities, near famous royal château.

The château at Chambord, with its park, is certainly impressive and well worth a visit. The nearby Château de Marais campsite is also well situated to visit other châteaux in the 'Vallee des Rois'. The recently designed site, providing some 200 large pitches, all with electricity (5A), water and drainage and with ample shade, is situated in the pine wood grounds of its own small château (in which there are rooms to let all year round). It boasts a heated swimming pool, a pleasant bar/restaurant, bicycle hire, fishing lake, excursions by coach to Paris and an entertainment programme in high season. The village of Muides sur Loire, with a variety of small shops, etc. is within a five minute walk. There are four modern, purpose built sanitary blocks with the latest facilities. These include some large showers and washbasins en-suite, British WCs, washing machine, etc. with hot water throughout. English is spoken and the reception from the enthusiastic owners and staff is very welcoming. The site is extensively used by tour operators (50%). As well as the rooms in the château (breakfast included), there are neatly furnished apartments to let - useful out of season.

Directions: From the A10 autoroute take exit 7 to Mer, then cross the Loire to join the D951 and follow signs.

Charges 1996:
-- Per pitch including vehicle and 2 persons Ffr. 115.00; extra person 30.00; child (under 5 yrs) 20.00; dog 10.00; electricity (5A) 20.00.
-- Credit cards accepted (over Ffr. 1,000).
Open:
1 May - 15 September. (Rooms, etc: all year.)
Address:
41500 Muides sur Loire.
Tel:
54.87.05.43.
FAX: as phone.
Reservations:
Advised for July/Aug - with 30% deposit.

4110M Camping Municipal de Tournefeuille, Romorantin-Lanthenay

This is a fairly typical town-type municipal, situated on the outskirts of this fairly large town, opposite the 'summer' swimming pool and tennis court. It provides 130 reasonably sized pitches, of which about 80 have electrical connections (6 or 10A), on flat grass with some shade from mature trees, but not a lot. There is an adjacent small lake, not suitable for swimming however. There is little by way of on-site facilities, but shops, cafes, etc. are within walking distance and there is a twice-weekly market. Sanitary facilities were more than adequate, if a little austere, with British style WCs, washbasins in cabins and hot showers with dividers, etc. A conveniently situated municipal for exploring the Loire valley area.

Directions: Site is on western outskirts of the town just off D724 Salbris road.

Charges guide:
-- Per pitch incl. 1 or 2 persons Ffr. 37.00; electricity 10.00.
Open:
27 March - 30 Sept.
Address:
Rue Long Eaton, 41200 Romorantin-Lanthenay.
Tel:
54.76.16.60.
Reservations:
Advised for July/Aug; with Ffr. 60 deposit.

117

4103 Sologne Parc des Alicourts, Pierrefitte sur Sauldre

Secluded 21 hectare site in the heart of the forest with many sporting facilities.

This site is situated in a very secluded, forested area midway between Orleans and Bourges, about 20 km. to the east of the A10. There are 250 pitches of which 200 have electricity (2-6A) and provisions for water are good. Most pitches are 120 sq.m. (min. 100) and vary from wooded to more open areas, thus giving a choice of amount of shade. There are three sanitary blocks, the oldest of which has British and continental type toilets, whilst the two newer ones have all British. The washbasins (open and in private cabins) have razor points, hair dryers and hot water, showers are controllable. In addition, there are three baby/toddler bath rooms plus washing machines and drying facilities. There is a restaurant using fresh produce and traditional cuisine (July/Aug) plus a takeaway service in a pleasant bar with terrace. The shop has a good range of produce in addition to the basics (essential as the nearest good sized town is some distance). Leisure facilities are exceptional: three swimming pools (open 20/5-15/9) with 25 m. shute, plus a paddling pool; a 7 hectare lake with fishing, bathing, canoes, pedaloes and children's play area, a 5 hole golf course (a very popular feature), football pitch, volleyball court, tennis, minigolf, table tennis, boules, cyclo-cross and mountain bikes and a way marked path for walking and cycling. In addition, there are lots of organised competitions for adults as well as children. In high season there is a club for children with an animateur twice a day, a disco once a week and a dance for adults. Some 26 pitches are taken by tour operators (10%).

Directions: Site is on a back road, 5 km. from Pierrefitte sur Sauldre and is well signed from this village. From the A71 take the Lamotte-Beuvron exit.

Charges 1996:
-- Per unit (incl. 2 persons) Ffr. 88.00 - 115.00; extra person over 18 yrs 32.00 - 39.00, 7-18 yrs 20.00 - 26.00, under 7 15.00 - 18.00; electricity 4A 22.00, 6A 27.00; dog 18.00; extra car 20.00; local tax 1/6-15/9 1.00.

Open:
1 May - 15 September.

Address:
Domaine des Alicourts, 41300 Pierrefitte sur Sauldre.

Tel:
54.88.63.34.
FAX: 54.88.58.40.

Reservations:
Made for min. 7 days for July/Aug. only.

4105 Camping des Grands Prés, Vendôme

Well situated site for visiting lovely town on the Loir.

Vendome is a fascinating and beautiful old town situated on, and criss-crossed by tributaries of, the River Loir (not to be confused with the Loire!). It is well worth a visit and is only 42 minutes from Paris on the TGV. Camping des Grands Prés was originally the town's municipal site but is now under private management. It is popular and is conveniently situated near the river, next door to the swimming pool, canoeing centre, etc. and only a short walk from the main areas of the town. The 200 pitches, mostly with electricity, are on mainly flat grass, clearly marked, but not actually separated. There is variable shade from a variety of trees. It has a very modern, purpose built sanitary block which is well equipped. However, we thought the maintenance a little suspect in terms of cleanliness when we inspected - partly a fault of the design, partly as a result of use by a number of apparently unsupervised children.

Directions: Site is signed from the N10 through the town.

Charges guide:
-- Per person Ffr. 14.00; child (5-12 years) 6.50; pitch 15.00; electricity 4A 12.00, 6A 16.00, 10A 24.00.

Open:
1 May - 30 September.

Address:
Rue Geoffrey-Mantell, 41100 Vendôme.

Tel:
54.77.00.27 (low season: 47.27.24.71).
FAX: 47.28.42.99.

Reservations:
Advisable in main season - contact site.

4201M Camping Municipal de Charlieu, Charlieu ✳

Charlieu is a very attractive little town, well worth a visit, and the municipal site here would make a good base for exploring the area. There are 100 pitches, all with 4/10A electricity, of which about half are occupied by French seasonal visitors. The pitches are reasonably large and well spaced, on level grass. Most are separated by trim hedges with some shade. Immediately opposite the site is an open-air, heated, municipal swimming pool with a grass bank for sunbathing, which was very popular when we visited in late June. Sanitary facilities are reasonably adequate (no special chemical disposal point). There are few other facilities as the lovely little town is within about 5 minutes walk.

Directions: Charlieu is 20 km. northeast of Roanne. The site is west of the town next to a sports stadium and is signed from the town centre. From Pouilly, on the D482, take the D487 to Charlieu (5½ km).

Charges guide:
-- Per pitch Ffr. 6.20; vehicle 3.70, twin axle vehicle 20.00; person 10.30; child (under 7) 5.20; electricity 4A 8.40, 10A 17.00.
Open:
1 April - 30 September.
Address:
Rue Riottier, 42190 Charlieu.
Tel:
77.69.01.70.
Reservations:
Probably unnecessary.

4202M Camping Municipal Le Surizet, Montbrison

This is a useful municipal site, situated on the outskirts of the town, used almost exclusively by the French, including a fair proportion of seasonal pitches. The most unusual feature is the 'plan d'eau' whereby the stream which runs alongside the site has been dammed to create a small pool with artificial beach, picnic tables, etc.. It is much used by children for swimming, paddling and generally enjoying themselves. The site has about 90 quite large pitches, 70 with 5 or 10A electrical connections, on level grass, with some neat hedging and a reasonable amount of shade from mature trees. The modern sanitary block includes rather small hot showers, with dividers, washbasins in cubicles, British type WCs, dishwashing sinks, and chemical disposal point. There is a large `salle de reunion' opposite the site entrance, used for table tennis, discos, etc.

Directions: Site is signed from D8 St. Etienne road in the direction of Moingt (2 km. south of Montbrison). The camping signs bear no name, only the tent and caravan logos.

Charges guide:
-- Per person Ffr. 8.00; child (under 7 yrs) 4.00; tent or caravan 4.00; car 4.00; electricity 5A 17.00 - 10A 30.00; visitor 10.30.
Open:
1 April - 31 October.
Address:
42600 Montbrison-Moingt.
Tel:
77.58.08.30.
Reservations:
Contact site; 35 pitches kept for tourists.

4310M Camping Municipal d'Audinet, Brives-Charensac, nr Le Puy ✳

This is a modern site on the edge of a very attractive, small spa town. Offering a total of 150 mainly flat, grassy pitches, all with 10A electrical connections, this site is actually a combination of two smaller sites. Situated within walking distance of the centre of this most attractive spa town, it is on two levels alongside a small lake and is pleasantly laid out with pitches mainly in small bays. The three sanitary blocks, of modern purpose-built construction are of a generally good standard which varies slightly from block to block. They provide some British type WCs, hot showers with dividers, hooks, etc., washbasins in private cabins, washing machine and dryer. Although close to the town's many and varied facilities, the site has its own attractive bar with snacks and restaurant, beside a stream which runs through the lower part of the site.

Directions: Site is 4-5 km. east of Le Puy, signed off N88 Valence-St. Etienne road. Cross the bridge at Brives-Charensac to reach site.

Charges guide:
-- Per person Ffr. 15.60; car 7.30; pitch 9.00; electricity 13.00; m/cycle 5.10; motor-caravan 25.00; double axle caravan 50.00.
Open:
15 May - 15 October.
Address:
43700 Brives-Charensac.
Tel:
71.09.10.18.
Reservations:
Said to be unnecessary.

43 Haute-Loire / 44 Loire-Atlantique

4301 Camping La Fressange, St. Didier en Velay

Pretty site in rolling Haute-Loire countryside, with swimming pool.

This site is worth considering as a base for touring this area or as a night-stop to visit St. Didier. It has the advantage of being situated some 2 km from the town centre, opposite the municipal swimming pool complex, which includes one pool of Olympic size (main season only) and tennis courts. The site itself is on quite steep grass terraces and the 100 or so pitches all have electricity and are of reasonable size. Despite the terracing the ground is steep and the pitches themselves are not that level. There is some shade from the trees that border the site and some further shade from smaller trees within it. The two modern sanitary blocks include showers with dividers, British type WCs, washbasins in cabins (warm water), dishwashing sinks (with one hot tap) and a washing machine. There are no tour operators and the site is extensively used by the French. There are few other facilities, but the site is only some 5-10 minutes walk from the town.

Charges guide:
-- Per person Ffr. 10.50; child (2-7 yrs) 5.00; pitch 8.50; vehicle 7.00; electricity 12.00; local tax 1.00.
Open:
1 May - 30 September.
Address:
43140 St. Didier en Velay.
Tel:
71.66.25.28.
Reservations:
Contact site.

Directions: Site is signed from N88 via La Séauve, southwest of Semène. Or from Firminy, southwest of St. Etienne, take the D500 to St. Didier.

4401M Camping du Val du Cens - Petit Port, Nantes

This modern municipal site, which is within the town limits, is well maintained and of good quality in a parklike area with mature trees. It has some 122 flat good sized, hedged hardstandings for caravans, all with electricity, water and drainaway. From Easter - 30 Sept. it also takes about 80 tents on separate grass areas. At certain times the caravan pitches become full with those working in the town or visiting for commercial reasons; however, in the holiday season, it is said that about half are available for tourists and one should usually find a space. The four sanitary blocks are good, with British toilets, individual basins in cubicles or cabins with shelf and light (a little cramped), and free hot water throughout including the showers. Facilities for disabled. Amenities on site include a shop for basics (high season only), a launderette, TV room, children's play area and football pitches on the nearby Hippodrome can be used for play areas. Telephones (for handicapped also). A swimming pool, ice rink (both free for campers under 18 yrs in July/Aug), bowling alley and café are very close, a bakery 100 m. and a restaurant is opposite. Golf easily accessible via the tramway. The new tramway system within the town is cheap and reliable and the site is easily reached by bus from the railway station.

Charges 1996:
-- Per caravan incl. car or motorcaravan Ffr. 45.00; tent plus car 34.00, without car 22.00; per person 17.00; child (under 7) 11.00; electricity 18.00.
-- Credit cards accepted.
Open:
All year.
Tel:
40.74.47.94.
FAX: 40.73.44.19.
Reservations:
Not made, but you could phone the previous day.

Directions: Site is on the northern edge of the town on the Bvd. Petit Port, near the university (ring road east). Follow camping signs `Petit Port'. From autoroute use exit signed for university.

4403 Castel Camping Le Pré du Château, La Baule

Select, quiet, little site for caravans and motorcaravans only.

In the grounds of the Château de Careil, a building dating from the 14th century which may be visited, this small site, shaded by mature trees, contains less than 50 good sized individual pitches. All are equipped with electricity, water and drainaway and, strictly speaking, it is only open to caravans or motorcaravans, though children's tents beside caravans are permitted and they may accept tents outside the main season. It is a simple site with a quiet atmosphere. Some essential provisions are kept (supermarket near). Children's playground. Washing machine - laundry service at times. TV Room. Volleyball. The sanitary facilities, in converted outbuildings, are small with British toilets, cubicles for washing, and free hot water everywhere. Facilities have been added for the disabled. Small swimming pool (11 x 5 m. open 10/6-15/9) and a sauna on site.

Charges 1996:
-- Per unit all-inclusive with 2 persons Ffr 115.00, extra person 25.00; child (under 10) 15.00; local tax 2.00.
Open:
1 April - 30 September.
Address:
Careil, 44350 Guérande.
Tel:
40.60.22.99.
FAX: as phone.
Reservations:
Necessary for July/Aug; min. 1 week, with deposit and fee.

Directions: Take D92 road from Guérande to La Baule and turn east to Careil before the town. From the D99 Guérande - St. Nazaire road, turn on to D92, following signs to `Intermarche'. Site is signed after the store.

120

4404 Castel Camping Parc Sainte-Brigitte, La Turballe, nr La Baule

Well established site in the grounds of a manor house, 3 km. from beaches.

A fairly small site, Ste. Brigitte has about 200 individual pitches, which are of good size. Some are in a park-like setting near the entrance, about 25 with electricity (4/6A) and water. A further 25 (rather undefined) are in a wooded area under tall pine trees which add to the fresh, open air feel. The remainder are on more open grass, with an unmarked area near the pool. One can walk around much of the estate not used for camping and there is a TV/sitting room next to the manor house. The main sanitary block has free hot water and is of fair quality with British toilets, washbasins in cabins; fully controllable showers, 2 bathrooms and sinks. Water taps around. Washing machines and dryer (no washing to be hung out on pitches - lines provided). Children's playground and table tennis. Solar heated swimming pool with children's pool, shop (July/Aug. only but baker calls) and a restaurant/bar with takeaway (15/5-15/9). A quiet place to stay outside the main season, with few facilities open; in high season, however, it is mainly used by families with its full share of British visitors and it can become very busy. Facilities then are put under considerable pressure. Inland from the main road, it is a little under 3 km. from the nearest beach; there is a variety of sandy ones near with safe bathing. Advance booking will normally be required for July and August.

Charges 1996:
-- Per person Ffr 23.50 plus 1.00 tax; child (under 7) 17.00; pitch 25.50; with water and electricity 55.50; car 13.50; dog 9.50.
Open:
1 April - 30 September.
Address:
44420 La Turballe.
Tel:
40.23.30.42.
Reservations:
Made for any length with exact dates and recommended for July/Aug, with deposit (Ffr. 310) plus fee (90).

Directions: Off the La Turballe-Guérande road D99, 3 km. east of La Turballe.

PARC SAINTE-BRIGITTE
★ ★ ★ ★ N.N.
De Luxe Camping Site

HEATED SWIMMING POOL

Close to the fishing village of La Turballe and neighbouring beaches. 10 km. from the well-known resort of La Baule. The charm of the countryside with the pleasures of the seaside. Sanitary facilities as in a first-class hotel.

4402M Camping Municipal du Vieux Moulin, Clisson

This excellent value, small site is conveniently located on one of the main north - south routes in the interesting old town of Clisson. The site has between 60 and 70 good sized, marked and level pitches with electricity (10A), divided by hedges and trees giving a good degree of privacy. Also an unmarked area for small tents. The single unisex toilet block is spotless and includes British and continental WCs, washbasins (some with hot water in private cabins, others with cold water only in a separate open room), both hot and cold showers in roomy cabins, plus a unit for the disabled. Dishwashing and laundry sinks, baby baths. A barbecue and camp fire area (with free wood) is to the rear of the site above the river where one can fish or canoe. Table tennis, table football, volleyball, and small children's playground. The warden lives on site. The attractive old town is within easy walking distance, a supermarket just across the road, and bread is delivered daily. No double axle or commercial vehicles accepted.

Charges 1995:
-- Per tent, car and 2 adults, incl. electricity Ffr. 54.00, without 44.00; caravan 55.00.
Open:
1 April - 31 October.
Address:
Routes de Nantes, 44190 Clisson.
Tel:
40.54.44.48.
FAX: 40.80.17.66 (local Office du Tourisme).
Reservations:
Contact site.

Directions: Entering Clisson from the north on N149 (Nantes-Poitiers), turn right at roundabout after supermarket on left. Access is directly off roundabout.

4405 Camping La Falaise, La Turballe, nr La Baule

Site beside beach and a short walk from resort centre.

This camp is unusually situated right by the edge of the sea with direct access to a beach of sand and rocks and it is also a walk of only some 600 m. to the centre of the village of La Turballe. It may therefore appeal to many. There is good bathing from a beach just along from the site, especially at high tide. The 150 pitches, on flat sandy/grassy ground with very little shade, are individual ones in rows separated mainly by low hedges but some by stones on frontage. They vary a bit in size but are mostly near 100 sq.m.; about 120 have water taps and 80 electricity. The central toilet block is of good size and fair quality, with mixed continental and British WCs, washbasins not in cabins but with free hot water, and good fully controllable free hot showers. Washing machine and dishwasher. Only bread, milk etc. are kept on site and there is a limited takeaway and drinks service in season. TV room. Exchange facilities. There are few other special on-site amenities as the village, with a supermarket (100 m.) and restaurants, is so near. No tour operators but a few mobile homes to let.

Directions: Site is where main D99 road joins western exit road from town.

Charges guide:
-- Per unit, up to 3 persons with water 117.00 Ffr; with electricity (4A) also 136.00; extra person 19.00; local tax 1.00.
Open:
25 March - 31 October.
Address:
1 Bvd. de Belmont, 44420 La Turballe.
Tel:
40.23.32.53.
Reservations:
Min. 7 days, Sat. - Sat. only with fee payable.

4407 Parc du Guibel, Piriac-sur-Mer

Unusual site in mature parkland, with swimming pool.

Parc du Guibel has spacious grassy pitches, left to look `au naturel' with good shade and many wild shrubs and plants. There is bird life in abundance, varied species of trees and even red squirrels, giving the impression of camping in a forest, although there are many sunny areas. It is situated 1 km from the beach and 3½ km. from Piriac. The site is divided by a minor road, one part being more mature and containing reception and a heated pool (10 x 20 m.) with two smaller children's pools joined by a small slide. Overlooking the pool is a bar/restaurant and takeaway with a terrace incorporating a small fountain and barbecue area.

Charges 1995:
-- Per pitch incl. 2 persons Ffr 79.00; extra person 22.00; child (under 7) 12.50; local tax (15/6-15/9) 3.00; electricity (3A) 16.00.
-- Less 20% before 26/4, 10% outside 29/6-30/8.

continued overleaf

4407 Parc du Guibel continued

Shop, TV room and telephones. The other part of the site has a more open aspect. There are 321 pitches, of which 250 have electricity and some, all services. There are four toilet blocks, all of slightly different design, with facilities for the handicapped in one. They have British toilets and free hot water and should be an adequate provision. Laundry facilities also. Amenities include minigolf, bicycle hire, petanque, volleyball and table tennis. Entertainment is organised in season. Mobile homes for rent. Recommended perhaps for a longer stay - it is some distance from the nearest town.

Open:
Easter - 30 September
Address:
44420 Piriac-sur-Mer.
Tel:
40.23.52.67.
FAX: 40.15.50.24.
Reservations:
Made with deposit (Ffr. 320) and fee (80).

Directions: Take the D52 road from Piriac towards Mesquer and site is signed; also from D452 in the direction of Kerdien.

4409 Castels Camping Château de Deffay, Pontchâteau

Quiet, family managed site, near the Côte Armor and Brière Regional Natural Park.

Château de Deffay has a rural setting and has been developed to blend into the natural environment of the estate. The 90 large pitches (150 sq.m) are either wooded and terraced or open, with views of the lake or farm land, most with electricity (4A), some fully serviced. The natural wild life and old farm buildings combine to produce a quiet relaxed atmosphere. The main sanitary block has been designed to be unobtrusive, in an old barn, but is well equipped with modern free controllable hot showers, British type toilets, washbasins in cabins with hooks and shelves. Provision for the handicapped and a baby bathroom have been added and there are washing machines and a dryer. Extra facilities are available in the old courtyard area of the smaller château (which dates from before 1400) which is also where the bar/restaurant with takeaway, well stocked shop (all July/Aug. only) and the solar heated swimming pool and paddling pool are located. The larger château (built in 1880) and another lake stand away from this area providing pleasant walking and there are weekly dinners in the château. The reception has been built separately to contain the camping area. There is a play area for children on grass, a TV room with table tennis, `animation' in season, tennis and swimming, paddle boating and fishing in the lake. Riding. Golf 5 km. The Guérande Peninsula, La Baule Bay and the natural wilderness of the `Grande Brière' are all nearby. Alpine type chalets (20) for letting have been built overlooking the lake and fit well with the environment. A reader reports problems with maintenance towards the end of last season - comments welcome.

Charges 1996:
-- Per pitch simple Ffr 26.00 - 52.00, with electricity (4A) 47.00 - 73.00; with 3 services 55.50 - 91.00; per adult 11.00 - 22.00; child (2-12 yrs) 7.00 - 14.00.
Open:
4 May - 6 September.
Address:
Ste. Reine,
44160 Pontchâteau.
Tel:
40.88.00.57.
(winter: 40.01.63.84)
FAX: 40.01.66.55.
Reservations:
Accepted for a min. period of 6 nights with deposit (Ffr. 300) and fee (100).

Directions: Signed from D33 Pontchâteau-Herbignac road near Ste. Reine.

4410 Camping Caravaning International Le Patisseau, Pornic

Friendly quiet site near fishing port of Pornic with its own pool.

Le Patisseau is an increasingly popular site, rurally situated 2½ km. from the sea. The older part of the site has an attractive woodland setting, although the pitches are slightly smaller than in the newer 'field' section, but most have water and electrical connections (4, 6 or 10A). Hedges have been planted in the newer section, which has good views. A railway line does run through the bottom half of the site with trains two or three times a day, although they do finish at 10.30 pm. and the noise is minimal. The site has a small indoor restaurant (open July/Aug.) and bar on a terrace near the medium sized pool (all season); also a games area with volleyball and table tennis and a children's play area on grass With a new reception area and two new sanitary blocks, the site continues to improve its facilities. The toilet blocks are modern, tiled and well cleaned. They have special children's toilets and baby baths with free hot showers and private cabins with washbasins. New laundry room, fully equipped. Shop (all season). Pornic itself is a delightful fishing village and the coastline is interesting with secluded sandy coves and inlets. Chalets (all year), mobile homes and bungalow tents for hire. Used by tour operators (5%).

Charges 1996:
-- Per unit incl. 2 persons Ffr. 74.00 - 105.00; extra adult 25.00; child (under 7 yrs) 16.00; electricity 4A 16.00, 6A 20.00 or 10A 30.00. Credit cards accepted.
Open:
16 May - 1 September.
Address:
Le Patisseau,
44210 Pornic.
Tel:
40.82.10.39.
FAX: 40.82.22.84.
Reservations:
Contact site.

Directions: Site is signed at the roundabout junction of the D751 (Pornic - Nantes) road, and from the town centre.

4501 Les Bois du Bardelet, Gien

Attractive, lively family run site with lake and pool complex in eastern Loire.

This site, in a rural setting, is well situated for exploring the less well known eastern part of the Loire Valley. A lake and pools have been attractively landscaped in 20 acres of former farmland blending old and new with natural wooded areas and more open 'field' areas with rural views. Bois du Bardelet provides 200 pitches, all more than 100 sq.m. with 80 electrical connections (15A) and some serviced (electricity, water and waste water). The communal areas are based on attractively converted former farm buildings and include two sanitary blocks with controllable hot showers, washbasins in private cabins, British type WCs, facilities for the disabled and for babies. Free hairdryers. Washing machines. The range of leisure facilities includes two swimming pools, one with a child's pool, archery, a lake for canoeing and fishing, tennis, table tennis, bicycle hire and pony rides (some activities high season only). A family club card can be purchased to make use of these activities on a daily basis. Shop for basics only (supermarket 5 km). Snack bar (1/5-5/9). Pizzeria and takeaway service. Pleasant terraced bar. Various excursions are organised, the most popular being to Paris on Wednesdays, which can be pre-booked.

Charges 1995:
-- Per unit incl. 2 persons Ffr 100.00; extra person (over 2 yrs) 23.00; electricity 22.00.
Open:
1 May - 30 September.
Address:
Rte. de Bourges, 45500 Gien.
Tel:
38.67.47.39.
FAX: 38.38.27.16.
Reservations:
Write to site with deposit (Ffr. 270).

Directions: From Gien, take D940 towards Bourges, turning left after 5 km. by a Peugeot garage - follow signs to site (narrow road and turning from main road).

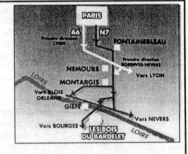

les bois du bardelet ★★★★

Club Vacances

With the Family Card:
Canoeing, Archery, VTT, Tennis
Pony rides, Mini-golf, Fishing
Visit Paris Wednesdays in high season
Evenings with entertainment

POILLY, 45500 GIEN (FRANCE)   TÉL: 38 67 47 39 - FAX: 38 38 27 16

4510M Camping Municipal du Château, La Chapelle St. Mesmin, nr Orléans

Within an hour's walk, along a footpath beside the Loire, of the centre of Orléans, this is a really delightful little site, ideal for visiting Orléans and/or this stretch of the Loire Valley. The site itself is small with 90 marked and separated pitches for caravans, mostly with electricity, plus an area for 20 tents. These are attractively arranged alongside the river, beside which runs a footpath to the nearby village (a must!) and on to Orléans - the opposite direction leads to a forest leisure park. There are three sanitary blocks, two of which, at either extremity of the site, are tiny. However, together they provide good controllable hot showers of a reasonable size, washbasins (H&C) and mainly Turkish type WCs, apart from one British type, officially designated for the handicapped. Overall, it is a reasonable, if not particularly luxurious, provision. For a site close to a large city, it is not only remarkably pretty, but security seems to be good too, despite the adjacent riverside footpath. Apart from a small children's play area and a telephone box, the site itself has no amenities, but shops, restaurants, etc. are all within reasonable walking distance.

Charges guide:
-- Per person Ffr. 12.00; child 7.00; pitch 10.00 - 20.00; electricity 14.00.
Open:
1 April - 30 September.
Address:
45380 La Chapelle St Mesmin.
Tel:
38.43.30.31.
(Mairie: 38.43.60.46).
Reservations:
Contact site.

Directions: Site is at Chapelle St Mesmin, 7 km. southwest of the city, from the N152, signed 'Camping Loisirs'. From the A10 autoroute, use exit for Orléans in the direction of Blois on the N152 - watch for 'Camping Loisirs' signs.

4601 Castels Camping de la Paille Basse, Souillac, nr Sarlat

Site in high rural situation with panoramic views and good swimming pools.

Some 8 km. from Souillac, this family owned and managed site is accessible from the N20 and well placed to take excursions into the Dordogne. It is part of a large Domaine of 80 hectares, which is available to campers for walks and recreation. The site has a high location and there are excellent wide views over the surrounding countryside. The 250 pitches are in two main areas - one is level in cleared woodland with good shade, and the other on grass in open ground without shade. They are all min. 100 sq.m., numbered and marked, about 80 having electricity, water and drainaway; electricity is available near all the others. A good swimming pool complex, has a main pool (25 x 10 m.), a second one (10 x 6) and a paddling pool; they are unheated. Solarium and crêperie adjacent. Shop. Restaurant, bar with terrace and takeaway. Disco (twice weekly in season). TV (satellite) and cinema rooms. Archery (free) and tennis (charged). Children's playground. Laundry facilities. Doctor calls. The main sanitary installations (also a small night unit at one end) are in three sections, all central and close to reception. With very modern equipment, all are kept very clean. Activities and entertainment organised in season. The site can get very busy in season and is popular with tour operators, but there is space from mid August.

Directions: From Souillac take D15 northwest towards Salignac-Eyvignes and after 6 km. turn right at camp sign on 2 km. approach road.

Charges 1995:
-- Per person Ffr. 31.00; child (under 7) 19.00; pitch 50.00 or with 3 services 62.00; electricity 18.00.
-- Less 20% outside 15/6-5/9.
Open:
15 May - 15 September.
Address:
46200 Souillac-sur-Dordogne.
Tel:
65.37.85.48.
FAX: 65.37.09.58.
Reservations:
Made for min. 1 week with deposit and Ffr. 90 booking fee.

4603 Camping Les Pins, Payrac-en-Quercy

Site in wooded parkland, suitable for a Dordogne holiday or overnight stop on way south.

Camping Les Pins named after its pine trees, has impressive views. The level pitches (100 sq.m) are clearly marked, all have electricity and 34 water and drainage connections also. On terraces, most are shady but there is a fair number of sunny places. A heated pool (15 x 17 m.), with sunbathing area and a smaller children's paddling pool are on site and a separate, small leisure park (Aqua Follies) adjoins the site with water chute, jacuzzi pool, contra-current pool and trampoline which is free for campers. Good tennis court (charged). An attractive, reasonably priced bar/restaurant with views over surrounding area also provides takeaway (extensive menu). Three toilet blocks, two recently modernised, are very well maintained providing British WCs, showers, complete with stools, and washbasins in cabins. Hot water for dishwashing sinks and laundry. Washing machines and dryers. Shop. TV. Library. Table tennis. Pétanque. Boules. Volleyball. Some entertainment in season. Nearby fishing, horse riding and canoeing on the Dordogne. Discos. Mobile homes to let.

Directions: Site is by N20 south of Payrac-en-Quercy, 16 km. from Souillac.

Charges 1996:
-- Per person Ffr. 15.00 - 30.00; child (under 7) 10.00 - 17.00; pitch 20.00 - 45.00; electricity 16.00; local tax 1.00.
-- Low season less 30%.
Open:
1 April - 30 September.
Address:
46350 Payrac.
Tel:
65.37.96.32.
FAX: 65.37.91.08.
In UK: 01722-322583.
Reservations:
Min. 1 week; deposit (25%) and fee (Fr. 100).

4604 Camping-Caravaning Moulin de Laborde, Montcabrier

Small site developed round an old watermill, with swimming pool.

The watermill and its outbuildings here have been sympathetically developed to provide a courtyard and terrace with a small bar, restaurant (with takeaway) and a shop. There are 90 pitches of 100 sq.m on level grass, well marked by shrubs and trees. All have electricity and they are bordered by woods, hills and a small river. As the trees grow, shade is developing. Swimming pool with sunbathing area and paddling pool. The sanitary block is good with well designed showers, British toilets and washbasins in cabins. Free hot water for washing dishes and clothes. Washing machine and dryer. Unit for the disabled. Mountain bike hire and mountaineering lessons, plus organised activities daily. Rustic children's play area on grass and small lake for recreation. Volleyball and badminton court. Boules. Petanque. Recreation room and table tennis. Barbecue facilities. Riding, tennis and canoeing on the Lot, near. No mobile homes, no tour operators.

Directions: Site is near Montcabrier, which is just south of the D673, 12 km. from Fumel. Follow D673 north for 2-3 km. towards Cazals, and site is on left.

Alan Rogers' discount
Extra 10% in low season

Charges 1995:
-- Per person Ffr. 28.00; child (under 7) 14.00; pitch 35.00; electricity (4A) 14.00; local tax (over 9 yrs) 1.00.
-- Low season less 20%.
Open:
15 May - 15 September.
Address:
46700 Montcabrier.
Tel:
65.24.62.06.
FAX: 65.36.51.33.
Reservations:
With deposit (Ffr. 35 p/night) by Eurocheque or postal draft.

4608 Camping Château de Lacomté, Carlucet

Welcoming English-run site near Rocamadour with excellent pool and restaurant.

Château de Lacomté is the closest site in the guide to the remarkable town of Rocamadour; indeed a 15 minute drive along the back road out of the village gets you to the lower car park. A little further on is the Gouffre de Padirac, with its underground rivers and concretions. It is close to Gramat and Cahors for supermarkets and other shops. Strange as it may seem, our most enjoyable meal in recession-hit France last year was cooked here by an Englishwoman, and throughout the year local residents sustain the owners' income by eating here regularly. The restaurant and bar make up part of the converted outbuildings of the Château, which also contain a small shop and the reception area. The restaurant is fronted by a large terrace where clients can eat or take drinks, and from which there are steps down to a swimming pool with children's paddling area. Views from the terrace over mature woodland are memorable, and the pool and terrace are beautifully lit at night. Below the pool is a new tennis court, and there is a table-tennis table by the reception area.

Charges 1995:
-- Per pitch Ffr. 40.00; person 20.00; child (under 7 yrs) 15.00; electricity 20.00.
Open:
All year.
Address:
46500 Carlucet.
Tel:
65.38.75.46
Reservations:
Made with deposit - contact site.

The main camping field is down a hill behind the bar area, so any noise from here (not that there is much) would not disturb those who relish quiet surroundings. The 85 pitches are marked out on slightly sloping ground, most with flat areas and six have hardstandings. The majority have good shade, electricity is available on all pitches and all are close to water taps. The toilet block is new and well equipped, with plenty of hot water, good showers, and clothes washing facilities - it was spotlessly clean when inspected. There are a few mobile homes for hire. This is a relatively new site, and the owners, Stuart and Sheila, have had struggles with bureaucracy and French builders that would make any of Peter Mayle's seem like `un déjeuner sur l'herbe'. Already many who have discovered it have booked to come back, so it may soon be necessary to reserve. Somehow, although run by an English family (all the children help out wherever and whenever they can) the ambience of this site is quintessentially French in its respect for its clients' palates and desire for a mixture of relaxation and bonhomie in a holiday - highly recommended.

Directions: Follow the main N20 from Souillac to Cahors and approx. 8 km. after Payrac, take the D1 towards Gramat. After approx. 12 km, turn left onto the D677 and soon after turn left on the D32 to Carlucet. The site is clearly signed from the village. (Note: you can get to the site via Rocamadour, but it is not recommended if you are towing or for large units).

4605 Camping Le Rêve, Le Vigan

Very peaceful, clean site with pool far from the madding crowd.

Le Rêve is situated in the heart of rolling countryside where the Perigord runs into Quercy. Pitches are divided by shrubs, and a variety of attractive trees have grown well to provide shade. With plenty of space, some pitches are very large, all having access to electrical connections. There are now 13 pitches in the woods. The toilet block is modern and kept very clean, with free hot showers and washbasins in private cabins, plus special cubicles for the disabled and a baby room. Washing machine and drying facilities. Small swimming pool with a separate children's paddling pool with large `mushroom' fountain. The reception area houses a small shop, a pleasant bar and restaurant and takeaway, serving snacks and more substantial dishes, which can be eaten on the terrace outside. Small children's playground but the woods and a field are used for games. Boules area, table tennis and volleyball facilities. Barbecues, tournaments, etc. organised. A few cabins for hire. Le Rêve impressed us with its tranquillity and the young Dutch owners are keen to develop the site in such a way that this would not be lost. Particularly suitable for families with young children.

Charges 1996:
-- Per adult Ffr. 20.00; child 7.00 - 10.00; pitch 25.00; electricity 3A 8.00, 6A 12.00.
-- Less 15-25% outside July/Aug.
Open:
1 May - 23 September.
Address:
46300 Le Vigan.
Tel:
65.41.25.20.
Reservations:
Made for any length with deposit (Ffr. 320) and fee (20).

Directions: Follow the N20 from Souillac towards Cahors. About 3 km. south of Payrac, turn right on D673 (signed Le Vigan and Gourdon). After 2 km, Le Rêve is signed on the right down a small lane and the site is some 3 km. further on.

4606 Camping Les Trois Sources, Calviac, nr Sousceyrac

Comfortable 'middle of nowhere' site in peaceful surroundings.

Situated some 2 km. from the hamlet of Calviac (with a small shop and cafe/ tabac) this is an ideal site for those wishing to get away from it all, yet be in comfortable surroundings with plenty to do if you choose. The site itself is on sloping ground and, although some of the 150 pitches are on flat terraces, some are not, but the helpful Dutch owners are only too willing to assist with siting and levelling your unit. All pitches have electrical connections. There is quite a lot of shade from the many tall trees (the site has been created within an area of woodland) and an interesting feature is a separate small field, within the site near the pool, where teenagers can pitch tents away from the rest of the pitches and where they can be relatively loud without disturbing others. A room for use by younger children for organised activities in the mornings and for discos in the evening is similarly well separated from the pitches. Likewise the swimming pool, with surrounding sunbathing area, is some little distance from, and below, the pitches nearby a stream with a small beach. All is designed to ensure that campers who want peace and quiet are not disturbed. There is an attractive bar/restaurant with a variety of menus, takeaway and shop for essentials - other shops are in Sousceyrac, 9 km. Sanitary facilities are modern and of somewhat unusual design. They include hot showers with dividers and curtains, washbasins in cabins, British type WCs, washing machines and dishwashing sinks. All were very clean when inspected. There is an extensive activities programme of walks, etc. for the more energetic and much to see and do in the surrounding area.

Charges 1996:
-- Per pitch Ffr. 35.00; person over 7 yrs 30.00, 3-7 yrs 20.00; dog 10.00; electricity (5A) 15.00.
-- Discounts out of main season.
Open:
15 May - 1 October.
Address:
46190 Calviac.
Tel:
65.33.03.01.
FAX: 65.33.06.45.
Reservations:
Recommended for July/Aug. and made with deposit (Ffr. 425 and fee (75).

Directions: From St Céré take the D673 signed Aurillac **past** Sousceyrac and watch for signs to the left for Calviac and site. From the N120, north of Aurillac at Laroquebron, take D653 to St Céré and site is signed before Sousceyrac.

46190 Calviac
Tel: 65 33 03 01
Fax: 65 33 06 45

In the Lot, close to the Dordogne and green Auvergne

♦ accompanied hikes in the Gorges of the Cère
♦ organised canoeing on the river Dordogne
♦ near places of pilgrimage like Rocamadour and Conques
♦ Rough nature areas.   Separate field for teenagers above 14 yrs

SPECIAL OFFER: 3 weeks for the price of two available from 15 May-7 July and 10 Aug-30 Sept. English spoken. BUNGALOWS FOR HIRE

4610M Camping Municipal Soulhol, Saint-Céré

Saint-Céré is an interesting small town, overlooked by the old château of the same name. It is actually in the département of Lot but is still in that area considered by the British to be the 'Dordogne'. The municipal site is now under privatised management, an increasingly popular system in France. It is ideally located within less than 100 m. of the swimming pool and tennis courts and only about 200 m. from the village centre with its shops, restaurants, etc. The site is neatly and attractively arranged, with large, flat pitches, 50% with 6A electricity. They are marked by rose bushes and have quite a lot of shade from avenues of mature trees. The site has its own small snack bar and takeaway and bread can be ordered. A further separate area is used mainly for rallies, etc., with its own sanitary block. There are two other sanitary blocks, the main, central one being of modern design, including hot showers with dividers, washbasins (H&C) in private cabins, British-type WCs, dishwashing sinks and washing machine.

Charges 1995:
-- Per person Ffr. 16.00; child (under 7 yrs) 8.00; pitch 15.00, with electricity 27.00.
-- Credit cards accepted.
Open:
1 April - 30 September.
Address:
46400 Saint-Céré.
Tel:
65.38.12.37.
FAX: as telephone.
Reservations:
Contact site.

Directions: Site is well signed from the centre of Saint-Céré.

4701 Moulin du Périé, Sauveterre-la-Lémance, Fumel

Immaculate, pretty little site tucked away in rolling wooded countryside.
Now under French ownership (formerly Dutch), this site has some 125 pitches,
well spaced and marked on flat grass. Most have good shade, though inevitably
pitches on a newer section have less, while trees and shrubs are growing. Grass
areas and access roads are kept immaculately clean, as are the three modern, well
appointed toilet blocks, which also contain baby and disabled facilities. The
attractive main buildings are converted from an old mill and its outhouses.
Flanking the courtyard, as well as the restaurant (open air, but covered), are the
bar/reception area in which people can meet and keep younger children under
supervision (there is even a Lego pit). Small shop selling such essentials as
bread, milk, gas, and various other groceries. Snacks and takeaway food are
available at the bar. Good small supermarket in the village, with hypermarkets in
Fumel. The site has a clean but rather small swimming pool, with a children's
pool much the same size. A small lake next to the pool is used for inflatable
boats and swimming. Next to this is a large games field for football, volleyball,
etc. New 'boulodrome'. Two table tennis tables, a trampoline and a children's
playground. The site organises a number of activities on and off site in season,
including a weekly French meal and barbecues round the lake. Some tour
operators (7%) and a few tents and a caravan for hire. Many clients return again
and again, so it is advisable to book early.

Charges 1995:
Per person Ffr 31.00;
child (under 7 yrs)
16.00; pitch and car
43.50; extra car 20.00;
animal 20.00; electricity
(6A) 16.00.
-- Credit cards accepted.
Open:
6 May - 30 September
Address:
Sauveterre-la-Lémance,
47500 Fumel.
Tel:
53.40.67.26.
FAX: 53.40.62.46.
Reservations:
Advisable for Jul/Aug.

Directions: Sauveterre-la-Lémance lies by the Fumel - Périgueux (D710) road,
midway between the Dordogne and Lot rivers. From the D710, cross the railway
line, straight through the village and turn left (northeast) at the far end on to a
minor road. Site is 2 km. up this road.

★★★★
Moulin du Périé
47500 SAUVETERRE-LA-LEMANCE

SITES & PAYSAGES
DE FRANCE

FOR FURTHER INFORMATION CONTACT:
Henri or Anne Marie BAUDOT
Tél. 00.33.53.40.67.26

4710M Camping Municipal Le Robinson, Tonneins

Close to the River Garonne, this small site has a rather formal charm, with neat
flower beds, well mown lawns and a generally extremely well cared for
appearance. It has only 40 pitches, all with electricity (12-15A) plus a meadow
for small tents. Pitches are of a reasonable size, mostly separated by hedges and
shrubs, with a variable amount of shade from many poplar trees. The sanitary
facilities were spotlessly clean when seen (in high season) and include hot
showers, some British WCs (for ladies' only, Turkish for men) and washbasins in
private cabins, under cover dishwashing sinks (H&C), all purpose built but of a
fairly old design and adequate rather than luxurious. Other than a children's play
area, there are few other facilities but the site is on the outskirts of the town and
only a 15 min. drive of the charming old riverside town of Port Ste Marie.

Charges guide:
-- Per pitch incl. 2
persons Ffr. 30.00; extra
person 10.00; electricity
10.50.
Open:
1 June - 30 September.
Address:
47400 Tonneins.
Tel:
53.79.02.28.
Reservations:
Contact site.

Directions: Use the RN113 in the direction of Agen from the town of Tonneins.
Take either exit 5 from autoroute to Marmande then the N113 south or exit 6 to
Aiguillon and the N113 north. Site is on the south side of Tonneins.

4702 Camping Les Ormes, Villeréal, nr Villeneuve-sur-Lot

Country site with various amenities, some 35 km. southeast of Bergerac.

This is a smallish site in a quiet country situation where the Dutch owners have developed a number of amenities and which seems to appeal to many British campers and caravanners. The 140 pitches, 110 with electricity, are in various situations. The majority are of standard size on terraces or gently sloping ground in a field, with a wide variety of shrubs and trees giving shade and separating pitches. Some 40 very large pitches are in well shaded woodland, and yet others are unmarked in a remote field. A toilet block of good quality in the main field includes a baby washing room and plentiful washing-up and clothes sinks. Both this and the original central block in the wood, have British WCs, washbasins in cabins with free hot water, shelf and mirror, free hot showers with screening and seat; pre-set water with pushbutton. Unit for disabled. Hot water also free for sinks. There is a small lake on site with a good sandy beach which can be used for bathing or boating with inflatables, etc; also for fishing (stocked by camp). There is also a swimming pool (200 sq.m.) with sun terrace, onto which a new bar opens, serving a good range of snacks and ice creams. Self-service shop, bar, restaurant, to eat there or takeaway (all perhaps from late May). Tennis. Table tennis. Room for young. TV room. Domestic and wild animals kept. Washing machine. Organised games for children in season. Horse riding. Villeréal, a little town with some atmosphere, is 3 km. away and Monpazier and Monbazillac under 20. Chalets for hire.

Directions: Site is signed from Villeréal itself on the D676 from Monflanquin and the D255 from Devillac.

Charges 1995:
-- Per person Ffr. 25.00; child (under 7) 14.00; pitch 36.00; animal 8.00; electricity (4A) 15.00.
-- 30% less outside 20/6-20/9.

Open:
1 April - 30 September.

Address:
47210 St. Etienne-de-Villeréal.

Tel:
53.36.60.26.

Reservations:
Made for any length with deposit (Ffr. 400).

Self-catering accommodation also available

camping – caravanning

★ ★ ★ ★

"les ormes"

4703 Castel Camping Château de Fonrives, Rives, Villeréal

Neat, orderly site with swimming pool, in southwest of the Dordogne.

This is one of those very pleasant Dordogne sites set in pretty part-farmed, part-wooded countryside. The park is a mixture of hazelnut orchards, woodland with lake, château (mostly 16th century) and camping areas. Barns adjacent to the château have been tastefully converted - the restaurant particularly - to provide for the reception, the bar, B&B rooms, shop and games areas. The swimming pool is on the south side of this. When visited there were 100 fair sized pitches (average about 120 sq.m. and all with electricity) but the site reports that there are now 100 new ones, all with water and electricity. Those near the woodland receive moderate shade, but elsewhere there is little to be gained from hedges and young trees. All pitches have their own rubbish bin and there are also bottle bins in places. Some 'wild' camping is possible in one or two areas. The original sanitary block is clean and adequate with free hot water, pushbutton showers and washbasins in well appointed private cabins. The site reports that there are now two additional blocks. The lake has a small beach and can be used for swimming, fishing or boating. A small field is set aside by the pool for volleyball and football. New children's play area. Reading room. Minigolf. Plenty of organised activities in season. Some tour operators (8%). Mobile homes and bungalows for hire.

Directions: Site is about 2 km. northwest of Villeréal, on the Bergerac road (D14/D207).

Charges 1996:
-- Per adult Ffr. 20.00 - 28.00; child (under 7 yrs) 15.00 - 20.00; pitch 32.00 - 45.00; electricity 4A 18.00; dog 10.00.
-- Credit cards accepted.

Open:
11 May - 21 September.

Address:
Rives, 47210 Villeréal.

Tel:
53.36.63.38.
FAX: 53.36.09.98.

Reservations:
Advisable for Jul/Aug.

CASTELS & CAMPING CARAVANING
Fonrives
FRANCE

Camping du Château de Fonrives
QUIET, COMFORT, and PLENTY of SPACE
in the PERIGORD NOIR AREA
Bed and breakfast accommodation
and mobile homes and bungalows
available for hire
★ ★ ★ ★

47210 Rives, Villeral — Tél.: 53.36.63.38 Fax: 53.36.09.98

4805M Camping Municipal de L'Europe, Marvejols

This is a smart, very neat and tidy site with 57 touring pitches, all with electricity (5A) and water connections, rather formally arranged and hedged, with most (not all) on level grass. Some front a small river and shade is developing in parts. There is a small snack bar, open in high season only, a tennis court, TV room and the municipal swimming pool is about 2 km. away. Sanitary facilities are in one modern, purpose built block and include fairly large hot showers (but without divider), washbasins in private cabins, British and Turkish style WCs, dishwashing sinks (H&C), and a washing machine, ironing board, etc. This is generally a useful site for night stops or touring the area. The town is twinned with Cockermouth in Cumbria, so Wordsworth is known!

Directions: Follow directions from N9 in town centre for 2-3 km. Site is on eastern outskirts of the town with a difficult, sharp right turn into the access road to the site. A turning point is indicated further on if necessary.

Charges guide:
-- Per unit incl. one person Ffr. 45.00, 2 persons 50.00; extra person over 5 yrs 19.00, under 5 free; electricity (5A) 15.00; local tax (over 18 yrs) 1.50.

Open:
1 June - 15 September.

Address:
48100 Marvejols.

Tel:
66.32.03.69.
FAX: 66.32.33.50.

Reservations:
Made from 1 March - contact site for details.

4901 Castel Camping L'Etang de la Brèche, Varennes-sur-Loire, nr Saumur

Peaceful, spacious family site with swimming pool, adjacent to the Loire.

Towards the western end of the Loire Valley, about 6 km. from Saumur, L'Etang de la Brèche provides an ideal base from which to explore the châteaux for which the region is famous and also its abbeys, wine cellars, mushroom caves and Troglodyte villages. Developed within a 12 ha. estate on the edge of the Loire, the site has a feeling of spaciousness and provides 175 large, level pitches with shade from tall trees, facing central grass areas used for recreation and less shaded. Electrical connections to most pitches, water and drainaway on some. The three toilet blocks have all been modernised to a high standard, providing showers with washbasins, hooks, mirrors, and dividers, and separate British WCs. Good hot water supply to washing up sinks, laundry, baby facilities and there are 2 units for the handicapped. A recently extended restaurant (used by locals as well) blends well with the existing architecture and, together with the bar area, provides a social base and is probably one of the reasons why the site is popular with British visitors. The site includes a small lake (used for fishing) and wooded area ensuring a quiet, relaxed and rural atmosphere. The enlarged swimming pool complex provides 3 heated pools for youngsters of all ages and there is a well organised entertain- ment programme. Shop, epicerie, takeaway, pizzeria, general room, games and TV rooms. Tennis, field for football and BMX track. Child minding is arranged in the afternoons. Torches required at night. Used by tour operators (36%)

Directions: Site is 100 m. north off main N152, about 5 km. southeast of Saumur on north bank of the Loire.

Charges 1996:
-- Per unit incl. 2 persons Ffr. 92.00 - 105.00 - 140.00.00; extra adult 25.00; extra child (2-7 yrs) 13.00; electricity 15.00; water and drainage 12.00; extra car 20.00.
-- Less in low season.
-- Credit cards accepted.

Open:
15 May - 15 September.

Address:
49730 Varennes-sur-Loire.

Tel:
41.51.22.92.
FAX: 41.51.27.24.

Reservations:
Made for min. 7 days with deposit and fee.

Alan Rogers' discount
Ask at site for details

4905M Camping Municipal les Frenes, Le Lion d'Angers

This very pleasant and tidy site is by the River Oudon in a pleasant town which is within range of a number of châteaux. The 100 pitches are well shaded and on level ground. Facilities include a modern toilet block, swimming pool, tennis and horse riding, with space for football and other games.

Directions: Take the N162 south from Laval for 30 km. The site is signed left from the main road just before the town.

Charges guide:
-- Per pitch Ffr. 10.00; person 7.00; electricity (5A) 10.00.

Open:
1 May - 30 September.

Address:
49220 Lion d'Angers.

Tel:
41.95.31.56 or 41.95.83.19.

Reservations:
Not normally necessary.

CAMPING LE VAL DE LOIRE ★★★★
49350 LES ROSIERS SUR LOIRE
Tel. 51 51 94 33. Fax. 41 51 89 13
Between Angers and Saumur, near the Loire River.
Road D.952 or D.59

Opens 15 April to 30 September. Snack, Ice creams, Children's entertainment, Minigolf, Swimming pool, Tennis.

<u>Nearby</u>: Fishing, Nautic Base (boats, canoe, kayak, escalade, hiking, VTT) Loire châteaux, Saumur and its National Riding School, Cave dwellings

4902 Camping de Chantepie, St. Hilaire-St. Florent, Saumur

Pleasant site with swimming pools, close to Saumur with lovely views over the Loire.

This medium sized site, created from open, flattish meadows on a high terrace with a panoramic view over the Loire, offers a choice of sunny or more shady pitches as the many trees planted grow to maturity and could provide a good base from which to visit the attractions of the western Loire. The Vendée coast is possible for a day's run. The 190 spacious, grassy pitches, 170 with electrical connections, on one place are clearly marked and separated by a variety of well chosen flowers and shrubs, with gravel tracks linking them. Sanitary provision is exceptionally good in both quantity and quality - if a little scattered between buildings. Hot water is free to washbasins in private cubicles and the many showers of the pushbutton, pre-mixed type. Unisex facilities for the handicapped are particularly noteworthy and are to be extended - the site in fact actively welcomes custom from either institutions caring for, or families with one or more handicapped persons. Other facilities on site include 3 pools (not heated), a bar/restaurant which also serves takeaway food and ice creams, and a small shop (all open all season). Leisure activities for all ages are well organised with daily entertainment in high season. Activities include canoe excursions, mountain biking, table tennis, pony rides, donkey or horse and cart rides and an organised family barbecue each week. There are TV, games, video games and reading rooms, picturesque minigolf, volleyball, well equipped children's play area, BMX bicycles to hire and track, a football field and table tennis. Bureau de change. Fishing permits obtainable. Used by by tour operators (10%).

Charges 1996:
-- Per adult Ffr 23.00; child (under 7 yrs) 11.10; pitch incl. car 58.60; electricity 16.00.
-- Less in May.
-- Credit cards accepted.
Open:
15 May - 15 September.
Address:
St. Hilaire-St. Florent, 49400 Saumur.
Tel:
41.67.95.34.
FAX: 41.67.95.85.
Reservations:
Made for min. 3 nights with 30% deposit.

Directions: Site is 4 km. from Saumur, downstream (northwest) of St Hilaire-St Florent. From traffic lights at southern end of N147 bypass bridge in Saumur, follow signs to St Hilaire-St Florent. Continue northwest, beyond village limits on D751 and site is signed off this road soon after. A further 2 km. to site.

4903 Camping Caravaning Le Val de Loire, Les Rosiers-sur-Loire

Select, quiet site midway between Angers and Saumur.

This is an attractive, well managed site which is ideally situated for exploring many of the Loire châteaux and the Troglodyte villages of the area. The 100 tourist pitches, all over 100 sq.m. and with water, electricity and drainage, are level, grassy and divided by hedges providing some shade. Motorhome facilities are very good. The three sanitary blocks have British toilets and the first-class fittings include washbasins in private cabins with hot water, razor points, shelves and mirrors. Showers are pre-set, pushbutton type and each has a dressing area with hooks. There are excellent facilities for the disabled. Washing machines, dryers, iron and ironing board are provided. No shop, but milk and bread are delivered daily in July/Aug. and a small supermarket is 400 m. away. No bar or restaurant either - the nearest are at Gennes and Les Rosiers - but there is a small takeaway service. Amenities include a children's play area, 2 adjoining pools (1 adult, 1 children and open 15/5-15/9), table tennis, volleyball, tennis, boules and minigolf. Extensive water sport facilities may be found on the Loire nearby. TV room with books. Chalets (5) and mobile homes (10) for hire.

Directions: From Saumur cross the Loire to northern side and take the D952 (signed Angers) to Les Rosiers. In Les Rosiers turn left (north) onto D59 (signed Beaufort en Vallée, Longue). Site is a few hundred metres on left, well signed.

Charges 1996:
-- Per pitch incl. up to 3 persons Ffr. 90.00; extra adult or child over 1 yr 23.00; electricity (5 or 10A) 10.00.
-- Credit cards accepted.
Open:
15 April - 30 September
Address:
49350 Les Rosiers sur Loire.
Tel:
41.51.94.33.
FAX: 41.51.89.13.
Reservations:
Made with deposit and Ffr. 50 booking fee; no min. length.

Alan Rogers' discount
5-10% discounts

5002M Camping Pré de la Rose, Villedieu-les-Poëles

Villedieu is 28 km. inland on a route followed by many who use the port of Cherbourg, and to a lesser extent Le Havre. The Pré de la Rose is a small, well kept site taking some 100 units on individual pitches; these are of good size, marked out and separated by low hedges. A small river, La Sienne, runs alongside the site (fenced off). Electrical connections are available in all parts, although long leads may be necessary. One good sized toilet block with continental WCs for men and British for women (plus bidets), and a smaller one with British WCs for all, make up a good provision. A few washbasins are in private cabins with free hot water, the others are not enclosed and with cold. Free hot showers preset and chain-operated. Like the site itself, the blocks have a cared for look. Tennis adjacent. TV room. Children's playground on sand. Table tennis. Volleyball. Shops are 400 m. in town centre, with a market on Tuesdays. It becomes full in main season but there are departures each day and places for early arrivals.

Directions: Site is an easy walk from the town centre; the entrance is past the market place car park.

Charges guide:
-- Per adult Ffr 12.50; child (under 7) 5.10; pitch 12.50; car 4.10; electricity 10.50.
Open:
Easter - 30 September.
Address:
50800 Villedieu.
Tel:
33.61.02.44.
Reservations:
Made for about a week or more without deposit.

All the sites in this Guide are regularly inspected by our team of experienced site assessors, but we welocme your opinion too.
See Readers' Reports on page 205

5001 Camping-Caravaning L'Ermitage, Barneville-Carteret

Family oriented site close to beach.

This corner of Normandy is short of good sites either for overnight stops before or after the ferry or for longer stays. Most of the 100 pitches here have electricity (3 or 6A) and 80 also have water and drainaway; about a third are taken by long stay units. The oldest part of the site has been supplemented by three additional fields where shade and hedges are not as developed. The one central toilet block is well maintained and provides free hot water, showers with dividers, washbasins (some in cabins), British toilets (fewer in number), baby bath and laundry facilities. Washing-up and clothes sinks have hot water. Near the entrance and reception is a bar with simple takeaway service in season and the owner's family run a good restaurant nearby (Le Clos Rubier). On site are a children's play area on sand, a half tennis court, table tennis, pin-table and pool. Nearby are horse riding, tennis, golf, fishing and sailing. A hydrofoil service to the Channel Islands runs from either Carteret or Portbail and there is an attractive beach at Carteret.

Directions: Site is signed from the D903 after Barneville-Carteret and before Portbail.

Charges 1995:
-- Per pitch incl. 2 persons Ffr. 70.00; xtra person 20.00; child (under 7) 12.00; electricity 15.00.

Open:
1 May - 15 September.

Address:
St. Jean de la Riviére, 50270 Barneville Carteret.

Tel:
33.04.78.90.

Reservations:
Made for a min. of 1 week, with Ffr. 200 deposit. (Please do not ask for reservations for less than a week).

CAMPING
L'ERMITAGE ★★★
BARNEVILLE - CARTERET

Attractive site near the lovely resort of Barneville-Carteret, only half an hour's drive from Cherbourg.

Reservations: write to site at St Jean de la Rivière 50270 Barneville-Carteret. Tel: 33.04.78.90

5004M Camping Municipal Ste Mère Eglise

A typically unpretentious municipal site, providing 77 pitches set on level grass amongst apple trees, all with electricity (8A), this site is adjacent to tennis courts and the gymnasium. The sanitary facilities are adequate rather than luxurious, providing hot showers, some washbasins in cabins and continental style WCs. Games room and small children's play area. Bread may be ordered and ice creams are sold at reception. The site is ideally situated within about 5 minutes level walking distance of the centre of this historic little town, (the first town in France to be liberated by the Allies), with its war museum and strategic position near to the Normandy landing beaches. Look for the parachutist hanging from the 13th century church!

Directions: Site is signed from the town centre.

Charges guide:
-- Per person Ffr 10.00; child 5.00; tent/caravan plus car 15.00; motorcaravan 25.00; electricity 12.00.

Open:
All year.

Address:
50480 Ste Mère Église.

Tel:
33.41.35.22.

Reservations:
Not normally necessary.

5003 Castel Camping Lez Eaux, Granville

Family site with swimming pools just back from sea on Cotentin coast.

Set in the spacious grounds of a château, Lez Eaux lies in a rural situation just off the main route south, under 2 hours from Cherbourg. The nearest beach is 3 km, St Pair is 4 km. and Granville 7, and it is a very pleasant situation from which to explore this corner of the Contentin peninsular. However, because of its location, Lez Eaux receives much 'en-route' trade, both from tour operator clients and independent campers on their way further south and at times this can put heavy pressure on the facilities. It has 192 pitches, 50% taken mainly by British and some Dutch tour operators with special places provided for late arrivals and early departures. Most pitches are of a good size, semi-separated by trees and shrubs on either flat or very slightly sloping, grassy ground overlooking Normandy farmland. All have electrical connections and some have drainage. Two modern toilet blocks have British WCs, washbasins in private cabins and showers with free hot water throughout. They are cleaned three times daily. Full provision for the handicapped. There is a small heated swimming pool (12 x 6 m.) and an attractive fun pool with slide and water shute. Shop. Small bar. Takeaway with set meal each night (order in advance). Adventure play area. Good tennis (Ffr. 40 per hour in high season). Games room with table tennis. Jacuzzi. Fishing in lake. TV room. Washing machine and dryer. Torches required at night. Note: facilities not fully open until 15/5.

Directions: Site access is signed west about 7 km. southeast of Granville on main D973 road to Avranches.

Charges 1996:
-- Per pitch incl. 2 persons Ffr. 105.00 - 110.00, pitch with all services 140.00 - 147.00; extra person 32.00 - 33.00; child (under 7yrs) 17.00 - 18.00; electricity 5A 22.00 - 23.00, 10A 31.00 - 33.00.

Open:
1 April - 15 September.

Address:
50380 St. Pair-sur-Mer.

Tel:
33.51.66.09.
FAX: 33.51.92.02.

Reservations:
Advisable for high season and made for min. 5 days with deposit (Ffr. 200) and fee (100).

CASTEL CAMPING
Lez Eaux

A family site not far from the ports of St. Malo, Caen, Cherbourg and only 3 kilometres from the beach. Set in the grounds of a Chateau with heated swimming Pool, Tennis Court, Bar and small Restaurant. You are ensured of a warm welcome by the owners Monsieur and Madame de la varde.

MOBILE HOMES FOR HIRE

Reservation direct to the site/or through the guide/Eurocamp Independent/Select Sites.

5000 Camping L'Etang des Haizes, St. Symphorien, La Hayes-du-Puits

Small, attractive, informal site with heated pool.

L'Etang des Haizes offers 150 good size pitches on level ground with 100 electrical connections (3 or 6A). They are set in a mixture of conifers, orchard and shrubbery, with some very attractive slightly smaller pitches near a private lake. There are 45 mobile homes inconspicuously sited, 25 of which are for hire. The two sanitary blocks are of modern construction, open plan and mixed, with British WCs, one with free controllable showers and washbasins in private cabins. The smaller block was enlarged in 1994 and now includes showers. Unit for the disabled, washing up under cover and small laundry with two washing machines and a dryer. The lake offers good coarse fishing for huge carp (we are told!), swimming (with a long shute) and pedaloes. Other facilities include a heated swimming pool, an attractive bar with terrace overlooking the lake and pool (both from 25/5), two children's play areas, table tennis, TV lounge, pool table, boules, volleyball, archery and minigolf. Only milk, bread and snacks available on site, but supermarket in La Haye-du-Puits (1 km). Gate locked 10 pm.- 6 am. Site is just 8 km. from a sandy beach and a 25 km. drive will take you to the Normandy landing beaches. Used by tour operators (40%).

Charges 1996:
-- Per adult Ffr 29.00; child (under 9 yrs) 15.00; pitch plus car 42.00; electricity 3A 18.00, 6A 25.00; dog 12.00.
-- Less 20% outside July/Aug.
Open:
1 April - 15 October.
Address:
50250 St. Symphorien-le-Valois.
Tel:
33.46.01.16.
FAX: 33.47.23.80.
Reservations:
Made with 25% deposit.

Directions: Site is signed off the D900 from St. Sauveur le Vicomte, 1 km. before La Haye-du-Puits.

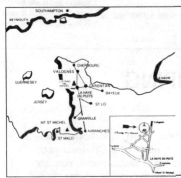

5101 Camping Airotel de Champagne, Reims

Satisfactory overnight site on city outskirts.

This can be a useful site for overnight stops or short stays for visiting the fine Gothic cathedral where most of the French kings were crowned, or to visit the Champagne houses for which the region is famous. It has about 300 pitches (115 with 4A electricity) on flat grass with hard access roads. Some are divided by hedges on three sides, others are on open meadows. The two toilet blocks, although fairly old, are satisfactory but may be hard pressed when the site is full. British WCs and free hot water in washbasins and showers. The site has an attractive entrance and was well cared for when seen. There is now no restaurant but, during the main season, frozen meals are available in the shop and there is a room with microwave ovens nearby.

Charges 1995:
-- Per caravan or tent Ffr. 18.00, car 4.50; person 20.00; child (under 7 yrs) 9.50; electricity 18.00.
Open:
1 April - 30 September.
Address:
Ave. Hoche, 51100 Reims.
Tel:
26.85.41.22.
FAX: 26.82.07.33.
Reservations:
Made without deposit; write to Office de Tourisme, 1 Rue Jadart, 51100 Reims.

Directions: From the north leave autoroute at `Cathedrale' exit, turn left at traffic lights, cross motorway and turn right onto road by canal for 2½ km. and follow site signs. From south take `Cormontreuil' exit from where site is signed.

5102M Camping Municipal, Châlons-sur-Marne

A pleasant, well kept site, between Reims and Vitry-le-Francois, this makes an excellent stopover on the new autoroute (A26) from Calais/Boulogne to Germany, Switzerland or southern France. Sited on flat ground on the river plain, 130 pitches are mainly in rows between access roads, with hardstandings for caravans and grass for tents. There is sparse shade in parts, electrical connections (5A) are available and 40 pitches have water connected. Some long-term French caravans, but also much transit trade and the site says it does not turn people away. The two main sanitary blocks are well equipped with free hot showers, washbasins in cubicles and facilities for the disabled. A third, small new block for ladies has a washing machine. One block can be heated in winter. No shop, nearest 150 m. Snacks and takeaway in season. Children's playground. Tennis. Table tennis. Volleyball. Boules. TV room. Fishing and boating in pool. 'Snack van' in high season. Telephones (Telecarte). A very clean, orderly and quiet site which makes an excellent overnight stop or for a short stay.

Charges 1995:
-- Per person Ffr. 23.00; child (under 7) 10.00; pitch 20.00; car 14.00; electricity 17.00.
Open:
Week before Easter - October.
Address:
51000 Châlons-sur-Marne.
Tel:
26.68.38.00.
Reservations:
Write to site.

Directions: Site is south of Châlons; the easiest way is from the N44. If using the autoroute use La Veuve exit from the A4, connecting with the N44. Site is signed from town but the route is a little tortuous. Watch carefully for all signs.

5201M Camping de la Presqu'ile de Champaubert, Braucourt

This is one of those 'magnificent municipals' which the French seem to excel at. It is situated beside what we believe to be the largest man-made inland lake in Europe (4,800 ha.), the Lac du Der Chantecoq. This provides superb facilities for windsurfing, sailing, etc. and even for swimming from a 100 m. beach alongside the site (lifeguard in main season). The site itself is situated on the shores of the lake, with fairly level grassy pitches of a good size, mostly with electrical connections (7A). They are separated by hedges and trees which also provide a fair amount of shade. The general appearance and the views across the lake are very attractive. The sanitary facilities, in two modern blocks, are of a good standard with individual small buildings for WCs (British type), hot showers with dividers, hooks, etc, and washbasins in private cabins, plus washing-up and laundry facilities. There is a small shop for essentials in the reception area and a bar/fast-food service during the main season.

Charges guide:
-- Per pitch Ffr. 18.00; person 20.00; child (under 7 yrs) 10.00; car 14.00; m/cycle 10.00; electricity 12.00.
Open:
1 April - 15 October.
Address:
52290 Eclaron-Braucourt.
Tel:
25.04.13.20.
FAX: 26.72.64.69.
Reservations:
Required for high season - write to site with Ffr. 350 deposit.

Directions: From St. Dizier, take the D384 past Eclaron to Braucourt and follow camp signs on to the site (3 km).

5300M Camping Municipal de Mayenne, Mayenne

The old port town of Mayenne, with a castle and cathedral, is built on the steep banks of the river of the same name. It is 200 km. from Cherbourg and its small municipal site could make a very pleasant night stop or possible base for visiting the Le Mans 24 hour race (70 km.). Also known as Camping M. Raymond Fauque, it is well cared for with a tranquil, peaceful atmosphere. Tall poplars and weeping willows over the river lend it a charm that lifts it out of municipal mundaneness. The 100 pitches are on fairly level grass and include a number right by the river. Most have electrical connections (5 or 10A). There is a fair amount of shade from the many tall, but 'narrow' trees. The river offers good fishing and canoeing (but could be dangerous for young children) and a footbridge crosses to green fields and countryside that invites walks and picnics with log-built picnic tables provided along the river bank. The substantially constructed, tiled sanitary block, has hot showers, continental style WCs and, in the ladies section, some washbasins in private cabins. Children's play area, football, volleyball, small shop/café and a salle de jeux. The town, with all its amenities, is just 800 m.. Large municipal pool right by site (open July/Aug).

Charges guide:
-- Per unit incl. 3 persons Ffr. 40.00 with pool entry, 26.00 without; extra person 8.80; electricity (10A) 8.80.
Open:
15 March - 30 September.
Address:
Rte de Brives, 53100 Mayenne.
Tel:
43.04.57.14.
Reservations:
Write to site.

Directions: Site is 800 m. north of Mayenne, off D23 to Caen, signed from town.

5501 Hotel de Plein Air Les Breuils, Verdun

Pretty site beside small fishing lake, close to famous town.

The defence of Verdun during the First World War cost half a million French casualties and the city is justly proud of its determined resistance. Camping Les Breuils is situated close to the Citadel and provides 120 flat pitches, on two levels. Separated by hedges, they are situated beside a small fishing lake and most offer the possibility of 5A electrical connections. The overall appearance is attractive. The site has a small swimming pool and children's pool. Little shop in season, which doubles as reception, selling essentials with various local guide books, histories, etc. Snacks are provided in July/Aug. Sanitary facilities, in two blocks, are a mixture of old and new, the newer parts being of a very high standard with roomy showers, including dividers and hooks, washbasins in private cabins, British type WCs, washing machines and dryers. The other, older facilities, upstairs, were adequate. An unusual feature of the site is a number of groups of four washing up sinks, under attractive pitched roofs, conveniently situated among the pitches. Attractive play area. The town centre is 1 km.

Directions: The RN3 forms a sort of ring road round the north of the town. Site is signed from this on the west side of the town (500 m. to site).

Charges 1995:
-- Per person Ffr. 18.00; child (under 7 yrs) 7.00; caravan 17.00; tent 13.00; electricity 15.00.
-- Credit cards accepted.
Open:
1 April - 31 October.
Address:
55100 Verdun.
Tel:
29.86.15.31.
FAX: 29.86.75.76.
Reservations:
Contact site.

Alan Rogers' discount
Discounts for longer stays

5605 Camping Kervilor, La Trinité-sur-Mer, nr Carnac

Quieter, more spacious site, slightly inland from busy resort.

Kervilor may be a good alternative for those who find the beachside sites in La Trinité too busy and lively. In a village on the outskirts of the town, it has 200 pitches on flat grass and is attractively landscaped with trees (silver birches) and flowers. The pitches, 180 with electricity (3 or 6A), are in groups divided by hedges, and are separated by shrubs and trees. There is a feeling of spaciousness. Sanitary facilities are in two good, modern blocks with further older facilities by the entrance. They offer pre-set, free hot showers, washbasins, many in cabins, British WCs (with some continental for men) and facilities for the disabled. Dishwashing under cover and small laundry. Centrally placed is a bar with terrace, a medium sized swimming pool, a children's pool and a pool with a water slide. Solarium. At one end is a play area with children's play equipment on sand and with minigolf, pétanque, tennis, volleyball and table tennis outside and under cover. Mobile homes for hire. Used by tour operators (22%). The site only has a small shop for basics and takeaway food in season, but the facilities of the town are not far away by car (1½ km.). The sandy beach is 2 km.

Directions: Site is north of La Trinité-sur-Mer and is signed in the town centre. From Auray take the D186 Quiberon road; turn left at camp sign at Kergrok on D186 to La Trinité-sur-Mer, and left again at outskirts of town.

Charges 1995:
-- Per person Ffr 22.00; child (under 7) 14.00; pitch 50.00; car 13.00; electricity 11.00 - 14.00.
-- Low season less 25%.
Open:
15 May - 15 September.
Address:
56470 Trinité-sur-Mer.
Tel:
97.55.76.75. (winter: 97.55.76.94).
FAX: 97.55.87.26.
Reservations:
Made with deposit (Ffr. 300) and fee (120).

Alan Rogers' discount
Ask at site for details

5601 Castel Camping La Grande Métairie, Carnac

Good quality site in southern Brittany with many facilities.

La Grande Métairie is quietly situated, a little back from the sea, close to some impressive rows of the famous 'menhirs' (giant prehistoric stones). It has much to offer on site and is lively and busy over a long season. There is a feeling of spaciousness with a wide entrance and access road, with 575 individual pitches (with electricity - 30 m. cables needed in parts), surrounded by hedges and trees. Paddocks with ponds are home for ducks, goats and ponies to watch and feed and there is a large playing field with football posts. A heated swimming pool of 200 sq.m. is supplemented by two smaller pools and a children's paddling pool. An entertainment area including an outside amphitheatre has been developed for musical evenings and barbecues. The three large toilet blocks are good, with free hot water, and have British toilets; washbasins in private cabins; free preset, warm showers, hairdryers, and facilities for the disabled. Three laundry rooms. Other amenities include a shop, boutique, restaurant, a good takeaway, a bar lounge and terrace and adjoining TV room and games room. Occasional dances, etc. (pitches near these facilities may be noisy late at night - the bar closes at midnight). Pony rides from site. Horse riding and golf near. Two tennis courts. Minigolf. Clubs for children (free) and two playgrounds. BMX track. Bicycle hire. Table tennis. Fishing (on permit). Organised events daytime and evening. Motorcaravan service points. Mobile homes for hire. The nearest beach is about 3 km. by road, so one would normally go by car. Local market at Carnac on Sundays. The site, although large and not cheap, is well known and popular so reservation from late June is necessary. Limited services before late May. American motorhomes accepted up to 30 ft. It has a large British contingent with about 45% of the pitches taken by tour operators and many British touring caravanners and campers.

Directions: From N165 take Quiberon/Carnac exit onto D768. After 5 km. turn left on D781 to Carnac and, following signs, turn left at traffic lights to the site.

Charges 1996:
-- Per person Ffr. 27.00; local tax (over 15) 2.00 1/6-30/9; child (under 7) 17.00; pitch incl. car 114.00, with electricity (6A) 130.00.
-- Less 25% 25/5-30/6 and Sept, 40% before 28/5.
-- Credit cards accepted.

Open:
29 March - 14 Sept, (all services 25/5-14/9).

Address:
B.P. 85,
56342 Carnac-Cedex.

Tel:
(02) 97.52.24.01.
FAX: (02) 97.52.83.58.

Reservations:
Made (min. 1 week) with deposit (Ffr. 300 per week booked) and fee (120).

**Alan Rogers'
discount**
Ask at site
for details

5602 Camping de la Plage, La Trinité-sur-Mer, nr Carnac

Family run site with direct access to beach.

The area of Carnac and La Trinité is a popular one with holidaymakers. The two sites at the sea front of La Trinité, La Plage and La Baie, are both owned by the same family and have the great asset of direct access to a good sandy beach. There are also shops, takeaway and a site owned bar and crêperie very close, with a scenic outlook across the beach. La Trinité village is 1½ km. The available area at both sites has been fully utilised for camping with narrow, one-way access roads, particularly at the entrance, which may become congested in high season (American motorhomes not accepted). Beyond the entrance at La Plage, however, the 200 pitches are separated by hedges and bushes giving some privacy and shade. All have electricity and water, 70% have drainage also. The two sanitary blocks have British toilets, washbasins in cubicles or cabins with hot water, free pre-set hot showers and facilities for the disabled. They should be an adequate provision, except perhaps at the busiest times. Washing machine and dryer. Freezer service. The site has a well established, mature feel, with a small swimming pool and water slide and a good children's playground to add to the attractions of the beach. Play area for the under 6s with ball pool. Two tennis courts. Volleyball. Table tennis. Minigolf. TV room with satellite and large screen for videos. Sailboards and bicycles for hire. Organised activities and entertainment in July/Aug. Shop 150 m. Used by tour operators (33%).

Directions: Site is signed in different places from the D186 coast road running from La Trinité to Carnac-Plage but entrance is easy to miss. Access inside camp can be congested.

Charges 1996:
-- Per person Ffr. 21.00; child (under 18) 15.00; local tax 2.00 (over 10 yrs) in July/Aug; pitch 49.00 - 99.00; electricity 9.00 - 16.00.
-- Credit cards accepted.

Open:
11 May - 16 September.

Address:
56470 La
Trinité-sur-Mer.

Tel:
97.55.73.28.

Reservations:
Made (from Dec.) for at least a few days, with exact dates; deposit (Ffr. 600) and booking fee (120).

See advertisement opposite

5604 Camping de Penboch, Arradon, nr Vannes

Quietly situated site on the Golfe du Morbihan with good facilities.

Penboch is situated 200 m. by footpath from the shores of the Golfe du Morbihan where there is plenty to do, including watersports, fishing and boat trips to the islands. There are also old towns, with weekly markets near. The site is in a peaceful, rural area and is divided into two parts - one in woodland with lots of shade, and the other main part, across a minor road on more open ground with hedges and young trees. The site is well kept and offers 175 pitches on flat grass, mostly divided into groups; electricity is available on most pitches (6/10A) and there are plenty of water points. Three sanitary blocks, the largest on the main part of the site, offer good showers with free hot water, washbasins in cabins and British WCs. There is a friendly bar with snacks and takeaway and basic food supplies are kept (all 15/5-16/9). A heated swimming pool with water slide and children's pool (15/5-15/9) are in the centre of the site and a good children's playground is provided with interesting play equipment. Games room. Washing machines and dryers. American motorhomes accepted in low season. Popular with British tour operators (33%). Site owned mobile homes and bungalows for rent.

Directions: From the N165 at Auray or Vannes, take the D101 road along the northern shores of the Golfe du Morbihan; or leave the N165 at D127 signed Ploeren and Arradon. Take turn to Arradon, and site is signed.

Charges 1995:
-- Per person Ffr 21.00; child (under 7 yrs) 14.00; pitch 68.00; electricity 6A 15.00, 10A 17.00; water/ drainage 11.00; extra car 10.00; dog 6.00; local tax (over 18) 2.00.
-- Less in low seasons.
-- Credit cards accepted.

Open:
6 April - 22 September.

Address:
56610 Arradon.

Tel:
97.44.71.29.
FAX: 97.44.79.10.

Reservations:
Recommended for high season and made for min. 7 days for the period 10/7-18/8.

CAMPING DE PENBOCH ★★★★
F 56610 ARRADON

At the heart of the picturesque region of Southern Brittany, 200 m from the Gulf of Morbihan, and 5 km from Vannes (excursions to the islands, fishing, sailing ...)

On the camp site there is:
◆ Heated swimming pool with water toboggan.
◆ Children's playground - Minigolf - Bar - Young people's room - Service area for motorhomes.
◆ Caravans and Bungalows for hire.

Tel: 97 44 71 29   Fax: 97 44 79 10

5705M Terrain de Camping Municipal de Metz-Plage, Metz

As this site is just a short way from the autoroute exit and within easy walking distance for the city centre, it could make a useful night stop if travelling from Luxembourg to Nancy or for a longer stay if exploring the area. By the River Moselle, the 200 pitches are on level grass, most are under shade from tall trees and 87 electrical connections at 10A. Tent pitches have a separate place on the river banks. The two sanitary blocks, one newer than the other, have free hot water in washbasins and showers. They are acceptable if not luxurious.

Directions: Take Metz-Nord exit from the autoroute, follow `Autres Directions' sign back over the motorway and follow camp signs.

Charges guide:
-- Per caravan or motorcaravan incl. 1 person Ffr. 50.00, incl. electricity 66.00; tent and vehicle 35.00, extra person 15.00; child (2-7 yrs) 10.00.

Open:
1 May - 30 September.

Address:
57000 Metz.

Tel:
87.32.05.58.

Reservations:
Contact site.

5803 Castel Camping Manoir de Bezolle, St. Péreuse-en-Morvan

Well situated site for exploring the Morvan Natural Park and the Nivernais area.

This site has been attractively landscaped to provide a number of different areas and terraces, giving some pleasant views over the surrounding countryside. Clearly separated pitches are on level grass with some terracing and a choice of shade or otherwise. The majority have electricity (6A or more). Several features are worthy of special mention including a large swimming pool and a smaller one (1/6-30/9), with a terrace overlooking, a special restaurant with a varied menu and also good value snack meals, and a collection of unusual animals. These include deer, peacocks and angora goats - which provide mohair used to make designer clothing displayed and sold locally - and a pony for rides. The goats, particularly the young ones (clearly under the patronage of a large male known as `His Excellency'!), are kept with the deer in a fenced field providing much entertainment especially for younger children. A pair of black swans reside on one small lake, with another used for fishing.

The site continues its updating programme including a new drainage system and roads with aid of the village and département. Two sanitary blocks, one new and purpose built, the other adapted in an older building but with modern fittings, provide hot, pre-set showers, basins in private cabins (cold water), continental style WCs, provision for the handicapped and a baby bath. Shop. Horse riding. Minigolf. Games room. Bicycle hire for children. Table tennis. Fishing. Laundry facilities. Mobile homes for hire. The site is popular with British tour operators (50%). Full services provided 15/6-15/9.

Directions: Site is mid-way between Châtillon-en-Bazois and Château-Chinon, just north of the D978 by the small village of St. Péreuse-en-Morvan.

Charges 1996:
-- Per pitch incl. 2 persons Ffr. 80.00 - 107.00; extra person 20.00 - 26.00; child (under 7 yrs) 15.00 - 20.00; electricity (6A) 24.00, extra 4A 12.00; water connection 14.00; animal 10.00; visitor 15.00, extra car 10.00; local tax 1.00.
-- Credit cards accepted.

Open:
15 March - 15 October.

Address:
58110 Saint Péreuse en Morvan.

Tel:
86.84.42.55.
FAX: 86.84.43.77.

Reservations:
Made with deposit (Ffr. 300) and fee (100); min. 1 week in high season.

5804 Le Village Européen, Montigny-en-Morvan

`Village vacances' near the banks of the Pannecière lake.

The `village vacances' is a distinctly French concept, usually associated with activity holidays with accommodation in chalets or bungalows. The Village Européen does indeed provide static accommodation in the form of a range of 45 apartments, but it is unusual in also offering 120 touring pitches as well. The original village was built some fifty years ago as accommodation for the manager and staff when building the barrage across the lake which forms a reservoir to provide water for Paris. The original stone houses have now been converted into apartments, a restaurant, small hotel, etc. The village includes a wide variety of facilities and amenities, including a restaurant/pizzeria/bar offering a choice of dishes at very reasonable prices, a large swimming pool with sunbathing area, two excellent tennis courts, mini-golf, pony and horse riding and watersports in July and August from the site's own marine base on the nearby lake. There are also plenty of amusements by way of pool, billiards and a well secluded disco and a theatre.

The good sized touring pitches, all with electricity, are mainly terraced and separated by small trees or hedging. Some of the newer ones in a quiet area served by its own new sanitary block have more shade from mature trees, but are not yet separated. The sanitary facilities comprise two blocks, both of which were clean and functional, if fairly simple, with hot showers, basins in cabins and continental style WCs. There are ample dishwashing facilities plus a laundry room with washing machines, etc. One of the most unusual, interesting and enthusiastically run sites we have added in recent years, this site should appeal to those looking for value for money and an extensive range of activities for all the family.

Directions: Site is near the Barrage de Pannecière. From Château-Chinon, follow D944 northward towards Montigny-en-Morvan and watch for site signs.

Charges 1995:
-- Per unit incl. 3 persons, water, 5A electricity Ffr. 120.00; extra person 25.00; child (under 10 yrs) 20.00; extra tent 25.00; dog 15.00.
-- Less 20% in low season.

Open:
1 April - 30 October.

Address:
Barrage de Pannecière, 58120 Montigny-en-Morvan.

Tel:
Site: 86.84.79.00.
FAX: 86.84.79.02.

Reservations:
Are made: contact reservations numbers: 86.84.79.01 when open or (1) 48.42.06.67 in winter.

see advert in previous colour section

5801 Camping Des Bains, St. Honoré-les-Bains

Attractive 'green' family run site with pool, close to small spa-town.

With 120 large (100 sq.m.) separated pitches, 100 with 6A electricity, and many trees, this is an attractive site, owned and run by the Luneau family who are keen to welcome British visitors and it is well situated for exploring the Morvan area. There are opportunities for horse riding, fishing, etc. or for 'taking the waters' which, combined with the clean, pollution free environment, are said to be very good for asthma sufferers (cures run for three week periods). The site has its own small swimming pool, with a separate aqua slide (from 15/6), a children's play area, and two small streams for children to fish in, one of which is warm from the thermal springs. The actual thermal park is next door with added attractions for children. The site has a traditional family bar (with Hungarian pianist playing a variety of music) and takeaway food which is also available in the bar (all season). Table tennis. Minigolf. Entertainment for children in July/Aug. Archery twice weekly in season. The modern sanitary facilities comprise three separate blocks with British WCs, washbasins in separate cabins and ample hot showers with dividers. There are dishwashing sinks (with hot water), a baby bath, facilities for the disabled and laundry. Modern gites on site for hire all year.

Directions: From the north approach via D985 from Auxerre, through Clamecy and Corbigny to St. Honoré-les-Bains, from where site is signed 'Village des Bains'.

Charges 1996:
-- Per unit incl. 2 persons Ffr. 90.00; extra person 22.00; child (under 7 yrs) 12.00; local tax extra; extra vehicle 8.00; electricity (6A) 16.00.
-- Less in low seasons.
-- Credit cards accepted.
Open:
1 April - 30 September.
Address:
B.P. 17, 15 Av. Jean Mermoz, 58360 St. Honoré-les-Bains.
Tel:
86.30.73.44.
FAX: 86.30.61.88.
Reservations:
Write with deposit (Ffr. 420) and fee (80).

Alan Rogers' discount
20-30% discounts

Camping des Bains
★★★

Burgundy – Morvan
at the spa & tourist resort of
SAINT-HONORE-LES-BAINS

SITES & PAYSAGES DE FRANCE

☆ Peaceful family holiday, individual shaded pitches in hedged bays ☆ 300 metres from the Thermal Park ☆ On the edge of the MORVAN REGIONAL NATURE PARK with abundant flora and fauna for the rambler to see, whether on foot, bicycle or even horseback ☆ 65km from the vineyards of BOURGOGNE, and VEZELAY Basilica ☆ Swimming pool, Paddling pool, waterchute, volley ball, table tennis, pony-riding, children's playground ☆ Crazy golf ☆ RESERVATION ADVISED

CAMPING LES BAINS, Route de VANDENESSE, 58360
ST-HONORE-LES-BAINS Tel. 86 30 73 44

5905M Camping Municipal de Maubeuge, Maubeuge

This is an attractive site convenient for night-stop or longer stays close to the RN6 road. It is one of the neat and tidy municipal sites and has 92 marked pitches of fair size. They are on mainly level ground and are separated by trim hedges. Most have electrical connections (3, 6 or 10A) and some have hard-standing. There is a variety of broadleaf trees providing shade when needed. Two circular sanitary blocks provide good modern facilities, with British style WCs, hot showers with dividers, hooks and mats, washbasins with warm water, undercover dishwashing sinks and washing machines. There are four pitches with private facilities (WC and washbasin) for a small supplement. When inspected, reception was friendly and helpful. Although there are few amenities on the site, the interesting town centre of Maubeuge itself is only about 1 km.

Directions: Site is on the N6 road north of the town, on the right going north towards Mons.

Charges guide:
-- Per unit Ffr. 13.00; person 13.00; child (4-7 yrs) 7.00; electricity 3A 12.00, 6A 17.00, 10A 22.00.
Open:
All year.
Address:
Route de Mons, 59600 Maubeuge.
Tel:
27.62.25.48.
Reservations:
Not normally made or necessary, but if in doubt telephone site.

5906M Camping Municipal `The Beach', Grand Fort Phillippe

This site is situated midway betwen Calais and Dunkerque and is therefore an ideal night stop. It has the usual good sanitary block, typical of municipal sites, with continental style toilets, pushbutton showers and some washbasins in private cabins. There are also facilities for the disabled. The block was clean, but a bit smelly when we visited! The site is quite open, flat and grassy with 84 tourist pitches all with electricity and water connections. Bread is delivered at breakfast time and there are restaurants and bars nearby in the town of Gravelines (2 km). A swimming pool and sports complex are 5 km. Public transport to the town and beach operates twice a day from just outside the site.

Directions: From the main N1/E40 Calais - Dunkerque road, turn in Gravelines where camping signs are shown.

Charges guide:
-- Per pitch Ffr. 16.50; car 8.50; adult 21.50; child (under 7) 10.00; electricity 16.00.

Open:
April - October.

Address:
59153 Grand Fort Philippe.

Tel:
28.65.31.95 or 40.00.

Reservations:
Contact site.

6001 Camping Campix, St. Leu-d'Esserent, nr Chantilly

Unusual, modern site recently developed in old sandstone quarry, with good access to Paris.

Only opened in 1991 this attractive, informal site is still being developed within the striking confines of an old sandstone quarry on the outskirts of the small town. The quarry provides a very sheltered, peaceful environment and trees have grown to soften the slopes. The 170 pitches are arranged in small groups on the different levels with gravel access roads (fairly steep in places). Electricity is provided on 150 pitches. There are many secluded corners for additional smaller units and plenty of space for children to run around, although parents should supervise as some of the slopes could be dangerous if climbed. A footpath leads from the site to the town where there are shops and restaurants and an outdoor pool (in season). At the entrance to the site a modern building houses the reception, a large social room with open fire and two sanitary units (just one open in low season). These units have free, premixed hot showers and washbasins in rows with hooks and mirrors. Laundry facilities. Bread and milk delivered daily except Wednesdays and snack van calls in July/August. Motorcaravan service area. Bungalow tents are available to rent. The friendly, English speaking owner will advise on places of interest to visit which include Chantilly (5 km.) and the nearby Asterix Park. Disneyland is 70 km. It is possible to visit Paris by train (max. 50 mins) from the station in St. Leu.

Directions: St. Leu d'Esserent is 11 km.west of Senlis, 5 km. west of Chantilly. From the north on the A1 autoroute take the Senlis exit, from Paris the Chantilly exit. Site is well signed in the town.

Charges 1995:
-- Per unit Ffr. 20.00 - 30.00, acc. to season; small tent 5.00 - 25.00, acc. to season and location; person 15.00 - 25.00; child (under 12 yrs) 10.00 - 15.00; electricity 15.00.
-- Credit cards accepted.

Open:
7 March - 30 November.

Address:
B.P. 37, 60340 St. Leu-d'Esserent.

Tel:
44.56.08.48.

Reservations:
Advisable for July/Aug. Write for details.

Alan Rogers' discount
Free entry to Chantilly Living Horse Museum

6101M Camping La Campiére, Vimoutiers

This small, well kept site is situated in a valley to the north of the town, which is on both the Normandy Cheese and Cider routes. Indeed the town is famous for its cheese and has a Camembert Museum, 5 minutes walk away in the town centre. The 40 pitches here are flat, grassy and mostly openly laid out amongst attractive and well maintained flower and shrub beds. There is some shade around the perimeter and all pitches have electricity. The one central, clean sanitary block provides British WCs, free hot water to showers and open washbasins. There is a separate bathroom for the disabled. Good children's playground complete with thematic sculptures of the region. No shop but large supermarket 300 m. Tennis courts and park opposite. Extensive water sports facilities 2 km., also riding and ski slope.

Directions: Site is on northern edge of town, signed from main Lisieux-Argentan road next to large sports complex.

Charges 1995:
-- Per person Ffr 13.00 - 14.50; child (under 10) 50%; pitch 8.20 - 10.20; car 6.40 - 8.20; electricity 10.20 - 16.30.
-- Reductions for 7th and subsequent days.

Open:
All year.

Address:
Bvd. du Docteur Dentu, 61120 Vimoutiers.

Tel:
33.39.18.86. FAX (Mairie): 33.36.51.43.

Reservations:
Not normally necessary.

6102M Camping Municipal Le Clos Normand, Sées

This small municipal site provides 50 pitches, 35 of which have electricity. Sizes vary up to 100 sq.m. plus and they are all level, grassy and separated by hedges. The two toilet blocks are at either end of the site and are attractive modern buildings but in the typical Normandy colombage style. Toilets are continental style for both men and women and washbasins, some in private cabins, some communal, have hot water, razor points, mirrors and hooks. Showers are pre-set, pushbutton type and each has a dressing area with hooks. There is no shop but a supermarket is 300 m. away. The site is well situated, a few minutes walk from the centre of this attractive town which has several good restaurants and bars. Boules pitch and large central grass area for children to play, but no other amenities. Near are tennis, horse riding and golf (8 km.). There are 120 km. of way-marked walks from Sées (pronounced SAY) - details from the tourist office. The town has a superb cathedral and an interesting museum.

Directions: Site is well marked from all main approach roads to Sées and is the only camp site in the town.

Charges 1996:
-- Per adult Ffr. 13.00; child (over 6 yrs) 8.50; car 10.00; tent/caravan 10.00; motorcaravan 20.00; electricity 12.00.
Open:
1 May - 30 September.
Address:
Rte. d'Alencon, 61500 Sées.
Reservations:
Made by letter to the Syndicat d'Initiative, Place du Général de Gaulle. (No min. length, no deposit or fee).

6103M Camping Municipal de Guéramé, Alençon

With 60 quite large pitches arranged in hedged bays of 4 or 5 each and all with 4-15A electricity, this rather pleasant site is about 15 minutes walk from the centre of Alençon. This is a town famous for its lace which lies at the intersection of north-south and east-west through routes. An unusual and attractive feature is the small outdoor swimming pool and surrounding terrace (free to campers) which is accessed through the café/bridge club immediately opposite the site entrance. Other amenities include two hard tennis courts and a motorcaravan service point. Shops for essentials are within a 5 minute walk. Sanitary facilities include hot showers, British-type WCs, washbasins (cold water only) in semi-private cubicles, and a washing machine. All were very clean when we inspected on Bastille Day!

Directions: Follow 3* Camping signs from the D112 Le Mans road.

Charges 1995:
-- Per unit Ffr. 22.00; adult Ffr. 10.00; child (1-10 yrs) 6.00; electricity 9.00 - 26.00.
Open:
1 May - 30 September.
Address:
65 rue de Guéramé, 61000 Alençon.
Tel:
33.26.34.95.
Reservations:
Write to site.

6202 Camping Le Canchy, Licques, nr Calais

Small, unpretentious, rural site in peaceful chalk downland.

Ideally situated for the tunnel, this small, recently developed site provides a reasonably priced stopover en-route south, but anyone looking for rural tranquillity may be tempted to a longer stay. The 72 grassy, individually hedged pitches of fair but variable size, are on a flat meadow, mostly around a gravelled circular perimeter track. All areas have electricity (3/4A) and trees and shrubs are maturing, providing some shade. The site has a pleasing ambience with a warm welcome. The central sanitary block is very clean with free hot water to basic, pre-set showers, but not to the washbasins to which it has to be ferried by container from a single tap in the block. Toilets are British and continental type. Good facilities for the handicapped. The block is not heated in winter. There are few on site amenities, though the office does stock some drinks, ice creams and gas, and bread, milk and basics can be ordered. Little bar in July/Aug. Washing machine. Boules. Telephone. Fridge for ice. Fishing near, beaches 25 km..

Directions: Site is 1 km. southeast of Licques from where it is signed. Licques is on the D224, 24 km. SSE of Calais and is a village on the Route de Drap d'Or - a tourist route. Calais, 25 km. Boulogne 26 km. From A26 use exit 2 or 3.

Charges 1995:
-- Per person Ffr 15.00; child (under 7) 7.00; pitch 15.00; electricity 8.50.
-- Less outside July/Aug.
Open:
15 March - 31 October.
Address:
Rue de Canchy, 62850 Licques.
Tel:
21 82.63.41.
Reservations:
Usually space available.

6204 Caravaning du Château, Condette, nr Boulogne

Useful small site on the coast, south of Boulogne.

Within about 15 minutes drive of the Hoverport at Boulogne and only 5 minutes by car from the long sandy beach at Hardelot, this is a particularly convenient site for those using the Seacat or Hovercraft services. A new small site, it has just 35 marked pitches with 6A electricity which are of variable size on level grass. Hedging plants between pitches have yet to grow to any size but there is a little shade from mature trees at the back of the site.   **continued overleaf**

Charges 1995:
-- Per unit incl. 2 persons Ffr. 55.00 - 75.00; extra person 15.00 - 18.00; child (under 7) 8.00 - 12.00; electricity (6A) 16.00.

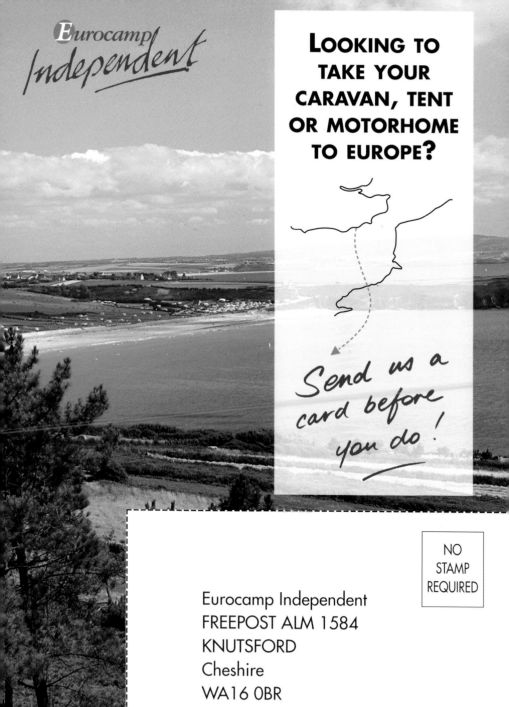

LOOKING TO TAKE YOUR CARAVAN, TENT OR MOTORHOME TO EUROPE?

Send us a card before you do!

Eurocamp Independent
FREEPOST ALM 1584
KNUTSFORD
Cheshire
WA16 0BR

NO
STAMP
REQUIRED

Eurocamp Independent

SITE AND FERRY RESERVATION SERVICE

Quality Sites Our brochure features 179 of Europe's best sites in 9 different countries. All are of the highest quality and offer an impressive range of facilities.

Flexibility You can visit as many sites as you like for as long as you like and choose from the widest selection of ferry routes and overnight stops.

Value for money Our competitive prices include maps, guides, personalised route directions, Fun Packs for the children, Children's Couriers on many sites, 24-hour emergency advice...

Easy to book Just one call to Eurocamp Independent will book everything - ferry crossings, sites, overnight stops and insurance. Our friendly, experienced staff will give you all the advice you need to plan your holiday.

Please send me a copy of your free colour brochure   GCF96

NAME Mr/Mrs/Miss _____

ADDRESS _____

_____

POSTCODE

Do you have: Tent ☐   Trailer Tent ☐   Caravan ☐   Motorhome ☐

How many times have you taken your own equipment abroad? _____

☐ Tick if you do not wish to receive direct mail from other carefully screened companies whose products or services we feel may be of interest

ABTA
V2310

**FOR A FREE BROCHURE
PHONE 01565 625544
OR RETURN THIS FREEPOST CARD**

AITO
THE ASSOCIATION OF INDEPENDENT TOUR OPERATORS

ONE CALL
BOOKS IT ALL

**01565
625544**

6204 Caravaning du Château continued

Sanitary facilities including large hot showers with dividers, washbasins (H&C), British WCs and a baby bath are in a smart, newly constructed block. Dishwashing sinks (H&C) and laundry facilities (washing machine and dryer). As yet, there are few other on-site facilities, but there is a pub/restaurant within walking distance, run by an Englishman!

Directions: South of Boulogne, take the N1 Amien (Paris) road, then on the outskirts take the right fork for Touquet-Paris Plage (D940). Watch for signs for Condette and Hardolot. Pass Condette signs to new roundabout, turn right and continue to next roundabout (after Elf garage). Turn right again to site on left.

Open:
1 April - 31 October.
Address:
21 Rue Nouvelle,
62360 Condette.
Tel:
21.87.59.59 (in season)
or 21.31.74.01.
Reservations:
Contact site.

6201 Castels Camping Caravaning La Bien-Assise, Guînes, nr Calais

Site with pool and excellent amenities close to cross channel links, worth a longer stay.

This site is a good choice for those looking for a camp close to Calais (15 mins) and the Channel Tunnel exit (less than 6 km.). Boulogne is also only 20 mins away. With a recent extension, it provides 200 pitches, all numbered and marked out, on flat grass and of a good size with many electrical connections. The three sanitary blocks are of excellent quality - the newest with facilities for small children and also provision for disabled visitors. The facilities provide amply for the size of the site and are of a standard one would expect from a site of this quality. They have British toilets, washbasins all in private cabins with free hot water in these and also in good, fully controllable showers, a small bath, and sinks for clothes and washing up. Launderette. The site is run personally by the proprietors who strive to improve it. A heated swimming pool (16 x 6 m.) is in an enclosed position and a small pond may be developed for fishing. Facilities include tennis, minigolf, table tennis, children's playground and mountain bike hire. Crêperie/snack bar and takeaway on site (from early May) as well as an excellent restaurant, `La Ferme Gourmande' which provides quality service and food at reasonable prices (open all year, closed Mondays). Hotel rooms also available (all year). TV room and library. Shop (from 1/5). Some entertainment in July/Aug. A popular site with very good facilities, reservations at peak times may be advisable. Reception is open long hours to meet the requirements of those crossing the Channel. Limited use by UK tour operators (25%).

Directions: From Calais ferry terminal follow signs for autoroute A16 in the direction of Boulogne. At junction 15 (St Pierre de Calais) follow signs for Guînes, passing under autoroute on D127. Continue beside canal to Guînes. Site is just southwest of the village on D231 towards Marquise. From south, on autoroute A26, use exit no. 2 signed Ardres and Guînes onto N43 and D231 (15 km).

Charges 1996:
-- Per pitch Ffr. 52.00;
adult 22.00; child (under 8) 16.00; electricity (6A) 16.00.
-- Less 7% in low season.
-- Credit cards accepted (not Diners or Amex)
Open:
25 April - 25 Sept.
(full facilities: 6/5-16/9).
Address:
62340 Guînes:
Tel:
21.35.20.77.
FAX 21.36.79.20.
Reservations:
May be advisable for July/Aug: deposit required for stays of about a week or more. Rooms in the house (annex) and restaurant open all year.

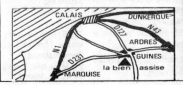

62 Pas-de-Calais / 63 Puy-de-Dôme

6203 Camping Château de Gandspette, Eperlecques, nr St Omer

Family run site in grounds of château with swimming pools.

Conveniently situated for the Channel Ports and the Tunnel, this family run site provides useful overnight accommodation as well as a range of facilities for a longer stay. It has the benefit of a large, heated swimming pool - an addition to a smaller older one with paved, sheltered sunbathing area (from 1/5). There is also an attractive bar, restaurant and takeaway in a 17th century building adjacent to the château (mid-day and evenings in July/Aug, otherwise evenings from 1/5). There are 120 pitches (100 sq.m.), half with semi-permanent caravans which intermix with some of the touring pitches giving a real French ambience. All have electricity (6A) and are delineated by trees in the corners and some hedging, with circular gravel access roads and central open spaces. The sanitary block is somewhat utilitarian looking but appears satisfactory with continental WCs, some basins in cabins with H&C, others with cold only and free push-button hot showers. Covered dishwashing sinks with hot water point. Washing machine. Small supermarket in the village (1 km). Children's play area; riding near (on site at weekends if reserved), walks in the site's 4 ha. of mature woodland. Petanque, tennis, children's room with electronic games and darts! Entertainment in season. Rooms in the château (B&B). Used by tour operators (20%). Market at Watton on Fridays, St Omer and Dunkerque on Saturdays.

Charges 1995:
-- Per unit incl. 2 persons Ffr. 90.00; extra person (over 4 yrs) 25.00, under 4 free; extra car 10.00; electricity (6A) 20.00.
-- Credit cards accpeted.
Open:
1 April - 30 September.
Address:
62910 Eperlecques.
Tel:
21.93.43.93.
FAX: 21.95.74.98.
Reservations:
Necessary for July/Aug - write to site.

Directions: From N43 St Omer-Calais road (southeast of Nordausques) take D221 (east) and follow camp signs for 5-6 km.

6302 L'Etang de Flechat, Orcival, nr Clermont-Ferrand

Remote, rural site, yet close enough to some major attractions, with lake bathing.

L'Etang de Flechat takes some finding but a friendly welcome awaits. Set in hilly country, just southwest of the Puy de Dôme itself, it provides a good base for exploring this region, both countryside and town. The 83 pitches are arranged either on hillside terraces or around the lake margins. Most are of good size and shadiness; some 48 have electricity and, although not numbered, are well separated. The one modern toilet block is adequate and includes a laundry room, general TV room and phone kiosk. Free hot water. The medium sized lake is available for bathing, fishing and boating (pedaloes for hire) and there is a beach with play area next to it. A drinks terrace off the bar, snack bar (basic menu and lake trout) and takeaway, and the reception room overhang the water's edge. Small shops (limited hours). Children's playground. Table tennis. Some organised activities. One or two caravans and mobile homes plus a chalet for hire, but no tour operators. A pleasant, quiet, if somewhat unspectacular site.

Charges 1995:
-- Per pitch Ffr. 30.00; person 20.00; child (under 5 yrs) 10.00; electricity (3A) 15.00; pet 6.00; local tax 1.00.
Open:
1 June - 15 September.
Address:
Orcival, 63210 Rochfort-Montagne.
Tel:
73.65.82.96.
(winter: 50.60.38.76).
Reservations:
Advisable at peak season.

Directions: Site is about 2 km. WNW of Orcival on an unmarked road linking D555 (D27E) Gioux - Orcival road and the D74 east out of Rochefort-Montagne.

6303 Hotel de Plein Air L'Europe, Murol

Spacious site with pool high in the Auvergne.

The site is a few minutes from the centre of the village, and just 15 minutes walk over the hill to the delightful Lac Chambon, with sandy beach and watersports. It has a swimming pool, with paddling pool, and a tennis court. There is a large football field and volleyball court at one end of the site, close to one of the three modern toilet blocks. There are 200 good sized, grassy pitches, marked out by trees and bushes, with plenty of shade. Small shop selling basics, some local specialities, and bread in the morning. The takeaway food service also operates from the shop, which abuts a bar/restaurant with poolside terrace. The site is ideal for visits to the southern Auvergne, being only a short drive from St Nectaire, the Puy de Sancy, Le Mont Dore, or the pretty spa town of La Bourbolle - you could of course hike, since this is famous walking country, and a number of excursions are organised by the site. Local markets at Murol (Wednesday), Chambon (Friday) and Saint-Nectaire (Sunday).

Charges 1996:
-- Per unit + 2 persons Ffr. 99.00; extra person 21.00; child (under 5) 16.00; electricity 3A 17.00, 5A 27.00.
-- Less in low season.
Open:
25 May - 8 September.
Address:
63790 Murol.
Tel:
73.88.60.46 (or low season: 73.61.61.18).
Reservations:
Made for min. 1 week with 25% deposit.

Directions: Take exit 6 from the A75 motorway and drive through St Nectaire and on to Murol. The left turn towards the site is signed in the village.

6310M Camping Municipal du Mas, Issoire

This pleasant site comes as a welcome surprise, a few hundred metres from exit 12 (Issoire) on the A75 autoroute - there could be some road noise, but it was not intrusive when we visited in late June. The nicely spacious site is on fairly level grass, with most of the 140 pitches arranged in bays of two or four, about half with 6A electrical connections, and having some shade. - very welcome in the heat! A useful grassy area beside a lake is immediately opposite the site for sunbathing or picnicking under the trees. The lake is used for fishing and is probably unsuitable for swimming. There is a `salle de reunion' with a machine dispensing cold drinks (not working when we visited), a children's play area and table tennis - not much else, but Issoire is only a short drive away and a supermarket is within a longish walk. Sanitary facilities in three blocks, one heated in winter, were quite adequate with large hot showers (no dividers), some British type WCs (but mainly Turkish) and some washbasins in private cabins (H&C), dishwashing and laundry sinks (cold water only) - as yet there is no washing machine, but one is planned for the future. Sports complex nearby.

Charges guide:
-- Per person Ffr. 10.60; child (under 7 yrs) 5.30; tent 5.30; caravan 7.00; car 5.30; m/cycle 3.60; electricity (6A) 7.00.
Open:
1 March - 15 December.
Address:
63500 Issoire.
Tel:
73.89.03.59.
Reservations:
Seldom required and discouraged.

Directions: Take exit 12 from the A75 in the direction of Orbeil, just beside the autoroute.

6401 Europ Camping, St. Jean-Pied-de-Port

Neat, purpose designed site in the foothills of the Pyrénées near the border.

Opened in 1987 with well designed facilities, including a swimming pool, Europ is a quiet, tranquil, 4 star site, attractively situated with views of mountains and vineyards. It is 2 km. from St. Jean-Pied-de-Port and 20 km. from the Forest of Iraty. The owner has a 4-wheel drive jeep for hire to explore the mountains or the Basque coast close at hand. Family run, the owners offer a friendly welcome. The site is maturing and all 93 pitches (100 sq.m.) are clearly marked and equipped with electricity, water and drainage. The swimming pool is of a reasonable size (20 x 8 m) with a smaller children's pool (4 x 4 m), at present with gravelled surround, and a sauna. The one large, mixed toilet block has pre-set hot water and a good supply of hooks and shelves in the showers, individual washcabins, British WCs and separate facilities for the disabled. Covered clothes and washing up sinks, two washing machines and one dryer. Bar and restaurant (all season). Takeaway. Small shop. Children's play area. Volleyball. Petanque. Barbecue areas. Car wash area. Telephone. Riding and tennis near. Used by tour operators (28%).

Charges 1996:
-- Per adult Ffr 32.00; child (under 7) 16.00; pitch and car 46.00; second car 22.00; dog 11.00; electricity 23.00.
-- Less in low seasons..
Open:
7 April - 31 October.
Address:
Ascarat, 64220 St. Jean-Pied-de-Port.
Tel:
59.37.12.78 or 59.37.16.29.
FAX: 59.37.29.82.
Reservations:
Made in writing with 30% deposit.

Directions: Site is 1 km. northwest of St. Jean-Pied-de-Port in the hamlet of Ascarat and is signed from the D198 Bayonne road.

6402 Camping-Caravaning Ametza, Hendaye Plage

Large, spacious site, near the beach and the border with Spain.

Only fully open in the main season, this neat, well laid out site is on sloping terrain, terraced where necessary, giving views of both the sea and the inland Basque countryside. The 320 pitches are on grass, with shade and are well marked, some with hedging. There is a large pool with sun bathing area and a tennis court. It is within walking distance of the beach (700 m). When seen there were no tour operators but some mobile homes. Two well maintained toilet blocks, one newer, provide a mixture of continental and Turkish style toilets, adequate pre-set hot water, with push button system for showers, not all of which had dividers and shelves and basins in cabins. Facilities for the disabled are provided in the new block. Washing machines. Small shop. Bar/restaurant with takeaway available. Children's play area. Some organized entertainment.

Charges guide:
-- Per unit incl. 2 persons Ffr. 84.00; extra person 18.00; child (under 7) 10.00; electricity 14.00, plus water and drainage 26.00; local tax 1.00.
Open:
15 June - 15 September.
Address:
64700 Hendaye Plage.
Tel:
59.20.07.05.
Reservations:
Made with deposit and Ffr. 24.00 cancellation insurance.

Directions: From Bayonne, use RN10 and D912 Corniche road to Hendaye Plage, turning left in the direction of Hendaye town before beach. Site is immediately on left over railway line. If using autoroute, take exit for St. Jean-de-Luz (sud).

64 Pyrénées-Atlantiques

6405 Airotel International d'Erromardie, St. Jean-de-Luz

Good seaside site close to some well known Basque resorts.

Sites right by the sea in this region are not all that numerous but this is a good one with only the access road to cross to reach a beach of fine shingle. It is said to be safe for bathing (there are some submerged rocks at low tide) although, as usual around here, it is supervised by lifeguards. The beach is public and can be busy at weekends. The site is mainly flat, grassy, and consists of several different parts separated by hedges with little shade. All pitches are now individual ones, with electricity, mainly adjoining access roads and backing onto hedges etc., so the site does not become overcrowded. The two large sanitary blocks are very satisfactory with washing facilities in private cabins. The newer block is of particularly good quality with free hot water in all facilities. British WCs. Individual basins with mirrors and shelves in private cabins. Free hot showers, some but not all pre-set, and free hot water for some basins and sinks. Swimming pool (25/5-30/9) and solarium. Shop and takeaway (both July/Aug). Restaurant (15/6-10/9). Boules. Children's play area. Golf near. Caravans and mobile homes for hire. St Jean-de-Luz, an attractive, lively little seaside resort with plenty of history and character, is a short drive. The more select and sedate Biarritz is about 15 km. as is the Spanish frontier at Hendaye and Behobia. San Sebastian, parts of the Pyrénées, and many charming old Basque villages in the interior can be reached easily on day trips. Used by tour operators (10%).

Directions: Turn off main N10 north of St. Jean-de-Luz towards sea by sign to 'Campings' and 'Plage d'Erromardie', then 1 km. to site. From autoroute A63, take exit for St. Jean-de-Luz Nord.

Charges 1995:
-- Per pitch incl. 2 persons and electricity (5A) Ffr. 90.00 - 134.00; extra person 15.00 - 20.00 (under 5 yrs free); local tax (over 10s) 1.00; extra car 20.00; dog 10.00.
-- Credit cards accepted.
Open:
15 May - 30 September.
Address:
64500 St Jean-de-Luz.
Tel:
59.26.07.74.
Reservations:
Made for foreigners with substantial deposit and small booking fee for periods of at least a week.

International d'Erromardie (St Jean-de-Luz) - *General view of camp and beach*

6404 Camping Les Gaves, Laruns

Small site set high in Pyrennean walking country.

This clean, well managed site has 97 flat, marked pitches, all with electricity. The toilet block has the demeanour of a 1940's school dormitory, but contains modern installations, plenty of hot water, and is heated in colder months. There is a small bar, bread is sold in the mornings, and for recreation, a volleyball court, some children's play equipment, indoor table tennis tables and a boules area. The Gave d'Ossau runs alongside the site and fishing is interesting for both practitioners and spectators. The site is only 25 km. from the Spanish border (via the picturesque Col du Portalet) and within easy walking distance from the town centre. Laruns is a very pleasant and bustling centre for walkers, with good restaurants including arguably the best crêperie outside Brittany!

Directions: Take N134 from Pau towards Olorons, branch left onto D934 at Gan. Follow road to Laruns, and just after town turn left, following signs to site.

Charges guide:
-- Per pitch Ffr. 38.00; person 18.00; electricity 11.00.
Open:
All year.
Address:
64440 Laruns.
Tel:
59.05.32.37.
Reservations:
Necessary for most of the year.

6407 Castel Camping Le Ruisseau, Bidart, nr Biarritz

Pleasant, busy site with swimming pool, just back from sea, with reasonable charges.

This site, just behind the coast, is about 2 km. from Bidart and 2½ km. from a sandy beach but it does have three swimming pools on the terrain: two (15 x 7 and 12 x 6 m.), both heated, on the main camp and one (18 x 10 m.), with slide, on the newer area opposite. There is also a little lake, where boating is possible, in the area at the bottom of the site which has a very pleasant open aspect and now includes a large play area. Pitches on the main camp are individual, marked-out and of a good size, either on flat terraces or on a slight slope. The terrain is wooded so the great majority of them have some shade. There are 300 here with a further 100 on a second area where shade has developed and which has its own good toilet block. Electrical connections are available nearly everywhere. The sanitary facilities (unisex) consist of two main blocks and some extra smaller units. They have British and some continental WCs, washbasins in private cabins with free hot water, free hot showers, nearly all pre-set, and are regularly refurbished and maintained. Shop. Large self-service restaurant with takeaway and separate bar with terraces and TV. Activities include 2 tennis courts (free outside July/Aug), volleyball, table tennis, riding from the site, TV and games rooms, minigolf, a small practice golf course, sauna, solarium and a children's playground. Washing machine. `Animation' during main season: organised sports and evening entertainment twice weekly in season. Bicycle and surf board hire. Site is very popular with tour operators. Mobile homes to rent.

Directions: Site is east of Bidart on a minor road towards Arbonne. From autoroute take Biarritz exit, turn towards St. Jean-de-Luz on N10, take first left at traffic lights and follow camp signs. When travelling south on N10 the turning is the first after passing the autoroute entry point.

Charges 1996:
-- Per unit incl. 2 persons Ffr. 105.00; extra adult 27.00; child (under 7) 14.00; electricity 19.00; dog 6.00; local tax (over 10) 1.50.
-- Less 20% in May, June and Sept.
Open:
15 May - 15 September, with all amenities.
Address:
64210 Bidart.
Tel:
59.41.94.50.
FAX: 59.41.95.73.
Reservations:
Made for exact dates, for min. a week or so in main season, with deposit (Ffr 350), fee (62) and cancellation insurance (18). Total Ffr. 430.

IN THE BASQUE COUNTRY:
CAMPING—CARAVANING LE RUISSEAU ****N.N.

64210 Bidart   Attractive wooded terrain close to a lake—

1,100 sq.m. pool with slides
Indoor pool
Tennis - Minigolf
Sauna - Restaurant
Hot takeaway food
Provision shop

Mobile homes and bunglows for hire

6403M Camping Municipal Ur-Alde, St Palais

Ur-Alde is a flat site by a river, adjoining a sports complex with swimming pool and tennis courts. There are about 50 individual pitches on one side heavily shaded by tall poplars, 25 large caravan pitches on the other with electricity, water and drainaway, separated by hedges, and some open meadows, not divided up, for the overflow. The toilet block is a good one, with free hot water. No shop. General room with beer/soft drinks bar. Playground. Washing machines. Barbeque. The site gets full in July/Aug. and reservations are not made.

Directions: Site is on eastern edge of town towards Mauléon.

Charges guide:
-- Per unit incl. 3 persons: caravan pitch with all services Ffr. 65.00; extra person 12.00; child 6.00.
Open:
15 June - 15 Sept.
Reservations:
Not made.

6406 Camping Le Pavillon Royal, Bidart, nr Biarritz

Comfortable, popular camp by a sandy beach with excellent toilet blocks and swimming pool.

Le Pavillon Royal has an excellent situation on raised terrain overlooking the sea, and with good views along the coast to the south and to the north coast of Spain beyond. Beneath the camp - and only a very short walk down - stretches a wide sandy beach. This is the Atlantic with its breakers and a central marked-out section of the beach is supervised by lifeguards. There is also a section with rocks and pools. If the sea is rough, there is a swimming pool (20 x 10 m.) on the camp. The site is divided up into 335 separate pitches, many with electricity, all marked out and many larger than before and levelled. They include some special ones for caravans with electricity, water and drainaway. Much of the camp is in full sun - shade in one part only. Roads are asphalted. No dogs are taken. All sanitary blocks are of the highest quality with mainly British WCs, washbasins in cabins with shelf and mirror, and free hot water in basins, and fully controllable showers, sinks and baby baths; good units for disabled all thoroughly cleaned twice daily. Washing facilities closed at night except for night units. Well stocked shop and restaurant with takeaway food also (open all season). General room. TV room. Games room with table tennis, also usable for films etc. Children's playground. Washing machines and dryers. Sauna. Reservation in high season is advisable.

Charges guide:
-- Per unit incl. 2 persons and electricity Ffr 115.00 - 135.00, with water also 136.00 - 160.00; extra person (over 4 yrs) 17.00 - 20.00; extra car 25.00.
Open:
mid-May - 25 Sept
Address:
Av. du Prince-de-Galles, 64210 Bidart.
Tel:
59.23.00.54.
FAX: 59.23.44.47.
Reservations:
Made for exact dates with deposit and fee.

Directions: Do not go into Bidart, as the camp is on the Biarritz side. Coming from north, keep on main N10 by-passing Biarritz, and then turn sharp back right on last possible road leading to Biarritz. After 600 m. turn left at camp sign (easy to miss). From A63 motorway take C4 exit.

6410 Caravaning Playa, Acotz, St. Jean-de-Luz

Excellent site in an idyllic location overlooking the sea.

This family run site offers the type of environment that can make the perfect holiday - friendly owners and a well run establishment in natural surroundings. Situated on the sweep of the bay between Biarritz and St. Jean-de-Luz, this is a terraced site. The pitches are level, separated by shrubs and have a sandy base and electric hook-ups. From reception a tarmac roadway slopes downwards to the various levels, but with care there is no problem should you wish to place an outfit alongside the wall close to the water's edge. There are some pitches at a higher level with a restricted sea view.

The sanitary facilities, which were exceptionally clean when we visited, are well maintained, modern and tiled with tasteful colour co-ordination between walls, floors and fittings. There are WCs (British style), washbasins in cabins, hot showers and facilities for the disabled. The proprietors are friendly, jovial people and, although they speak no English, during the high season they employ staff who speak English, Dutch, German and Spanish. Catering facilities on site are to be found on the opposite side of the road from reception and where there are several holiday caravans for hire. There is a pleasant bar/restaurant and patio area with an extensive, reasonably priced menu, also a takeaway. Whilst there is a magnificent, supervised beach at this site, within 5 km. at St. Jean-de-Luz is the commencement of the spectacular Corniche road which follows the cliff tops to Hendaye and its impressive 3 km. long sandy beach.

Charges guide:
-- Per unit Ffr. 60.00; person 25.00; electricity 20.00.
-- Less 30% outside July/August.
Open:
1 April -- 15 November.
Address:
Acotz, 64500 St. Jean-de-Luz.
Tel:
59.26.55.85.
Reservations:
Are accepted - contact site.

Directions: Leave the A63 autoroute at St. Jean-de-Luz nord exit onto the RN10. Proceed for approx. 500 m. north and turn west onto an unclassified road signed Guéthary. Site is clearly signed on the left.

6409 Camping La Chêneraie, Bayonne

Good class site with swimming pool in pleasant situation 8 km. from sea.

A good quality site in a pleasant setting, La Chêneraie is only 8 km. from the coast at Anglet where there is a long beach and big car park. It also has a medium sized free swimming pool on site, open June-Aug, longer if the weather is fine, which makes it a comfortable base for a holiday in this attractive region. Bayonne and Biarritz are near at hand. There are distant mountain views from the site which consists of meadows, generally well shaded and divided partly into individual pitches and with some special caravan plots with electricity, water and drainage. In the sloping part of the site terraces have been created to give level pitches. A wooded area, not used for camping, is available for strolls. The sanitary installations consist of one very large central block of good quality with British toilets and free hot water in the washbasins (in private cabins) and in fully controllable hot showers, and three smaller units in other parts all of which are kept very clean. Baby baths and facilities for the handicapped. Shop, general kiosk and restaurant with all day snacks service and takeaway (shop, restaurant and pool 1/6-15/9). Tennis (free outside July/Aug). Small pool for fishing, boating with inflatables etc. Table tennis. Children's playground. TV room. First aid room. Washing machine and dryer. Fully equipped tents for hire and site is used by tour operators (10%). English spoken. This is a good site to know and it may have room if you arrive by early afternoon.

Directions: Site is 4 km. northeast of Bayonne just off the main N117 road to Pau. From new autoroute A63 take exit 6 marked `Bayonne St. Esprit'.

Charges 1996:
-- Per person Ffr. 21.00; child (under 7) 12.00, local tax (over 18s) 1.10; pitch 50.00; electricity 18.00.
-- Less 20% outside 1/6-15/9.
Open:
Easter - 30 September, full services 1/6-15/9.
Address:
64100 Bayonne.
Tel:
59.55.01.31.
FAX: 59.55.11.17.
Reservations:
Made for min. 1 week with deposit (Ffr. 400) and fee (100).

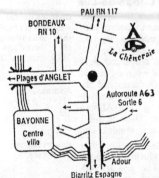

BAYONNE **Airotel La Chêneraie** ★★★★

Camping Caravaning
Route de Pau RN117
Tel: 59.55.01.31
(Take exit 6 `Bayonne Saint-Esprit'
from autoroute A63)
★
SWIMMING POOL ON SITE
Most modern sanitary facilities. Boating - Fishing
Beaches only a few minutes' drive
Corridas and folklore festivals
Tennis - Archery - Entertainment

Fully equipped BUNGALOWS for hire

Absolute quiet - view of Pyrénées

6423M Camping Municipal de Mosqueros, Salies-de-Béarn

In scenic surroundings convenient to A64, this is a 3 star municipal site, worthy of its grading and attractively located in a parkland situation 1 km. from the pretty little town of Salies de Béarn. It has an immaculate appearance, welcoming wardens and spotlessly clean facilities. Tarmac roadways lead from the entrance barrier (locked at night), past reception to spacious pitches. These are numbered, have electricity and water connections and are separated by tall shrubs and hedges giving complete privacy. The toilet block is in a central position and maintained to a high standard. It offers adequate WCs (British), washbasins, showers, etc. Washing up and laundry area with sinks, washing machine, dryer and iron. On site is a TV and recreation room, plus a swimming pool and tennis courts adjacent. For all shopping, Salies-de-Béarn, with its old houses overhanging the river and its thermal baths, is only minutes away.

Directions: Well signed in town, on D17 Bayonne road, northeast of the town.

Charges guide:
-- Per person Ffr. 13.00; child 7.50; pitch 11.00; with electricity 28.00; local tax 1.50.
Open:
15 March -- 15 October.
Address:
64270 Salies-de-Béarn.
Tel:
59.38.12.94.
Reservations:
Advisable for July/Aug. Contact site.

6411 Camping du Col d'Ibardin, Urrugne

Family owned site with swimming pool at foot of Basque Pyrénées

This is a highly recommended site which justly deserves praise. It is well run with emphasis on personal attention, the smiling Madame, her staff and family ensuring that all are made welcome. It is attractively set in the middle of an oak wood. Behind the forecourt, with its brightly coloured shrubs and modern reception area, various roadways lead to the pitches. These are individual, spacious and enjoy the benefit of the shade, but if preferred a more open aspect can be found. There are electric hook-ups and adequate water points distributed around, with rubbish disposal near the entrance gate. The two toilet blocks are kept very clean and house WCs (British), a WC for the disabled, washbasins, free pre-set hot showers and sufficient shelves, hooks, razor points, etc. Dishwashing facilities are in separate open areas close by and a laundry unit with washing machine and dryer is located to the rear of reception. A small shop sells basic foodstuffs and bread orders are taken, but a large supermarket and shopping centre is within 5 km. In July and August there is a catering and takeaway service on site, also a bar and occasional evening entertainment which includes Flamenco dancing. Other amenities include a swimming pool, paddling pool, tennis courts, bicycle hire, boules, table tennis, video games and a children's playground and club with adult supervision. From this site you can enjoy the mountain scenery, be on the beach at Socoa within minutes or cross the border into Spain approximately 14 km. down the road.

Directions: Leave the A63 autoroute at St. Jean-de-Luz sud, exit no. 2 and join the RN10 in the direction of Urrugne. Turn left at traffic lights onto the D4 and site is on right after 5 km.

Charges guide:
-- Per unit incl. 2 persons Ffr. 82.00; extra adult 18.00; child (2-7 yrs) 10.00; electricity (4A) 14.00; local tax 1.00.
-- Less 20% in June and Sept.
Open: 1 May - 30 September.
Address: 64122 Urrugne.
Tel: 59.54.31.21. FAX: 59.54.62.28.
Reservations: Are accepted - contact site.

6421M Camping Municipal Chibaou-Berria, St Jean-de-Luz

The first impression of this large site is one of neatness. From the entrance tarmac roadways lead to the spacious pitches which are divided by hedges with plenty of room for awnings. Pitches to the left hand side beyond reception are placed at different levels, whilst those to the right have a sea view, Of the 300, there are 220 with electric hook-ups and water points, rubbish points and night lights are distributed around. Sanitary facilities are modern and when we visited were spotlessly clean. They include showers, individual wash cabins and hot water. WCs are a mixture of British and continental style. Open dishwashing sinks. Laundry facilities including washing machines and ironing room. Also on site are a food store, bar, restaurant, takeaway and TV room. There is direct access to the beach for surfing and windsurfing. Nearby are discos, tennis courts and often Basque folk festivities or Corridas with Landes cows.

Directions: Follow the RN10 from Bayonne for 2 km. After Guéthary take the third road to the right. From the south take motorway exit St Jean-de-Luz north in the direction of Bayonne, then the first road to the left.

Charges guide:
-- Per person Ffr. 20.00; child (under 10 yrs) 10.00; car and caravan 23.00; electricity 11.50.
Open: 1 June - 15 September.
Address: 64500 St Jean-de-Luz.
Tel: 59.26.11.94 or 59.51.61.71.
Reservations: Contact site.

6420M Camping Municipal de la Vallée d'Ossau, Izeste

This site is located between Pau and mountains, with the Gave d' Ossau running beside it and surrounded by attractive hedges. Most of the marked pitches are flat and well shaded. Facilities were clean and well maintained. Small shops and a restaurant are nearby in the village of Izeste.

Directions: Take the N134 from Pau to Olorons and turn left on the D934 to Laruns. Site is just south of Izeste on the left.

Charges guide:
-- Per pitch Ffr. 10.00; person 7.00; electricity (5A) 12.00.
Open: 15 June - 31 August.
Address: 64260 Izeste.
Tel: 59.05.62.84.
Reservations: Advised for July/Aug.

6422M Camping Municipal de Plaza Berri, St Jean-Pied-de-Port

This is a basic 2 star municipal site, secluded beneath the ramparts and shaded by an assortment of trees and shrubs. Roadways are tarmac and the Bureau is to the left as you drive in. Should this be closed, you choose a pitch and report to the warden later. A notice should give opening hours. The 50 pitches are grass, mostly level and have electrical hook-ups. The sanitary facilities are to the rear but are not in the conventional toilet block style. Showers (free), WCs and wash cubicles with mirrors and shaver points are individually housed and kept very clean. The dishwashing area, laundry sinks and clothes lines are in the open alongside. Warm water is available 9 am. - 7 pm. A park area is on the ramparts above, a sports centre with swimming pool beside the site and a Roman bridge within 500 m. St Jean-Pied-de-Port is one of the Basque country's most appealing old towns, surrounded by the splendid scenery of the Pyrénées.

Directions: Site is well signed in the town.

Charges guide:
-- Per adult Ffr. 13.00; child (under 7 yrs) 8.00; car and caravan 16.00; motorcaravan 15.00; electricity 11.00.

Open:
Easter - September.

Address:
64220
St. Jean-Pied-de-Port.

Tel:
59.37.00.92 or
59.37.11.19.

Reservations:
Not normally necessary.

N6501 Domaine Naturiste L'Eglantiere, Ariès-Espénan

Pretty riverside site in the Vallée du Gers, near Castelnau-Magnoac

This site is situated in the valley between the Pyrénées and the plain, within easy reach of Lourdes and the mountains, alongside a small, fast flowing river, in wooded surroundings. It comprises 12 ha. for camping and caravanning, with a further 28 for walking and relaxing in woods and fields. The river is said to be suitable for swimming, canoeing and fishing. The 120 pitches are of mixed size on fairly level grass, the older ones secluded and separated by a variety of tall trees and bushes, the newer ones more open, with a natural tenting area across the river. About 60 pitches have 12A electrical connections. There is a central medium sized swimming pool, with sunbathing areas both on paving and grass, and a children's pool, overlooked by the attractive, traditional style clubhouse and terrace. The clubhouse provides a bar and snacks, an indoor activities area, play room for young children and table tennis for the older ones. There are restaurants in the nearby village. The two existing sanitary blocks for either end of the site are in typically naturist style, providing under cover, open plan hot showers, washbasins (H&C) in vanity units, continental style WCs and sinks for washing up (cold water). Shop in main season. Children's play area beside the pool and children's animation in season. Volleyball. Badminton. Table tennis. Pétanque. Archery. Activities on the river. Trekking and cross-country cycling. Telephones. Studios, mobile homes, chalets and tents to rent. A torch is useful.

Directions: From Auch take D929 southward in the direction of Lannemezan. Just after Castelnau-Magnoac watch for signs to the hamlet of Ariès-Espénan on the left and follow site signs.

Charges 1995:
-- Per pitch incl. 2 persons - 'traditional' Ffr. 76.00 - 107.00, 'wild' 67.00 - 94.00; young person (over 8 yrs) 20.00 - 28.00; child (3-8 yrs) 10.00 - 15.00, under 3 yrs free; animal 5.60 - 8.00; electricity 20.00.

Open:
27 April - 13 October.

Address:
65230 Ariès-Espénan.

Tel:
62.99.83.64 or
62.39.88.00.
FAX: 62.39.81.44.

Reservations:
Made with Ffr. 600 deposit.

6505M Camping Municipal, St Lary-Soulan

Near the centre of this pleasant town, this is a rather pretentious 4 star municipal site with many mature trees. It has a very grand, modern, architect designed sanitary block. More grand than functional however - don't French architects go camping? It was not as clean as we would expect either, but there is not a great choice of campsites in this area apparently. Readers reports and suggestions welcomed.

Directions: From Arreau take the D929 road south, via Vielle-Aure, to St Lary Soulan (13 km.) and site is signed.

Charges guide:
-- Per pitch 24.00; adult 23.00; child 10.00; electricity (2 or 10A) 15.00 - 33.00.

Open:
All year
except 19 Oct - 11 Dec.

Address:
65170 St. Lary Soulan.

Tel:
62.39.41.58.

Reservations:
Contact site.

6502 Camping Les Trois Vallées, Argelès-Gazost

Developing site with good pool between Lourdes and the mountains.

We felt this was the most promising site along the valley road from Lourdes into the Pyrénées, and one of few with room and plans for development. It has a rather unprepossessing entrance, (to be redesigned), and pitches near the road suffer from noise, but at the back, open fields allow views of surrounding mountains on all sides. A good pool complex has two flumes and a small bar with snacks and takeaway (July/Aug). Bread is available on site and there is a large supermarket across the road. There are 150 flat, grassy, marked out pitches of good size, all with electricity. Water points were scarce, but the owner hopes to remedy this, given the go-ahead by local officialdom. Two very clean modern toilet blocks have good clothes washing and handicapped facilities.Volleyball, football, boules, minigolf and archery. Good children's playground. The proximity to the road is at least advantageous for touring the area, being by a roundabout with Lourdes one way, Luz-St-Sauveur and mountains another way, and the dramatic Pyrénées Corniche Col d'Aubisque going off to the west. Argelès-Gazost is an attractive town with good restaurants and cultural interests.

Directions: Take the N21 from Lourdes to Argelès Gazost. As you approach Argeles, pass a Champion supermarket on your right, and then a roundabout - take the furthest left exit and the site entrance is 100 m. or so on the left.

Charges 1996:
-- Per pitch Ffr. 23.00; adult 23.00; child (0-7 yrs) 13.00; electricity 5.00 per amp.
Open: Easter - 30 September.
Address: 65400 Argeles-Gazost.
Tel: 62.90.35.47.
FAX: 62.97.53.64.
Reservations: Advised for July/Aug.

6503 Airotel Pyrénées, Esquièze Sere, Luz-St-Sauveur

Small high quality site with pools in the heart of the Pyrénées.

The site is located on the main road south from Argelès-Gazost, just before Luz-St-Sauveur, which is very much the centre of tourism in the Haute Pyrénées. There are 165 pitches, some quite large and all with electricity. They are marked by hedges and shrubs, and terraced around an excellent toilet block, which is heated in colder months. Facilities for the disabled are very numerous and installations are very modern. Adjacent to the toilet block is an indoor heated pool, open twice a day. An outdoor pool is to be found near the entrance - it is larger, but rather close to the road. Also on site are to be found a climbing wall, half-court tennis, table tennis and volleyball . An extensive program of outdoor activities is organised, including canyonning, mountain biking, rafting and mountain walking. Skiing can be arranged in winter. The site is close to facilities in the town, but provides a small shop, takeaway service and bar; a small restaurant is open each evening except Saturdays - a larger one is planned.

Directions: Take the N21 from Lourdes through Argelès-Gazost towards Luz-St-Sauveur. The site is on the left at Esquièze-Sere, just outside Luz-St-Sauveur.

Charges 1995:
-- Per pitch incl. 2 persons Ffr. 75.00 - 85.00; extra person 20.00; child (0-2) 10.00; electricity 3A 12.00, 6A 29.00; local tax 1.00.
Open: All year.
Address: 65120 Esquièze-Sere.
Tel: 62.92.89.18.
FAX: 62.92.96.50.
Reservations: With deposit (Ffr. 300) and fee (125).

6601 Camping-Caravaning California, Le Barcarès, Perpignan

Family owned site with swimming pool, not far from beach.

This small site is attractively laid out with much green foliage, like an orchard, and has some 200 hedged pitches on flat ground. Cool and shaded, the site is acquiring a mature look with an attractive terraced pool bar area. The pitches, all with electricity and shade, vary a little in size and shape but average about 100 sq.m. The two toilet blocks are of standard modern construction with continental style WCs, free pre-mixed hot water in the washbasins with shelf and mirror, in the showers with pushbutton, and in the sinks. Baby bath and small toilets. The camp is about 900 m. from a sandy beach and has a swimming pool of 200 sq.m. and children's pool (from 15/5), with free water slide in a small separate pool. Restaurant/bar with takeaway and shop (all 25/6-5/9), wine store and pizzeria at entrance to site. Tennis. TV room. Small multi-gym. Sailboards and mountain bikes for hire; BMX cycle track on site. Archery. Washing machine. Car wash. Exchange facility. Children's animation in season, some evening entertainment. Bungalows and mobile homes of different sizes to let.

Directions: Site is on the D90 coast road 2 km. southwest of Le Barcarès centre.

Charges 1996:
-- Per unit with 2 persons Ffr 102.00, with electricity 117.00; extra person 27.00; child (under 7) 17.00; local tax Jul/Aug 1.00.
-- Less 20-50% outside July/Aug.
Open: 20 April - 27 September
Address: Route de St. Laurent, 66420 Le Barcarès.
Tel: 68.86.16.08.
FAX: 68.86.18.20.
Reservations: Any period with deposit (Ffr. 400) and fee (60).

6602 Camping Caravaning Ma Prairie, Canet, nr Perpignan

Site 3 km. back from sea among the vineyards, with various amenities.

The Gil family provide a warm welcome and pleasant atmosphere at Ma Prairie. It lies some 3 km. back from the sandy Canet beaches, with two swimming pools - a small children's one (120 sq.m.) and a large one for adults (10 x 22 m.), across a small road from the camping area. There are 260 pitches of nearly 100 sq.m. average, on flat grassy ground with various trees and bushes separating them and providing shade (possible road noise). Most have electricity; water and drainage are available on 35. Three sanitary blocks have mixed British and continental WCs, washbasins in private cabins and hot showers. Baby bath. Ample free hot and cold water in basins, showers, washing-up sinks and clothes sinks. Washing machines. There is extra provision near reception. Quite a few pitches are taken by tour operators and there is a busy atmosphere. A large bar overlooks the terraced pool area. Satellite TV. Table tennis, billiards and amusement machines. Disco, dancing etc. about 3 times weekly and daily animation in season. Shop for basics only. Covered snack bar and open air restaurant service or takeaway next to reception. Tennis. Children's play area. Mobile homes and equipped tents for hire. Bus/tram service to the modern resort of Canet, with first class restaurants, etc. including one owned and run by the same family. The attractive, old 'Canet Village' is within walking distance.

Directions: Site access is from D11 Perpignan road close to the junction with D617 in Canet-Village.

Charges 1995:
-- Per unit with 2 persons Ffr. 116.00; extra person 30.00; child (under 7) 17.00; local tax 1.00; electricity (6A) 24.00 or (3A) 18.00; fully serviced pitch 30.00.
-- Less 30% in May, June and Sept.
Open:
1 May - end-Sept.
Address:
66140 Canet en Roussillon.
Tel:
68.73.26.17.
FAX: 68.73.28.82.
Reservations:
Any length with deposit (Ffr. 400) and fee (80).

6607 Camping-Caravaning Le Brasilia, Canet Plage en Roussillon

Large, well developed, self sufficient site with direct access to sandy beach.

This is an ideal site for those seeking a seaside holiday with all facilities and amenities within walking distance - in most cases, actually on-site. Le Brasilia has some 900 pitches, all with 5A electricity, mostly of good size and with a fair amount of shade from a variety of trees and many flowering shrubs. The numerous modern sanitary blocks are all well equipped, with British WCs, washbasins in cabins and showers with dividers, etc. The latest block is definitely 'state of the art', with some of the best facilities we have seen, particularly for children. The beach here is busy with a beach-club, but with plenty of room even in high season, and there is also a large pool with sun-bathing areas, aqua-gym, aerobics and tennis. The pool is charged for in high season (adult Ffr 50 per week, child 4-10 yrs 30). With a bar/restaurant, night club, entertainment and shops, the site is almost a resort in itself with a lively atmosphere but without being 'tacky'. Used by tour operators (15%).

Directions: Site is north of Canet Port. From Canet Plage follow signs for Port then Canet Village to pick up site signs.

Charges 1995:
-- Per unit incl. 2 persons Ffr. 87.00 - 125.00; electricity (5A) 15.00; extra person (over 3 yrs) 17.00 - 25.00; local tax 1.00.
-- Credit cards accepted.
Open:
8 April - 7 October.
Address:
B.P. 204, 66140 Canet Plage en Roussillon.
Tel:
68.80.23.82.
FAX: 68.73.32.97.
Reservations:
Contact site for details.

66 Pyrénées-Orientales

6606 Camping Les Dunes de Torreilles-Plage, Torreilles, nr Perpignan

Seaside site near Perpignan with swimming pool and pitches with own sanitation.

This is an unusual site in several respects. It is quite large, with some 600 pitches, all of 100 sq.m. minimum but of varying size and shape, all having electricity and drainage. The pitches are all marked and most are separated by foliage except near the beach and dunes where vegetation is sparse. The site has the advantage of direct access to sandy beaches with good bathing and boating, including a naturist beach. The facilities on site are numerous and include a swimming pool (20 x 10 m. 15/5-30/9), with children's pool, a restaurant, bar, pizzeria and several takeaways. A 'Centre Commercial' with supermarket, shops and small restaurant is adjacent. Tennis courts. Windsurfing lessons; boards for hire, also pedaloes. Kiosk/bar by beach. Disco. Launderette. Treatment room; doctor calls June to Sept. Entertainment programme and organised excursions. Another unusual feature of the site is that each pitch has its own sanitary unit with shower (heated and adjustable), washbasin, British WC, mirror and hooks. Clients keep these units clean during their stay but the site takes a deposit to ensure that they are left clean, however they are cleaned for incoming clients. There is a number of static units on the site devoted to tour operators, some leased on a semi-permanent basis and others for hire. However, with over 300 pitches for tourists, apart from the mid-July to mid-August peak season, there is usually ample space and the opportunity to choose your own pitch. In many respects this is an ideal site for families, in a developing tourist area, with plenty of activities on the site and nearby but without being too intrusive for those who prefer just to relax. There may be some evening noise on pitches at one side from an adjoining campsite which operates a disco. This is not a site you are likely to forget - we like it, but it may not be to everyone's taste - it can be windy and dry.

Directions: From autoroute A9 take exit for Perpignan-Nord, then D83 towards Le Barcarès for 9 km. then south on D81 towards Canet for 3 km. before turning left to site.

Charges 1995:
-- Per unit all-inclusive with electricity Ffr. 70.00 - 189.00; deposit refunded on departure 350.00; local tax 1.00.
Open: 15 March - 15 October
Address: 66440 Torreilles-Plage.
Tel: 68.28.30.32 or 68.28.38.29.
Reservations: Made with deposit (Ffr. 350) and fee (85), min. 1 week in July/Aug.

6620M Camping Municipal de la Plage, Ste-Marie en Roussillon

Quite one of the most unusual and prettiest municipals we have ever seen, de la Plage has an excellent swimming pool (surrounded by portraits of international rugby players by the English artist Leslie Dyke who lives nearby), with an extensive blue and white ceramic tiled sunbathing area. The main buildings contain a variety of shops, bars, etc. around a piazza with trees providing welcome shade. The ambience is essentially French, or perhaps Catalan. The 378 pitches are mainly of a good size with shade on most from the variety of trees and colourful flowering shrubs, mostly oleander. There are several access points directly onto the blue flag beach which has a sailing school. A naturist beach is 250 m. There is a surprisingly wide range of sports facilities actually on site during the season (15/6-15/9), including volleyball, archery, judo, tennis and table tennis. Also much animation - the jovial Director is a rugby player (clearly a front row forward!) and promotes the game actively - even the roads are named after rugby players. The site has shops, a health centre and free mini-club for under 5s. Sanitary facilities are adequate and relatively modern. All were clean when seen in high season. We have tended to think of municipal sites mainly in terms of night stops and for visiting towns and cities or in remote areas, rather than as a base for a seaside holiday - this one made us rethink. Reservations will be essential for high season visits as it can get very busy.

Directions: From the D81 Port Barcarès - Canet-Plage coast road follow signs for Ste-Marie-Plage and the site is signed to the left.

Charges guide:
-- Per unit incl. 2 persons Ffr. 90.00; extra person 27.00; child (under 4 yrs) 11.00; animal 14.00; electricity 14.00; local tax adult 2.00, child (4-10 yrs) 1.00.
Open: 1 March -- 31 October.
Address: 66470 Ste-Marie la Mer en Roussillon.
Tel: 68.80.68.59. Information: 68.73.14.70.
Reservations: Made with 25% deposit.

6603 Camping Cala Gogo, St. Cyprien-Plage, nr Perpignan

Site by beach, with own swimming pool and varied amenities.

This site has an agreeable situation by a sandy beach where bathing is supervised and boats can be launched. Also on site is a good-size free swimming pool with children's pool and a pleasant terrace bar area adjoining. The 700 pitches, on flat ground, are individual ones of around 100 sq.m. They are now more fully marked out with easier access and electrical connections everywhere and shade has developed. The five toilet blocks are basically good and provide toilets, washbasins in private cabins and free hot, controllable showers. Maintenance may vary in high season. Large bar complex with disco and TV, which becomes very busy in season and could be noisy (popular with young people), and an attractive small shopping mall and supermarket. Full restaurant plus self-service restaurant with simple menu and takeaway. Small bar by beach. Organised programme of events in season: sports, etc. during day, dancing or entertainment in bar some evenings. Wine boutique. Tennis. Table tennis. Children's playground. Cycle hire. Boat excursions and courses in skin-diving, windsurfing, sailing near. Treatment room; doctor calls daily in July/Aug.

Directions: To the south of St. Cyprien, site is well signed from roads around.

Charges 1995:
-- Per person (any age) Ffr. 36.00, plus local tax 2.00 per adult, 1.00 per child; pitch (any unit) 51.00; electricity 15.00. -- 20% less June/Sept.
Open:
1 June - 30 September, with all services.
Address:
66750 St. Cyprien.
Tel:
68.21.07.12.
FAX: 68.21.02.90.
Reservations:
Sat. to Sat. with deposit and fee.

6604 Camping Le Soleil, Argelès-sur-Mer, nr Perpignan

Pleasant, family owned site with good size pitches and direct access to beach.

Le Soleil is certainly one of the best of the 40 odd sites that are available around Argelès and it has been much improved in the last few years. A large site, it has over 700 individual numbered pitches of ample size, on sandy/grassy ground and with shade except, perhaps, in the newer extensions, and electrical connections in all areas. With direct access to a sandy beach with safe bathing, this is an established, mature site. Access for caravans sometimes needs care on the narrow tree lined roads. It has a wide range of amenities and Spain and the Pyrénées are near enough for excursions. The six sanitary blocks are of the type with external access to individual units and should give good coverage. They have plentiful hot showers in four blocks. Washbasins in private cabins, some with only cold water. A large, impressive swimming pool complex (Californian style) is on site and a supermarket, general shop and restaurant with takeaway. Bar with dancing nightly in season. Children's adventure playground. TV room. Tennis. Minigolf. Riding near. Facilities for mooring boats on adjacent river. Washing machines. Bureau de change. English spoken. Comprehensive reservation system and this is advisable for most of July/Aug. No dogs taken.

Directions: Site is at north end of the beach 1 km. from Argelès-Plage village.

Charges guide:
-- Per person (any age) Ffr. 37.00; local tax 2.20; pitch 55.00; electricity 15.00. Pool deposit Ffr. 100 p/pitch.
Open:
15 May - 30 September.
Address:
Rte du Littoral, 66600 Argelès-sur-Mer.
Tel:
Season: 68.81.14.48.
FAX: 68.81.44.34.
Winter: 68.95.94.62.
FAX: 68.95.92.81..
Reservations:
Made from Sat. to Sat. only, with large deposit and small booking fee.

6611 Camping Le Dauphin, Argelès-sur-Mer

Quieter site with views of the Pyrénées and good swimming pools.

Near Taxo in the quieter, northern part of Argelès (a somewhat frenzied resort in season), this site enjoys good views of the Pyrénées, particularly from the terrace area surrounding its excellent complex of swimming pools. About a third of the 300 level, grassy and well shaded pitches (all with 3A electricity) have the benefit of what amounts to their own individual sanitary block with hot shower, washbasin and WC and with adjacent washing up sink. The other pitches are served by a central sanitary block which, though quite old, has been refurbished to provide excellent, modern facilities including a number of showers and washbasins en-suite, British WCs, etc. A good range of facilities includes a bar/restaurant, pizzeria with takeaway, shops (all season), tennis, large children's play area and minigolf. Table tennis. Entertainment twice weekly in July/Aug. Although 1½ km. from the town and beach, there is a regular connecting `train' service throughout the day up to midnight. Used by tour operators (20%).

Directions: From autoroute take exit Perpignan-Nord for Argelès and follow directions for Plage-Nord and Taxo d'Avall (similarly from the N114).

Charges 1996:
-- Per pitch incl. 2 persons Ffr. 130.00; extra person 28.00; child (under 5) 15.00; electricity 23.00; water 20.00; indiv. sanitation 50.00; local tax 2.00.
Open:
25 May - 30 September
Address:
Rte. Taxo d'Avall, 66701 Argelès-sur-Mer.
Tel:
68.81.17.54.
FAX: 68.95.82.60.
Reservations:
Write to site.

 Alan Rogers' discount Less 20% in June or Sept

6600 Camping Pujol, Argelès-sur-Mer

Quiet well managed site with ornamental swimming pool complex.

We say quiet because in itself it is. However, Argelès is a busy tourist area and in high season it doesn't matter which of the 93 sites you are on, there are various loud open air discos and activities which may impinge on the wrong side of midnight for a while. However, it is possible to avoid the standard hectic seaside site in otherwise attractive Argelès, and Pujol may represent the best chance of doing so. There are around 250 pitches, all larger than 100 sq.m. and on flat grass. Numbered and marked, nearly all have electrical connections. The main sanitary blocks contain a good modern provision of all facilities and are kept very clean. A second block (affectionately known as the Taj Mahal) has been built in a recently extended section of the site, and is very well appointed in all respects except its lack of cold water, though there is a tap nearby. Washing machines in each block, and free electric irons.
The site boasts a good terrace restaurant and friendly bar. Care is taken to ensure this is a family bar rather than one overrun by youngsters, who are catered for in a covered meeting area which also houses animation and dances. A small supermarket sells cheap wine by the flagon, all basic needs, and excellent hot bread twice a day, baked on the premises. The site's pride and joy is a delightful pool complex with a fairly large L-shaped pool, children's pool, and for adults, a spa pool on an overlooking terrace. Semi-tropical shrubs and fountains make the area very attractive. There are two table tennis tables, a volleyball court, children's playground and boules pitches. The site is very close to an interesting fortress and only 2 km. from the fast N114, via which the pretty ports of Collioure and Port Vendres are but a short distance to the south, and Perpignan not far in the other direction (watch out for traffic jams in the mornings going north). Argelès Plage and the quiet resort of Racou are a short distance if you want to exchange the pool for a Mediterranean beach.

Directions: Take N114 from Perpignan and turn to Argelès at Taxo d'Avall. Site is signed from roundabout just before town - turn left off roundabout and the site is 200 m. on right before the castle. Use exit Perpignan-Nord from autoroute.

Charges 1995:
-- Per pitch incl. 2 adults Ffr. 95.00; extra person 24.00; child (under 3) 12.00; electricity 20.00.
Open:
1 June - 30 September.
Address:
Rte. du Tamariguer, 66700 Argèles-sur-Mer.
Tel:
68.81.00.25.
FAX: 68.81.21.21.
Reservations:
Advised in high season and made with Ffr. 500 deposit. Write or 'phone for information.

6613 Hotel de Plein Air L'Eau Vive, Vernet-les-Bains

Well kept small site at the spa town of Vernet in the Pyrénées.

Enjoying dramatic views of the towering Pic du Canigou (3,000 m.), this site is 1½ km. from the centre of Vernet-les-Bains. It is approached via a twisting and not too well made up lane through a residential area, which should not be allowed to put you off. The site is well kept with first class sanitary facilities in two modern blocks with British WCs, hot showers with dressing area, washbasins (hot water) in private cabins, dishwashing (hot water) under cover, facilities for the handicapped and with a washing machine in each block. The 58 tourist pitches, all with electricity (4/10A) and water, are on level grass, hedged but without a lot of shade. Although there is no swimming pool as such, the site has a more or less natural pool (created by pumping and circulating running water from the nearby stream - very attractive) and even providing a tiny beach with water slide, cordoned off for children. Bar/reception with pool table, amusement machine, library, etc. An attractive open air (but under cover) bar/restaurant has waiter service and takeaway in main season and although there is no shop as such, fresh bread can be ordered. Chalets to let. Well situated for touring this area of the Pyrénées and with very comfortable amenities, this small site quickly becomes fully booked in season and advance reservation is essential. The medieval, walled town (Ville-Franche-de-Conflent), the Grottes des Canalettes and the hillside fort with its many steps are well worth visiting.

Directions: Following the N116 to Andorra, 6 km. after Prades, take turning at Ville-Franche-de-Conflent for Vernet-les-Bains. Continue up hill for 5 km. and keep right avoiding town centre. Turn right over bridge in direction of Sahorre. Immediately, at one end of small block of shops, turn right into Ave de Saturnin and follow for about 1 km. past houses to more open area and site is signed.

Charges 1996:
-- Per unit incl. up to 3 persons and electricity (4A) Ffr. 85.00 - 125.00, with tent 50.00; extra person (over 7 yrs) 15.00; child 10.00; animal 10.00; electricity (10A) 10.00.
-- Less for weekly stays.
Open:
All year except 12 Nov-31 Dec.
Address:
Chemin de Saturnin, 66820 Vernet Les Bains.
Tel:
68.05.54.14.
FAX: as phone.
Reservations:
Made with deposit (20% of charges), Ffr. 100 fee (high season only) and cancellation insurance (details from site).

6614 Hollywood Camping International, Amélie-les-Bains

Pretty, small site with pool on outskirts of famous spa town.

Don't be misled by the name - this is an unpretentious little site in a rural setting. It enjoys good views of the nearby mountains (Mont Albères), yet is within 2 km. of the rather elegant spa town of Amélie-les-Bains. There are some 100 mainly level pitches all with electricity, water and drainage, arranged on small, grassy terraces with a variety of trees and shrubs providing variable amounts of shade. The site has the benefit of a recently built pool (14 x 8 m.) with paved sunbathing area and a modern sanitary block. This has free hot showers, with dressing area, washbasins in cabins with hot and cold water, washing up sinks (H&C) and a laundry with washing machine and ironing board. WCs are mixed continental and Turkish style. Although the site does not claim to have its own restaurant, it is adjacent to an auberge run by the same family providing a range of meals and takeaways. Children's playground. Caravans, tents and bungalows to let.

Directions: Site is between Amélie les Bains and Pont Céret on the D115. Turn left up partly made-up road immediately after the small village of La Forge de Reynés approaching from the direction of Le Boulou.

Charges guide:
-- Per unit inc. car and 2 persons Ffr. 63.00; extra person 21.00; child (under 7 yrs) 10.50; electricity 4A 16.00, 6A 19.00; drainage 5.50.
-- Low season less 10%.
Open: 15 March - 15 Nov.
Address: B.P. 3, La Forge de Reynès, 66110 Amélie-les-Bains.
Tel: 68.39.08.61.
Reservations: Made with deposit (Ffr. 400) and fee (40).

N6612 Camping Naturiste La Clapère, Maureillas

Very attractive naturist site in the lower ranges of the Pyrénées.

Situated in a valley in the Albères, this site occupies a large area (50 hectares), includes a fast flowing small river and offers a choice of 200 good sized pitches on no less than eight separate terraces. They are all slightly different in character; two for example are alongside the river, one is among greengage trees, another vines. Electricity is available on five of the terraces, the others being more suitable for tents. There is a large swimming pool with smaller children's pool, and ample paved sunbathing areas, alongside which is the attractive bar and restaurant (with simple, basic `plat du jour' menu and takeaway) and the shop which, although small, is very well stocked. Table tennis. Boules. Volleyball. Organised rambles (Wednesday mornings). Children's playground. Fishing. Caravans for hire. There are three modern sanitary blocks of unusual design providing first class facilities including some of the best (open plan) hot showers we have come across. Washbasins have hot and cold water as do the washing up and laundry sinks - there is also a washing machine. The nearby town of Céret has a Saturday morning market. This is one of a small number of very attractive, unspoiled naturist sites located in beautiful, wild countryside. It is little wonder that more and more campers and caravanners are turning to naturist sites for their holidays in these more environmentally conscious times.

Directions: Take the last autoroute (A9) exit before Spain (Boulou exit). Leave Boulou on N9 in the direction of Le Perthus for 3 km. Turn right onto the N618 to Maureillas, then the D13 in the direction of Las Illas. Site is 2 km.

Charges 1995:
-- Per pitch incl. 2 person Ffr. 96.00; extra adult 32.00; child (0-14 yrs) 21.00; animal 5.00 - 8.00; electricity 17.00; local tax 1.00, child (4-10) 0.50.
-- Less in low seasons.
Open: 1 April - 31 October.
Address: Route de Las Illas, 66400 Maureillas.
Tel: 68.83.36.04
Reservations; Made with deposit (30% of charges).

6702M Camping Municipal Le Hohwald, Le Hohwald

It is difficult to see how this site has 4 stars in the French classification system, but it is in a scenic, remote situation, high up in the hills of Alsace. Pitches, many with good shade, are either on four small terraces or in individual, levelled places. It is quite a tortuous drive whichever road is taken - narrow and slow rather than steep. The one, central sanitary block is of average standard with the usual provision, but might be hard pressed if the site was full. Almost half the places are taken by static caravans but you should find space. There is an excellent community room with a kitchen. Two restaurants are very near the site entrance, with others in the village a short distance away.

Directions: Site is at the southwest end of the village on the D425.

Charges guide:
-- Per person Ffr. 13.00; child (under 7 yrs) 7.20; car or m/cycle 7.20; pitch 8.20; electricity 4.80 - 31.00, acc. to amps; local tax 1.00.
Open: All year.
Address: 67140 Le Hohwald.
Tel: 88.08.30.90.
Reservations: Contact the site.

6701M Camping Eichelgarten, Oberbronn, nr Niederbronn

This is an attractive, inexpensive and well run site, set amidst the mountains and forests of northern Alsace, not far from the German border. There are good views over the valley to one side with trees sheltering the other. The circular internal road has pitches around the outside, some on terraces, as well as space in the centre where there is also a children's playground. Two well appointed sanitary blocks are heated in cool weather, with British WCs, washbasins (some private cabins for ladies), good free showers, washing machines and dryers. Baby room and facilities for the disabled. Solar-heated swimming pool (open July/Aug) and children's pool of excellent quality. General purpose room with billiards, table tennis and table football. Minigolf and two hard tennis courts on site and fitness circuit in the nearby forest. Small shop, supermarket in village (1 km). Bungalows to let.

Charges 1995:
-- Per person Ffr. 14.20;
child (under 7) 8.00;
pitch 9.40; vehicle 7.00;
electricity (per amp)
5.00; local tax 1.00
Open:
All year.
Address:
67110 Oberbronn.
Tel:
88.09.71.96.
Reservations:
Send precise dates; no
deposit needed.

Directions: Travel northwest from Haguenau on N62 for approx. 20 km. Near Niederbronn turn left on D28 for Oberbronn-Zinswiller - site signed from here.

Alan Rogers'
discount
10% for stays
over 10 days

6801M Camping de l'Ile du Rhin, Biesheim, nr Colmar

In pleasant situation by Rhine, between the Vosges and the Black Forest, this is a well kept site. With 233 pitches, it has many seasonal static caravans but there are 68 tourist pitches. They are individual plots which vary in size, all on flat grass with good shade and many electrical points. The three sanitary blocks are well kept and have free hot showers, British toilets and individual basins (cold water) with shelves, mirrors and separators. Amenities include washing machines, a shop, sports ground, table tennis, tennis and boules. Restaurants near. It is a useful overnight stop or for exploring the area. Used by tour operators (25%).

Charges 1995:
-- Per unit incl. 2
persons Ffr. 53.00;
electricity 17.40.
Open:
All year.
Address:
68600 Biesheim.
Tel:
89.72.57.95.
Reservations:
Made for longer stays.

Directions: Site is close to bridge into Germany and is well signed. Turn off N415 road close to French frontier post and proceed along river to north.

6804M Camping Municipal Les Trois Châteaux, Eguisheim

The three châteaux from which the site gets its name are clearly visible on the distant hill above the site and add to the interesting surroundings. This nice little site with 120 tourist pitches slopes slightly but has a level terrace and good tree cover. Caravans over 7 m. and/or 1 ton in weight are not accepted. A busy site, the facilities appear to cope well and it has a neat, well tended appearance, with a single sanitary block at its centre. This has continental style WCs, hot showers (on payment) but cold water elsewhere. Children's playground. The facilities of the fascinating walled town of Eguisheim are close and the site is well positioned for exploring this delightful part of Alsace.

Charges 1995:
-- Per person Ffr. 13.00;
child (under 7) 7.00;
pitch 15.00; electricity
(4A) 15.00; tax 1.00.
Open:
Easter - 30 September.
Address:
10 Rue de Bassin,
68420 Eguisheim.
Tel:
89.23.19.39.
Reservations:
Contact site..

Directions: Site is well signed in the village and easy to find.

6803M Camping Municipal Masevaux, Masevaux

As one approaches the appearance promises an excellent site and one is not disappointed - this must rank amongst the best municipals. On the quiet edge of town next to the indoor pool, the pitches, marked by trees which give good shade, are on flat grass. The 110 places for tourists all have electrical connections (3 or 6A) and are surrounded by hills and trees. The glory of the site is the new sanitary block, heated in cool weather and of exceptional quality. It has British WCs and free hot water, with most washbasins in private cabins. No shop (supermarket very close) but soft drinks and ices at reception and a baker calls in high season. The attractive town centre is a short walk away.

Charges guide:
-- Per unit Ffr. 14.00;
person 14.00; child
(under 7 yrs) 6.50;
electricity (3A) 14.00.
Open:
Easter - 30 September.
Address:
Rue du Stade,
68290 Masevaux.
Tel:
89.82.42.29.
Reservations:
Write to site.

Directions: Site is well signed around the town - 'Camping Complexe Sportif'.

6805M Camping Municipal de L'Ill, Colmar

If you are travelling between Colmar and Freiburg (Germany) and looking for a night stop or are wishing to explore this part of Alsace, this would be a good place to stay. It is situated on the banks of the river with an unguarded edge (which could be dangerous for young children). At the time of our visit the new Colmar motorway ring road was under construction on the opposite bank of the river but we were assured that noise would be screened out. A hard tarmac road leads to three level terraces - two of which are under tall trees - and the 220 tourist pitches are on level grass and have electrical connections (3/6A). Unusually for a municipal site, there is a well stocked shop and an excellent restaurant. Sports facilities are about 5 minutes away. Good community/lounge room. An older sanitary block is near the entrance and two newer ones situated at intervals through the rectangular site, with more modern conveniences. One block has facilities for the handicapped. One hesitates to say that one received a friendly welcome as staff change on municipal sites but during our visit we were well received. Used by tour operators (20%).

Directions: Site is to east of Colmar on N415 Colmar-Freiburg road, by bridge.

Charges 1995:
-- Per pitch Ffr. 15.50; person 13.50; child (under 10 yrs) 8.00; animal 6.00; electricity 3A 13.50 6A 22.50.
Open:
1 February - 30 Nov.
Address:
Horbourg-Wihr, 68000 Colmar.
Tel:
89.41.15.94. (Tourist Office: 89.20.68.92).
Reservations:
Contact site or L'Office de Tourisme, rue des Unter linden, 68000 Colmar.

6901M Camping International de Lyon, Lyon

Camping International is kept busy with overnight trade and reception and the café (in main season) are open until quite late. There are 150 separate numbered plots with electricity in most parts. Those for caravans are mostly on hardstandings on a slight slope, with another small grassy part, while those for tents are on a flatter area of grass. The three sanitary blocks are good, with free hot water (solar heated) in all washbasins (in cabins), good showers and sinks. The block under reception has baby facilities and washing machines. Amenities include a TV room, table tennis, children's playground, medical service and a smallish swimming pool. Some basic provisions are kept in the café, but a very large commercial centre is just outside the site, with 8 hotels, restaurants, supermarket, petrol station etc. Possible road noise. Mobile homes to rent.

Directions: Do not take new A46 motorway around Lyon, but continue on A6 autoroute and take exit marked 'Limonest, Dardilly, Porte de Lyon' about 8 km. north of the Lyon tunnel; at once turn left for Porte de Lyon.

Charges 1995:
-- Per person Ffr. 16.00, child (7-15 yrs) 10.00, under 7 free; tent pitch 32.00; motorcaravan 42.00; caravan: 1 axle 42.00, 2 axles 85.00; electricity 13.00 - 32.00 (winter); local tax 1.00.
Open:
All year.
Address:
Porte de Lyon, 69570 Dardilly.
Tel:
78.35.64.55.
FAX: 72.17.04.26.
Reservations:
Made if you write, but there is usually space.

6902M Camping Municipal La Grappe Fleurie, Fleurie-en-Beaujolais

With the benefit of easy access from both the A6 autoroute and the N6, this site is ideally situated for night stops, or indeed for longer stays to explore the vineyards and historic attractions of the Beaujolais region. Virtually surrounded by vineyards, but within walking distance (less than 1 km.) of the pretty village of Fleurie, this is an immaculate small site with 96 separated 'delimité' touring pitches. On fairly level grass, all have the benefit of 10A electrical connections. Sanitary facilities, in two modern purpose built blocks, are of a good standard and were as they should be when we visited in high season, in terms of cleanliness and sufficiency. Catering and shopping facilities are available in the village, although the nearest swimming pool is 8 km. away.

Directions: From the N6 at Le Maison Blanche/Romanech-Thorins, take the D32 to the village of Fleurie, from where site is signed.

Charges 1995:
-- Per adult Ffr. 16.00; child 5-10 yrs 10.00; caravan or motorcaravan 28.00; tent 17.00.
Open:
20 March - 25 October.
Address:
69820 Fleurie.
Tel:
74.04.10.44 (or La Mairie: 74.69.80.07. FAX: 74.69.85.71).
Reservations:
Contact site.

7001M Camping Municipal La Maladiere, Port sur Saône

La Maladiere is situated on the edge of town in a quiet location near a river marina and with good shade in parts. The level, grassy pitches, some of which are marked by hedges and most with electrical connections (3A), are on either side of hard access roads. There are two sanitary blocks of rather average standard, one at each end of the site, with British and Turkish WCs, free hot water in showers but cold water only in the washbasins and sinks. A bar/restaurant is at the site entrance.

Directions: Site is off the D6 near municipal bathing area, signed in the village.

Charges guide:
-- Per person Ffr. 8.50; child (under 7 yrs) 4.50; car 5.50; pitch 8.50; electricity (3A) 13.00.
Open:
Mid-May - mid-Sept.
Address:
70170 Port sur Saône.
Tel:
84.91.15.32.
Reservations:
Contact the site.

7102M Le Village des Meuniers, Dompierre-les-Ormes, nr Mâcon

Opened in 1993, this site is a good example of current trends in French tourism development. The 97 neatly terraced, large pitches are on fairly level grass and all have electricity, 37 with water and drainage also. They enjoy some lovely views of the surrounding countryside - the Beaujolais, the Maconnais, the Charollais and the Clunysois. The site is 500 m. from Dompierre-les-Ormes, a small village of 850 people, with all services (banks, shops, etc). Sanitary facilities are mainly in an unusual, purpose designed hexagonal block, with the most up-to-date furniture and fittings, all of a very high standard. A small unit has now been added in the lower area. There is a bar, shop, takeaway, etc. plus minigolf and other recreational activities. An attractively designed, upmarket swimming pool complex has three pools with a toboggan run (open from end-June). The site has its own high quality wooden gites, operated by Gites de France. This site is one of the better municipals we have seen, particularly as the hedges have grown to provide shade. This is an area well worth visiting, with attractive scenery, interesting history, excellent wines and good food. Used by tour operators (15-20%).

Charges 1996:
-- Per adult Ffr. 25.00; child 15.00; pitch 30.00; electricity 10.00.
-- Special family rate (4 or more persons) Ffr. 120.00.
-- Credit cards accepted.
Open:
15 May - 15 September.
Address:
71520 Dompierre-les-Ormes.
Tel:
Site: 85.50.29.43 (winter: 85.50.21.34). FAX: 85.50.28.25.
Reservations:
Contact site.

Directions: Town is 35 km. west of Macon. Follow N79/E62 (Charolles, Paray, Digoin) road and turn south onto D41 to Dompierre-les-Ormes (3 km). Site is clearly signed through village.

7101M Camping Municipal, Mâcon

Always useful and well cared for, this site has been greatly improved in recent years and must now rank as one of those 'magnificent municipals'. For a large site near a big town it has a neat, well cared for appearance, with 285 good sized pitches, all with 5A electricity and including a number of 'super pitches'. They are on mown, flat grass, accessed by tarmac roads, with a generally bright and cheerful ambience. The sanitary facilities, hitherto the site's weakest feature, are now in three fully modernised blocks. They have been greatly improved and are bright and cheerful, with all the latest facilities, although a few Turkish style WCs remain, as well as modern British ones. Washing machine and dryer. Facilities include a shop/tabac, bar, takeaway, a nice restaurant (le Tipi) open midday and evenings, a good TV lounge and a children's playground. Gates closed 10 pm.-6.30 am. Swimming pool, sports stadium and supermarket nearby.

Charges guide:
-- Per unit incl. 2 persons and electricity Ffr. 49.00 - 75.00; extra person 15.10; child (under 7) 7.60.
Open:
15 March - 31 October.
Address:
71000 Mâcon.
Tel:
85.38.16.22.
Reservations:
Not normally required.

Directions: Site is on the northern outskirts of Mâcon on the main N6.

7105 Camping Moulin de Collonge, Saint-Boil

Well run, family site in the heart of the Burgundy countryside.

This site offers an 'away from it all' situation. Surrounded by sloping vineyards and golden wheat fields, it has instant appeal for those seeking a quiet, relaxing environment. There are 50 pitches which are level and most have electrical hook-ups. Reception and sanitary facilities are housed in a converted barn which is tastefully decorated and immaculately kept. White tiled floors and whitewashed walls give it a spotlessly clean appearance. There are curtained wash cubicles, shaving points and showers. Sinks for dishes and laundry are outside with washing machine and dryer inside. Hanging flower arrangements are in abundance and, like the shrubs and grounds, are constantly being attended to by the proprietor and his family. Beyond the stream which borders the site are a swimming pool, pizzeria and patio. Ices and cool drinks can be purchased but there is no food shop - baguettes and croissants arrive by van at 8.30 each morning. Other on-site activities are minigolf, table tennis and pony trekking.

Charges 1995:
-- Per unit Ffr. 22.00; adult 17.00; child (under 7 yrs) 9.00; electricity 15.00.
Open:
4 April - 30 September.
Address:
71940 Saint-Boil.
Tel:
85.44.00.40.
Reservations:
Accepted - contact site.

Directions: From Chalon-sur-Saône travel 9 km. west on the N80. Turn south onto the D981 through Buxy (6 km). Continue south for 7 km. to Saint-Boil and site is signed at south end of the village.

7106 Camping du Château de Montrouant, Gibles

Delightful site with range of activities for adults and children.

This small pretty site is in a steep valley in the rolling Charollais hills, beside a small lake in the grounds of an imposing château. There is ample shade from the many mature trees and the 45 pitches are of a good size on reasonably flat grassy terraces, mainly separated by small hedges, all having electrical connections (min 6A). The whole appearance is attractive with some pitches overlooking the lake, some by the field where ponies graze. A swimming pool, with secluded sunbathing area has been sympathetically landscaped. There is also a very small open-air bar/restaurant for evening barbecues, half-court tennis and pony riding. The enthusiastic owner organises several unusual and interesting activities during the main season, including stone masonry, model boat building, walks, wine tours, etc. Essentials are available from reception but the village of Gibles, with shops, restaurant, etc. is only 2 km. Sanitary facilities, housed in part of the château, include washbasins in cabins (H&C), hot showers, stainless steel dish-washing sinks, British style WCs, washing machine, dryer, etc. - all of a more than acceptable standard. Regrettably the season here is short and the site becomes quickly full from mid-July to mid-Aug, so the best times could be from late June - mid July or the second half of Aug. Used by a Dutch tour operator.

Charges 1995:
-- Per person Ffr. 20.00; child (under 7 yrs) 14.00; pitch 20.00; vehicle 17.00; electricity (6A) 19.00; dog 10.00.
-- Special weekly charges.
Open:
23 June - 31 August.
Address:
71800 Gibles.
Tel:
85.84.54.30 or 85.84.51.13.
FAX: 85.84.52.80.
Reservations:
Essential for 8/7-25/8 and made with 25% deposit.

Directions: Site is to the west of Macon and can be reached from the A6 via the N79 to Charolles (approx. 55 km). Take the D985 road south from Charolles for 19 km. to La Clayette, then follow signs for Gibles and site (approx. 7 km). Alternatively the site can be reachd from the D982 Roanne - Digoin road. Exit for Pouilly, pass through Charlieu and Châteauneuf to La Clayette.

7107 Camping-Caravaning Château de l'Epervière, nr Bourgogne Sud

Enthusiastically run rural site in the grounds of a château.

We are fortunate to have been able to identify a number of good sites in an area where these are somewhat scarce, and it is nice to be able to add another to our selection. Château de l'Epervière is peacefully situated on the edge of the little village of Gigny-sur-Saône, yet within easy distance of the A6 autoroute. With 100 pitches (about 25% taken by tour operators), nearly all with 6A electricity, the site is essentially in two fairly distinct areas - a smaller one with semi-hedged pitches on reasonably level ground with plenty of shade from mature trees, close to the château and fishing lake, and a larger, more open area, still with good shade, with very big, hedged pitches, on the far side of the lake.

There is a smallish, unheated swimming pool, partly enclosed by old stone walls which protect it from the wind and a good restaurant in the château with a distinctly French menu, but a very helpful young English waiter! The sanitary blocks, a large one beside the château and a small one near the lake which was not completed when we visited in May '95, provide modern facilities, including free hot showers, washbasins in private cabins, British type WCs, and undercover dishwashing and laundry areas, including a washing machine and dryer. Perhaps the most striking feature of this attractive site is the young owner's enthusiasm and the range of activities he lays on for visitors. These include wine-tasting and a special programme of 'French Flavour Holidays' designed to provide an insight into the French culture (see advert on page 20 for details). Perhaps not surprisingly, this seems to appeal more to the British and other nationalities than to the French, as when we visited in mid May there were few French campers there! Apartments to let in the château.

Directions: From the N6 between Châlon-sur-Saône and Tournus, turn east on to the D18 (just north of Sennecey-le-Grand) and follow site signs for 5 km.

Charges 1995:
-- Per adult Ffr. 16.00; child 8.00; pitch 26.00; dog 9.00; electricity 15.00.
Open:
12 April - 30 Sept.
Address:
Gigny-sur-Saône, 71240 Bourgogne Sud.
Tel:
85.44.83.23 or 85.44.78.79.
FAX: 85.44.74.20.
Reservations:
Contact site.

7203 Castel Camping Le Château de Chanteloup, nr Savigne l'Evèque

Peaceful, pleasant site 15 km. from Le Mans from which to explore La Sarthe.

Situated in the park of an old château in the heart of the Sarthe countryside, this site has a certain elegance with the old château in the process of renovation. There are 100 pitches, some well wooded, some on the lawn and completely open, plus some overlooking the lake, so the degree of shade varies. All are more than 100 sq.m. and about 80% have electricity. Three sanitary blocks have been formed in the château outbuildings, all with good, tiled facilities. All toilets are British and washbasins are in private cabins with hot water, razor points and mirrors. Some showers are push button, some operate by chain and all have dressing areas with hooks and shelf. There are undercover dishwashing facilities, a washing machine and facilities for the handicapped. A small shop sells necessities (baker calls daily), there is a pleasant bar with terrace in the château and a new restaurant with takeaway chicken and chips also available (all July/Aug). Leisure facilities on site include a swimming pool (all season), children's play area, a room for teenagers, tennis, volleyball, table tennis and the hire of mountain bikes. Fishing (free), squash and badminton can be arranged. Tours of the château grounds and the village by pony and cart are arranged. Organised activities from 5 July-25 Aug. include Disneyland trips, canoeing, riding, tours of the Loire Châteaux and barbecues. Games room with baby foot, flipper, pool, draughts, etc. Golf and horse riding 6 km. Tour operators take 30% of the pitches.

Directions: Site is 15 km. northeast of Le Mans. From the autoroute take the Le Mans Est exit, then follow the Yvré l'Evèque, Savigne l'Evèque and Bonnétable road (D301). Site is halfway between these last two villages.

Charges 1996:
-- Per pitch Ffr. 49.00; adult 29.00; child (under 8 yrs) 17.00; electricity 18.00.
-- Visa credit cards accepted.
Open:
1 June - 7 September.
Address:
Parc de l'Epau, Sillé-le-Philippe, 72460 Savigne l'Evèque.
Tel:
43.27.51.07.
FAX: 43.89.05.05.
Reservations:
No min. length - contact site.

7201M   Camping de la Route d'Or, La Flèche

This is a useful site to know as La Flèche lies at the junction of the Le Mans-Angers and Laval-Saumur roads, along which Britons frequently travel. Readers report a very friendly welcome and reasonable charges. The site lies on the south bank of the Loir, only a short walk from the town centre where there are plenty of shops and restaurants (neither on site). There are about 300 pitches on flat grass, many in excess of 100 sq.m. and these may now be fully marked out. Electrical connections in all parts but long leads needed in certain places. There are two, original sanitary blocks and an extra new block has been added so facilities should be more than adequate. Also a very good separate sanitary block for the disabled. Amenities on site include tennis, boules, a children's playground, pedaloes and canoes for hire on the river, bicycle hire and a laundry room. Caravans and bungalows for hire.

Directions: Site lies in southwest outskirts of town just off D938 road to Saumur and is signed from a junction on the bypass.

Charges 1995:
-- Per person Ffr. 15.50; child (under 7) 7.75; car 4.10; tent 4.50; caravan 6.70; motorcaravan 14.90; electricity 6A 7.30 - 14.70; local tax 2.00.

Open:
All year except 16/11-14/2.

Address:
Allée de la Providence, 72200 La Flèche.

Tel:
43.94.55.90.

Reservations:
Made without deposit but space usually available.

7202M   Camping Municipal du Lac, St Calais

St Calais is a small town some 37 km. east of Le Mans with a small municipal site. Camping du Lac has some 60 marked pitches, all with electricity, on level grass and close to a lake and river. It offers very good value in terms of price. There is a swimming pool adjacent and the site is within walking distance of the town and restaurants. There are two sanitary blocks with British WCs, large hot showers with dividers and some washbasins in private cabins. There are few 'on-site' facilities, but being so close to the town centre this hardly matters. Reception is very welcoming, the value is excellent and this would make a good night stop or base for visiting the Le Mans 24 hour race.

Directions: Well signed from N157, site is by lake north of town, near station.

Charges guide:
-- Per pitch Ffr. 3.70; adult 6.00; child (under 10 yrs) 3.60; vehicle 3.50; electricity 10.00 (6A), 6.20 (3A).

Open:
1 April - 15 October.

Address:
72120 St Calais,

Tel:
43.35.04.81.

Reservations:
Write to site.

7205   Camping Caravanning Brulon le Lac, Brulon

Small, picturesque site overlooking an attractive lake.

Previously a municipal site, but now privately managed, Brulon le Lac offers 65 good size pitches set on flat grass and numbered, some divided by new shrubs and bushes; 45 have electrical connections. The sanitary block, operated by a key system, has British WCs, roomy, pre-set showers and vanity style washbasins, plus a washing machine and dryer. Since our visit a second block has been added. The site is alongside and has direct access to a large lake and sits in a very attractive valley. Swimming is allowed in the lake, with a lifeguard each afternoon in July and August. Activities arranged include sailing, windsurfing, canoeing, fishing and archery (tickets from reception). A children's play area on sand is by the lake and there is a public tennis court. Further additions in 1995 included a small, swimming pool, minigolf, TV and library room, and a bar/restaurant with lake views. Mobile homes (5) for hire.

Directions: From the A81/E50 (Lavel - Le Mans) road, take the D4 (south) to Brulon, where site is signed.

 Alan Rogers'
discount
3rd person
free all season

Charges guide:
-- Per pitch Ffr. 30.00 - 50.00; extra person 10.00 - 15.00; child (under 7 yrs) 5.00 - 10.00; electricity 8.00 - 13.00; visitor 5.00.

Open:
1 April - 30 October.

Address:
Bord du Lac, 72350 Brulon.

Tel:
43.95 68 96
FAX: 43.92.60.36.

Reservations:
Contact site.

73 Savoie / 74 Haute-Savoie

7301 Camping Le Bois Joli, La Chambre, nr St. Martin-sur-la-Chambre

Very pleasant rural site in mountain area.

If you are looking for somewhere different, off the beaten track or happen to be passing on the N6 from Albertville to Modane and the Frejus tunnel to Italy, this might well be a good stopping place. Le Bois Joli is in wooded country in a most peaceful situation. There are 100 grass pitches, all with electrical connections, in small terraced clearings and the site is divided by a minor road. Every effort has been made to disturb the natural habitat as little as possible and, although the camping area could be increased to accommodate more people, the owners like it as it is and will not do this. There are two sanitary blocks, one older one near the heated swimming pool (free) and a new, pre-fabricated one in the other section. British and continental toilets, room for the disabled and a baby room. Laundry and dishwashing sinks. There is a kiosk with a terrace for drinks, takeaway and basic food supplies and a bar with rest room which offers local cuisine from time to time. Two children's play areas and table tennis. A delightful site run by a very helpful and pleasant family who organise guided walks (qualified guide) and games for children in high season.

Directions: From the N6 take road D213 at Le Chambre and follow signs to camp, 1 km. northeast of St. Avre.

Charges 1995:
-- Per unit incl. 2 persons Ffr. 65.00; extra person 20.00; child (under 7 yrs) 12.00; electricity 15.00 - 20.00, acc. to amps; local tax 1.10.
Open:
1 June - 15 September.
Address:
73130 La Chambre Savoie.
Tel:
79.59.42.30 or 79.56.21.28.
FAX: 79.59.42.30.
Reservations:
Write to site.

7302 Camping-Caravaneige Le Versoyen, Bourg-St. Maurice, Les Arcs

Good quality mountain site open all year.

Bourg-St. Maurice is on a small, level plain at an altitude of 830 m. on the River L'Isère, surrounded by high mountains. For many years a winter ski-ing resort, it now caters for visitors all year round. The Parc National de la Vanoise is near, along with a wealth of interesting places. Le Versoyen attracts visitors all year round (except for a month when they close). Trees typically seen at this altitude give shade in some parts. The 200 flat, grass pitches, divided by young trees and numbered by stones, are on either side of tarmac roads. Duckboards are provided for snow and wet weather and hardstandings for motorcaravans (also service area). Some 75% of the pitches have electrical connections. The two acceptable sanitary blocks are in separate places and the provision may be hard pressed in high season. They have continental and Turkish style WCs. There is a heated rest room with TV, a new small bar with takeaway in summer. Laundry facilities. Restaurants and shops are 200 m. Tennis and swimming pool 300 m, horse riding 800 m. and there is a park for walking. A good base for winter ski-ing and summer walking, climbing, rafting or canoeing, plus car excursions.

Directions: Site is 1½ km. east of Bourg-St. Maurice on CD119 Les Arcs road.

Charges 1995:
-- Per person Ffr. 22.00; child (2-7 yrs) 13.00; pitch 20.00; electricity 21.00 - 44.50, acc. to amps; local tax 1.10.
Open:
All year except 14/11-13/12.
Address:
73700 Bourg-St. Maurice.
Tel:
79.07.03.45.
FAX: 79.07.25.41.
Reservations:
Write with deposit (Ffr. 200) and fee (60).

7401 Camping Les Deux Glaciers, Les Bossons, nr Chamonix

Well kept mountain site close to popular resort.

A pleasant little summer or winter site, Les Deux Glaciers has 135 individual pitches on terraces or single plots, levelled out of quite steeply rising ground, with electricity available in all areas. Pleasantly laid out with different trees - and floral displays in their season - it is well tended and maintained. It is quietly situated with fine views of the high mountains around but being a northern slope it loses the sun a little early. The two small sanitary blocks, both heated in cool weather, should suffice and have British toilets, at least half the washbasins in private cabin with shelf and mirror, and free hot water in all basins and showers and most of the sinks. Facilities for the disabled. Snack restaurant (11/6-15/9). Mobile traders call in season, otherwise the village shop is 500 m. On site is a general room, table tennis and a washing machine and drying room. The site becomes full for much of July/Aug. and is not keen on reservations but could make some for Britons, so try. In season, if not reserved, arrive early.

Directions: From west take second road leading off main N506 to right for Les Bossons, which takes you direct to site. From east turn right at sign for Les Bossons, then left at T-junction, and on to site.

Charges 1996:
-- Per unit with 2 persons Ffr. 62.00; extra person 21.00; child (0-7) 11.00; local tax 1.00; electricity (2A) 13.00.
Open:
All year except 15/11-15/12.
Address:
Rte. des Tissières, Les Bossons 74400 Chamonix.
Tel:
50.53.15.84.
Reservations:
May be possible - see text.

7403 Camping Le Bélvèdere, Annecy

Hillside camp with good views over lake, in lovely area.

Annecy is an attractive town in a beautiful setting at the head of the lake of the
same name. The old centre is intersected by flower decked canals and also has
historical interest. There is much to see and do in this region in both summer and
winter with Geneva and the high Alps near. Le Bélvèdere, as its name implies,
overlooks the lake and is the nearest camp to the town. It is now under private
management, on lease from the authorities. There are hardstanding terraces for
80 caravans, where all pitches have electricity, and grass areas for tents where
space may be limited if the site is busy. One small area is reserved for groups.
Tall pines and steep hillside back the site on the west and small trees decorate
without giving much shade. Three modern sanitary blocks are around the site,
one heated in cold weather and with a washroom for the disabled. Games room,
good children's playground and one may swim in the lake. Shop (from May) and
laundry facilities. A neat and tidy site ideally placed for visiting Annecy.

Directions: From the town centre follow signs for 'Camping Municipal' towards
Albertville on road N508. Turn right to follow sign for 'Hopital' up hill and take
first left after passing this towards Semnoz and site.

Charges 1995:
-- Per person Ffr. 20.00;
child (under 7) 10.00;
tent, caravan or motor-
caravan 31.00; small
tent 20.00; electricity
20.00; local tax 1.00.
Open:
February - 30 October.
Address:
Rte. de Semnoz,
74000 Annecy.
Tel:
50.45.48.30.
FAX: 50.45.55.56.
Reservations:
Necessary for July/Aug.
- write to site.

7404 Camp de la Ravoire, Doussard, nr Annecy

Quality site with pool, overlooking Lake Annecy.

De la Ravoire, some 800 m. from the lake, has gained the coveted 4 star rating
by the quality of its sanitary block, its neat tidy appearance and the quietness of
its location in this popular tourist region. The 100 numbered pitches, on well
mown grass and separated by small shrubs, have little shade, although there are
trees on the lake side of the site. The sanitary block in the centre of the camp is
very good with British WCs and hot water in washbasins (in cabins), sinks and
showers. There are special facilities for the disabled and a laundry room with
washing machines, dryers and irons. The outdoor pool is overlooked by the
terrace of the snack bar where limited basic food items may be stocked. Near this
building is a children's play area. There is a good restaurant on the lake-side
where the camp road leaves the main road and others near, with shops in
Doussard village. Those looking for a quiet, quality site in this most attractive
region without the 'animation' programmes which so many French camps feel
are necessary will find this a peaceful base, although disco noise from a camp by
the lake may drift across under some weather conditions.

Directions: Site is signed from the Annecy-Albertville road, just north of
Bout-du-Lac. (Watch carefully, signs are small!)

Charges 1995:
-- Per unit incl. 2 adults
and electricity (5A) Ffr.
135.00, plus 1 child
under 10 yrs 140.00;
water/drainage 20.00;
extra person 30.00;
child (under 10) 11.00.
-- Low season -15-20% .
Open:
1 May - 30 October.
Address:
Bout-du-Lac,
Rte de la Ravoire,
74210 Doussard.
Tel:
50.44.37.80.
Reservations:
Made for min. 10 days;
details from site.

7406 Camping La Colombiere, Neydens, nr St Julien-en-Genevois

Good small site with pool, near Geneva.

La Colombiere, on the edge of the small residential village of Neydens, is a few
minutes from the A40 autoroute and only a short way from Geneva. It is a neat,
tidy, rectangular site with four rows of pitches of grass on small stones between
hard access roads with 100 numbered places separated by fruit and other trees.
With mountain ridges to both east and west and a good variety of trees between,
this is a quiet peaceful site, well run by the Bussat family. Two good quality
sanitary blocks have British WCs, the usual amenities, a baby room and facilities
for the disabled. Excellent bar/restaurant with terrace overlooking the heated
pool. Guided cycle tours and mountain walks are arranged during high season
when French country music evenings are also held. The owner has a small
vineyard about 300 m. from the camp, has the wine made in Switzerland and
sells this by glass or bottle in the restaurant. Neydens makes a good base for
visiting Geneva and the Lac Leman region and is a very pleasant, friendly site
where you may drop in for an en route night stop - and stay for several days!

Directions: Take exit 13 from A40 autoroute south of Geneva, turn towards
Annecy on N201 and follow camp signs (Camping Neydens, **not** name of site).

Charges 1995:
-- Per unit incl. 2
persons Ffr. 80.00; extra
person 20.00; child
(under 7 yrs) 14.00;
extra car or tent 14.00;
dog 8.00; electricity 3A
15.00, 5 or 6A 20.00.
Open:
1 April - 31 October.
Address:
74160 Neydens.
Tel:
50.35.13.14.
FAX: 50.35.13.40.
Reservations:
Write to site.

7405M Camping Municipal, Saint-Ferréol

This is a value for money site in a very popular area. It is well run and well maintained with a high standard of cleanliness and friendly Bureau staff. Surrounded by glorious alpine scenery, it offers a relaxing environment away from the busy lakeside roads around Lake Annecy. Reception is located on the forecourt beside the security gate. also within this area is the St Ferréol village hall and boule club. Pitches on the site are grass, numbered and have electric hook-ups. The ground is level and there is some shade from the tall fir trees in the centre. Two spotlessly clean toilet blocks are fully tiled. An electronic barrier is in operation and campers are issued with a key. Two supermarkets are a few minutes away by car at Faverges where you will also find banks, post office, etc. This is an excellent base from which to explore the high mountain passes, visit Chamonix or linger by the turquoise coloured lake.

Directions: Leave Faverges on the N508 Albertville road. Site is clearly signed to the left within 2 km.

Charges guide:
- Per unit incl. 2 persons and electricity Ffr. 59.00.
Open: 15 June - 15 September.
Address: 74210 Saint-Ferréol.
Tel: 50.27.47.71 or 50.44.56.36.
Reservations: Are accepted - contact site.

7502 Parc de Camping Paris-Ouest, Bois de Boulogne, Paris

Attractively situated camp beside the Seine and close to the city limits.

This site is the nearest camp to the city, lying in a wooded area between the Seine and the Bois de Boulogne. One can reach the Champs Elysees in 10-15 minutes by car or there is usually a shuttle bus running from the site to the Metro station. The camp is quite extensive but nevertheless becomes very full with many international visitors of all ages. There are about 500 pitches of which 280 are marked, with electricity (10A), water, drainage and TV aerial connections. 60 mobile homes are available to rent. No reservations are made for the pitches so arrival early (in the morning) in season is necessary. The four toilet blocks are of necessity rather utilitarian and are of mixed type, with various types of WCs, washbasins partly open, some in cabins and free pre-set hot showers. These facilities suffer from heavy use in season and require continuous maintainance. Small supermarket and snack bar (April-Oct). Washing machines and dryers. Bureau de change. Children's playground. Organised excursions. No dogs.

Directions: Site is on east side of Seine between the river and Bois de Boulogne, just north of the Pont de Suresnes. Follow signs closely and use a good map.

Charges guide
-- Per unit incl. 2 persons Ffr 65.00; special pitch incl. 4 persons and all services 140.00; extra person 15.00.
Open: All year.
Address: Allée du bord de l'eau, 75016 Paris.
Tel: (1) 45.24.30.00. FAX: (1) 42.24.42.95.
Reservations: Not made.

7604 Camping La Source, Petit Appeville, Hautot sur Mer, nr Dieppe

Flat, shady site, convenient for Newhaven ferries.

This site is just 4 km. from Dieppe and is useful for those using the revitalised Newhaven - Dieppe ferry crossing. It is flat, shady and quiet, in a valley with the only disturbance the occasional passing train. A shallow stream flows along one border (not protected for young children). There are hardstandings for motorcaravans and electricity is available (3, 6 or 10A). The one toilet block (males to the left, females to the right) is good and kept clean, providing washbasins in cubicles (H&C), pre-set showers with dividers and mixed British and continental WCs (less in number). Facilities under cover for dishwashing (H&C) and laundry. Toilet, shower and basin for the disabled but unmade gravel roads may cause problems. The site has an arrangement with Stena Sealink Line and therefore stays open for late night ferries so there could be some noise late at night. A small bar, attractively renovated, also provides snack meals and is open for late ferries. Small play field for children. TV room (French programmes) and room for young people with table tennis and amusement machines.

Directions: On leaving the dock, follow one way system bearing left at Canadian War memorial, below the castle. Follow signs to Paris and Rouen and, after long hill, at large roundabout take first exit to right on D925, Av. St. Jaures. After 2 km. turn left at traffic lights on D153 (Pourville sur Mer to right). Just past railway station turn left under bridge (signed) into narrow road with stream on right. Site is a short distance on the left.

Charges 1995:
-- Per caravan or motorcaravan Ffr. 24.00; tent 18.00; person 18.00; child 12.00; car 6.00; electricity 15.00.
Open: 15 March - 15 October.
Address: Petit Appeville, 76550 Hautot sur Mer.
Tel: 35.84.27.04.
Reservations: Write to site.

7601M Camp Municipal Forêt de Montgeon, Le Havre

This is a good spot to spend the first or last night of your holiday or perhaps a bit longer. In a pleasant quiet setting within a wooded park in the upper part of the town, the site is well laid out with tarred access roads. There are 40 caravan pitches on hardstandings with electricity, water and drainaway plus some 35 on grass, and five tent lawns taking well over 220 units. It can become full with much transit trade but you should find space if you arrive early. The 5 identical, small sanitary blocks provide plentiful facilities of a reasonable standard which include some washbasins in private cabins and 8 free hot showers (these appear to be much used by local sportsmen). Small shop (open nearly all season) with take away snacks and outdoor eating area. Tennis. Table tennis. Games room. TV room. Good children's play area. Bicycle hire. Animation. Gates closed 11 pm. - 6.30 am. A sandy beach is 7 km.

Directions: The site and the Forêt de Montgeon are not too easy to find as approaches from most directions are circuitous and signposts easy to miss. Approaching from Tancarville Bridge, follow ferry signs and bear left at rotating advert sign along Quai Colbert. Turn right into Cours de la République, following signs to Montvilliers and Fecamp (N115), past Gare Central. From the ferry turn right and then, shortly after, left into Cours de la République. Pass through Tunnel Jenner (taller vehicles keep in right hand lane). Turn right shortly after the tunnel following signs to the Forêt and camp. The last section of through the forest park is circuitous with a one way system at weekends.

Charges guide:
-- Per caravan and car incl. 2 persons Ffr. 71.00 (2 axles 81.00); tent and car 50.00; extra adult 18.00; child 9.00; local tax 1.00; electricity (5A) 12.00 - (10A) 24.00.
-- Discounts for 2-6 nights, more for over a week.
Open:
1 April - 30 September.
Address:
76620 Le Havre.
Tel:
35.46.52.39.
Reservations:
Only made for the special caravan pitches for 2 or more nights.

7603 Camping International du Golf, Le Tréport, nr Dieppe

Attractive, wooded site on edge of resort near Dieppe.

This site is about 1 km. from the centre of the resort of Le Tréport and is well worth considering for a holiday in this area. It has some 250 pitches, all about 100 sq.m., some on flat grass, separated by fencing markers and many in wooded areas giving more privacy and good shade. There are about 70 pitches with electrical connections (5A). There are two principal sanitary blocks providing continental style WCs, free hot water to washbasins (many in private cabins with shelf, mirror and light) and to the showers. These facilities are supplemented by three small toilet blocks of rather basic quality; water points around. Shop and cafe (1/7-20/8). A large bar with an hotel opened in 1994. Sports/play field. Bureau de change. Despite the site's name, the nearest golf course is 30 km. at Dieppe.

Directions: Site is on the southwest edge of Le Tréport, by D940 Dieppe road.

 Alan Rogers' discount Less 10% after 3 days

Charges 1995:
--Per pitch incl. 2 adults Ffr 58.00 - 82.00; extra person 20.00 - 24.00; child (1-7 yrs) 14.00 - 18.00; electricity (5A) 28.00.
-- Credit cards accepted
Open:
Easter/1 April - 20 Sept.
Address:
76470 Le Tréport.
Tel:
35.86.33.80.
FAX: 35.50.33.54.
Reservations:
Write with Ffr. 100 deposit.

7605M Camping Municipal Parc du Château, Eu

Situated in the grounds of the Château d'Eu, the setting for this site is quite lovely, even with the main town of Eu only minutes away. On entering the site, there is a long woodland area and park providing excellent picnic opportunities with lots of shade. The Château itself houses reception, the recreational rooms and the toilet facilities. These offer free hot water and continental style WCs, with some facilities shared by both sexes. The showers are of good quality with an adequate provision for the size of the site which is quite small despite its initial appearance. Previously the property of the Princes of Orleans, the Château now also houses the Town Hall and museum, and some rooms, the gardens and the grounds are open to the public. The park gates are closed 10 pm. - 7 am. Mobile homes to rent.

Directions: Take the D925 from Le Tréport into the town centre from which the Château and site are signed.

Charges guide:
-- Per person Ffr. 10.40; child (2-10 yrs) 5.20; pitch 10.40; vehicle 10.40; electricity (6A) 18.30.
Open:
1 April - 31 October.
Address:
76260 Eu.
Tel:
35.86.20.04.
Reservations:
Policy not known - contact site.

7606M Camping Municipal de Martigny, Martigny

Well located by a lake and the river Arques, for those keen on sailing or fishing, this reasonably sized site has facilities for both. There is a sailing school opposite the site and access to the river and lake for canoeists or small boats, but not for swimming (nearest pool is 2 km). There are 110 pitches, 48 with electrical connections. The two sanitary blocks have controllable hot and cold showers with dressing areas and British WCs. There are some washbasins in private cabins, laundry and washing up sinks under cover and a washing machine. A small shop and limited bar and takeaway operates in July and August and there is a games room and boules court.

Directions: From the Arques la Bataille-Torcy road (D154) turn off to Martigny and site is signed.

Charges guide:
-- Per adult Ffr. 11.75; child (under 7 yrs) 5.45; car 6.10; caravan pitch 21.50; tent 10.00; animal 4.95; local tax 1.00 per person.
Open:
1 April - 15 October.
Address:
76880 Martigny.
Tel:
35.85.60.82.
Reservations:
Contact site.

7607M Camping-Caravaning Municipal Le Mesnil, St Aubin sur Mer

This site does not give the impression of the usual municipal site, having a personality very much of its own with the reception and toilet blocks proudly displaying the thatched roofs of Normandy. The site is on a steep hill but the ground has been levelled into terraces for the 155 pitches which are separated by tall, manicured hedges and have ample shade from trees. Electricity (10A) is available for caravans, not for tents. Three small toilet blocks are situated around the site, each having 6-8 toilets and showers for men and women, with free hot water. Laundry and dishwashing sinks are under cover. Laundry room with washing machine. Previously a Norman farm, the old buildings have been restored and converted to provide the site's facilities, including a small shop also offering a boulangerie, snacks and takeaway. A large, octagonal, open sided games and community room is at the top of the hill and a children's playground on grass is at the bottom. Other facilities include volleyball, boules and table tennis. Some mobile homes to let. Restaurant/bar 200 m. A footpath leads from the site through fields to the coast or there is the lively beach at St Aubin.

Directions: From the D925 Veules Les Roses-Dieppe road turn off onto D75 to St. Aubin sur Mer. Site is signed 2 km. on the D68 road to Veules Les Roses.

Charges guide:
-- Per person Ffr. 20.20; child (under 7 yrs) 10.10; car 10.10; pitch 14.00; pitch with services 18.20; electricity (10A) 18.00; local tax 2.00 per person.
Open:
1 April -- 31 October.
Address:
76740 St Aubin sur Mer.
Tel:
35.83.02.83.
Reservations:
Contact site.

7701 Davy Crockett Ranch, Disneyland Paris, Marne-la-Vallée

Disney quality site, with excellent indoor pool close to Disneyland

Disney's campsite is on the south side of the A4 autoroute, but far enough from it to be untroubled by traffic noise. Most sectors of the wooded site contain log cabins (498) which are very well equipped and quite attractively priced, but one sector, the Moccassin Trail, provides 97 numbered tourist pitches. Each consists of a long, narrow hardstanding with a roughly 25 sq.m. sand-topped tent area at the far end (awnings are not therefore possible). Each pitch is separated from the next by an area of small trees and shrubs and the whole site is well endowed with tall trees for shade. Each place has its own individual electric point, water supply and drain, a large picnic table and an equally robust iron barbecue. At the centre of the oval Trail is a modern, quality toilet block of ample proportions and containing every facility, including washing machines (free).

The touring sector is furthest away from the main services complex (styled like a Western movie set!), but a 400 m. walk is well rewarded. The shop provides a rather wider choice of Disney souvenirs than food, but all the basic requirements can be obtained, and there are a number of supermarkets and hypermarkets within a short drive. However, most campers will be tempted into using the self-service restaurant, which offers both American and French style food. A major attraction is the large leisure pool, with flume and jacuzzis, built inside a huge log cabin, which opens out onto a terrace with chairs and sunbeds. The terrace overlooks Indian Meadows, a large field, with adventure play equipment, basketball and football goals. Farm and pony rides. Campfire sessions (summer only) sound like fun! Bicycles and electric golf carts can be hired on a daily basis. There is a good covered tennis court and a half court.

Connection with the Magic Kingdom is via the autoroute taking 10 minutes (with free regular bus service, or there is free car parking at Disneyland for campers). We avoided queuing to get in by buying entry tickets from the cycle hire shop on the campsite the night before. It is for other publications to review its attractions, but we had a marvellous time. Nowhere else does Coca-Cola taste quite the same, or are staff quite so polite. This politeness and attention to cleanliness, comfort and visitors' needs were equally in evidence throughout the operation of the Ranch. There may be cheaper sites within range of Disneyland, but this one offers you the Disney magic throughout your stay. The site is also eminently suitable for visits to that other magic city, Paris, only 35 km. away by autoroute or train. However, in the main season the campsite will be busy and may be noisy with cars and motorcaravans returning from the late evening shows (possibly also some aircraft noise). In high season you must reserve, and early.

Directions: From Paris take the A4 eastwards, following signs for Metz/Nancy. For Disneyland itself take exit 14, but for the Davy Crockett Ranch, turn right at exit 13. From Calais, follow Paris signs until just before Charles de Gaulle airport, then follow signs to Marne la Vallée - eventually you should join the A4.

Charges 1995:
-- Per pitch, all incl. Ffr. 375.00; 6-berth cabin from 575.00 per night.
Open:
From 1 April (contact Disney for closing date), log cabins all year.
Reservations:
For information and reservations phone 0171-753-2900 (UK).

7705M Camping Municipal, Samoreau

A small site with large pitches and adequate toilet facilities (little else, it must be said), it is on one of the prettiest stretches of the river Seine. It is close to commuter lines to Paris, good for visiting the Fontainebleau forest and within range of Disneyland. The pitches are partly delineated on gently sloping grass. There is a small café beside the river in high season.

Directions: The scenic route is by the D39 south from Melun. Follow the river for about 20 km. to Samoreau. Site is through the village behind the beautifully restored barn, La Grange aux Dimes.

Charges 1995:
-- Per adult Ffr 12.00; child (under 10) 6.00; caravan 25.00; tent 15.00; motorcaravan 35.00; vehicle 10.00; electricity 4A 8.00.
Open:
15 March - 30 Sept.
Address:
77210 Samoreau
Tel:
(1) 64.23.72.25.
Reservations:
Not normally necessary.

7702 Camping Les Courtilles du Lido, Veneux-les-Sablons, nr Fontainebleu

Useful site in convenient location southwest of Paris.

An adequate site in most respects, Les Courtilles du Lido provides a suitable place for shortish stays, situated 23 km. southeast of Melun. The 100 good sized pitches, all with electricity (2 or 6A), are laid out on flat level ground. Many more long stay units are well screened from the touring area. The sanitary block is some distance from the furthest pitches and is a little ugly on the outside (fortunately it is screened from most pitches by trees). Inside, however, clean, modern installations are provided. A new block for ladies has recently been added with hot showers (token on payment). A fair sized pool (15/5-15/9), half-court tennis, boules area and children's playground provide amusement. There is no shop but a bread van calls each morning and it is a short walk/cycle ride to either of two villages along the river. The better village to head for is the delightful Moret-sur-Loing at the confluence of the Loing and the Seine. The location puts Paris and Disneyland just in range by train (station a 10 min. walk) or by driving (1 hour). It is also ideal for cycling or walking in the Forest of Fontainebleu. Sunday market at St Mammes. Dogs and pets are not accepted. Used by tour operators (50%).

Charges 1995:
-- Per caravan Ffr. 18.00; tent 15.00; car 12.00; adult 19.50; child 15.50; electricity 2A 14.00, 6A 15.50.
Open:
1 April - 30 September.
Address:
77250 Veneux-les-Sablons.
Tel:
(1) 60.70.46.05.
FAX: 64.70.62.65.
Reservations:
Not normally necessary.

Directions: Take the N6 south from Fontainebleau towards Sens. After about 6 km. turn left towards Veneux-les-Sablons. Site is well signed from Veneux (left off the main street).

7703 Léon's Lodge Camp Hotel, Camping and Golf Parc, Crécy-la-Chapelle

Unusual site, very convenient for visits to Disneyland.

For some years we have been investigating possible sites to stay at for visits to Disneyland Paris, and Leon's Lodge represents a good bet! Quite attractively situated and with a direct 15 minute bus connection to Disneyland (the bus calls at the site), one could hardly find a more convenient location, added to which, it is also easy to get into the centre of Paris by train (about 25 mins). Having been developed from a former municipal, the site itself is quite unusual, the dominant feature now being a number of `permanent' Trigano type tents for hire. These are unusual as the interiors are specially designed for Leon's Lodge in a very colourful Arabian Nights style, continuing the Disney theme, which should certainly appeal to the kids!

The touring pitches are currently on fairly level open ground with lots of electrical connections, but not marked or separated. There are plans to relocate these pitches in a wooded area (drainage may be a problem). We visited the site twice in 1995 - once in March, just before it was open, and again in May, in a downpour. Given these somewhat unfortunate circumstances, our impressions were generally favourable, although one of the two refurbished sanitary blocks was already showing signs of wear and its actual design is distinctly draughty. The other block is enclosed and can be heated. The facilities themselves, however, were comprehensive, adequate and clean, particularly given the awful weather at the time. The catering facilities, with the restaurant sited in an Arabian Nights marquee, provide a range of fairly simple, well cooked (mainly grilled) meals at very reasonable prices, plus a children's menu and takeaway meals. Although there is no shop, basics such as bread milk and butter can be bought from the restaurant. The enthusiastic and knowledgeable Dutch owner has some ambitious plans for this site and the nearby luxurious golf complex. All in all, our impression is that if one is looking for a reasonably comfortable and interesting venue for visiting Disneyland or Paris, this site is well worth considering.

Charges 1995:
-- Per pitch incl. 4 persons Ffr. 90.00 - 150.00 acc. to season.
-- Contact site for details of `Ali Baba' tents.
-- Special price Disneyland tickets.
Open:
1 April - 30 September.
Address:
N-34 Rte de Serbonne, 77580 Crécy-la-Chapelle.
Tel:
(1) 60.43.57.00.
FAX: (1) 60.43.57.01.
Reservations:
Contact site.

Directions: From the A4 motorway take Crécy exit and follow signs to Crécy-la-Chapelle and Coulommies. Léon's Lodge is just after the 12th century church in La Chapelle (approx. 5 km).

7801 Parc Montana Laffitte, Maisons-Laffitte, Paris

Busy site on the banks of the Seine with good train service to central Paris.

Previously Camping International, this site is now under the ownership of the Parc Montana group. Maisons-Laffitte is a pleasant suburb which has a château, a park, a racecourse and some large training stables, and there is a good and frequent train service, including an express service, to the Gare St. Lazare (station is 1 km. from the camp). Normally taking about 18 minutes on the journey, it returns until 12.30 am. The site occupies a grassy, tree covered area bordering the river. Most of the pitches in the tourist parts (there is also a permanent section) are marked out with separators and of good size. Only the meadows at the end of the site, intended mainly for tents, are not marked and could become more crowded. There are three sanitary blocks, all with free hot water in all services. Two are well insulated and heated for winter use, the third is a more open block better suited for the summer months. Self-service shop (closed in winter). Restaurant/bar with takeaway food also; some live entertainment. Launderette. Table tennis. Billiards. Used by all the main tour operators. A busy site, facilities could be overstretched at times. Some railway noise. Mobile homes available for rent (tel: (1) 39.62.90.75).

Directions: From autoroute de l'ouest take exit to Poissy, then follow signs to Maisons-Laffitte. From N14 from Rouen take St. Germain exit from the Pontoise by-pass motorway and turn left at big roundabout in Forêt de St. Germain. From north or east, take boulevard périphérique to Porte Maillot exit then via Pont de Neuilly and Pont de Bezons which is more complicated and map really needed.

Charges 1995:
-- Per tent or caravan incl. 1 or 2 persons Ffr. 85.00 - 120.00; motorcaravan 100.00 - 130.00; extra person 10 yrs or over 27.00 - 32.00, child under 10 free; extra tent 15.00; extra car or m/cycle 13.00 - 18.00; electricity (4A) 20.00, (10A) 30.00; local tax 3.00.
Open: All year.
Address: 1, Rue Johnson, 78600 Maisons-Laffitte.
Tel: (1) 39.12.21.91. FAX: (1) 34.93.02.60.
Reservations: Advisable for July/Aug. and made with deposit and fee (Ffr. 100).

Alan Rogers' discount
Ask at site for details

Remember - to claim your discount you will need to show your 1996 discount voucher

78 Yvelines / 79 Deux-Sèvres

7803 Domaine d'Inchelin, St. Illiers la Ville, nr Bréval

Quiet, family run site in the Seine valley within 60 km. of Paris.

This area, within easy reach of Paris and Versailles, is one of rolling countryside and small villages made famous by th artist Monet. On the outskirts of one of these is Domaine d'Inchelin where an attractive camp site has been developed around charming old farm buildings. The 135 pitches, almost all with electricity and water connections, are large (250 sq.m.) and arranged amongst ornamental trees and shrubs with well kept hedges providing privacy and shelter. Peacocks (rather noisy in spring!) and other tame birds parade the site and roost in the trees. A wooded area provides play equipment and space for children to play. Tennis and riding are available nearby. Neatly arranged in the timbered buildings which surround three sides of the old farm yard are a small shop, bar, takeaway (all May-Sept), an under cover play area and the main sanitary facilities. An attractive, new swimming pool lies sheltered in the centre. Sanitary facilities are split into two areas - one room with toilets (mixed), the other with showers, washbasins in cabins, a dishwashing area and a laundry room. Hot water is free throughout and whilst the high ceilings and old beams remain, the facilities are well kept and clean. A modern block was added in 1995. The Daniel family provide a friendly welcome and will advise on what to see in the area and how to reach the attractions of Paris (45 mins by train, 55 km. by road) and Versailles. Some seasonal caravans. Used by British tour operators (60%).

Charges 1996:
-- Including car, unit and pitch: per adult Ffr. 60.00 - 75.00; child (4-12 yrs) 25.00 - 30.00, under 4 yrs free; dog 10.00; electricity (4A) 25.00, (6A) 40.00.
Open:
1 April - 31 October.
Address:
St. Illiers la Ville, 78980 Bréval.
Tel:
34.76.10.11.
Reservations:
Write to site for details.

Directions: From A13 autoroute take Chaufour exit (no. 15) onto N13. Turn off within 1 km. into centre of Chaufour and take D25 to Lommoye, then D89 to St. Illiers. Take Bréval road and road to the site is almost immediately on the left.

7901M Camping Municipal de Noron, Niort

A good example of the better type of municipal site, this well kept and agreeable camp should be highly satisfactory for overnight or a bit longer. On flat ground, in a quiet setting beside the River Sèvre (fenced, with gate) with mature trees and next to exhibition grounds, it has individual pitches with good shade over most of the site and a general meadow with play area. Electrical hook-ups available (5, 10 or 15A). The sanitary block is of very fair standard, with free hot water throughout, continental style toilets, many washbasins, some in cabins, and plentiful free showers with pre-set hot water. Washing machine and ironing board. Two children's playgrounds. When we visited a mobile snack bar and takeaway service was working well (open 15/6-15/9). No other facilities on site but a shopping centre is close. The barrier is closed 10 pm.- 7 am.

Charges 1995:
-- Per person Ffr 15.00; child (under 8 yrs) 9.00; pitch 6.00; tent/caravan 7.00; vehicle 6.00; motorcaravan 18.00.
-- Credit cards accepted.
Open:
15 April - 15 October.
Address:
21 Bd. Salvador Allende, 79000 Niort.
Tel/Fax:
49.79.05.06.
Reservations:
Write to site.

Directions: Site is west of the town, adjacent to the ring road running between N148 and N11.

7902 Camping de Courte Vallée, Airvault

Small, pretty British-run family site on the Route d'Or.

Strategically situated in a river valley on the outskirts of Airvault, on the Route d'Or from Dieppe to Bordeaux and convenient for Futuroscope, we first visited this small site when it was originally opened some three years ago, but delayed its inclusion on the grounds that it was then somewhat 'immature'. Since our first visit, the owners (Richard and Wendy Curtis from Guernsey) have added an attractive swimming pool and the site has matured very nicely, with small trees and an abundance of flowers and shrubs providing more shade and better separation of the pitches. There are, in fact, just 41 pitches on gently sloping grass. All of a good size, more than half have electrical connections (8 or 16A). The single, unisex sanitary building is of a de-luxe standard with facilities to match - one of the best we've seen. Apart from the swimming pool and facilities to purchase essentials, the site has few amenities but the town of Airvault is only 10-15 minutes walk away. There is plenty to see and do in this little known area.

Charges 1995:
-- Per person Ffr. 16.00; child (under 7 yrs) 8.00; pitch and vehicle 35.00; animal 9.00; electricity (8A) 15.00.
Open:
Mid May - mid Sept.
Address:
79600 Airvault.
Tel:
49.64.70.65.
FAX: 49.70.84.58.
Reservations:
Contact site for details.

Directions: Site is 50 km. south of Saumur, signed off the D938 road in Airvault. Watch for 'Courte Vallée' signs with logo.

8001 Castels Camping Domaine de Drancourt St. Valéry-sur-Somme

Popular site between Boulogne and Dieppe with swimming pools and other amenities.

This site will be at a convenient distance for many people from one of the Channel ports, but with all the amenities on the site, plenty stay for much longer periods. On fairly flat meadow with some large apple trees at intervals, the original section is marked out in 100 numbered individual pitches of good size. An extension of that area, with some seasonal caravans and taking 50 units, is in light woodland. Two newer sections are on flat or gently sloping grass, with little shade as yet. The total is now some 200 pitches and electricity is available in all areas. Sanitary installations consist of three blocks - the original enlarged block, a modern one of quite good quality, and a third in the newest sections. All have British WCs, free hot water (pre-set temperature in the newer blocks) to washbasins (in cabins or cubicles), showers and sinks. Amenities include two free heated swimming pools, (both 17 x 6 m. but of different depths), open 15/5-15/9 plus some weekends when weather is good. Shop. Takeaway all season with new pizzeria open until late. Restaurant closing at 9 pm. (late June-end Aug). Bar in château, small bar with longer hours and bar by the pools with karaoke in season. Three TV rooms, one for children. Separate disco for the young with free entry. Games room with table tennis. Tennis court. Golf practice range and new minigolf in enclosed setting. Bicycle hire. Washing machines and dryers. Riding in season and free fishing. Organised activities and weekly excursions to Paris, June-Aug. Bureau de change. Well known and deservedly popular, reservation is advisable for main season. Most tour operators present. Stony beach at Cayeux, 8 km or sandy beach 25 km. Run very personally by the energetic proprietor, English is spoken. Tents and bungalows for hire.

Charges 1995:
-- Per person Ffr. 26.00
+ local tax (over 10 yrs)
1.00; child (under 7)
20.00; pitch 42.00; car
12.00; electricity (6A)
14.00.

Open:
Easter - 15 September.

Address:
80230 St. Valéry-sur-Somme.

Tel:
22.26.93.45.
FAX: 22.26.85.87.

Reservations:
Made for any length, with deposit for longer stays.

Directions: Site is 2½ km. south of St. Valéry, near Estreboeuf, and is signed from the St. Valéry road N40.

A quiet country touring site within easy reach of the Channel ports.
2 Swimming pools, Golf Driving range and animations, restaurant etc.

Camping du
Domaine de Drancourt
ST. VALERY-SUR-SOMME
✳ ✳ ✳ ✳

Member of Chaine Castels et Camping

Excursions to Paris every week from June to August

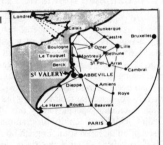

8003 Camping-Caravaning Port de Plaisance, Péronne

Conveniently situated, attractive town site.

Now run by a non-profit making association under the auspices of the Chamber of Commerce, this former municipal site is informally laid out beside the Canal du Nord on the outskirts of the small town of Péronne, on the river Somme. The associations with the Great War (including a museum) are strong and the First World War battlefields and cemeteries are numerous in this area, a vivid reminder of the folly of war. Only some 2-3 hours drive from the Channel ports and Tunnel, this site is conveniently situated for overnight stops en route to or from destinations further south or east. The site itself is surprisingly pretty, being surrounded by trees, with 94 marked pitches of varying shapes and sizes on mainly level grass, some being seasonal. There are 64 electrical connections (5/10A). The sanitary facilities are fairly typical of a former municipal site and, although somewhat dated, are gradually being improved, with free hot showers including a divider, but somewhat cramped. There are some washbasins in private cabins (hot water) and British WCs in an area which can be heated in winter. Covered dishwashing sinks with both hot and cold water and a washing machine and dryer. It is generally an adequate provision. Small children's play area on grass. The gates are open 7 am. - 10 pm, and although reception is said to be open from 3-10 pm. it is best to arrive before 8 pm. Public telephone. Van with bread and a mobile shop/charcuterie call. Motorcaravan service point.

Directions: From north and the ferries, on autoroute A1, take exit 14 and follow N17 (south) to Peronne. Take signs for town centre and continue through (watching for 3 star camp signs). Pass over river Somme and Canal du Nord and site is on right, just past garage at Porte du Plaisance (2 km. from town centre). From south use exit 13 and follow D79 to Barleux, the D370 to pick up the N17 going north. Watch for site signs on left before crossing Canal du Nord.

Charges 1995:
-- Per pitch Ffr. 11.45; person 12.50; child (under 7 yrs) 6.80; vehicle 5.00; m/cycle 2.45; animal 2.45; electricity 5A 15.25 (winter) - 11.25 (summer), 10A 30.50 - 22.45.
-- Less in low seasons.
-- Credit cards accepted.

Open:
All year except 23/12-1/1 (but check with tourist office).

Address:
Route de Paris, 80200 Peronne.

Tel:
22.84.19.31.

FAX: 22.83.14.58.

Reservations:
Possibly necessary in main season.

8101 Camping Relais de l'Entre Deux Lacs, Teillet, nr Albi

Small, quiet, family run site between the Rassisse and Bancalié lakes.

This is a lovely little site, run by the Belgian family of Lily and Dion Heijde-Wouters. Situated in part meadow, part semi-cleared woodland, with a small farm alongside, the site now offers a range of modern amenities including a good sized swimming pool (1/5-30/9) and an excellent bar/restaurant specialising in Belgian cuisine. It also serves a range of no less than 30 different Belgian beers as well as French wine. Lily is developing quite a reputation for her very good special recipes using the beers and is attracting local French to eat at the restaurant. Special family oriented attractions include a weekly barbecue evening, children's activity programme and 'It's a Knockout' contests. A library in reception includes some English books and board games.

The 54 pitches, all with electricity, are on level terraces, possibly with ample shade. They are of varying size, up to 100 sq.m. The site and activities are very well managed, the owners at pains to ensure the generally tranquil atmosphere is not disrupted by noise late at night. Late arrivals or those wishing to leave before 8 am. are therefore sited in an adjacent small meadow. There are two sanitary blocks, with extra toilets at the lower part of the site. The main one is of new construction with the latest fittings including free, pre-set hot showers, washbasins in cabins, British WCs and dishwashing sinks under cover (H&C). The older, smaller block, in the converted pigeon house, has similar, though older style fittings and is heated in winter when the new block is closed. It also has facilities for the handicapped and washing machines. Volleyball. Table tennis. Boules. Children's farm (they can help feed the animals) and playground. Bread to order, shop in village. Bicycle hire. Canoes and kayaks for hire on the Rassisse lake. Caravans and chalets to rent. This site is well situated for a variety of interesting excursions in an area not that well known to British visitors.

Directions: From Albi ringroad, take the D81 going southeast to Teillet (approx. 20 km). Continue through the village on the D81 and site is on the right.

Charges 1996:
-- Per unit incl. 2 persons Ffr. 71.00, with electricity 82.00 - 93.00; extra person 23.00; child (under 7 yrs) 11.00; extra tent 10.00; dog 10.00; electricity 3A 10.00, 6A 20.00.
-- Less 20% outside 15/6-31/8 for stays of min. 5 days.

Open:
All year.

Address:
81120 Teillet.

Tel:
63.55.74.45.

FAX: 63.55.75.65.

Reservations:
Made with deposit (Ffr. 100 per week booked) and fee (70).

PARC MONTANA
4 Star Campsites

Maisons-Laffitte

Aureilhan · · Villeneuve Loubet
· Gassin

For Holidays in
Magnificent Natural Settings

Camping Club

LES PARC MONTANA
Time for holidays. Time for fresh air. Time to relax
Les Parcs Montana offer all this and more in a
beautiful environment.
The 4 star campsites are situated in natural countryside and
provide places for touring, mobile homes or chalets to hire
and a range of activities to enjoy.

- Maisons Laffitte
  1 Rue Johnson,   *See Page 173*
  78600 Maison - Laffitte
  Tel: (1) 39 12 21 91 Fax: (1) 34 93 02 60

- Aureilhan
  Promenade de L'Etang   *See Page 113*
  40200 Mimizan
  Tel: 58 09 02 87 Fax: 58 09 41 89

- Villenuve Loubet
  Route de Grasse   *See Page 29*
  06270 Villenuve-Loubet
  Tel: 93 20 96 11 Fax: 93 22 07 52

- Gassin
  Route de Boutrian-Gassin *See Page 181*
  83580 Gassin
  Tel: 94 56 12 49 Fax: 94 56 34 77

Camp du Domaine

ELECTED CAMPING OF THE YEAR 94
by readers of Caravanier

10% discount in low season

A 45 ha large pine-wood bordering a sandy beach and facing the "Iles d'Or".
COTE D'AZUR: RIGHT BY THE SEASIDE.

A top quality camp with luxurious installations. Large pitches with connections for electricity, water, drainaway. Most comfortable toilet blocks with cleanliness of the utmost importance. Comprehensive bar and restaurant in Spanish style, with takeaway food. Swimming pool of over 200 sq. m. and children's pool, both heated. Tennis court, Volley Ball, Table Tennis, etc… Wooden chalets for 5/6 persons for hire.

Daily recreational programme in main season, with sporting competitions, evening events until midnight, organised excursions, etc…

HOTELLERIE DE PLEIN AIR # LA PUERTA DEL SOL ★ ★ ★ ★ 'great comfort'

LES BORDERIES, 85270 ST. HILAIRE DE RIEZ, VENDÉE. Tel: 51 49 10 10
Fax: 51 49 84 84

Selected by "Le Caravanier" Magazine for review as one of the 30 BEST CAMP SITES IN EUROPE.

Reservations taken from January onwards for any length of stay.

From 3/1 to 15/4 write to us at: 47 rue de Candale prolongé, 93500 PANTIN, tel. and fax: 1-48 44 33 22 After 15/4 write or telephone Vendée address.

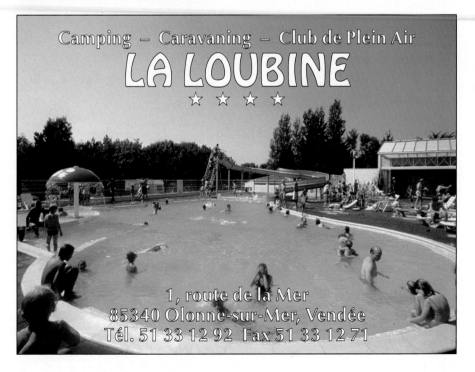

Caravaning
★★★★
l'Étoile d'Argens

TENNIS AND GOLF FREE LOW-SEASON

TEL: 94.81.01.41
83370 ST.AYGULF

8307 Camping-Caravaning L'Etoile d'Argens, St Aygulf

Large, well equipped yet peaceful site near beach, with good pool complex.

L'Etoile d'Argens lies just back from the sea, a little over 2 km. from the sandy beach at St. Aygulf. A river runs along one side of the site and in peak season a boat provides a free service from the site to the beach; moorings for small boats and fishing are available on the river. For a large site with almost 500 pitches, many of which are very large (up to 250 sq.m.), it is surprisingly tranquil and ideal for families. Its main feature is a large swimming pool complex and tennis club, with several pools, large paved sunbathing area, attractive bar, restaurant-pizzeria and disco. The site, which is actually family run, is formally designed with pitches marked and separated by hedges, most with electrical connections and some with water and drainage as well. Those in the older part have ample shade from the variety of tall, mature trees, those in the newer parts having increasing shade from younger trees with a more park-like appearance and larger pitches. For each 25-30 pitches there is a small sanitary block with British style WCs, washbasins in cabins and hot showers in well appointed cubicles. Although somewhat elderly, the sanitary blocks are a good provision and are all well maintained and a process of refurbishment, including the addition of new facilities, is well under way. The site also provides its own small supermarket, four tennis courts, minigolf (both free in low season), table tennis, football pitch and a children's playground. Although used by several tour operators, these only take up about 20% of the available pitches and do not dominate. Entertainment is organised in season.

Directions: Site is 4½ km. NNW of St. Aygulf, where camp signs are not easy to find. You can also approach by turning off the N98 coast road midway between St. Aygulf and Fréjus, or from the N7 just outside Fréjus to west, taking a turning to south over a level crossing, and left after 3½ km.

Charges 1995:
-- Per 'comfort' pitch (100 sq.m.), incl. 3 persons, water, drainage and electricity (10A) Ffr 199.00, 'luxury' pitch (c. 180 sq.m.) incl. 4 persons 256.00 - (c. 250 sq.m.) 273.00, basic pitch with electricity (100 sq.m.) 135.00; extra person 35.00; child (under 7) 25.00.
-- Less 25% in low seasons.
-- Special low season price for 2 persons.
Open:
1 April - 30 September, with all services.
Address:
83370 St. Aygulf.
Tel.
94.81.01.41.
FAX: 94.81.21.45.
Reservations:
Any period with large deposit and fee.

8302 Castels Camping Caravaning Esterel, Agay, nr Fréjus

Attractive, good site for caravans only, in hills east of St. Raphaël with pools, 3½ km. from sea.

Set among the hills at the back of Agay, in an attractive quiet situation with good views around, this site is 3½ km. from the sandy beach at Agay, where parking is perhaps a little easier than at most places on this coast. In addition to a section for permanent caravans, it has some 200 pitches for tourists, on which caravans of any type are taken but not tents. Pitches are on shallow terraces, attractively landscaped with good shade and a variety of flowering plants, giving a feeling of spaciousness and all with electricity connection and tap. There are 18 special ones which have their own individual washroom with WC, basin and shower (both with hot water) adjoining. Amenities include five heated, circular swimming pools, one large for adults, one smaller for children and three arranged as a waterfall. They are much used, attractively landscaped (floodlit at night) and are open all season. A pleasant courtyard area contains the shop, takeaway and the bar/restaurant and terrace which also overlooks the pools . Disco, volleyball, minigolf, 2 tennis courts, petanque and - most unusual for France - a squash court. The two toilet blocks plus one smaller one adjacent to the tourist section are very satisfactory ones which can be heated and have British toilets, most basins in private cabins, and free hot water in all facilities, though the temperature varies a little at busy times. Facilities for the disabled. Cleaning of these blocks and dustbin emptying are very good. Laundry room. Service point for motorhomes. Car wash. Organised events and entertainments in season. Children's playground. Good golf courses very close. Trekking by foot, bicycle or by pony in the surrounding natural environment of L'Esterel forest park. Mobile homes with 2 bedrooms to let. A good site, well run and organised in a deservedly popular area. Some tour operators.

Directions: You can approach from St. Raphaël via Valescure but easiest way is to turn off coast road at Agay where there is good signing. From Fréjus exit on autoroute A8, follow signs for Valescure, then Agay, and you come to site on left. (Readers comment: If in doubt, follow golf complex signs - or Le Clerc).

Charges 1995:
-- Per unit incl. 2 persons Ffr 145.00; extra person 30.00 or child (under 7) 20.00; Special pitch with own washroom 25.00 extra; local tax 1.00.
Open:
Easter/1 April - 30 Sept.
Address:
Agay, 83700 St. Raphaël.
Tel:
94.82.03.28.
FAX: 94.82.87.37.
Reservations:
Necessary for high season and made for min. 1 week with large deposit and Ffr. 50 fee.

8312 Camp du Domaine, La Favière, Le Lavandou

Site by a sandy beach with plenty of shade, 3 km. south of town.

For a seaside camping site, the individual pitches which the Domaine provides are in most parts large. There are some on sandy ground very near to the beach, and some specially large ones on a level hard surface a little further back, both of which have some artificial shade and electricity available. There is also a large number of levelled plots throughout the vast wooded estate which covers most of the site: some not so large, and maybe more suitable for tents. Those at the back can be up to 700 m. from beach and shop. The second main asset of the Domaine is the sea, for the site has direct access to a good beach of considerable length. This has become narrower following the major construction of the La Favière marina but it offers good bathing and is cleaned by the site. The sanitary blocks have undergone extensive renovation in recent years, and 8 of the 10 are now in modern style, with private cabins, though some still have individual, open basins. All blocks have WCs virtually all of the Turkish type, in which the site firmly believes. Free hot water, mostly premixed, throughout. Facilities for the disabled. Washing machine. Supermarket and restaurant serving simple fare, either to eat there or take away (all season). Pleasant separate bar with pizzeria. Sports field. Animation for children and adults in season. Boats and pedaloes for hire. 6 tennis courts. Doctors will call. American motorhomes not accepted. Site is strict in forbidding all barbecues. Very early reservation is necessary over a long season - say late June to early Sept. - as regular clients book from year to year. The site is entirely for tourists with no hire units and should be strictly managed and maintained.

Directions: Just outside and to west of Le Lavandou, at new roundabout, turn off N559 towards the sea on road signed to `Favière, Bénat'. After some 2 km. turn left at camp signs.

see advert in previous colour section

Charges 1996:
-- Per person Ffr. 23.00
- 26.00, plus local tax 2.00; child (under 7)
12.00 - 14.00; pitch incl. car + tent/caravan 30.00
- 35.00; special pitch with electricity, water and drainage, near beach 70.00 - 78.00; extra car 7.00 - 9.00.
-- Credit cards accepted.
Open:
23 March - 31 October.
Address:
La Favière B.P. 207, 83234 Bormes les Mimosas.
Tel:
94.71.50.58.
FAX: 94.15.18.67.
Reservations:
Made Sun.- Sun. only, by letter from Jan.-March, with booking fee (Ffr. 150). Regular clients have right to re-book for following year.

8301 Camping-Caravaning Les Pins Parasols, Fréjus

Family owned site with pool, 5 km. from beach; some pitches with individual sanitary units.

Not everyone likes very big sites, and Les Pins Parasols with its 189 pitches is of a size which is quite easy to walk around. Although on very slightly undulating ground, virtually all the plots are levelled or terraced and separated by hedges or bushes with pine trees for shade. They are of around 100 sq.m. and all with electricity. What is particularly interesting, as it is the most unusual feature of the camp, is that 48 of the pitches are equipped with their own fully enclosed, tiled sanitary unit, consisting of British WC, washbasin, hot shower and washing up sink, all quite close together. These naturally cost more but may well be of interest to those seeking extra comfort. The normal size toilet blocks, in three different places, are of good average quality and give a plentiful supply with continental style WCs, washbasins in private cabins and free hot showers with pre-set hot water and pushbutton. Facilities available for the handicapped. On site is a swimming pool of 200 sq.m. with attractive rock backdrop and sun-bathing terrace, a separate long slide with landing pool and a small children's pool. Small shop with reasonable stocks and restaurant with takeaway (both from 15/4). General room with TV. Half-court tennis. Tax free exchange facility. The nearest beach is the once very long Fréjus-Plage, now reduced a little by the new marina, which is some 5½ km. away and adjoins St. Raphaël. (See note on La Baume entry concerning traffic delays at the D4/N7 road junction.) Used by tour operators (25%).

Directions: From west on autoroute A8 take Fréjus-Ouest exit (junction 37) and turn right at roundabout. Turn right at junction and site is on right. From east take exit for Fréjus - St. Raphaël (junction 38), turn right immediately on leaving pay booths on a small road which leads across to D4, where right again and under 1 km. to site.

Charges 1995:
-- Per normal pitch with electricity incl. 2 persons Ffr 119.00; special pitch with sanitary unit incl. 2 persons 150.00; extra person 32.00; child (under 7 yrs) 20.00; car 9.00; dog 11.00.
-- Less 10% outside 16/6 - 31/8.
Open:
1 April - 30 September.
Address:
Route de Bagnols, 83600 Fréjus.
Tel:
94.40.88.43.
FAX: 94.40.81.99.
Reservations:
Necessary for July/Aug. only and made for min. 10 days for exact dates with deposit (Ffr 600) but no fee.

8306 Camping-Caravaning de la Baume + La Palmeraie, Fréjus

Busy, large site back from sea with excellent swimming pool complex and other amenities.

This large site has been well developed, and much money has been spent on it. It lies about 5½ km. from the long sandy beach of Fréjus-Plage, but it has such a fine and varied selection of five swimming pools on site that many people do not bother to make the trip. The pools, with their palm trees, are a feature of this site and were remarkable for their size and variety (water slides, etc.) even before the addition of the latest, very large `feature' pool which is one of the highlights of the site. This large pool, surrounded by sunbathing areas, is overlooked by the extremely pretty terracing for the bar, restaurant, etc. The site has nearly 500 pitches of varying but quite adequate size with electricity, water and drainaway, with another 200 larger ones with plumbing in to mains sewerage to take mobile homes; separators to divide plots are being installed. Shade is available over most of the terrain. Although tents are accepted, the site concentrates mainly on caravanning. The 7 toilet blocks should be a satisfactory supply, two have recently been enlarged and the others refurbished. They have British toilets with a few continental; washbasins in private cabins with hot and cold water; free hot showers and sinks for clothes and dishes with hot water at pre-set temperature (which varied a bit when tried). Supermarket and several other shops. Bar with external terrace and TV. Restaurant and takeaway. Tennis courts. Archery. Organised events - sports, competitions, etc. in daytime and some evening entertainment partly in English. Amphitheatre for shows. Discos daily in high season. The site is likely to become full in season, but one section of the site with unmarked pitches is not reserved and there is plenty of space off-peak. La Baume's convenient location has its `downside' however as there is some traffic noise from the nearby autoroute: somewhat obtrusive at first but we soon failed to notice it. A popular site with tour operators.

Adjoining La Baume is its sister site La Palmeraie, which is not for campers but is for those who wish to hire self-catering accommodation. It has some 80 small chalet-type units for 4 - 6 persons (full details from site). It also has its own landscaped swimming pool and provides some entertainments to supplement those at La Baume.

Directions: Site is 3 km. up D4 road, which leads north from N7 just west of Fréjus. From west on autoroute A8 take exit for Fréjus/St. Raphaël (junction 37), turn towards them and after 4 km., turn left on D4. From east take exit for Fréjus/St. Raphaël (junction 38); after exit turn right immediately on small road marked `Musée' etc. which leads you to D4 where right again.

Charges guide:
-- Per unit incl. up to 3 persons on pitch with electricity, water and drainage Ffr 155.00 - 190.00, without services 132.00 - 165.00; extra person 28.00 - 33.00; child (under 7) 18.50 - 23.00; extra car or m/cycle 17.00 - 20.00; electricity 17.00 - 20.00; plus local tax in July/Aug.
-- Min. stay 3 nights.
-- For La Palmeraie charges apply to site.
Open:
1 April - 30 September, with full services.
Address:
Route de Bagnols, 83618 Fréjus Cedex.
Tel:
94.40.87.87.
FAX: 94.40.73.50.
Reservations:
Essential for high season; made for exact dates with substantial deposit and fee (Ffr 180), from 1 Jan.

8305 Camping-Caravaning des Aubrèdes, Fréjus

Smaller, family managed site with pool, 5 km. from sea, which welcomes British visitors.

This site has now become known and has its fair share of campers, though being just back from the sea, it may still have some space when others are full. It has a small swimming pool, open nearly all season, and is about 5 km. from the long beach at Fréjus-Plage and from St. Raphaël. Mainly on slightly sloping ground and quite close to the motorway (though not too much noise), the site has individual pitches without much to divide them. There are now about 30 special 'plateformes' - pitches with electricity, water and drainaway. Although the site has an open aspect, a reasonable amount of shade is available from mixed, tall trees over most of the terrain. Three sanitary blocks have free hot showers, continental and Turkish style toilets, washbasins in cabins with cold water (some now with hot water also) and a hot water point for sinks; reasonable quality but only just enough. Shop, bar/pizzeria with occasional dancing, and restaurant (all open from 8/6) with takeaway facility also. Tennis. Children's playground. Washing machines. Organised activities in season: sports competitions, shows, dancing etc. and children's entertainer in July/Aug. Caravans and mobile homes for hire; no tour operators. Telephones.

Directions: Turn off N7 to north just east of Puget sur Argens autoroute entry and follow blue camp signs across motorway to site.

Charges 1996:
-- (probable) Per pitch with 2 persons Ffr. 103.00; extra person 21.00; child (under 7) 16.50; plateforme pitch, water and drainage extra; electricity (8A) 20.50; animal 8.00; local tax 1.00.
-- Less 10-30%. (not electric) in low season.
Open:
1 April - 30 September.
Address:
83480 Puget-s-Argens.
Tel:
94.45.51.46.
FAX: 94.45.28.92.
Reservations:
Sat. to Sat. (min. 1 week) with deposit (Ffr. 800) and fee (100).

Alan Rogers' discount
Low season 3rd week discount (if reserved)

8308 Au Paradis des Campeurs, La Gaillarde Plage, nr Fréjus

Agreeable small site with direct access to sandy beach.

Just across the coast road from a sandy beach with direct access by an underpass for pedestrians, this well kept little site in an attractive and popular area is family owned and run. It has 125 pitches, all with 3 or 6A electricity, of varying but satisfactory size and shape (they have made the most of the space), 70 of which have their own water tap and drainaway as well. Some shade on most pitches. The two toilet blocks have been refurbished to a very high standard with good quality fittings. They are very well maintained with WCs of various types, washbasins with hot water mainly in cabins or cubicles, free hot showers at pre-set temperature and facilities for babies. Shop and full restaurant with takeaway service; both front onto main road and are open when the site is open. Fresh bread is baked on site. TV room. Washing machines. Children's playground. Telephone. Service point for motorhomes.

Directions: Site is signed from N98 coast road at La Gaillarde, 2 km. south of St. Aygulf.

Charges 1995:
-- Per unit incl. 3 persons Ffr. 76.00 - 116.00, incl. water and drainage 92.00 - 147.00; extra person 27.00; child (under 4) 17.00; extra tent 13.00; electricity 3A 15.00 - 6A 20.00; plus local tax.
Open:
25 March - 1 October.
Address:
La Gaillarde Plage, 83370 St Aygulf.
Tel:
94.96.93.55.
Reservations:
Advised main season.

8310 Camping de la Plage, Grimaud, nr St. Tropez

Popular site by a sandy beach opposite St. Tropez.

This site near Ste. Maxime is right by the sea with its own sandy beach, which can become crowded. The site is divided into two parts by a main road (N98), but there is a pedestrian underpass which avoids the rather dangerous crossing. All pitches in both parts are numbered and can be reserved. Except perhaps for those by the beach, they are of good size, and many are pleasantly grassed and shaded. Electrical connections available (2, 4, 6 or 10A). There are three sanitary blocks in the part near the sea and four on the far side. They have mixed British and continental WCs, washbasins with free hot water (some in private cabins), and free hot showers - a satisfactory supply. Supermarket, bar and restaurant, with takeaway (not all season). Volleyball. Children's playground. Tennis. Doctor calls daily. Boat hire close to site. Studios and apartments to let.

Directions: Site is on the main coast road (N98) about 6 km. southwest of Ste. Maxime. Take care - this road is very busy in main season.

Charges 1995:
-- Per unit with 2 persons Ffr 100.00; extra person 26.00; local tax 2.00; child (under 7) 13.00; electricity 15.50 - 34.00.
Open:
23 March - 30 Sept.
Address:
83360 Grimaud.
Tel:
94.56.31.15.
Reservations:
Exact dates with fee, Oct.- March only.

8311 Camping de la Baie, Cavalaire

Busy site, with pool, within the resort of Cavalaire and only a short way from the beach.

This site is only a short walk from the beach and from the main street of a pleasant little holiday resort where there is a new harbour and restaurants and shops. A long, sandy beach runs right round the bay and there are plenty of watersports activities nearby. The site has an attractive, free, kidney-shaped swimming pool with sunbathing terrace (open Easter - end Sept.) and a small children's pool. Pitches are individual ones on slightly sloping ground with terracing and access roads, nearly all with electricity. Trees have grown well to give plenty of shade. There are four main toilet blocks, two of which have been refurbished, with free hot showers and with washbasins in tiled private cabins, and four smaller units with toilets and open washbasins behind. British toilets, with some continental. Small shop with baker on site; town shops are close. Restaurant (all season) and bar, with takeaway. 'Animation' with dance evenings. Full launderette. Children's playground. Table tennis. TV room. Exchange facilities. Doctor at 150 m. Mobile homes for hire - details from site. English spoken. Used by tour operators.

Directions: Site is signed from Cavalaire main street, in the direction of the harbour.

Charges guide:
-- Per unit with up to 3 persons Ffr 126.00; extra person 28.00; child (under 7) 14.00; electricity 25.00. local tax 2.00
Open:
15 March - 15 Oct.
Address:
Bd. Pasteur, BP.12, 83240 Cavalaire.
Tel:
94.64.08.15 or 10.
FAX: 94.64.66.10.
Reservations:
Made from Jan, min. 1 week, Sat.-Sat with deposit (Ffr. 1,000 incl. fee 200).

8315 Camping International de la Sainte-Baume, Nans-les-Pins

Holiday style site with excellent swimming pools.

This is a family oriented 'holiday' site in Provencal countryside, some 30 minutes by car from the coast at Cassis. Somewhat smaller than other sites of this type, there are some 130 good sized pitches with 6 or 10A electricity on mainly level, rather stony ground, with variable shade. There is an attractive large complex with 3 swimming pools (1 for children), solarium and jacuzzi, surrounded by ample paved sunbathing area with some shade from the trees. A restaurant overlooks the pools with a varied and full menu, also snacks and takeaway service (July/Aug). A separate, renovated building houses a bar, disco, shop (July/Aug) and TV room and is fronted by an entertainment area for shows, cabarets, etc. Sporting facilities include tennis, table tennis, archery, volleyball, boules and, for children, a mini-club. The two main sanitary blocks, including a new super de-luxe one, are good, with free hot showers, washbasins in private cabins and British WCs, plus dishwashing and laundry. Although having all the facilities, activities and entertainment expected of a holiday site, the atmosphere is very relaxed and much less frenzied than some other similar sites. Mobile homes and bungalows for hire (80).

Directions: Take St. Maximin exit from A8 and head for Auriol on the N560, turning after 9 km. for Nans-les-Pins (D80); site is on left just before this village.

Charges 1995:
-- Per unit incl. 2 persons Ffr. 75.00 - 130.00; extra person 22.00 - 35.00; child (under 7) 19.00 - 23.00; electricity (6A) 19.00 - 23.00; drainage/water or extra vehicle 15.00; plus local tax (15/6-15/9).
Open:
4 May - 8 September.
Address:
83860 Nans-les-Pins.
Tel:
94.78.92.68.
FAX: 94.78.67.37.
Reservations:
With deposit (Ffr. 600) and fee (90).

8317 Camping Domaine de la Bergerie, Roquebrune-sur-Argens

Well organised site with a holiday environment to suit all ages and tastes.

This is yet another excellent site in this region which takes you away from all the bustle of the Med. to total relaxation amongst the natural perfumes of Provence. Here, where cork oak, pine and mimosa flourish, is a 70 ha. campsite which varies from landscaped areas for mobile homes to flat, grassy terrain with avenues of separated pitches for caravans and tents. All pitches average over 100 sq.m. and have electrical connections, with those in one area also having water and drainage connections. The four sanitary blocks are kept very clean, the newest with an attractive green and white colour scheme, and include hot showers, washbasins in private cubicles, facilities for the handicapped and for babies, chemical disposal points, plus dishwashing and laundry areas with washing machines. A well stocked supermarket (daily fresh bread) is uphill behind the touring pitches. To the right of this adjacent to the restaurant are parking areas, as being a spread out site walking can be tough going. The restaurant/bar, a converted farm building, is surrounded by shady patios, whilst inside it oozes character with high beams and archways leading to intimate corners. Takeaway service. Alongside is an extravagantly designed complex with three swimming pools and a keep fit centre (body building, sauna, gym, etc). There are five tennis courts and two half courts, volleyball, mini football and more. Tournaments and programmes are organised daily and in the evening, shows, cabarets, discos and dancing at the amphitheatre prove popular. Horse riding, water skiing and rock climbing are available nearby - in fact, few activities have been forgotten. When all that the site has to offer has been exhausted, either St Aygulf or Ste Maxime are 7 km. or drive inland and discover the delights of the hinterland.

Charges 1995:
-- Per unit incl. 2 persons and electricity (5A) Ffr. 95.00 - 125.00; 3 persons and electricity 120.00 - 165.00; 3 persons and electricity, water and drainage 140.00 - 195.00; extra adult 23.00 - 32.00; child (under 7 yrs) 17.00 - 22.00; electricity (10A) 12.00; local tax 1.00.
Open:
1 April - 30 September.
Address:
Vallée du Fournel, 83520 Roquebrune-sur-Argens.
Tel:
94.82.90.11.
FAX: 94.82.93.42.
Reservations:
Made with deposit (Ffr. 800 by Eurocheque or bank draft).

Directions: Leave A8 at Le Muy exit on N7 towards Fréjus. Proceed for 9 km., then right onto D7 signed St Aygulf. Continue for 8 km. and then right at roundabout onto D8; site is on the right.

8316 Parc Camping-Caravaning Les Cigales, Le Muy

Family run site in a quiet location, convenient for the attractions of this popular area.

In a natural setting of 10 ha. this site is well tucked in, 1 km. from the busy N7. Whilst it offers the opportunity for a peaceful and relaxing stay, it also makes an excellent base for exploring the coast or the hinterland and the Gorges du Verdon. On entering the site (electronic gate operated by card), reception is on the left. Sand based, gravel roads lead to the numbered pitches which vary in size, with some terracing. The terrain is typical of the area with rough, sloped and stony, dry ground, but pitches are mostly level and benefit from the shade given by the abundance of trees which include cork, oak and pine, plus the sweet smelling mimosa and many shrubs that fill the air reminding us that this is Provence. The site has six modern sanitary blocks which more than serve the 180 pitches. Facilities include showers, washbasins in cabins and facilities for the disabled. Dishwashing sinks are outside, but covered, Laundry area with washing machine. A feature of Les Cigales is the swimming pool and sunbathing area, and also the patio at the restaurant/bar which is popular in the evening. Entertainment is organised each evening in season, with a disco twice weekly and daytime activities for children and senior citizens. Salads, fresh food, etc. are available at the restaurant and there is a shop (June-Sept), but if wanting to get out and about, it is only 2 km. to Le Muy where a Sunday market is held. The N7 is on a bus route or take a train at Les Arcs (8 km). For sports enthusiasts, canoeing, riding and hang-gliding are organised. Bungalows to rent.

Charges 1995:
-- Per unit incl. 2 persons Ffr. 85.00; extra person 24.00; child (under 7 yrs) 15.50; electricity (6A) 20.00; plus local tax.
-- Less 10-20% outside July/Aug.
-- Credit cards accepted.
Open:
1 April - 31 October.
Address:
83490 Le Muy.
Tel:
94.45.12.08.
FAX: 94.45.92.80.
Reservations:
Advisable for July/Aug. Contact site.

Directions: Site is signed off approach to autoroute péage on A8 at Le Muy exit and is 2 km. west of Le Muy on N7.

8303 Camping-Caravaning Leï Suves, Roquebrune sur Argens

Quietly situated pretty site behind the coast.

Situated close to the unusual Roquebrune 'mountain', this site is adjacent to the D7 road, and convenient for those using the A8 autoroute or the N7, yet within easy reach of resorts such as St Tropez, St Maxime, St Raphaël and Cannes. The site is mainly individually terraced, on sloping ground, with some shade provided by the many cork trees which give the site its name. The 350 pitches are of a reasonable size, most with electricity and access to water. Facilities include a good sized pool open from May and surrounded by terracing with a snack bar, takeaway and shop (all 1/6-30/9), table tennis, tennis and a children's play area. The two identical, modern sanitary blocks provide hot showers with dividers and shelves, continental type WCs and washbasins in cabins, along with external washing-up sinks, a laundry room with washing machines and ironing boards and facilities for the disabled.

Directions: Leave the autoroute at Le Muy in the direction of St Raphaël. After Le Muy go left at junction towards La Boverie, then follow site signs.

Charges 1995:
-- Per unit incl. 2 persons Ffr. 145.00; extra adult 34.50; child (under 7 yrs) 19.50; electricity 17.00; animal 10.00; local tax 1.00.
-- Less in low seasons.
-- Credit cards accepted.
Open:
15 March - 15 October.
Address:
Quartier du Blavet, 83520 Roquebrune.
Tel:
94.45.43.95.
FAX: 94.81.63.13.
Reservations:
Write to site.

8401M Parc Municipal du Pont St. Bénézet, Avignon

This large, neat site, now run by the municipality, has an excellent situation with some fine views across the river Rhône to the Pope's palace and the famous 'Pont d'Avignon', which is in fact the Pont St. Bénézet. On flat, well tended grass, with space for 300 units, it has separate sections for caravans - with well sized, marked pitches with electricity (6A), mainly with hedges to separate them and good shade - and for tents a more open area. The five sanitary blocks were refurbished in 1994 after a very bad flood during the winter and are good except, as often in France, WCs seem fewer than other facilities. Individual washbasins in cubicles, no shelf, all with hot water, free pre-set hot showers, hot water for laundry sinks and facilities for the disabled. A shop and a bar with bar meals or takeaway (1/4-30/9), are in a pleasant central area, partly covered and with a terraced area. Telephones. Children's playground. Table tennis. Tennis with racquets for hire. Bicycle hire. Activities organised. Swimming pool nearby. The site becomes full from about 10/7-2/8 when the festival of Avignon is held, and reservation is then advisable for longer stays.

Directions: Site is northwest of town on an 'island' which is crossed by the N100 Nîmes road. The access road is at the start of the second bridge - there are other sites on the island so watch signs carefully.

Charges guide:
-- Per person Ffr. 17.00; child (under 7) 8.50; caravan/car 20.00; tent/car 14.00; motorcaravan 20.00; electricity (6A) 14.00.
Open:
1 March - 31 October.
Address:
Isle de la Barthelasse, 84000 Avignon.
Tel:
90.82.63.50.
FAX: 90.85.22.12.
Reservations:
Made for min. 2 weeks with deposit.

8403M Camping Le Brégoux en Provence, Aubignan, nr Carpentras

Generally speaking, reasonably priced sites of a good standard in this area are few and far between. This attractive municipal site is an exception and well worth considering as a base for exploring this region, being conveniently situated for visiting Mont Ventoux and the Dentelles de Montmirail, Orange, Carpentras, Vaison la Romaine, Avignon and even Aix-en-Provence. The site itself is about 10 minutes walk from the town, on level grass and fairly well shaded. The 200 or so pitches, most with electricity, are of a reasonable size and partially separated. Sanitary facilities, in three blocks, include pre-set hot showers, some washbasins in private cabins, covered washing up areas, and two washing machines, all very clean when inspected in July.

Directions: Site is on the southern outskirts of the small town of Aubignan, some 6 km. north of Carpentras via the D7. Signposted in Aubignan.

Charges guide:
-- Per person Ffr. 12.00; child (under 7) 6.00; pitch 10.00; extra car 10.00; electricity 9.70.
Open:
15 March - 31 October.
Address:
84810 Aubignon.
Tel:
90.62.62.50 (Mairie).
Reservations:
Telephone or write.

N8402 Domaine Naturiste de Bélezy, Bédoin, nr Carpentras
Excellent naturist site with enormous range of amenities and activities.

By any standards this is an excellent site and the extent to which the owners have created a site in harmony with the Provencal countryside is remarkable. The ambience is essentially relaxed and comfortable. English is spoken widely amongst the staff and customers. The site has been developed to provide an area in which to stay and an area in which to `play', joined by a short pedestrian tunnel. There are 200 pitches, all now marked and numbered amongst the many varieties of trees and shrubs - oaks, olives, pines, acacias, broom, lavender, etc. Electrical points (12A) are plentiful but you may need a long cable. The emphasis is on informality and concern for the environment, and during the high season cars (and pets) are banned from the camping area - there is ample parking nearby, mostly shaded - and this provides not only an air of tranquillity, but safety for children.

So far as naturism is concerned the emphasis is on personal choice (and weather conditions!), the only stipulation being the requirement for complete nudity in the pool and pool area. The facilities in general are what you would expect from a four-star site although some of the sanitary blocks are a little `different'. The newer ones are of a standard type and excellent quality, with free hot showers in cubicles with separators, washbasins (H&C) in private cabins and British WCs. One block has a children's section with baby baths, children's toilets, showers and low sinks. The older blocks are well maintained and different in so far as the hot showers are in the open air, separated by natural stone dividers. There are washing up areas, with H&C, again mostly in the open air. Laundry facilities.

The leisure park includes numerous sports facilities, including two good tennis courts and three swimming pools (one open and heated April - Sept.). The largest is for swimming and relaxation, the smaller one for watersports and the smallest for young children and there are ample, very attractive sunbathing areas around the pools. Apart from the pools, the old Mas (Provencal farmhouse) houses many activities including a virtually sound-proof disco and the restaurant/bar and terrace. The leisure park is an unspoiled area of natural `parkland' with an orchard, fishpond and woodland (with many small animals such as squirrels), and blends well with the surrounding countryside. It is possible to walk into Bédoin - the market is fascinating. The variety of activities available at Bélezy is one of the most extensive we have ever encountered. To mention but a few, they include painting courses, language lessons, archery, music (bring your own instrument), a sauna and guided walks. There is also a (little used) TV room and of course the usual boules and table tennis. A Hydrotherapy centre offers courses of massages, steam baths, acupuncture and a variety of other treatments including osteopathy and Chinese medicine (on payment). You can use your holiday to tone up and revitalise with qualified diagnosis. There is a reasonably priced shop and a small boutique selling a range of good quality souvenirs and even clothes! The restaurant provides both waiter service and takeaway meals again at reasonable prices. Child minding. Mobile homes, bungalows, etc. to let. All in all, we continue to be impressed both with the site itself and with the French approach to naturism and the environment.

Directions: From the A7 autoroute or the RN7 at Orange, take the D950 southeast to Carpentras, then northeast via the D974 to Bédoin. Site is signed in Bédoin, being about 2 km. northeast of the village.

Charges 1995:
-- Per 1 adult Ffr 43.50 - 90.00, 2 adults 87.00 - 123.00, 3 adults 130.50 - 162.00; extra adult 30.00 - 38.00; child (3-7 yrs) 21.50 - 26.50; electricity 20.00; large pitch + 18.50; pitch with water, drainage and sink + 24.00. Recreation fee free - 5.00 per night, per person (child free - 3.50); local tax 2.00 adult, 1.00 child.
-- Reductions large families or for longer stays outside high season.
-- Credit cards accepted.

Open:
23 March - 13 October.

Address:
84410 Bédoin.

Tel:
90.65.60.18.
FAX: 90.65.94.45.

Reservations:
Write with deposit of 25% of total charge.

Alan Rogers' discount
Less 5% in low season

8404 Camping Le Jantou, Le Thor, nr Avignon

Family run, attractive site beside River Sorgue.

The nicest feature of this attractive site is the 18th century `mas' (Provencal farmhouse) and outbuildings which, together with a huge plane tree, form a centre piece courtyard for the site facilities. The 143 pitches, around 120 for tourers, are somewhat unusually arranged in groups of mainly four pitches, the groups rather than the individual pitches being separated by tall hedges. They are mostly of a good size on flat grass, with the majority having 3, 6 or 10A electricity and some water and drainage. The site was originally designed and constructed in the late 70s (it has only been owned by the Tricart family for the last few years), but the two sanitary blocks have now been renovated and improved to provide the most modern of facilities, plus facilities for the disabled, dishwashing and laundry sinks with hot water and washing machines and dryers. Telephones. Snack bar and a small restaurant serving stews, plat du jour, etc. Whilst there is a small shop for essentials, a small supermarket is within a short walk. Some live entertainment is organised in season. Swimming pool. A quite fast flowing river runs past the site which is suitable for angling (short term licences available from the site), but not really for swimming due to the current. It is approached through a gate (unlocked!) in a fence for children's safety. No tour operators but some mobile homes for both tourists and long term visitors.

Directions: Leave A7 autoroute at Avignon Nord exit and join D942 in the direction of Carpentras. Turn immediately south on D6 and proceed 8½ km. to join N100. Turn east for 3½ km. to Le Thor. Site is signed before the village.

Charges 1996:
-- Per adult Ffr. 23.00; child (2-14 yrs) 12.00; pitch 28.00; electricity 3A 14.00, 6A 18.00; refrigerator 14.50; animal 6.00.
-- 15th night free in high season, 8th in low.
-- Credit cards accepted.
Open:
1 April - 31 October.
Address:
84250 Le Thor.
Tel:
90.33.90.07.
FAX: 90.33.79.84.
Reservations:
Advised for July/Aug;
with Ffr. 50 deposit.

Alan Rogers' discount
Less 5-10% acc. to season

8502 Camping du Jard, La Tranche-sur-Mer

Neat, developing site, halfway between La Rochelle and Les Sables d'Olonne.

Du Jard is a well planned, neatly laid out site with shade developing from the many attractive trees and hedges which have been planted. The 350 pitches are flat and grassy, and a minimum of 100 sq.m. Most are equipped with electricity, half with water and drainaway also. The site is 700 m. from a sandy beach and also has its own heated pool (20 x 10 m. no shorts allowed) with a small one (5 x 6 m.) for children. Good tennis court, minigolf, table tennis and a sauna, solarium and fitness room with instruction included. Children's play area and games and TV rooms. The three toilet blocks are well designed and maintained, with excellent facilities for the disabled and for babies. Ample free hot water; mixture of continental and British toilets; washbasins in private cabins. Owner managed, one receives a friendly welcome; English is spoken (in season!). Card operated barrier. There is a bar with terrace, restaurant and a small shop for basics (shops and restaurants nearby). Exchange facilities. Car wash. American motorhomes not accepted. Used by two British tour operators (25%).

Directions: Site is east of La Tranche-sur-Mer, 3 km. from the D747/D46 roundabout, on the D46.

Charges 1995:
-- Per pitch incl. 2 persons Ffr. 110.00, with electricity (4A) 125.00, full services 143.00; extra person over 5 22.50, under 5 15.00; tax 1.10.
-- Low season less 25%.
Open:
25 May - 15 September.
Address:
123, Route de la Faute, 85360 La Tranche.
Tel:
51 27 43 79.
FAX: 51.27.42.92.
Reservations:
Min.1 week, Sat.- Sat. with deposit (Ffr. 500).

8501 Camping Baie d'Aunis, La Tranche-sur-Mer, nr Les Sables d'Olonne

Small, seaside site with individual pitches and easy access to sandy beach.

One great asset of Baie d'Aunis is that it really is right by the sea - access to a sandy beach (which is safer than most here) is through the site wall (code number for barrier) and 50 m. across a car park. You can also walk quite easily into the town (400 m). A special lagoon has been developed in the bay for teaching windsurfing, as La Tranche is a major windsurfing centre. The site, on flat ground, has 155 individual marked pitches, many very sandy. Some trees give shade and electricity is available (10A). The main sanitary block has been completely rebuilt and is now of an excellent standard, with facilities for the disabled and for babies. There are also refurbished facilities in other places. Free hot water in basins, showers and sinks; washbasins in private cabins; continental and British toilets. A swimming pool has been added to the facilities, heated from early season. Shop (24/6-4/9) and restaurant/bar (1/4-15/9). The site is popular and reservations are essential from mid-June - late August. No dogs accepted in July/Aug. Chalets and mobile homes to rent.

Directions: Site is on eastern approach to La Tranche; from N747/D46 roundabout turn towards town and site is on left.

Charges 1995:
-- Per unit incl. up to 3 persons Ffr 118.00 - 121.00; extra person 22.00 - 23.00; child (under 7) 16.00 - 17.00; electricity (10A) 17.50; local tax (over 9) 1.10.
-- Less in low seasons.
Open:
1 April - 30 September.
Address:
85360 La Tranche.
Tel:
51.27.47.36.
FAX: 51.27.44.54.
Reservations:
Exact dates (min 7 days) with deposit and fee.

8504 Castels Camping La Garangeoire, St Julien-des-Landes

Parkland site, with swimming pool, 15 km. from the Atlantic coast.

The village of St Julien-des-Landes is about 20 km. from Les Sables d'Olonne, and 15 km. inland from the nearest point on the coast, where there are sandy beaches. The site is set in the parkland surrounding La Garangeoire, a small château. The peaceful, attractive grounds of many acres, where campers may walk, include three lakes, one of which may be used for fishing and boating. The site has a spacious, relaxed atmosphere and many use it as a quiet base. There are two heated swimming pools (both 200 sq.m.) with water slides, fountains, etc. and a child's pool. The camping area consists of three large meadows, edged with mature trees, and a smaller wooded section. The 300 pitches are especially large (most 150-200 sq.m.) and are marked and well spaced. All have electricity (6A) and some also water and drainage. The sanitary installations are quite satisfactory and are being gradually updated; where complete the facilities are very good. One block, which has been completely modernised, has facilities for the handicapped and the site reports further new blocks are now open. They have British toilets; basins in private cabins, baby bath. Free hot water throughout and laundry facilities. Full restaurant, takeaway and crêperie, with attractive courtyard. Large playing area for children, a games room, 2 tennis courts, bicycle hire, table tennis, minigolf, archery and volleyball. Good shop and exchange facilities. Popular with British tour operators (40%) but there is plenty of space.

Directions: Site is signed from St. Julien; the entrance is to the north off D21.

Charges 1996:
-- Per unit incl. 3 persons, with electricity Ffr. 152.00; extra person 30.00; child (under 7) 15.00; extra car 12.00; dog 12.00.
-- Less in low season.
-- Credit cards accepted.
Open:
15 May - 15 September.
Address:
St Julien-des-Landes, 85150 La Mothe-Achard.
Tel:
51.46.65.39.
FAX: 51.46.60.82.
Reservations:
Made up to 15/5 (min. 10 days in July/Aug), with deposit (Ffr. 300) and fee (100).

8505 Camping Les Dunes, Brétignolles-sur-Mer, nr St. Gilles-Croix

Large, busy site with swimming pools and direct access to good sandy beach.

Even in an area like the Vendée, where there are great long stretches of sandy beach, sites where one can walk directly to the beach with no roads to cross are not very numerous. This, however, is one where from several gates in the boundary fence, one can walk over some 150 m. of grass covered dunes onto the good beach. It is a large site and many of the 760 pitches have been sold for permanent mobile homes, which rather dominate the eye. Additionally some 20% of pitches are occupied by British tour operators. There are, though, about 450 pitches available for tourists and the present intention is that it should remain at this number. Pitches are of at least 100 sq.m. (some over 150 sq.m.), and all have electricity, water connections and drainaway. They are separated by light hedges. About a third of the site is shaded by tall trees, but the remainder is without shade and although closer to the beach, is perhaps a little exposed in high winds. There are 9 identical, modern sanitary blocks of a good standard, with mixed British and continental WCs, washbasins in private cabins with light, shelf, free hot water, pre-set hot showers with pushbutton. They should be an ample provision and each block has a washing machine. Two outdoor heated swimming pools (20/5-7/9), with sunbathing areas form an attractive complex together with an indoor pool, toboggan and jacuzzi (6/4-13/10). TV room. Supermarket, restaurant (both from 11/5) and takeaway, two tennis courts. Children's playground. Sailing and windsurfing school; boards for hire. Organised sports programme in July/Aug., with little tournaments, etc. for adults and children; some evening entertainments or dancing at times. A good site by a good beach is obviously attractive, and not surprisingly this one has become popular and is full over quite a long period. Perhaps because of its size, it has become a little impersonal.

Directions: Site is 2 km. south of Brétignolles, signed from the main D38 road.

Charges 1996:
-- Per person Ffr. 24.00; child (under 7) 14.00; pitch 122.00; animal 14.00; local tax (over 10s) 2.20.
-- Less in low season.
-- Credit cards accepted.

Open:
1 April - 27 October.

Address:
85470 Brétignolles-sur-Mer.

Tel:
51.90.55.32.
FAX: 51.90.54.85.

Reservations:
Made for min. 20 days with deposit (Ffr. 400) and fee (100). Video available from site.

8506 Airotel Domaine Le Pas Opton, Le Fenouiller, nr St. Gilles-Croix

Well established site with good installations and swimming pool, 6 km. from sea.

Le Pas Opton is family managed and run and much work has been carried out to make it worth considering for a stay in this popular region. It is 6 km. back from the sea at St. Gilles Croix de Vie and quietly situated. With a well established atmosphere, it is a select type of site but at the same time offers on-site amenities such as a heated swimming pool with water slide and child's pools and an attractive bar with some dancing. A recent addition is a new terrace overlooking the pool. There are 200 pitches, most of which have electricity and some hardstanding, water and drainage also. Those in the original part are well shaded by mature trees and tall hedges. The newer areas are developing well with a more spacious feel. The four toilet blocks are all of good quality. They have free hot water in all facilities and are kept very clean and in good order, with British toilets, individual washbasins with free hot water, mainly in private cabins for women, partly for men and free hot water in showers and sinks. Laundry facilities available. Other amenities include a shop, bar, café, takeaway (all open 1/6-1/9), basketball, table tennis, a children's playground and a car wash area. Entertainment is organised in season. The river Vie runs past the rear of the site (with fishing) and the owners have been improving the access to this. Non-powered boats can be put on the river, but there can be a current at times. Sailing centre close. Chalet and 3 large caravans for hire. Used by a tour operator (30%).

Directions: Site is northeast of St. Gilles, on the N754 about 300 m. towards Le Fenouiller from the junction with D32.

Charges 1995:
-- Per unit, incl. up to 3 persons: without electricity Ffr. 111.00; with electricity 133.00; with water and drainage also 148.00; extra adult 22.50; child (under 7) 11.50; local tax 2.20 per person (over 10 yrs) in July/Aug.
-- Less 25% before 30/6.
-- Credit cards accepted.

Open:
20 May - 10 September.

Address:
Route de Nantes, Le Fenouiller, 85800 St. Gilles Croix de Vie.

Tel:
51.55.11.98.
FAX: 51.55.44.94.

Reservations:
Advisable for main season and made from Jan. (min. 1 week) with deposit and fee.

8508 Camping La Puerta del Sol, St. Hilaire de Riez

Well designed, good quality site with swimming pool and other amenities.

La Puerta del Sol is a modern site developed on ambitious lines resulting in a very good, environmentally pleasing site with excellent amenities. It has about 193 individual pitches (and 32 chalets), most of about 100 sq.m., on reasonably grassy ground, with shade developing well from young trees. All pitches have electricity, water and drainaway. The three well designed, identical toilet blocks have mostly continental WCs, some Turkish style; washbasins in private cabins with free hot water, shelf, mirror and light; free hot showers (controllable, but operated by pushbutton which runs on for a short time) plus facilities for the disabled, laundry and babies' rooms. The facilities are very well cleaned and the site well regulated, with friendly staff. The Spanish camp name is reflected in the architectural style of the buildings which contain reception, bar lounge, restaurant and takeaway (all fully open in high season). A heated swimming pool of over 200 sq.m., with paddling pool, is by the bar with a terrace. There is a minimarket (20/6-31/8) and a general room also used for 'animation' events; sports competitions and games. Evening entertainment and dancing (until midnight) and organised excursions in July/Aug. Barbecue area with picnic tables, children's adventure play areas (on sand), tennis and games room with table tennis, amusement machines. The nearest sandy beach is 5 km. and St. Jean-de-Monts 7. American motorhomes accepted in limited numbers and with reservation. Chalets for 4-6 persons for hire. A good site perhaps for families with teenagers.

Directions: Site is 1 km. north of Le Pissot (which is 7 km. north of St. Gilles Croix-de-Vie on D38) on the D59 road towards Le Perrier.

Alan Rogers' discount
Less 5% in low season

Charges 1996:
-- Per pitch with up to 3 persons, car and caravan or trailer tent, incl. 3 services Ffr 70.00 - 170.00, 2 persons 60.00 - 100.00; extra adult 18.00 - 36.00; child (under 7) 8.00 - 24.00; extra tent free - 35.00; animal 7.00 - 24.00.
-- Credit cards accpeted.
Open:
11 May - 22 September.
Address:
Les Borderies, 85270 St. Hilaire de Riez.
Tel:
51.49.10.10.
FAX: 51.49.84.84.
Reservations:
Any period with deposit (Ffr. 900) and fee (150). Contact site when open or reservations address in low season: 47 Rue de Candale prolongée, 93500 Pantin. Tel or Fax: 48.44.33.22.

8509 Camping L'Abri des Pins, St Jean-de-Monts, nr Challans

Family run, well equipped site with pool on outskirts of popular resort.

L'Abri des Pins is situated on the outskirts of the pleasant, modern resort of St. Jean-de-Monts and is separated from the sea and long sandy beach by a strip of pinewood. One can walk about 600 m. through the wood to the beach from a back entrance of the site or drive slightly further and park. Bathing is said to be safer here than on most of the beaches on this coast, but is nevertheless supervised. The site has 225 pitches, of which 150 are larger, with electricity, water and drainaway. Electricity is also available in other parts where pitches are around 100 sq. m., fully marked out with dividing hedges and quite shady. The two sanitary blocks have mixed continental and British toilets, washbasins mainly in private cabins; free hot water in washbasins, fully controllable showers (no dressing area) and sinks. There is a good, heated swimming pool with water slide for adults and an adjoining pool for children, with a paved sunbathing area where loungers are supplied free of charge (open late May - end Aug). Shop. Modern bar/restaurant with takeaway. Tennis, table tennis, minigolf, TV room and games room. Children's playground. Exchange facilities and telephones. a new feature is the fitness suite equipped with a good selection of high standard, modern equipment (no instructor as yet, but free of charge). New, modern mobile homes and chalets for hire. Riding, sailing and windsurfing hire nearby. Shopping complex near.

Directions: Site is 4 km. from the town centre on the St. Jean-de-Monts to Notre Dame-de-Monts/Noirmoutiers road (D38).

Charges guide:
-- Per unit incl. 3 persons Ffr. 103.50 - 129.00, with electricity (4A) 109.00 - 136.00; with electricity, water and drainaway 115.00 - 144.00; extra adult 16.80 - 21.80; child (under 5) 10.00 - 12.00; local tax (over 10 yrs, July/Aug) 2.20.
Open:
15 May - 18 September.
Address:
85160 St Jean-de-Monts.
Tel:
51.58.83.86.
(winter: 40.71.98.04).
FAX: 51.59.30.47.
Reservations:
Min. 2 weeks in main season, otherwise 1, with deposit and fee.

8507 Camping Les Biches, St. Hilaire de Riez, nr St. Gilles-Croix

Site in a pinewood with good pitches and swimming pools, 4 km. from the sea.

Les Biches is covered by a pinewood, so nearly everywhere has good shade. The 380 individual pitches, which are mainly of very good size (most are equipped with electricity, water and drainaway), are on grassy or sandy ground under the trees and there is a spacious and peaceful atmosphere. This is a popular site and reservations for main season are necessary. There are special parts for tents and caravans, the tent part being particularly shady. The four sanitary blocks are of good quality and size and refurbishment and improvements continue. They have British WCs, individual basins, many in private cabins with free hot water in all basins and fully controllable showers, plus laundry facilities.

The site is not by the sea but several sandy beaches can be reached in a short drive, the nearest being 4 km. away. However, there is a new heated swimming pool on site near the entrance, with slides and jacuzzi. Further improvements in 1995 included a large new bar, disco and restaurant (all from 20/5). Other amenities include a shop with ice service, takeaway, crêperie, tennis courts, volleyball, table tennis and games room with amusement machines. There is a private fishing lake, car wash area, new children's playground, a treatment room, TV room with satellite TV, minigolf and bicycle hire. Mobile homes to let. It is a quiet and peaceful type of site, with not so many camp activities as in some places, but it is popular with British tour operators (60%), so can be busy at times. Site entrance is guarded.

Directions: Site is about 2 km. north of St. Hilaire, close to and signed from the main D38 road.

Charges 1996:
-- Per pitch incl. 3 persons and car Ffr. 150.00, with electricity (10A) also 175.00; extra person 30.00; child (under 7) 15.00; extra car 10.00; dog 10.00; m/cycle 10.00.
-- Less 20% May, June and Sept.

Open:
15 May - 15 September.

Address:
85270 St. Hilaire-de-Riez.

Tel:
51.54.38.82.
FAX: 51.54.30.74.

Reservations:
Made with dates of both arrival and departure required, with deposit (Ffr. 400) and fee (100).

Camping Les Biches, 85270 St. Hilaire-de-Riez
Tel: 51.54.38.82 Fax: 51.54.30.74
LARGE SHADY PITCHES - NEW SWIMMING POOL with SPA and 'TOBOGGAN AQUATIQUE'
TENNIS - COMFORTABLE TOILET BLOCKS WITH PLENTIFUL HOT WATER
RESERVATIONS ARE RECOMMENDED FOR MAIN SEASON

Alan Rogers' discount
Ask at site for details

Remember - to claim your discount you will need to show your 1996 discount voucher

85 Vendée

8503 Camping La Loubine, Olonne-sur-Mer

see advert in previous colour section

Friendly site with good atmosphere, near the facilities of Les Sables d'Olonne.

The original mature parts of this site have been added to, giving a total of 260 pitches, including 143 with all services, plus 40 mobile homes for hire. These individual, marked pitches are of particularly large size, on flat grass, and many now have shade. Two heated swimming pools, including a water slide and indoor pool with jacuzzi, add to its attraction. Original buildings around a courtyard area have been converted to provide a pleasant restaurant and bar, takeaway and small shop (15/5-15/9). The four toilet blocks are attractively designed and of commendable quality. Tiled throughout, and colour co-ordinated, they have mainly British toilets, large washbasins set in flat surfaces and all in individual cabins, free hot water in basins and sinks, and free pre-set hot showers. Facilities for disabled and babies. Washing machines and dryers. Tennis. Table tennis. Minigolf. Badminton net. Volleyball. Large children's play area (on sand and grass) and children's club in high season. TV with Eurosport channel. Organised activities and sports for adults and children all season. Horse riding and practise golf nearby. The site is under 2 km. from a sandy Atlantic beach, and 5 km. from the lively resort of Les Sables d'Olonne. No dogs taken. Used by tour operators (35%). Full facilities from 15 May.

Directions: Site is west of Olonne beside the D80 road.

Charges 1996:
-- Per pitch incl. 2 persons Ffr. 115.00, and electricity (4A) 130.00, all services 140.00; extra adult 23.00; child (under 7) 13.00; electricity (6A) 10.00.
-- Less in low seasons.
-- Credit cards accepted.
Open:
5 April - 30 September.
Address:
1 Route de la Mer, 85340 Olonne-sur-Mer.
Tel:
51.33.12.92.
FAX: 51.33.12.71.
Reservations:
With deposit and fee (min. 7 days Jul/Aug.)

8513 Camping Pong, Landevieille

Pleasant, well kept site 4 km. from the coast at Brétignolles.

This site, situated 12 km. south of St Gilles-Croix-de-Vie, has 162 pitches, of which 112 have electricity (4 or 6A). They are all of a good size with some extra large (130 sq.m.) ones costing a little more. Set on level, grassy/sandy ground with some terraced areas at the lower end, all are separated by shrubs and bushes. There are many mature trees, including attractive weeping willows, which provide shade. Three modern, unisex sanitary blocks provide mainly continental style toilets, free hot water for showers and washbasins (some open plan, some in private cabins), and facilities for the disabled. Separate baby room, washing up under cover and laundry room. New heated swimming pool (with jacuzzi), the original pool with water slide, a paddling pool and sunbathing area, bar and terrace, fishing, games room, TV lounge, small gym and children's play area on sand and grass. Small shop with bread, milk and takeaway meals. Mobile homes for hire. Tennis 200 m. Golf, markets, vineyards all near. Site is 2½ km. from the large Lac du Jaunay (canoeing and pedaloes) and 14 km. from Lac d'Apremont and its XVI century château. No tour operators.

Directions: Site is on D32 St. Gilles-Croix-de-Vie-La Mothe road just south of Landevieille, signed.

Charges 1996:
-- Per unit incl. 2 persons Ffr 83.00; extra person 16.50; child (under 6) 10.50; electricity 4A 14.50, 6A 19.00; plus local tax.
-- Less in low seasons.
Open:
Easter - 25 September.
Address:
Rue du Stade, 85220 Landevieille.
Tel:
51.22.92.63.
FAX: as phone.
Reservations:
Made with deposit and fee for exact dates.

Alan Rogers' discount
Less 5% before 15 July

8511 Camping Les Jardins de l'Atlantique, St. Jean-de-Monts

Attractive, family run site in woodland, with swimming pool.

With 310 pitches (250 with electricity), this site is in two sections, one wooded, the other more open divided by a road. In the former, tall trees and abundant natural growth make for relaxing, peaceful pitches, most of a good size. The owners encourage this theme with a small animal pound, housing a donkey and wild bird life. The other section also houses the bar/restaurant (from 15/6) and shop (1/6). The medium sized swimming pool and children's pool are between the two sections. The more open section comprises pitches on grass, some with hardstanding and a motorcaravan service point. The two sanitary blocks are of modern design, with free hot showers, British type WCs, and dishwashing and laundry facilities under cover and the site reports the addition of a further block. There is a bar grill, children's play area, games room, tennis, horse riding and various organised activities in the main season. Bungalows and mobile homes to rent (but these do not dominate) and no tour operators. Barbecues are restricted.

Directions: Site is off Sables d'Olonne-Noirmoutier road, via Rte de la Garenne.

Charges 1995:
-- Per unit incl. 2 persons Ffr. 64.00; extra adult 14.50; child (under 7) 7.00; electricity 15.00.
Open:
1 April - 30 September.
Address:
Plage des Demoiselles, 85160 St. Jean-de-Monts.
Tel:
51.58.05.74.
Reservations:
Contact site.

8512 Camping Le Bois Masson, St. Jean-de-Monts

Lively, modern site, with many facilities including indoor pool.

Le Bois Masson is a large, lively site with modern buildings and facilities in the seaside resort of St. Jean-de-Monts. As with other sites here, the long, sandy beach is a few minutes away by car, reached through a pinewood. This site, popular with tour operators, offers 480 good sized pitches, all with electricity. They are of sandy grass, mostly separated by hedges, with medium sized trees providing some shade. There are 10 pitches with water and drainage also and an area kept for those who prefer a quieter pitch around a pond used for fishing. The 4 sanitary blocks are of excellent design, with modern showers with mixer taps, washbasins in cabins and British WCs. They include a dishwashing room (with dishwashers), a laundry, facilities for the disabled and for babies and hot water is free throughout. The comprehensive site facilities are housed in modern buildings which front on to the road. They include a good supermarket, a large, lively bar with entertainment room above overlooking the pools, a restaurant and a crêperie. There is plenty of on-site entertainment over a long season. The swimming pool complex includes a large outdoor pool, a children's pool, a separate slide and landing pool and for cooler weather an indoor pool, with sliding doors to the outside. A jacuzzi, sauna and fitness room are also provided together with many other sports including tennis, volleyball, table tennis and bicycle hire. Fishing on small pond and riding, golf, squash, watersports near. No barbecues. Mobile homes and rooms to rent. Very busy in high season, this is not a site for those seeking somewhere quiet, but there is plenty to do for those perhaps with older children. Very popular with British tour operators. There is a sister site, Le Bois Dormant, a short distance up the road which may be slightly quieter.

Charges guide:
-- Per unit incl. 3 persons Ffr 95.00 - 152.00, incl. electricity (4A) 110.00 - 169.00, incl. electricity (6A) 118.00 - 175.00, incl. water/drainage 140.00 - 190.00; extra person 17.50 - 28.00; child (under 5) free - 13.00; extra car free - 13.00; tax (over 10s) 1.10.
Open:
Easter - 30 September.
Address:
B.P. 714, 85160 St. Jean-de-Monts.
Tel:
51.58.01.30.
Winter and reservations: 51.58.62.62.
FAX: 51.58.29.97.
Reservations:
Write for booking form.

Directions: From the roundabout at the southeast end of the St. Jean de Monts bypass road, turn into town following signs to 'Centre Ville' and site, which is on the right after 400 m.

8516 Camping-Caravaning Sol a Gogo, St Hilaire de Riez

Modern site with direct access to the beach and an attractive pool complex.

Sol a Gogo is owned by the family who also own Le Clarys Plage (8518) and Le Bois Tordu (8517). It has a well designed pool complex which also encompasses reception and the bar, and boasts a water chute which seems very popular. The unusually shaped pool with a central water fountain and a smaller children's pool are heated and provide areas for sunbathing, with chairs and sun beds. A sandy beach suitable for windsurfers is reached via the site's private path. Lifeguards patrol in the main season. The restaurant is of a good standard and decor and overlooks the pool, specialising in grills and salads and offering good value (from 1/6). There is a basic shop and takeaway in season (both from 22/5, supermarket, etc. near), tennis (half court), table tennis, pétanque and a play area on sand. Windsurfing is possible off the beach and minigolf near. The 196 pitches (100 sq.m), on sandy grass, with water, electricity and drainage, are clearly marked by newly planted bushes. These are growing slowly and will eventually provide shade and privacy, but at present the site is rather open and lacks shade, though reed type fencing has been used effectively. The site is very popular with tour operators (60%) so English is evident. There are two modern, well designed toilet blocks, with free hot water, British type toilets, and washbasins in cabins. They should be an adequate provision in the height of the season. Barbecues are permitted.

Charges 1995:
-- Per pitch with all facilities, 3 persons and car Ffr. 162.00; extra person 23.50; child (under 5) 12.50; dog 7.00; extra car 7.00; local tax (over 10 yrs) 1.87.
Open:
15 May - 15 September.
Address:
61 Avenue de la Pege, 85270 St. Hilaire-de-Riez.
Tel:
51.54.29.00.
FAX: 51.54.88.74.
Reservations:
Possible except in high season.

Directions: Site is on the D123 road, between St. Hilaire de Riez and St. Jean de Monts.

8517 Camping Le Bois Tordu, St Hilaire-de-Riez

Small family site 300 m. from sandy beach.

Located near to its sister site, Le Bois Tordu provides comfortable shade, more of a family type atmosphere with a short walk to the beach and a supermarket and bar/restaurant adjoining the site. The beach is across the D123 but there is a heated pool on site, with water chute and children's paddling pool, with a sunbathing area, chairs, etc. provided. All of the 104 pitches (100 sq.m) have electricity, water and drainage, and they are clearly marked by hedges and trees. The sanitary block is not as modern as at Sol a Gogo, but provides free controllable hot showers, some washbasins in cabins, the rest in rows. Toilets (continental and British) are at the rear of the block with separate entrance. There are facilities for the handicapped, a bath for children and a laundry room. A children's play area is on sand and table tennis and minigolf on the opposite side of the road. Used by British tour operators (60%).

Directions: Site is on D123, midway between St. Hilaire-de-Riez and St. Jean-de-Monts, near Sol a Gogo (no. 8516).

Alan Rogers' discount
Less 20% outside July/Aug.

Charges 1995:
-- Per unit incl. 3 persons and full services Ffr. 162.00; extra person 23.50; child (under 5) 12.50; dog 7.00; extra car 7.00; local tax (over 10 yrs) 1.87.
Open:
15 May - 15 September.
Address:
La Pege, 85270 St Hilaire-de-Riez.
Tel:
51 54 33 78.
Reservations:
Possible **except** between 1-15 Aug.

8518 Le Clarys Plage, St Jean-de-Monts

Quiet family site with swimming pool, 300 m. from the beach.

Set a little way back from the beach, on the outskirts of the town, the main feature of Le Clarys Plage is its attractive, heated pool complex which is imaginatively designed in `rocky mountain' style with slides, chutes, bridges, etc. and surrounded by a paved sun bathing area (sun loungers and chairs provided). A new, indoor pool and jacuzzi have been added. The site has been extended to provide a total of 304 pitches. The original ones have comfortable shade from attractive trees and brush fences, the newer ones are more open. All have electricity and some water and drainage also. The three toilet blocks are modern, tiled and spacious with free hot water in the pushbutton showers, some with no dividers or hooks. There are British and continental toilets and facilities for the disabled and babies. Washing machines and dryers. Shaded play area. `Centre commercial' adjacent. The site has a bar with terrace and snacks are available in high season. Barbecue areas. Mobile homes for rent. Popular with British tour operators (60%).

Directions: Signed off the D123 coast road between St. Hilaire-de-Riez and St. Jean-de-Monts.

Charges 1996:
-- Per unit incl. 2 persons and services Ffr. 138.00; extra person 25.50; child (under 5) 15.50; extra car 7.00; dog 7.00; tax 2.20 (over 10 yrs).
-- Less 20% outside July/Aug.
Open:
15 May - 15 September.
Address:
85160 St Jean-de-Monts.
Tel:
51.58.10.24.
FAX: 51.54.88.74.
Reservations:
Write to site.

8515 Camping La Yole, Orouet, St. Jean de Monts

Attractive site 1 km. from sandy beach.

This site offers 278 pitches all with 6A electricity and water, some with drainage as well. Arranged off avenues of trees, separated by hedges and shrubs, they are about 100 sq.m. There are 100 holiday caravans and many British tour operator pitches (50%). Three tiled, fairly modern sanitary blocks have British WCs, free hot water to pre-set showers and washbasins (in private cabins) and 2 units for the disabled. Laundry room with washing machine, dryer and iron. Outside but under cover are baby baths. There are two swimming pools (unsupervised), one with water slides, and a children's paddling pool - no T-shirts allowed. Plans for 1996 include a new pool complex with indoor pool and jacuzzi. Bar with terrace, restaurant, takeaway and well stocked shop. Good sized children's play area on sand and a grassy area for ball games and picnics. Table tennis, pool, electronic games room and entertainment in high season. A pleasant walk through pine trees leads to two fine sandy beaches. St. Jean de Monts, popular for fishing and watersports and with two golf courses, is 6 km. Site gate closed 22.00-0800.

Directions: Signed off the D38, 6 km. south of St. Jean de Monts.

Charges 1995:
-- Per unit, 2 persons, electricity and water Ffr 90.00 - 131.00; extra person 20.00 - 23.00.
-- Less in low seasons.
Open:
15 May - 15 September.
Address:
Chemin des Bosses, Orouet, 85160 St. Jean de Monts.
Tel:
51.58.67.17.
FAX: 51.59.05.35.
Reservations:
Advised, particularly for July/Aug.

8521 Camping Les Ecureuils, Jard-sur-Mer

Attractive site in quieter part of South Vendée.

Les Ecureuils is perhaps the prettiest site on this coast, with attractive vegetation and large, hedged pitches with plenty of shade. The good sized swimming pool is surrounded by a sun terrace and the friendly bar overlooks it. Snacks and ice-creams are available from the bar, and there is a small shop with essentials. The toilet blocks are very well equipped and kept very clean. Facilities include a children's play area, table tennis, pool table. The site is popular with tour operators (50%). Dogs are not permitted and only gas barbecues are allowed. Jard is rated among the most pleasant and least hectic of Vendée towns and there is a town beach with other good beaches a short distance away. The harbour contains fishing boats and rather more pleasure craft, and has a public slipway for those bringing their own boats. There is a range of places to eat in the town and a morning market. And in case you are curious, yes there are squirrels on site, including red ones!

Directions: Jard is off the D21 road from Les Sables d'Olonne to La Tranche. The site is well signposted from the main road - caravanners will need to follow these signs to avoid tight bends and narrow roads.

Charges 1996:
-- Per person over 10 yrs Ffr. 25.00; child 0-4 yrs 11.00, 5-9 yrs 19.00; pitch 63.00, with electricity 78.00; extra car 9.00; local tax. (over 10) 2.20.
-- Less 10% outside 30/6-1/9.
Open:
18 May - 9 September.
Address:
85520 Jard sur Mer.
Tel:
51.33.42.74 or 51.33.64.38.
Reservations:
Advised for July/Aug.

8519 Le Marais Braud, St Hilaire de Riez, nr St Gilles-Croix

Small, quiet and unsophisticated site with swimming pool, near the sea.

Le Marais Braud occupies a peaceful wooded setting with level, grassy pitches, slightly inland from the busy coastal areas. The good sandy beaches are within easy reach by car. The facilities include a heated swimming pool with a slide and a children's pool (from 15/6), tennis court and a small lake for fishing. The friendly bar and crêperie incorporate a games area with a skittle alley and there is a little shop for basics (all from 25/6). There are 150 pitches here, of 100 sq.m., half with electricity, with shade and some hedges. One large and one smaller toilet block, both with hot water, provide showers and wash cabins with shelves and hooks and mixed continental and British toilets and there is a washing machine. Wooden chalets for rent. No tour operators. The site has a family atmosphere being managed by the owners, M. & Mme Besseau, but is only open for a very short season.

Directions: From St Hilaire de Riez, take the D38 north to Le Pissot, site is signed from the D59 road from Le Pissot to Le Perrier.

Charges 1995:
-- Per unit, incl. 2 persons Ffr. 70.00; extra adult 19.00; child 2-10 yrs 15.00, under 2 yrs 10.00; extra car 5.50; electricity (6A) 14.00.
-- Less in low seasons.
-- Credit cards accepted.
Open:
1 June - 15 September.
Address:
298, Route du Perrier, 85270 St Hilaire de Riez.
Tel:
51.68.33.71.
FAX: 51.35.25.32.
Reservations:
Write to site.

8520 Camping La Petite Boulogne, St Etienne-du-Bois

Small, attractive site beside the Petite Boulogne river.

The 27 pitches on this small site are set out on semi-terraced grass and are of good size, separated by bushes and shrubs. All have electricity, water and drainage connections. There are 8 mobile homes for hire at the top of the site at the furthest point from the river. Although only in their second season, the owners are justly proud of this attractive little site with its profusion of beautiful rose beds and flowers. Leading from the site, a little wooden bridge takes you across the Petite Boulogne river and, after a few minutes walk, to the village of St. Etienne-du-Bois with its restaurant and bar. St. Etienne is about 24 km. northwest of La Roche-sur-Yon. The modern, centrally heated sanitary block has free hot water to the pre-set showers and the washbasins in both open style and private cabins, and excellent facilities for the disabled. Under cover washing up, small, but adequate, laundry room. Shop for essentials and fresh bread (supermarket 3 km at Legé). On site facilities are limited at present, with a children's play area on grass, table tennis and bicycle hire. Horse riding, lake and river fishing nearby. Tennis, volleyball and petanque are available at the local sports centre (300 m.) and an open-air heated pool is near. Large, safe beaches are about 20 km. Al fresco chef speciality nights and wine tasting evenings are arranged in peak season.

Directions: From Legé take D978 south towards Palluau for 7 km. then turn left onto D94 towards St. Etienne-du-Bois from where site is well signed.

Charges 1995:
-- Per unit incl. 2 persons Ffr 70.00, full services 80.00; extra person 10.00; child (under 5 yrs) 5.00; extra vehicle 10.00; electricity (6 or 10A) 10.00.
-- less 25% on pitch fee outside July/Aug.
Open:
All year.
Address:
85670 St. Etienne-du-Bois.
Tel:
51.34.54.51.
Low season or pm:
51.34.54.91.
FAX: 51.34.54.87.
Reservations:
Made with deposit (Ffr 200 or £25).

N8514 Camping Naturiste Le Colombier, St Martin-Lars

Countryside site in 125 acres in a valley for naturists.

Almost akin to 'Camping a la Ferme', but with the benefit of good facilities, this site provides around 110 pitches in seven very natural fields on different levels linked by informal grass tracks. However, there are some level areas for caravans but it is generally more suitable for tents. Pitches are unmarked and electricity up to 6A is available at various strategically located points. A bar/restaurant, serving a meal of the day (order before 13.00), home baked bread and pizzas, is situated in an old, very attractive converted barn, where there is also a small 'library' of local tourist information, table tennis facilities etc. Milk is available from the farm and grocer/baker calls daily (shop 1 km.). There are facilities for volleyball and boules and a children's paddling pool and playground. Fishing. Bicycle hire.

In the main season pony and trap rides around the woodlands and one day a week the bread oven is lit and children can make their own bread. There is no pool here but it is possible to swim in one of the small lakes within the confines of the site, although you have to share the water with the fish! For nature lovers the 125 acres in which the site is located provide the opportunity for many walks throughout the attractive, wooded valley. The sanitary installations are at present in two modern blocks and are good. They provide hot showers in cubicles, some solar heated, others on a normal system, British WCs. The local area is interesting, with antique 'Bocage Vendeen' and sculpture featuring prominently, and provides a very different view of the hectic coastal Vendée.

Directions: From the N148, La Roche sur Yon - Niort road, at St. Hermine, turn onto the D8 eastward for 4 km. Turn left on to the D10 to St. Martin-Lars where there are signs to site.

Charges 1995:
-- Per person Ffr 33.00; child (4-9 yrs) 15.00, (10-16 yrs) 21.00; electricity 13.00.
Open:
All year (reduced facilities 1/11-31/3)
Address:
Le Colombier - Centre de Vacances Naturiste, 85210 St. Martin-Lars en Ste Hermine.
Tel:
51.27.83.84.
Reservations:
Not considered necessary.

8601 Castels Camping Le Petit Trianon de St Ustre, Ingrandes

Family run character site with pool, close to main N10 between Tours, Poitiers and Futuroscope.

Le Petit Trianon, one of the Castels sites, is much used by the British as an overnight stop as it lies close to the N10, one of the main routes to the southwest, but is well worth considering for a longer stay. With reception housed in the château, the site consists of two large, slightly sloping fields and a wooded section. The 90 pitches are of a good size, partly shaded and separated by earth scrapings exposing bare chalk rather than hedges. Over 70 have electricity and 5 are 'grand confort'. The sanitary facilities are located in an old building close to the main house and are spacious and generous in their provision, particularly the showers. The main rooms can be heated and have washbasins in private cubicles and British WCs, as well as showers. Elsewhere in the same building are rooms with showers and washbasins in the same cubicle, baby bathrooms and washing machines. A new sanitary block was added in 1994 with facilities for the disabled.

The heated swimming and paddling pools (open at set hours) are located on the sunny side of a rather picturesque castled facade in which is a large, very cool reading room. There is a restaurant only 50 m. away with the menu displayed on the site. Shop - essentials and drinks kept; open till late. Takeaway cooked dishes. Children's playground. Table tennis, badminton, croquet (with a specially prepared lawn), 4 bicycles for hire, volleyball and boules. TV room with satellite (eg. Sky Sport). Minigolf. Organised excursions. Washing machines. Some self-catering accommodation, chalets and gite to let. Futuroscope at Poitiers is well worth at least a day's visit (if you stay for the after dusk laser, firework and fountain show, remember your late night entry code for the site gate). This site has grown in popularity in recent years and reservation is advisable in high season, especially since some 20-30 pitches are given over to tour operators.

Directions: Turnings to site east of N10 are north of Ingrandes, which is between Dangé and Châtellerault. From autoroute A10 take exit for Châtellerault-Nord.

Charges 1996:
-- Per person Ffr. 34.00; child (3-6 yrs) 17.00; vehicle 20.00; pitch 20.00; water and drainage for motorcaravan 10.00; electricity (6A) 21.00; local tax (over 3 yrs) 1.00.
-- Less for longer stays.
-- Credit cards accepted.

Open:
15 May - 30 September.

Address:
86220 Ingrandes-sur-Vienne.

Tel:
49.02.61.47.
FAX: 49.02.68.81.

Reservations:
Made with 25% deposit and fee (Ffr. 80); min. 5 days in July/Aug.

Alan Rogers' discount
Less 5% after 3 days

8605M Camping Municipal Le Riveau, La Roche-Posay

This 200 pitch site is in two parts, one new (flatter and more open), the other more mature on something of a slope but with the benefit of shade from tall trees. Each section has some electrical connections, allegedly 16A. The two sections are divided by a small stream with access to the river Creuse, on which boating and fishing are allowed. The two sanitary blocks, one in each section, offer free hot showers and good facilities for washing, dishwashing, etc. in clean, modern surroundings, with facilities for the disabled. There are few other facilities, apart from a children's play area, but the town is only about 1 km. away. An unremarkable site, but satisfactory enough.

Directions: Site is signed from the town centre on the D5 Lesigny-sur-Creuse road (1.2 km).

Charges guide:
-- Pitch incl. 1 person Ffr. 25.00; extra adult 17.00; child 6.50; electricity 17.00.

Open:
1 March - 31 October.

Address:
86270 La Roche-Posay.

Tel:
49.86.21.23 or.20.59.

Reservations:
Not made and said not to be necessary.

8606M Camping Municipal de Bonnes, Bonnes

Right on the bank of the Vienne river, (and not fenced off!) this small, peaceful and pretty site enjoys nice views towards the well known Bonnes Bridge. Some of the 65 pitches slope slightly towards the river, facilitating the launching of small boats, canoes, etc. - the river is reportedly good for fishing too. The site is fairly open, but with shade around the perimeter, 10A electricity is available on some pitches. The unisex sanitary facilities are modern and well maintained. There are no permanent on-site catering facilities or shop, but the village is only about 100 m. away. A much less busy and noisy site than the larger municipal at nearby Chauvigny.

Directions: Site is just south of the village of Bonnes, 5 km. from the N151 road, 22 km. from Poitiers and 5 km. from Chauvigny.

Charges guide:
-- Not available but likely to be inexpensive!

Open:
At least 15 May - 15 September.

Address:
86300 Bonnes.

Tel:
49.56.44.34.

Reservations:
Contact site.

8701M Camping Municipal de Montréal, Saint Germain-les-Belles

Situated on the edge of the town with good views across the small lake, this pleasant municipal site is ideal for an overnight stop or for a longer stay in the beautiful Limousin countryside between Limoges and Brive. There are 60 tourist pitches, all over 100 sq.m. and separated by well kept hedges, which afford good privacy and views of the lake. Arranged on two grassy terraces, they have little shade; 15 have electrical connections. The modern toilet block is well designed to be quiet and draught free and is well appointed with British style toilets, washbasins, some in private cabins and controllable showers with space for dressing, but not partitioned. Good facilities for the disabled. Washing up and laundry basins under cover but no washing machine or dryer. A restaurant with terrace and bar overlooks the lake (open to the public) and there is a takeaway service. No shop but the baker calls mornings in July/August and there are a supermarket, restaurants and a good range of shops in the town 10 minutes walk away. Leisure facilities on the site are centred on the 5 hectare lake with its 150 m. long sandy beach. A bathing area is marked out by two diving boards, there are pedaloes for hire, a large children's play area and two tennis courts. The tourist office on site gives updated information to local events.

Charges 1996:
-- Per person Ffr. 12.00; child (under 7 yrs) 7.00; vehicle 6.00; pitch 6.00; electricity 10A 12.00.
Open:
1 April - 30 September.
Address:
87380 St Germain-les-Belles.
Tel:
55.71.86.20.
Reservations:
Made by phone or letter (letter preferred) to the Tourist Office (address as site); no booking fee.

Directions: From Limoges take the N20 south and shortly after Magnac-Bourg (18 km.) take exit 42 onto D7. Continue about 6 km. to St Germain-les-Belles from where the site is well signed on a side road to La Porcherie.

8702 Castels Camping du Château de Leychoisier, Bonnac la Côte

Elevated site in the grounds of a château, 10 km north of Limoges.

Just 2 km. from the A20/N20, yet very quiet and secluded, the Château de Leychoisier makes an ideal staging point or a good base for a longer stay in the region. Pitches are very large, individual ones on grassy ground, marked out by trees. Of the 80 pitches, some 55 have electrical connections and some with water and drainaway too. The sanitary facilities are not all modern, but all the toilets are of British type and washbasins are in private cabins with mirrors and free hot water. The showers are good, also with free hot water. There are baby bath and nappy changing facilities and provision for the disabled. There is a restaurant and a pleasant bar with terrace in an old open-ended barn. Small shop selling basic foodstuffs and fresh bread every morning. Mini-market at 2 km, supermarket at 5 km. Swimming pool (unsupervised) and a 4 ha. lake with free fishing and a marked off area for swimming. Tennis, table tennis, TV room, babyfoot and bar billiards. The large estate is available for walks and there is good terrain in the area for mountain bikes, but none for hire. It is a friendly, quiet site where you have plenty of space and where there are no letting units and many people like it for these reasons.

Charges 1995:
-- Per pitch Ffr. 42.00; person 27.00; child (under 7) 18.00; extra car 20.00; dog 5.00; electricity (4A) 19.00.
-- Less 15% April, May, 1-15 June and Sept.
Open:
1 April - 30 September.
Address:
87270 Bonnac-La-Côte.
Tel:
55.39.93.43.
Reservations:
Made with deposit (Ffr. 100) and fee (80), short reservations accepted without charge in low season.

Directions: Take the exit (west) signed Bonnac-La-Côte from the A20/N20. The site is well signed from the village.

8801 Camping Les Deux Ballons, St. Maurice-sur-Moselle

Good mountain site for summer and winter activities.

St. Maurice-sur-Moselle is in a narrow valley 7 km. from the source of the River Moselle in the massif of Hautes Vosges on the main N66 which leads to the Col de Bussang. This is a pleasant leafy area for winter skiing and summer outdoor activities. Les Deux Ballons lies in a small valley surrounded by mountains and under a cover of trees which give shade in most parts. The 180 pitches are on stony ground under the firs or on two terraces, and all have electrical connections. Three sanitary blocks of average quality (continental style WCs) are spread around the site; a new block has been added recently. There is a bar with terrace. The large swimming pool (30 x 20 m.) with water slide and a smaller pool for children, are open in high season (July/Aug) when there are also organised walks, fishing, bowls, riding, and summer sledging. Ski hire in winter. TV room. Tennis. Table tennis. Volleyball. Washing machines and dryers. Motorcaravan service point. Chalets and caravans for hire.

Directions: Site is on main N66 Le Thillot - Bussang road on northern edge of St. Maurice near Avia filling station (entrance partly obscured - keep a look out).

Charges 1995:
-- Per person Ffr. 18.00; child (under 7 yrs) 12.00; pitch 22.00; electricity 4A 21.00; dog 8.00; extra car 11.00; local tax 1.50.
Open:
15 February - 2 Nov. and Xmas.
Address:
17 Rue du Stade, 88560 St. Maurice-s-Moselle.
Tel:
29.25.17.14.
Reservations:
Necessary for winter and July/Aug. Write with deposit (Ffr. 100) and booking fee (50).

8802 Camping de Belle Hutte, La Bresse, nr Gérardmer

Pleasant mountain site for summer and winter sports.

La Bresse, in the heart of the Vosges mountains, makes a good base for winter ski-ing and summer walking and although a little off the beaten track, is on one of the southern routes to the Col de la Schlucht. Camping de Belle Hutte, although surrounded by mountains and trees, occupies an open hill slope (900 m. above sea level) with 122 numbered grass pitches on six terraces. Places of about 90 sq.m. are divided by hedges and all have electrical connections. The reception office at the entrance carries basic food supplies with larger shops and restaurants in the village about 400 m. away. The well built, brick sanitary block is centrally placed, of excellent quality and heated in cool weather, with facilities for the disabled and babies. Here also is a laundry room with washing machines and dryers, a drying room, a play room with table tennis, rest room with open fire and TV and a ski storage room. Swimming pool open for July/Aug. Children's plaground. To reach the site you would have to depart from the usual main through routes but it is a good site in pleasant surroundings.

Directions: Site is about 9 km. from La Bresse on the D34 road towards the Col de la Schlucht.

Charges 1996:
-- Per person Ffr. 15.50 - 20.00; child 11.50 - 14.00; car 8.50 - 9.50; caravan 10.50 - 11.50; tent 9.50; motorcaravan 26.00 - 33.50; electricity 2A 8.00 - 10.00, 10A 32.00 - 40.00; local tax 1.10.
-- Higher in winter.
-- Credit cards accepted.
Open:
All year.
Address:
88250 La Bresse.
Tel:
29.25.49.75.
FAX: 29.25.52.63;
Reservations:
Necessary in winter (not summer). Write to site.

8805M Camping du Parc du Château, Epinal

A good stop-over between Nancy and Basel, this site, about 2 km. from the centre of Epinal, is set in the grounds of a ruined castle where, although there are a number of trees, shade is scarce at certain times of the day. There are 92 pitches available for tourists, some on sloping ground, some on levelled places on grass and divided by short, low fences which carry pitch numbers, and most with electrical connections (mostly 6A). There is also a large area of tarmac which could be used for one night stays. The one large and two smaller sanitary blocks have British style WCs and free hot water in washbasins, showers and sinks. There is a bar in high season and shops and restaurants in the town.

Directions: Site is on the D11 road to Gérardmer and signed from the centre of Epinal.

Charges guide:
-- Per person Ffr. 9.00; child 4.50; tent 7.00; caravan 12.00; mobile home 15.00; car 4.00; electricity 23.00 - 13.00.
Open:
All year.
Address:
Chemin de Chaperon Rouge, 88000 Epinal.
Tel:
29.34.43.65.
Reservations:
Write to site.

8806 Camping du Château, Les Chappes, Granges sur Vologne

Quiet, country site with swimming pool.

Opened in 1993, Du Château is set in the heart of the countryside 550 m. above sea level, on a hill with views across the valley to gently rolling, wooded slopes beyond, making a very pleasant setting. The Château from which the site gets its name, dates from the 1930s, stands just inside the entrance and houses reception, a small shop with basic supplies, two rooms for wet weather or quiet use and TV. A good quality sanitary provision is on the lowest floor with continental style WCs, free hot water in washbasins and showers and a separate WC and shower for the disabled. The 43 good size pitches, all with electrical connections (4A), stand on six terraces giving unobstructed views and are served by gravel roads. The main feature of the site is the 5 x 10 m. swimming pool with a depth of 1.5 m.. There is also a separate games room with table tennis just off the camping area. With no organised entertainment and a rural atmosphere, this is a peaceful, quiet camp which makes an excellent base for a restful holiday or from which to explore the delights of the Vosges region. Good walking country. Shops and restaurants about 3 km. away.

Charges 1995:
-- Per person Ffr. 15.00; child (under 7 yrs) 8.00; pitch 17.00; electricity 15.00.
Open:
14 June - 15 September.
Address:
Les Chappes, 88640 Granges sur Vologne.
Tel:
29.57.50.83.
Reservations:
Write to site.

Directions: Site is signed from the village of Granges-s-Vologne on the D423 about half way between Bruyeres and Gérardmer.

8901M Camping de Sous-Rôche, Avallon

This attractive site is in a low lying, sheltered, part wooded situation, 2 km. from the centre of Avallon. There is quite a choice of 100 pitches on the pleasant grassy terrain - on shady terraces, on flat open ground, or by a stream; 60 electrical connections (4A). It may be very busy. The single toilet block is being modernised and now includes continental WCs, including one with basin and ramp for the disabled, individual washbasins (4 in private cabins), showers, traditional sinks for clothes and dishes, all with free hot water. Shop, takeaway (July/Aug) and cooking facilities. Children's playground (on gravel). Information/reading room with phone. A very useful night stop on the way to or from Lyon and the south, worth a longer stay. Avallon is a picturesque town and good centre for visiting the wild valleys and lakes of the Morvan mountains.

Charges 1995:
-- Per person Ffr 17.00; child (under 7) 8.50; car 13.00; pitch 12.00; electricity 17.00.
Open:
15 March - 15 October.
Address:
Service Camping, Mairie, 89200 Avallon.
Tel:
86.34.13.50.
Reservations:
Write to La Mairie.

Directions: From centre of Avallon take N944 to south towards Lormes. After 2 km. turn left at camp sign (a fairly steep, downhill road to site).

8901

Sous-Rôche
Avallon

*The site's
peaceful setting*

8902M   Camping Municipal d'Auxerre, Auxerre

Very convenient for overnight stays, particularly for those using the nearby A6 autoroute, this well cared for site is strategically situated, close to shops and the leisure centre and the River Yonne. There are some 220 numbered and marked tourist pitches on flat grass and of reasonable size. They are situated amongst a variety of mature trees, giving a fair amount of shade when needed, and about half of them have 6A electrical connections. The sanitary facilities in two blocks are adequate rather than 'state of the art' and there is a small snack bar, shop and bar, plus takeaway food in season. Children's playground. The nearby leisure centre offers an Olympic size pool, tennis, etc. Auxerre itself is worth a visit, having a superb cathedral, harbour and wide choice of restaurants, bistros, etc. A small number of tour operator pitches.

Directions: Site is southeast of the town on the D163 towards Vaux, signed from the centre of Auxerre as 'L'Arbre Sec' with camp symbols.

Charges 1995:
-- Per adult Ffr. 14.00; child (under 7 yrs) 5.60 - 8.00; car 7.00; pitch 7.00; electricity 11.00.
-- Stay 6 days, 7th free.
Open:
1 April - 30 September.
Address:
Route de Vaux,
89000 Auxerre.
Tel;
86.52.11.15.
FAX: 86.52.18.34.
Reservations:
Contact site.

9100   Camping-Caravaning La Bois du Justice, Monnerville, nr Etampes

Clean site close to Paris and Versailles.

The site is situated in a wood in the middle of farmland and the 50 tourist pitches are laid out among the trees, well shaded and flat. Electricity is available throughout. The one large toilet block is very well appointed, and spotlessly clean, although it is some way from the furthest pitches. A medium sized pool, children's playground, open air table tennis and volleyball court provide sporting diversions and a bar is open during the day and early evening. There is no shop, but a bread and provisions van calls morning and evening. Shops and restaurants are to be found in the village 3 km. away, or a little further in Etampes. The site is ideal as an overnight stop, or for touring the area southwest of Paris - Chartres, Fontainebleau and Versailles are in easy range. Paris itself is only an hours drive, Disneyland not much more.

Directions: From the N20 (Paris - Orleans), turn left going south at Monnerville, then right as you come into the village. Site is signed, but the access road is very bumpy for 2-3 km.

Charges 1995:
-- Per caravan or large tent 30.00; 2 person tent 15.00; adult 30.00; child (under 7 yrs) 15.00; car 15.00; electricity (6A) 15.00.
Open:
1 March - 30 November.
Address:
91930 Monnerville.
Tel:
(1) 64.95.05.34.
FAX: (1) 64.95.17.31.
Reservations:
Contact site.

9500   Parc de Sejour de l'Etang, Nesles-la-Vallée, nr L' Isle Adam

Small, informal site in pretty valley 33 km. northwest of Paris.

This family run site is on the southern outskirts of the village of Nesles-la-Vallée in a pretty, tree lined river valley not far from L'Isle-Adam, a popular destination for Parisiens at weekends. In fact, most of the 150 pitches are occupied by seasonal caravans (plus a few British tour operator tents - 10%) and there are only 20 pitches available for touring units. However, with its pretty rural location and close proximity to Paris it is a comfortable and peaceful place to stay for a few days. The site is informally arranged around a duck pond with many trees to provide shelter and shade and semi-tame rabbits competing with the ducks for food and attention. Pitches are large and flat and electricity is available. The single, central sanitary block, which is well heated in the cooler months, is a substantial building and although rather dated in style the facilities are well maintained and kept clean. Hot water to all facilities is free. Plenty of play activities for children include a good playground, volleyball and basketball areas and an under cover play barn with table tennis tables. There are no other on-site facilities but the village and a restaurant are within walking distance. Fishing permits for the river are available in the village and riding stables are close by. Chantilly, Parc Asterix and Disneyland are easily reached by car. The nearest station for access to Paris (and Disneyland) is 15 minutes away.

Directions: From the A15 take exit 10, then the D927 and D79 to Nesles-la-Vallée. From the N1 take the L'Isle Adam exit. Site is on the southern outskirts of the village.

Charges 1996:
-- Per pitch Ffr. 15.00 - 24.00; person 15.00 - 24.00; child (under 7 yrs) 7.50 - 12.00; electricity 3A 18.00, 6A 22.00.
Open:
1 March - 15 November.
Address:
10 Chemin des Bellevues,
95690 Nesles-la-Vallée.
Tel:
34.70.62.89.
Reservations:
Write to site for details.

**Alan Rogers'
discount**
Less 10%

OPEN ALL YEAR

The following sites are understood to accept caravanners and campers all year round, although the list also includes some sites open for at least 10 months. Where this is the case we have given brief details. However, it is always wise to phone a site first to check details as, for example, facilities available may be reduced.

0200	Vivier aux Carpes	4009M	Lou Broustaricq
0405M	Municipal Les Relarguiers	4401M	Val du Cens - Petit Port
0601	Domaine Sainte Madeleine	4608	Château de Lacomté
0605	La Vieille Ferme	5004M	Municipal Ste. Mère Eglise
0802M	Lac des Vielles-Forges	5905M	Municipal de Maubeuge
N0901	Domaine de Pauliac	6101M	La Campiére, Vimoutiers
0905M	Municipal Sorgeat	6404	Les Gaves
1102	Le Moulin du Pont d'Alies	6503	Airotel Pyrénées
1105M	La Bernede except Dec. & Jan.	6505M	St Lary Soulan exc. 19 Nov-11 Dec
1303	Rio Camargue	6613	L'Eau Vive except 12 Nov-31 Dec
2000	U Farniente	6701M	Eichelgarten
2104M	Municipal de Fouché	6702M	Municipal Le Hohwald
2605M	Municipal de L'Epervière	6801	l'Ile du Rhin
2701	Le Vert Bocage	6805M	Municipal de L'Ill except Dec & Jan
2811M	Municipal de Bonneval	6901M	International de Lyon
2910	Manoir de Pen-ar-Steir	7201M	La Route d'Or except 16 Nov-14 Feb
2920M	Municipal du Bois de Pleuven	7302	Le Versoyen except 14 Nov-13 Dec
3001M	Domaine de la Bastide	7401	Deux Glaciers except 15 Nov-15 Dec
3105M	Municipal Bélvèdere des Pyrénées	7502	Paris-Ouest
3201	Le Camp de Florence	7801	Parc Montana Laffitte
N3204	Centre Naturiste Deveze	8003	Port de Plaisance exc. 23 Dec-1 Jan
3320M	Municipal de l'Eyre	8101	Relais de l'Entre Deux Lacs
N3405	Le Mas de Lignieres	N8514	Le Colombier
3406	L'Oliveraie	8520	La Petite Boulogne
3605M	Municipal Les Vieux Chênes	8801	Deux Ballons except 3 Nov-14 Feb
3802M	Municipal Porte de Chartreuse	8802	Belle Hutte
3803	La Cascade except 1 Oct-14 Dec.	8805M	Parc du Chateau, Epinal

How to use the 1996 Discount Voucher !

The Discount Card/Vouchers are in three parts:

Part 1   should be retained and must not be removed from the Guide. You should complete it by adding your name, address and signature. This part includes the printed Card Number, and should be shown to those parks indicating special offers for our readers as identified by an Alan Rogers' logo in the Guide.

Part 2   should be completed by adding your name, address, the card number as shown in part 1, and your signature. This part may then be used to claim your discount(s) for travel, breakdown, caravan or motorcaravan insurance.

Part 3   should be completed by adding your name, address, the card number as shown in Part 1, and your signature. This part may then be used to claim your FERRY DISCOUNT, as directed.

Note that the Discount Cards are valid from **1 January - 31 December 1996 only**

SITE BROCHURE SERVICE

The following sites have supplied us with a quantity of their brochures. These leaflets are interesting and useful supplements to the editorial reports and most contain colour photographs or other illustrations of the site which cannot be reproduced in this book. If you would like any of these simply cut out or copy this page, tick the relevant boxes and post it to us. Please enclose a large envelope (at least 9" x 6") addressed to yourself and stamped (on average, 5 brochures will weigh 60 gms). Send your requests to:

Deneway Guides Ltd, Chesil Lodge, West Bexington, Dorchester, Dorset DT2 9DG

0401	L'Hippocampe	☐	3901	La Plage Blanche	☐
N0404	Castillon de Provence	☐	4004	La Paillotte	☐
0601	Ste Madeleine	☐	4103	Parc des Alicourts	☐
0602	Caravan Inn	☐	4104	Châteux du Marais	☐
0603	La Bergerie	☐	4403	Pré du Château	☐
0605	La Vieille Ferme	☐	4409	Château de Deffay	☐
0704	Le Rouveyolle	☐	4603	Les Pins	☐
0706	Mondial	☐	4605	La Rêve	☐
0707	Les Ranchisses	☐	4608	Château de Lacomté	☐
1106	Au Pin d'Arnateuille	☐	4903	Val de Loire	☐
1202	Les Rivages	☐	5000	Etang des Haizes	☐
1403	Châteaux de Martragny	☐	5003	Lez Eaux	☐
1407	De La Vallée	☐	5603	De Penboch	☐
1603M	Le Champion	☐	5801	Des Bains	☐
1702	Puits de l'Auture	☐	5804	Village Européen	☐
1705	L'Orée du Bois	☐	6001	Campix	☐
2208	Le Ranolien	☐	6201	La Bien Assise	☐
2401	Château Le Verdoyer	☐	6203	Château de Gandspette	☐
2403	Les Périères	☐	6407	Le Ruisseau	☐
2409	Soleil Plage	☐	8101	L'Entre Deux Lacs	☐
2410	Le Moulinal	☐	8306	La Baume	☐
2603	Le Grand Lierne	☐	N8402	Belezy	☐
2901	Ty Naden	☐	8403	Le Jantou	☐
2906	Le Pil Koad	☐	8501	Baie d'Aunis	☐
3201	Camp de Florence	☐	8506	Le Pas Opton	☐
3301	La Dune	☐	8507	Les Biches	☐
3302	De Fontaine Vieille	☐	8508	Puerta del Sol	☐
3305	Les Ourmes	☐			
3403	Int. Le Napoleon	☐		Parc Montana Group	☐
3500	Le Vieux Chêne	☐		French Flavour Holidays	☐
3504	Le P'tit Bois	☐			

PLEASE NOTE

We would draw your attention to the fact that these are the sites' own brochures, the contents of which we have no control over. We cannot therefore accept any responsibilities for possible errors, omissions, inaccuracies or misleading information contained therein. Brochures are only available for the sites listed above. We will make every effort to fufill all requests as promptly as possible, but this offer is subject to stocks being supplied to us and to still being available at the time of receiving your request. Supplies are normally exhausted by the end of July/mid-August.

202

REQUESTS FOR INFORMATION

For your convenience, we have printed below some slips which you may cut out and fill in your name and address to obtain further information from any of the sites in the guide in which you are interested. Send the slip to the site concerned at the address given in the site report, not to us.

ALAN ROGERS' GOOD CAMPS GUIDE - 1996
ENQUIRY FORM

To (name of site): ....

Please send me a copy of your brochure and details of your conditions for making reservations.

We have our own trailer caravan/motor caravan/tent/trailer tent (delete as appropriate).

Name: ....

Address: ....

....

ALAN ROGERS' GOOD CAMPS GUIDE - 1996
ENQUIRY FORM

To (name of site): ....

Please send me a copy of your brochure and details of your conditions for making reservations.

We have our own trailer caravan/motor caravan/tent/trailer tent (delete as appropriate).

Name: ....

Address: ....

....

ALAN ROGERS' GOOD CAMPS GUIDE - 1996
ENQUIRY FORM

To (name of site): ....

Please send me a copy of your brochure and details of your conditions for making reservations.

We have our own trailer caravan/motor caravan/tent/trailer tent (delete as appropriate).

Name: ....

Address: ....

....

RESERVATION LETTER

 Although France probably has more campsites than any other country in Europe, it can sometimes be difficult to find a pitch at a popular resort in peak season. We would advise writing direct to your selected site enclosing an international reply coupon (obtainable from any post office). You may find it helpful to copy the letter below.

M. le Directeur

.... *address of site*

....

.... / /1996

Monsieur,

Je voudrais faire une réservation pour les dates suivantes:
I would like to make a reservation for the following dates

Arrivé le .... Départ le ....
Arriving *Departing*

Notre partie consiste de:
Our party consits of:

.... adultes et .... enfants de .... ans
   adults *children aged* *years*

Nous désirons réserver un emplacement pour:
We would kike to reserve a pitch for:

une voiture *(car)*
une caravan *(caravan)*
une caravan motorisée *(motorcaravan)*
une auvent de .... cm x cm *(awning and size)*
une petite tente *(extra small tent)*
avec une branchement de ampères *(electric hook-up of x amps)*

Ci-joint est une frais réservation de ....
en accordance avec vos conditions.
I enclose a booking fee of ... in accordance with your conditions

Veuillez me répondre directement á l'addresse ci-dessus.
Please reply to me at the address below

Veuillez agréer, monsieur, mes salutations les plus distingués
yours faithfully

Name:.......................................

Address: ....

....

....

REPORTS BY READERS

We always welcome reports from readers concerning sites which they have visited. These provide invaluable feedback on sites already featured in the Guide or, in the case of sites not featured in our Guide, they provide information which we can follow up with a view to adding these sites in future editions. Please make your comments either on this form or on plain paper. It would be appreciated if you would indicate the approximate dates when you visited the site and, in the case of potential new sites, provide the correct name and address and, if possible, include a site brochure.

Send your reports to:

Deneway Guides & Travel Ltd, Chesil Lodge, West Bexington, Dorchester, Dorset DT2 9DG

Name of Site and Ref. No. (or address for new recommendations):

....

....

Dates of Visit: ....

Comments:

Reader's Name and Address: ....

....

....

....

Caravan Insurance - it's not compulsory but it's a very good idea.

LOWER RATES FOR THE OVER 50's

U nfortunately touring caravans are extremely vulnerable to all sorts of damage and can be relied upon to lose arguments with gate posts, walls, overhanging trees and people with crowbars! The following quotations taken from recently submitted claim forms are proof, if proof is needed, that caravan insurance is a <u>must.</u>

"Turned too tight an angle coming out of driveway catching side of van on brick pillar"

"The caravan was in storage and was broken into with 37 others"

"Caravan door damaged, twisted and levered, lock smashed"

"The rear window of the caravan was blown out due to high winds"

"My wife and I were pushing the caravan onto the drive when we misjudged how close to the gate post we were"

CLAIM YOUR ALAN ROGERS READERS DISCOUNT

All of these situations and many others are catered for by the specialist policies of 'The Caravan Insurance Centre'. For full details, including a copy of the 'Guide to Caravan Insurance', complete and return the coupon below. By utilising this coupon you will benefit from a special discount for readers of an 'Alan Rogers' publication.

Please send me by return your 'FREE Guide to Caravan Insurance' and proposal forms

AR

Name ....

Address ....

....

....

Postcode ....

THE QUADRANGLE
IMPERIAL SQUARE
CHELTENHAM GL50 1PZ

THE CARAVAN INSURANCE CENTRE

BAKERS OF CHELTENHAM

The Regions of France

France is divided into larger areas known as Regions, each of which consists of one or more départements. For example, the Region known as Normandy comprises five départements (76 Seine-Maritime, 27 Eure, 61 Orne, 14 Calvados and 50 Manche). Tourist information is available from:

The French Tourist Office, 178 Piccadilly, London W1V 0AL

Listed alphabetically with the départements (each with its official number) within each, the Regions are:

ALSACE

67 Bas Rhin, 68 Haut-Rhin

Alsace first became French in the 17th Century, but over the intervening years it has swapped backwards and forwards between France and Germany many times. This 'duality' gives it a unique culture and intriguing style. It is no coincidence that Strasbourg, the heart of Alsace but so close to Germany, has been chosen as the home for so many European institutions. It brings together its European and International responsibilities with its individual Alsatian identity in a most sensitive manner. Alsace is a 'heaven on earth' for food and wine lovers but if over indulgence occurs there are many methods of 'recovery', particularly in the beautiful Vosges with its marked footpaths, outdoor activities and breathtakingly beautiful scenery.

AQUITAINE

24 Dordogne, 33 Gironde, 47 Lot-et-Garonne, 40 Landes, 64 Pyrénées-Atlantiques

This large sunny southern region extends from Périgord in the north to the Pyrénées in the south. Aquitaine is a diverse region of mountains and vineyards, vast beaches and fertile river valleys, rolling grasslands and dense forests. Within its boundaries are the beautiful valleys of the Dordogne and Vézère and the forest of the Landes, stretching from the Gironde estuary to the Basque country on the Spanish border, the Pyrénèes, some of the world's most famous vineyards around Bordeaux and the wonderful Atlantic coast beaches - truly a region with something for everybody.

AUVERGNE

03 Allier, 63 Puys-de Dôme, 15 Cantal, 43 Haute-Loire

This high, green and fresh region with spectacular scenery is at the very heart of France. Lovers of outdoor pusuits are catered for extensively with a seemingly endless range of activities from which to choose. Access to the Auvergne is much improved and the roads are well engineered, with little back ones taking the discriminating visitor to some magical places. The Auvergne was once isolated and inward looking but is now realising its potential as a holiday area, with nountains, rivers and lakes combining to make this one of France's most refreshingly natural areas. It would be difficult to think of a region more suited to camping and the outdoor life.

BRITTANY

35 Ille-et-Vilaine, 22 Côtes d'Armor, 29 Finistère, 56 Morbihan

Strong Celtic roots make this region very different from the rest of France and many Bretons are determined to keep it so, with a unique culture reflected in its music, dance, drama and language. If, like many tourists, you attend a 'Pardon' (a religious procession), you will understand some of the Breton history and piety and see beautiful traditional costumes. Surrounded on three sides by sea, Brittany is often the destination for those with young families or visiting France for the first time and has so much to offer in the way of sandy beaches, lovely islands (just right for exploring), towering cliffs, wooded estuaries and fascinating towns and villages.

The Regions of France

BURGUNDY   **21 Côte d'Or, 71 Sâone-et-Loire, 58 Nièvre. 89 Yonne**

Famous for wine and food and lying within easy reach of the Channel ports and tunnel, Burgundy, in the rich heartland of France, is also warm, beautiful and interesting and has been coveted as a place to settle since Roman times. Criss-crossed by navigable waterways and with the beautiful Parc Regional de Morvan to visit, there are many intriguing old towns with fascinating buildings, châteaux and shrines, with some of the most striking religious architecture in Europe to be found at Cluny, Vezelay and Fontenay.

CHAMPAGNE-ARDENNE 08 Ardennes, 51 Marne, 10 Aube, 52 Haute-Marne

The wooded Meuse valley, beautiful lakes between Troyes and St. Dizier, the meadows of the Marne and Haute-Marne and interesting towns like Langres, Chalon sur Marne and Rheims are good reasons to dally here a while, just a couple of hours drive from Calais, Boulogne and Dunkirk. The rich, productive soil is reflected in the high standard of food available in small country hotels and sophisticated urban restaurants, with Champagne itself being the 'piece de resistance'.

COTE D'AZUR   **06 Alpes-Maritime**

Much has been written about the overdevelopment here but it is still relatively easy to find lovely coves and beaches where you can enjoy the marvellous climate. The simplicity of days on the beach with a picnic can be contrasted with visits to sophisticated towns like Nice, Monte Carlo and Cannes which have interests for visitors of all ages. One should not forget the inland areas (l'arriere pays or back country) where life is not so fast moving and there are far fewer people, many of whom do not depend on tourists for their livelihood. A good example is the Massif des Maures` behind' Frèjus and St Tropez.

FRANCHE-COMTE   **90 Tre. de Belfort, 79 Haute-Saône, 25 Doubs, 39 Jura**

There are many attractions for the visitor to this relatively little known region with a chequered history yet undeniably French flavour. Two nature reserves and miles of trails, often leading to waterfalls and lakes or following rivers and mountain streams, cutting their way through beautiful, peaceful forests combine to offer many attractions to the nature seeker.The Saône and Doubs rivers are ideal for cruising and there are also fast flowing rivers for white-water canoeists. The spa towns of Salin les Bains and Besançon offer relaxation and a chance to 'take the waters'. The Region's position, bordering Switzerland and close to Germany, is reflected in its culture and the great diversity of architectural style in many of the fine buildings.

LANGUEDOC-ROUSSILLON 48 Lozère, 30 Gard, 34 Hérault, 11 Aude,
66 Pyrénées-Orientales

The Mediterranean coastline stretches from the Spanish border to the Rhône, whilst to the north lies the underpopulated Lozère with the cosmopolitan regional capital of Montpelier in the south. The high mountains of the Pyrénèes and Cevennes and the stark and arid uplands contrast with fertile vine covered coastal plains. Sleepy villages and interesting towns such as Nimes, Beziers, Carcassonne and Perpignan combine with the tranquility of the famous Canal du Midi, the Minerve and the Route of the Cathars, the awe inspiring Gorges du Tarn, and the ultra modern coastal resorts such as La Grand Motte, Cap d'Agde and Canet, to give this region a fascination all of its own.

LIMOUSIN

23 Creuse, 19 Corrèze, 87 Haute-Vienne

Whenever you enter this region, with its rural appeal, the first word that springs to mind is relaxation. There are no motorways in Limousin and there always seems to be plenty of room on the roads and freedom of the countryside, and it seems that only the discriminating have discovered the region as a holiday destination. It is said that in Limousin a discovery awaits you at the end of every path and we consider this to be a fairly accurate description. There are towns such as Limoges, famous for its porcelain, Brive la Gaillarde in the south, lively and with a thriving market, Aubusson with beautiful and intricate tapestries, and day trips to the Dordogne and Maronne Gorges, starting from Argentat or water sports and nature watching at the Lac de Vassiviere, 35 km east of Limoges.

LOIRE VALLEY

28 Eure-et Loir, 45 Loiret, 18 Cher, 36 Indre, 37 Indre-et-Loire, 41 Loir-et-Cher

The mild climate of this beautiful region makes the Loire Valley a favourite with visitors. Known as the Garden of France, it is a most productive and lush area with large farms. Famous for wine and châteaux, the Loire Valley rewards an extended stay, although it would be impossible to visit all of the châteaux as many are still in private ownership, but three to be recommended are Chambord, Chinon and Azay le Rideau. An enchanting area is the Sologne, southeast of Orleans - itself an historic and most interesting town. Tours, Chartres with its magnificent cathedral, Blois, Angers, and Amboise are all worth a visit. Contrasting with these towns are the sleepy and picturesque villages of the region. What could beat sipping a glass of local Muscadet or Sancerre and watching the Loire and the world flow by - 'A votre santé!'

LORRAINE VOSGES

57 Moselle, 54 Meurthe-et-Moselle, 88 Vosges, 55 Meuse

This is a region of great contrasts with hills, valleys, plateaux and mountains stretching into the distance. It has a peaceful feeling now, although it was not always so, with the beautiful valley of the Moselle with its vineyards, fascinating towns and large cities such as Metz and Nancy, the lakes and waterfalls of the Vosges and numerous castles providing evidence of its history. Easily reached from the Channel ports via the Autoroutes, it is well situated for excursions to both Luxembourg and Germany.

MIDI-PYRENEES

46 Lot, 12 Aveyron, 81 Tarn, 31 Haute-Garonne, 32 Gers, 09 Ariège, 65 Hautes-Pyrénées, 82 Tarn-et-Garonne

This huge region is one of many contrasts. Its eight départements make it France's most extensive administrative area. It is a region blessed by bright sunlight, fascinating settlements, a treasure chest for those interested in history and a fantastic range of scenery. High chalk plateaux, majestic peaks stretching up into the bright blue skies and tiny hidden valleys housing sleepy villages which seem to have changed little since the Middle Ages contrast with a high tech, industrial and vibrant university city like Toulouse. Its attractions are so numerous but here are five personal recommendations - Roquefort (Aveyron) for the cheese, Toulouse (Haute Garonne) for the sausage, Auch (Gers) for the Armagnac, Albi (Tarn) for the cathedral and Cordes (Tarn) for the sky.

The Regions of France

NORD / PAS-DE-CALAIS   59 Nord, 62 Pas-de-Calais

There is a temptation to drive quickly through this region en-route to destinations further south, or at best, to make a night-stop close to the Channel ports. To do so is rather a pity, as there is much to see and do, and it is an ideal area for a short break or for an extended stay at the start or end of a long holiday. The region is an intriguing combination of busy market towns, ferry and fishing ports, seaside resorts, sleepy villages and pretty countryside, all within easy reach of the Channel Tunnel.

NORMANDY   76 Seine Maritime, 27 Eure, 61 Orme, 14 Calvados, 50 Manche

As the history of Normandy is so closely linked with our own, it is not altogether surprising that so many British visitors feel comfortable in this fascinating and diverse region. Apart perhaps from the weather, which can often be rather too like our own, although a degree or two warmer, Normandy has everything for a first rate holiday; a superb coastline, with towering cliffs, vast sandy beaches and a variety of resorts from the most sophisticated to the most simple. Normandy is famous for its rich cuisine, lush countryside, interesting historic towns and cities, and of course the famous 'landing beaches' of 1944, but it also has a few 'secrets', such as the Suisse Normandie, the Pays d'Auge, and the forested Orne Valley, all of which amply reward a visit; and of course there are the 'three C's' - Crême, Camembert and Calvados!

PARIS / ILE-DE-FRANCE   75 Paris, 77 Seine-et-Marne, 78 Yvelines, 91 Essone, 92 Hauts-de-Seine, 93 Seine-St-Denis, 94 Val de Marne, 95 Val d'Oise

How many millions of words have been written about Paris? Quite simply, it is a marvellous place of infinite variety - the list of things to do is virtually endless and could easily fill many holidays - window shopping, the Eiffel Tower, Montmartre, the Louvre, trips on the Seine, pavement cafés, the Moulin Rouge, etc, etc! Both the bus and Metro systems are excellent, efficient and reasonably priced, so there is no need to take your car into the centre. The outskirts of Paris sprawl like most big cities but it is not too difficult to get into some attractive countryside like the beautiful forests at Fontainebleu or to new tourist attractions such as Disneyland or the Asterix Parc.

PICARDY   80 Somme, 02 Aisne, 60 Oise

Picardy is not simply a region of ruler-straight roads shaded by the ubiquitous poplars across rolling plains, it is a great deal more besides. Deep river valleys, numerous forests of mature beech and oak, peaceful lakes and sandy beaches provide plenty of contrast. It is a region steeped in history, recently much of which is tragic, and the acres and acres of immaculately tended war graves are a sobering reminder. At Marquenterre, near the mouth of the River Somme, is France's largest bird sanctuary outside the Carmargue, with over 300 species. The region is dotted with interesting towns characterized by their fine Gothic architecture. There is more to Picardy than roses!

POITOU-CHARENTES **79 Deux Sèvres, 86 Vienne, 16 Charente,**
17 Charente-Maritime

This region is the sunniest in Western France, and is ideal for beach holidays with lively resorts and quiet villages along its extensive Atlantic coastline. The islands off the coast of Charente-Maritime (Ile de Ré, Ile d'Oléron) are popular holiday destinations, particularly with the French themselves. The scenery inland is in marked contrast to the busy resorts and ports of the coast - wooded valleys, the vineyards of Cognac, the Vienne, the agricultural landscape and the heat in summer all seem to make a visit inland an essentially French experience. The towns and cities of the region are also fascinating - La Rochelle, Poitiers, Angoulême, Saintes, Niort and Cognac are all worth visiting.

PROVENCE **05 Hautes-Alpes, 04 Alpes-de-Haute-Provence, 83 Var,**
84 Vaucluse, 13 Bouches-du-Rhône

From the Alps to the Mediterranean, this large region seems to have everything. The often spectacularly beautiful (and sometimes spectacularly busy!) coastline includes famous resorts like St. Tropez and Fréjus. The distinctive cuisine, bright blue inland lakes, the breathtaking Gorges du Verdon, the majestic Alps, the impressive Vaucluse and fascinating historic towns such as Aix, Avignon and Arles provide a seemingly endless choice of attractions. If you are looking for the renowned peace and tranquility and the incomparable light that has made Provence so popular as a home for artists, it is still not difficult to find those `off the beaten track' places only a few miles inland from the busy coast.

RHONE VALLEY **01 Ain, 69 Rhône, 26 Drôme, 07 Ardèche, 42 Loire**

The Rhône Valley is one of Europe's main arteries - this traditional route carries millions of travellers and millions of tons of freight - by rail (TGV), by Autoroute and by water - to the Mediterranean area. However, either side of this busy corridor are areas of great interest and natural beauty; the sun-baked Drôme, with its ever changing landscapes, culminating in the isolated mountains of the Vercors, the spectacularly beautiful Ardèche, with its gorges, the Doubes ornothological reserve, with its rare waterbirds, and Lyons (France's third city). The Rhône Valley enjoys a very high reputation for food and wine and first rate meals can be had at simple country auberges, as well as at first-class restaurants.

SAVOY-DAUPHINY ALPES **38 Isère, 74 Haute-Savoie, 73 Savoie**

Winter sports are just some of the activities which attract thousands of visitors to the purpose built resorts of the `ceiling of Europe' with many peaks over 4,000 m. culminating in Mont Blanc at 4,807 m. It is also an area of pine and larch forests, fast running streams, glaciers, clean air and lovely lakes. Old and interesting towns such as Annecy, Aix-Les-Bains, Evian and Chambery and the lively University city of Grenoble are well worth visiting, as are the welcoming villages and the Chartreuse distillery at Voiron. In addition to winter sports, for the more active, the range of outdoor activities is impressive and includes climbing, caving, riding, fishing, walking and cycling. Italy and Switzerland are within easy reach for day excursions.

WESTERN LOIRE **53 Mayenne, 72 Sarthe, 49 Maine-et-Loire,**
85 Vendée, 44 Loire-Atlantique

The Western Loire region's five départements to the south of Brittany have become popular for British visitors, involving no more than a day's drive from the Channel ports. The region includes a wide range of attractions, including the beaches of the Vendée, châteaux on the Loire, the Le Mans 24 hour sports car race and the Parc Regional de Brière, north of St. Nazaire. The coastline extends from the sophisticated resort of La Baule in the north to La Tranche in the south. The inland areas are less well-known, but are well worth a visit.

The Regions and Départements of France

France is divided administratively into 95 `départements' (including Corsica) which are approximately the equivalent of our counties but with rather more autonomy. The départements are numbered in alphabetical order and these numbers form the first two digits of all post codes within each département. For example, the Dordogne is département 24, so every large town in the Dordogne has a post code commencing 24... We have adopted a similar system for numbering our French campsites; thus all our sites in the département of Dordogne start with the numbers 24..

Our Guide is now organised in départements for ease of use. The layout is therefore numerical and alphabetical: 01 Ain, 02 Aisne, etc. For the benefit of the majority of readers who are not experts on French geography, we include the map below indicating the location of each département, together with its official number. The map also shows in which Region each département is situated. We have also included a (necessarily very brief) description of each Region on pages 209-213.

THE REGIONS AND DEPARTEMENTS OF FRANCE

The Départements of France - Index

France

Calais
Boulogne
6204
8001
7603
Dieppe 7605M
Cherbourg 5004M 7607M 7064
Le Havre 7601 7606M
1402M 7601 Rouen
5001 1401
5000 1407 1405
5003 1403 Caen
1411M 6101M
2900 2208 2210 5002M 2701 2810M
Brest 2204/9 6102M 2811M
2913 2201 2205 1410M
2207 2200 3500/2/4 6103M A11
2908 2211 2206M 3503M 5300M 7203
2906 2907 2220M 7202M 2801
2905 2203 N12 7205 Le Mans 4105
2911/12 2901 3510M Rennes 7201M 4101
2920M 4905M 4903 Tours
2902-4/10 N165 4902 4901 3710M
2909 4409 4401M 4903 3701 3711M
5601-5 Nantes 4902 4901 8601 8605M
4404-7 4410 4402M 7902 8601 8606M
4403 8520 8514N Poitiers 3605M
8509/11/12/15 8504 7901M A10 N20
8506-8/16-19 8501/2 2305M
8505/13 1709M 1603M 8702
8503 1708
8521 1706 1605M Limoges
1707 1703-5 8701M
1702 1601M 1602 1905M
1701 2420M 2401
3306/7 2416 N89
3305 2402-5/9 2406
3302 3303 3308 /11-15/17
3304 Bordeaux 2407 4603 4601
3301 3320M 2408/10, 4604 4605
4009M 4702/3 4710M 4608
4007/8 4010 3201 4701
4011 N10 3204N
4005/6/12N 4020M 3203
4013 4004 3205M To
4021M 4001 4002/3
6406/7 6423 6501N 0901N
6405/10/21M 6409 3105M
6402 6403M A64 6502
6411 6420M 6505M N20
6401/22M 6404
6503

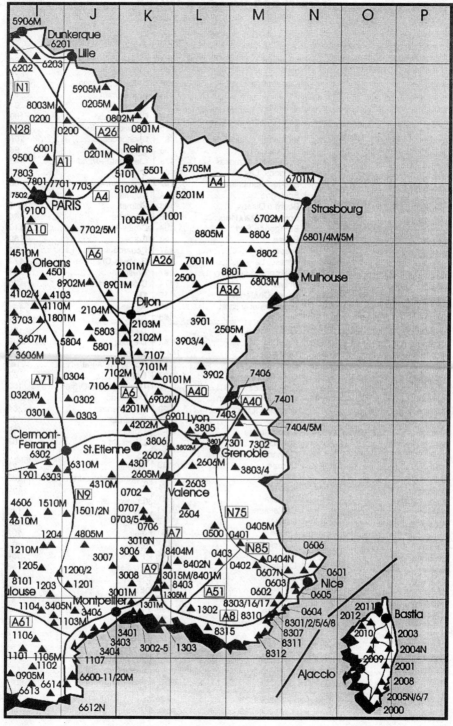

TOWN and VILLAGE INDEX

219

Maps and Index - new grid system

For 1996 we have introduced a grid system for our map, whereby each grid square is identified by co-ordinates in the form of two letters - one on the horizontal axis, and a different one on the vertical axis. In the index therefore each site is identified by two letters, indicating the map grid square in which it is located, followed by a number which identifies the actual site location within that square. We hope this will make it easier and quicker to identify the location of sites in unfamiliar areas.

INDEX OF CAMPSITES

Index of Campsites

Index of Campsites